TIES THAT BIND

Published in South Africa by:
Wits University Press
1 Jan Smuts Avenue
Johannesburg 2001
www.witspress.co.zawww.witspress.co.za

First published in South Africa in 2016
Compilation © Editors
Chapters and poems © Individual contributors 2016
Images © Individual copyright holders

ISBN 978-1-86814-968-1 (Print)
ISBN 978-1-86814-969-8 (EPUB – North and South America and China)
ISBN 978-1-86814-970-4 (EPUB – Rest of World)
ISBN 978-1-86814-971-1 (Web PDF)

Edited by Jill Weintroub
Proofread by Alison Lockhart
Indexed by Marlene Burger
Design and layout by Fire&Lion
Cover image courtesy of Mohau Modisakeng

TIES THAT BIND

Race and the Politics of Friendship in South Africa

EDITED BY SHANNON WALSH & JON SOSKE

WITS UNIVERSITY PRESS

CONTENTS

LIST OF FIGURES

Love itself, the subversive gift, is an important
public good, and loving is a significant political act,
particularly among those stigmatized and marked as
unworthy of love and incapable of deep commitment.

– Richard Iton, *In Search of the Black Fantastic*

From now on, all friendship is political.
  – Comité invisible, *L'Appel*

FANON'S SECRET

GABEBA BADEROON

The grape picker holds out
his hand full of fruit but turns
his face, the slight, unavailable cast
of his head his most precious possession.

The woman who cleans your house
all day is in the places you cannot be,
touches your sheets.

You hate
what is held back,
not known to you,
kept, stolen, enchanted.

1 THINKING ABOUT RACE AND FRIENDSHIP IN SOUTH AFRICA

JON SOSKE AND SHANNON WALSH

Writing in 1896, Olive Schreiner, arguably the most radical critic of imperial policy of her day, argued that a racial apocalypse could be averted only if South Africa's white population ruled the country in the spirit of friendship, 'a course of stern unremitting justice is demanded from us towards the native ... we [must] raise him & bind him to ourselves with indissoluble bonds of sympathy and gratitude'. By tying the responsibilities of colonial governance to the cultivation of an unbreakable emotional bond, Schreiner articulated a vision of friendship that served as both an instrument and outcome of the civilizing mission, replacing a precarious rule of violence with the cultivation of a 'native' subjectivity that was bound by affection and gratitude to the (former) colonial master.[1] Strikingly, a similar rhetoric can be found in the writing of white South Africans ranging from the segregationist Jan Smuts to the liberal author and politician Alan Paton, from apartheid ideologues of the 1950s to the young nonconformist Patrick Duncan. In the 1930s and 1940s, a social scientific version of this language developed under the sponsorship of the European-Native Joint Councils movement and the South African Institute of Race Relations. Whether articulated as a civilizing mission, separate development, or racial equality, each of these projects made claims on the emotional life of the colonized, and envisioned its outcome as generating bonds of affection between black and white. A history of colonial power in South Africa must therefore incorporate a genealogy of the language and practices of friendship.

At the same time, friendship is often understood to transcend the sphere of politics. Circulating affections and desires create connections that are not easily mapped onto existing power relations. Friendship can crystallize almost instantly both practices that resist structures of oppression and those that enable them: intimacies and complicities. This volume explores friendship as a mode of liberal colonial power, while still holding on to possibilities for insurgent, transgressive, and subversive friendships. How did the (generally homosocial) framework of colonial friendship function to police other forms of desire and articulate the gender dynamics of white settler society? How did African intellectuals, spanning from the work of S. M. Molema in the 1920s to Steve Biko in the 1970s, develop a critique of colonial friendship? How did the rhetoric, symbolism, and imagery of the liberation struggle attempt to subvert or reconfigure the expectations of friendship as a racial script? To what extent do languages and practices of solidarity – both during the anti-apartheid struggle and within the contemporary South African left – build on earlier visions of racial friendship? How has literature and art served as a space to disrupt the emotional economy of colonialism or experiment with alternate models of love and intimacy?

Writing from a diverse range of disciplinary, theoretical, and political perspectives, the contributions to this volume bring South African debates into conversation with three currents of scholarship developed in other contexts. First, we engage with a new generation of scholarship in settler colonial studies, critical race theory, and indigenous studies. These literatures, albeit in ways that differ significantly, have placed the 'structure of settlement' (Wolfe 2006) and the very definition of the human at the center of debates over core ideas of political theory: nation, civil society, sovereignty, citizenship, and recognition (Burton 2011; Byrd 2011; Simpson 2013; Stoler 2002). We consider ways in which the idea of the South African nation, both historically and following the 1994 transition, presupposes the structures of settler society – expressed in the project of 'civilization' or liberal civil society – and normalizes the underlying violence of whiteness. Second, we engage in a dialogue with queer theory and postcolonial feminism regarding the role of affect and intimacy in the operation of power. By looking at affect we bring a lens to the libidinal and emotional forces that circulate in often-invisible ways between and through how people relate to one another. Third, we reflect on the critique of solidarity that has emerged across a number of locations, including African American feminist activism and Palestinian studies. In developing such concerns, we read the question of nonracialism, an idea often treated as uniquely South African, within an international set of debates regarding over-identification, appropriation, and the denial of privilege. Several chapters struggle with what anthropologist Audra Simpson (2014) describes as refusal: the ethical and political rejection of the gift of friendship, a refusal that includes rejecting what is deemed good, rational, and sensible by a given social order. Finally, this volume asks: what forms of love, friendship, and mutuality can emerge from the rupture created by the failure of civil society, and solidarity, as universalizing projects?

Until the last decade or so, most scholarship on race in South Africa focused on the grand architecture of segregation or ideologies of white supremacy (Posel, Hyslop, and Nieftagodien 2001). By placing the question of friendship at the center of South African cultural life, past and present, this volume examines how power operates within everyday social relationships. These are not only historical questions. In a country profoundly divided by race, class, and gender-based violence, these issues are central to almost any discussion of South Africa's present. Interrogating friendship as a political space is not meant to hollow it out or stiffen the emotional and intimate flows that make friendship dynamic and hopeful. To the contrary, the chapters in this volume keep alive the promise of friendship and its possibilities, while also investigating what Lisa Lowe (2015: 18) calls the 'political economy of intimacies', in which affective relations are not only personal and interior, but also an essential part of the social reproduction of power.

There is no universal position from which to define a politics of friendship in South Africa. Friendship must be understood in the dynamics between diverse African cultures of affiliation as well as the complex formation of subjectivities that occurred through settler colonialism, indigenous genocide, African land dispossession, slavery, and Indian indenture. 'Friend' is an English language word and the valence of English, especially when tracking histories of affect and intimacy, should never be treated as neutral. Each of South Africa's languages has its own lexicon for describing and performing social bonds and their emotional entailments. In isiZulu, to take one case, many expressions for friendship invoke or crosshatch with other relationships: *umngani obalulekile* (an important friend), *untanga* (a friend of the same age), *umkhozi* (one who is close to the heart). The use of kinship as a vocabulary of friendship, for example the Afrikaans word *boetie*, sometimes ties personal intimacy to the community created by a shared way of inhabiting a language. The history of friendship in South Africa is also the story of these idioms and their multidirectional translations.

Given those caveats, considering friendship as a central site of the political in South Africa is crucial for a few reasons. First, it helps return historicity to race and its production through the lived experiences of evolving subjectivities. As such, the chapters in this volume are interested in mapping the overlapping genealogies of liberal colonialism, discourses of affection, and the bonds of intimate ties as they relate to settler colonial governance, the codifying of racial difference, white supremacy, and anti-blackness. Second, the ties of friendship are manifest from liberal colonial projects of the nineteenth century to the apartheid security police, but they also can be found between comrades in the underground, as intimate personal and political networks were essential to the clandestine nature of anti-apartheid activities (O'Malley 2007; Soske 2012). The bonds of loyalty, as well as the scars of betrayal, continue to be present in the everyday debates of political life in South Africa (see Hardy and Rampolokeng this volume; Dlamini 2014; Lewin 2011). So too, there are times when friendship is an essential space for subversion, improvisation, and resistance: a place where alternative subjectivities and 'affective communities' can flourish (Gandhi 2005).

Finally, friendship underlines the intersection between affect (the ability and potential to affect and be affected) and the very constitution of politics. Affect is not a fixed object that can be easily mapped and studied: it is a potential and a relation, found in circulations, intensities, and emotions that pass from body to body. Said simply, affects are experiential states (ranging from arousal to trauma) that are situated within social worlds and that bring bodies in relation with other bodies (Ahmed 2010; Massumi 2002). In South Africa the folding together of affect and the political can be seen, for example, when looking at the evolving public precepts and strictures around sexuality and romantic intimacy: from early racist panics over the black 'peril' to white women going back to the 1920s, to the policing of intimacy, romance, and sex across race with the successive 'immorality' laws of 1927, 1950, and 1957, to the HIV pandemic in the 1990s, which posed a range of questions around intimacy, sex, and desire that burst open the private space of the bedroom into the public arena of political life (Epprecht 2008; Fassin 2007; Walsh 2009). Mark Hunter's (2010) work brilliantly maps the geography of intimacy in South Africa in which love, sex, and gender identities are entwined with economic questions such as unemployment and poverty in the context of everyday realities of AIDS. While sex and its psychic, political, and social implications have been the focus of investigations into the dynamics of power (Burns 2007, 2012; Cole and Thomas 2009; Epprecht 2004; Posel 2005), the familiar bonds of friendship have received less critical investigation. Sex and modes of intimacy that were policed by the apartheid state possessed more transparent coordinates with which to track oppression and resistance than do the shifting and illusory bonds of friendship that often slip from view. Accounting for these conflicting, interwoven, and entangled spaces of intimacy and affection as they relate to political life is central to this volume.

As an increasingly rich body of literature demonstrates, friendship has long served as a privileged form for understanding political relations. In one sense, friendship reflects an attachment to the political: it is a desire for 'non-sovereignty', giving up independence for interconnection with others (Berlant 2011). Yet unlike familial, contractual, romantic, or professional relationships that assume prescribed obligations, the basis of friendship – especially as it has been understood across European cultural history – is a mutually given affection and respect for the other's autonomy (Silver 1989). As a result, philosophical and popular discussions often circle around a subversive paradox. While friendship exemplifies the pleasures of social life (and in some discourses society itself), it nonetheless remains radically dependent on the open-ended commitment of two individual wills. Debates over friendship have repeatedly centered on both its universal character – the possibility of an ethical commitment that truly escapes from personal interests and instrumentalism – and the question of who has the capacity for this universality (Caine 2011). Beginning with Aristotle's *Ethics*, a canonical concept limited the highest form of friendship to the virtuous subject: he who has the freedom and autonomy to enter into a relationship of true reciprocity.[2] Friendship between elite men thus was a way to define the borders of ethical life – the mode of life, unlike the woman or slave, to which Aristotle attributed universal value. As Jacques Derrida argues, this construction of friendship is one of political exclusions: it is phallocentric and rooted in concepts of brotherhood, family, territory, and (in later writers) the nation-state (1997).

Such exclusions are particularly acute in the context of settler colonialism, which privileges certain subjects and cultures as worthy, rational, civilized, and human, while simultaneously marking and distinguishing those who are deemed unfit or disallowed. In such a context, prohibitions and edicts around social relations are ways to reinforce and deepen social divisions in everyday life. As Lowe (2015) has argued in relation to British colonialism across four continents, the liberal idea of freedom and emancipation distinguished both those who were deserving of freedom and those who were unfree based largely on the construction of racial difference. Racialized bodies are expected to embark on a gradual (and ultimately endless) path of development toward full freedom, subjecthood, citizenship, and, it follows, the capacity for friendship. Social relations of affiliation thus become a central site for this production of difference. This politics of friendship is less about how friendship has been understood as an interior or personal space shared between two people and more about a model of affiliation as a mode of governance and a process of social control.[3] The liberal subject was able to assume and think freedom – identified with the very essence of the human – to the extent to which indigenous, colonized, and enslaved lives were denied such a possibility (Hartman 1997; Lowe 2015; Wilderson 2010).

In South African studies, Pumla Gqola, Gabeba Baderoon, Mark Sanders, Ashraf Jamal, Patricia Hayes, Jacob Dlamini, Gary Minkley, and Ciraj Rassool are scholars who attempt to think different modes of intimacy, complicity, affect, or emotion together with the political: from the slave owner's kitchen in the eighteenth-century Cape to Jacob Zuma's rape trial.[4] In a seminal contribution, Sarah Nuttall and Cheryl-Ann Michael's edited volume, *Senses of Culture* (2000: 5) provocatively reads South African culture through its 'intimacies and connectivities' , which, it is claimed, have been neglected in favor of a focus on struggle, segregation, and separation. Nuttall and Michael argue that the close proximity of different cultures has created cultural entanglement and creolization in South Africa. This focus on intermingling opened up a wide-ranging debate about whether their approach too quickly set aside the existing material realities of racial and class division (Jacobs 2002), as well as whether the notion of creolization, or hybrid identities, masked the violent processes that have particularly targeted and oppressed black bodies.[5] We argue that a focus on intimacy need not neglect material concerns, nor fall into a trap of celebrating hybridization. To the contrary, looking at intimacies as inherently part of the political economy and production of racial difference forces a careful attention to the nuances, processes, and constraints from which they emerge. As Baderoon (2014: 50) writes, these intimacies can be read as 'charged by silence and as coded trauma'. Rather than assume that cultural entanglement necessarily disrupts or diminishes difference, we are interested in the inverse: how intimacies expressed through friendship *produce* and *structure* difference.

FICTIONS OF FRIENDSHIP

There is a long and rich tradition of writing about the intersections of race and friendship in South Africa. The novel, in particular, has offered a medium for exploring the possibility and limits of empathy between oppressor and oppressed. Because fiction presupposes the ability to imagine another's experience, writers were frequently torn between attempting to depict the separation between worlds and the reaffirmation of literature's capacity to reach across the racial divide. Beginning with Schreiner (1883) and Sol Plaatje (1930), the question of whether friendship was possible across racial lines served as a vehicle for reflecting on the conditions for building a common society. In this mode of writing, the personal serves as a microcosm: it stands in for and makes possible a vision of social and political life. The failure of friendship therefore calls into question the emotional and ethical basis for a future nationhood. In different ways, Es'kia Mphahlele (1957), Lewis Nkosi (1963, 2002), and Nadine Gordimer (1976) have critiqued how English language writers, particularly the tradition identified with the liberal novel, denied the unbridgeable racial inequalities of colonial rule and apartheid. In a 1976 essay, Gordimer contended that the liberal novel's depictions of interracial friendship offered a nonrevolutionary resolution to white domination: the colonizer is redeemed not through the loss of power, but through the love and forgiveness of the oppressed. Gordimer's early portrayal of an interracial relationship, *Occasion for Loving* (published in 1963), depicted how intimacy, far from healing divisions, could resolve in an assertion of white impunity that underscored the chasm between worlds.

In a discussion of Gordimer's later work, Nkosi (1983) was skeptical of the capacity of white writers, such as Gordimer, to imagine a complete disintegration of interracial relationships. Clinging to the interpersonal, even in a failed form, was a way of continuing to assert their relevance. Nkosi's early critical essays argued that literary realism (and, in certain statements, any literary aesthetics) could not adequately represent the entrapment, malaise, and daily chaos of black life. The failure of literary empathy derived not only from the insularity and privilege of white writers, as Nkosi (1983: 109) has suggested, but also the sheer absurdity of black existence under apartheid conditions. At moments, he denied that friendship was possible between black and white: 'Such relationships are dogged by guilt, by equivocation, and the major problem of communication between a world deeply divided by color'. Writing after 1994, Nkosi nuanced and elaborated his argument by questioning whether a common experience existed, beyond the fact of division, which could express itself in a truly South African literature. Surveying post-apartheid literary developments, Nkosi (2002: 328) warned against the seductions of nation building based on a superficial performance of reconciliation. If the novel could help to prepare the space for the emergence of new subjectivities, it would require a fundamentally transformed social reality: 'The truth of recent South African history can only be told in novels of the abyss.' Nkosi's argument suggests that the liberal tradition should be read as an archive of imagination's failures: an archive of the abyss. These failures were not only individual, but also testify to the exorbitant nature of the structuring violence that drew black and white together.

As Njabulo Ndebele (1986) has warned, however, the hypnotic character of this violence poses its own set of dangers. An aesthetic fixated on the overwhelming spectacle of confrontation risked emptying characters, especially black characters, of interiority and complexity. In important respects, Ndebele's argument built on the new political and intellectual space created by the Black Consciousness (BC) movement of the late 1960s and 1970s. Reviving earlier debates over the role of minorities in the liberation struggle, BC leader Steve Biko denied that white South Africans could seek the destruction of a system that guaranteed their privileges. Despite friendships with white activists (such as the academic and anti-apartheid activist Richard

Turner), Biko maintained that the elusive quest for white solidarity was a trap. The BC movement inspired an enormous body of poetry, theatre, music, and autobiographical writing that emphasized consciousness building, community, and self-reliance among black South Africans. This work placed art and culture at the center of creating 'a true humanity' (Biko 2004).

Responding to a major debate during the 1980s over the concept of art as a weapon of struggle, Ndebele developed a pointed critique of writers who reduced politics to the spectacular battle of black and white. In contrast, Ndebele (1986) urged an aesthetic mode, and therefore a kind of political imagination, that eschewed the dramatic in favor of subtlety, the everyday, and psychological nuance. According to Ndebele, the ordinary is constituted through personal relationships in all their intricacy. This injunction located the political within the web of interconnections, both personal and formal, that make up quotidian existence. Ndebele's (1996, 2000) post-apartheid writings have extended this conception into a critique not only of the continued power of whiteness, but also of modes of reactive blackness that place a highly militarized conception of struggle at the center of political life. As Ndebele (2013) has recently suggested, South African history has taken the form of a 'fatal intimacy' between hostile and mutually dependent identities.

Ndebele's interventions have influenced an important direction in post-apartheid art, writing, and criticism. In her scintillating genealogy of the Muslim in South African culture, Baderoon (2014) reads the micro-political violence and erasures of colonialism in ordinary sites and objects including words (*kaffir*), food and cookbooks, landscape paintings, and family memories. By showing that each moment of erasure is simultaneously a point of contact and resistance, she lovingly depicts South African history, through all of its violence, as slowly, sometimes almost imperceptibly, shaped by the ordinary lives and struggles of black communities. In a related attempt to rethink the place of struggle in the South African cultural imaginary, Gqola (2009: 72) has urged new 'kinds of public spaces, conversations, and memories' that transform the masculinist and increasingly violent spectacle of post-apartheid politics. Her work contributes to this project by showing that the silences within the historical archive (around slavery, women, black interiority) can be claimed as sites for imagining more complex and vulnerable forms of subjectivity (Gqola 2010). These attempts to discover new modes of ethics and politics within the everyday are inflected by a profound dilemma theorized by Jamal (2004): the contradiction between the perversions and perverse fascinations of a country built on black suffering and the imperative of finding new ways to play and love. Developing this line of thinking, Dlamini (2009) and Thembinkosi Goniwe (2010, 2011) have argued for multifaceted depictions of black life under apartheid and motivated the political significance of depicting the affective bonds among black South Africans. By moving beyond the fixation on whiteness (including the white audience), the aesthetic of the ordinary enables the exploration of spaces, languages, idioms, practices, and styles of friendship outside of the linguistic and social worlds dominated by English and Afrikaans. In the context of prevalent depictions of black emotional life as emulative or pathological, images and practices of black love remain insurgent (see MADEYOULOOK in this volume).

TIMES, SCALES, AND SPACES OF FRIENDSHIP

In *Entanglement* (2009), Nuttall motivates a reading of historical temporality that stresses the interweaving of the past, present, and future as well as disturbances and interruptions. Following Nuttall, we suggest such a temporal mélange in relation to the *times of friendship*. Writing histories of friendship requires holding multiple temporal and spatial dimensions together: the chance encounter and the slow unfolding of intimacy, the immanence of togetherness, and the anticipation of a letter or meeting, the prolonged absence, and the counterpoint of remembering. There is no objective moment of friendship: its durations are neither linear nor impersonal. Rather, friendship offers the possibility of rethinking other temporalities (social, economic, political) through the events and memories of two interwoven, but discontinuous, lives. For this reason, friendship (and other forms of intimacy) can also point to a politics that is not located in the present or future, but is both continual and cyclical.

If friendships are often considered to be micro-political, they also provide key links within the structures and networks that enable large-scale, formalized politics. In this respect, the politics of friendship also requires rethinking the problem of *scale*. Affective relationships organize politics through family alliances, boys' clubs, political parties, business networks, student organizations, military units, and so on. Friendships frequently develop across multiple sites at once – public and private, visible and invisible – a fact that troubles the liberal conception of democracy with its distinct realms of political and cultural/private life. As a result, friendships can traverse levels of analysis that social scientists and historians often treat separately: the local and the national, the economic and the political, the affective and the material, structure and agency. In post-apartheid South Africa, this aspect of friendship has been discussed in terms of the relationship between the African National Congress's (ANC) political culture (characterized by strong bonds developed in exile, the underground, and prison) and the impersonal demands of constitutional legality (Booysen 2011). Among its other functions, the debate over corruption attempts to define and regulate the proper relationship between personal loyalties and the functioning of the bureaucratic state.

While friendships exists in multiple *times* and *scales*, they also provide *spaces* for emotional events, exchanges, fantasies, misunderstanding, confidences, and secrets: they create worlds with unique sets of assumptions and expectations. As Derrida (1997) suggests, friendship might be (in some sense) a universal form of relation, but one friend can never replace another. At the same time, certain kinds of friendships are frequently associated with particular sites, especially in contexts where space is policed. As a result, interracial relationships – but also political and artistic friendships that transgressed the conservative mores promoted by the regime – were closely tied to alternative social spaces. The most famous of these locations were the neighborhoods targeted for destruction by the 1950 Group Areas Act: Sophiatown, District Six, and Cato Manor. Celebrated by the *Drum* generation of writers, these areas came to symbolize a demimonde of dancing and jazz, interracial drinking, cosmopolitanism, and everyday freedoms. Other spaces played a similar social and symbolic role on a smaller scale: the 'grey areas' of the art world that developed in neighborhoods such as Hillbrow and the Market Theatre district (Peffer 2009); publications such as *Staff Rider* and Ravan Press (Vladislavić 2008); and student associations and the campuses of the liberal universities. Reflecting on an afternoon in Paris spent with the poet Breyten Breytenbach, Nkosi (1983) described exile as a space where relationships could develop that would have been impossible within the confines of South African society. Other memoirs recall the experience of prison in similar terms. Despite constrictions and regular abuse, activists from across the country lived together, debated, and developed new understandings of their country through the very different experiences of others (Caine 2011; Desai 2014). As Nelson Mandela (1995: 328) recalled: 'Prison is an incubator of friendship.' If each of these locations facilitated alternative forms of sociability and intimacy, they also became venues for intense struggles over privilege and disillusionment with the limitations of friendship.

Across its immense range of periods, contexts, and political organizations, the anti-apartheid struggle also provided a crucial space for the intersection of race, friendship, and the political. Because of its clandestine and semi-clandestine character, oppositional politics frequently operated through dense networks of close personal relationships that overlapped (in varying degrees and in different ways) with the ties of household, family, neighborhood, and workplace. At moments, particular friendships developed a public character and embodied the defiance of apartheid racial norms, for example the relationship between ANC leader Albertina Sisulu and the BC activist Dr Abu Baker Asvat (Soske 2012). Close relationships often drew people into politics. Many memoirs and interviews describe the experience of struggle in terms of the formation of unprecedented friendships that broadened political consciousness and challenged racial (and other) preconceptions. At the same time, influential political cultures within liberation politics, especially those influenced by some form of Leninism, demanded the disciplining of personal affections. Drawing on a Soviet language of the party as family, the ANC underground promoted the subordination of judgment, individual attachments, and intimacy to an impersonal love for the people demonstrated through revolutionary activity (Suttner 2008). Along similar lines, Rassool (2004) argues that a particular political culture, centered on the biography of the liberation organization's (male) president, either erased or subordinated personal relationships to the larger narrative of the struggle as the nation in the process of becoming. As exemplified by Donald Woods's (1987) controversial biography of Biko, friendship with a struggle icon could also be invoked to confer authority: writing oneself into the heroic life of the leader became a vehicle to disavow the author's own whiteness and ventriloquize on the hero's behalf. Inversely, the central place of affection, trust, and intimacy in liberation politics gave rise to the painful wounds of betrayal as Hugh Lewin (2011) and Dlamini (2014) have explored.

SETTLER COLONIALISM, THE NATIVE QUESTION, AND THE POLITICS OF RELATION

In 1895 a young Jan Smuts delivered his first published political address in Kimberley. Intended as a critique of Schreiner's views, Smuts's speech began by placing the defense of western civilization at the center of South African politics. He described South Africa as an imperiled white outpost surrounded by a sea of barbarism and savagery. A proper approach to the Native Question, therefore, began with building a common white identity, itself a kind of friendship, in order to strengthen civilization's resolve against the military and cultural-biological threat of African demographic superiority. If this celebration of white domination served to rebuke Schreiner and the color-blind franchise of the early Cape, it nonetheless accompanied a conception of trusteeship that shared Schreiner's insistence on the interwoven destinies of the settler and the African. The failure to gradually raise the native would ultimately lead to their mutual ruination:

> The Natives are our servants and nurses; they are to a large extent the playmates of our children; they dwell among us in towns and on our farms; in short, they constitute a permanent part of our moral and social environment. According to the character of that environment will be its influence on us. ... I mention these considerations to show that our white supremacy in South Africa has grave responsibilities which, for our own sake as well as for the sake of the aborigines, we are bound to discharge faithfully (Hancock and Van Der Poel 2007: 96).

The conclusion that Smuts drew from this formulation paralleled Schreiner's vision of a racial catastrophe. If exploitation and colonial violence threatened to plunge the country into a racial apocalypse, only a society based on the native's willing embrace of a shared civilizational project could guarantee a common future. Smuts argued that the pedagogy of 'civilizing labour' (see Barchiesi 2011, 2012), rather than education or culture, would 'discipline the Native into something worthy of our civilization and *his* humanity' (emphasis added). Because colonialism had produced the interdependence of white and black, the African's acceptance of a common future – the native's desire for entrance into civilization – was the very basis of its survival. At the time, the African's incorporation could only ever take the form of subordination: the process of assimilation was forever incomplete.

Schreiner's and Smuts' reflections underline the relationship between three questions that reoccur throughout the contributions to this volume: the Native Question, settler civil society, and the politics of relation. As Premesh Lalu (2009) has argued, the Native Question was consolidated during the early twentieth century as an administrative and academic discourse regarding the formation of African subjectivities. Lalu (2011) explains: 'Caught between a discourse on vanishing cultures and the story of progress, academic disciplines performed the role of trusteeship over the category of the native, which appeared resolutely bound to administrative decree and capitalist demand.' In other words, the Native Question defined the problem of colonial governance as the disciplining, management, and gradual uplift of populations no longer located in the idealized realm of African tradition, but not yet fully incorporated as modern subjects within liberal capitalism (see also Barchiesi 2012).

Despite their opposing political perspectives, Schreiner and Smuts's late nineteenth-century formulation of the Native Question adds two critical dimensions to our understanding of this discursive framework. First, this discourse presupposed the universality of bourgeois civil society or (in Smuts's language) civilization. A robust concept incorporating private property, the heteronormative nuclear family, Christianity, and western law, civilization provided the basis for the assimilation or exclusion of the native. In effect, the Native Question occurred at the limits of the universalization of bourgeois civil society as a political project: this limit was then projected onto the body of the colonized as an imminent danger to civilization. Second, Smuts and Schreiner understood the central problem of colonial governance in terms of the interdependency of colonizer and colonized. If segregation and indirect rule would emerge as the preferred solutions to the Native Question in the 1920s (Mamdani 1996), they nevertheless presupposed a more fundamental question of managing entanglement. This framework was a way of conceptualizing the relationship between those who enjoyed citizenship within settler civil society and the perpetually unassimilated bodies that must be both excluded and controlled. As a result, the Native Question placed the politics of relation at the center of imagining colonial power. It also required a fundamentally hypocritical disavowal of 'exploitation', that is, the forms of economic and political violence that underwrote civil society as a colonial project.

Situated at the fringes of European expansion (at least before the discovery of gold in the 1880s), South Africa emerged from a patchwork of European enclaves, frontier economies, colonial protectorates, and experiments in indirect rule over African societies (Keegan 1996). Over the course of the eighteenth and nineteenth centuries, the South African racial order gradually emerged from four founding moments of violence: the genocide of the San peoples, the instantiation of a slave society in the Western Cape, the deployment of Indian indentured labor in Natal, and the destruction of independent African landownership across southern Africa through either expulsion or indirect rule. While exterminating force was directed at the Cape San (Adhikari 2011), settler formations developed adjacent to and in conflict with African societies that the South African state (unified in 1910) brought fully under its control in the early twentieth century. Even then the dispossession of Africans was never fully completed: the reach of civil society was considerably less extensive and absolute than in other settler contexts. By attacking indigenous control of land, colonialism undermined the economic, political, and cultural foundations of pre-colonial existence (Landau 2010), while refusing Africans entry into a common social life as citizens. In relationship to settler civil society, African societies endured a form of collective social death. Frank Wilderson III (2010) reworks Orlando Patterson's use of the term social death in the context of Atlantic slavery, describing it as a state of general dishonor, natal alienation, the absence of protections created by mutually recognized social ties, and perpetual vulnerability to gratuitous violence.[6] Since settler civil society structurally and psychically maintains the violence that creates and perpetuates social death, it necessarily reproduces anti-blackness as a historical formation.

Despite the linguistic and political differences within the settler population, a shared commitment to European domination cohered in the nineteenth century around the idea of white civilization as an assemblage of property ownership, law, and Christianity. If South Africa differed from Canada, Australia, and the U.S. in terms of the demographic weight of the colonized population and its considerable economic integration into relations of capitalist exploitation, the civilizational ideal echoed and articulated with a global project of white supremacy. The foundation of anti-blackness was not a particular *form* of colonial power or political economy. Anti-blackness was produced by the whiteness – as a social formation and a political project –

that civil society both creates and defends. While insisting on the importance of political economy, embodiment, and everyday materiality, Wilderson's (2010: 18) approach understands 'anti-Blackness' as a relation of non-relation:

> But *African*, or more precisely *Blackness*, refers to an individual who is by definition already devoid of relationality. Thus modernity marks the emergence of a new ontology because it is an era in which an entire race appears, people who, a priori, that is prior to the contingency of the 'transgressive act' (such as losing a war or being convicted of a crime), stand as socially dead in relation to the rest of the world.

This analysis does not necessarily, as some worry, slide into essentialism by reducing black subjectivities to suffering and pathology (Moten 2014). Rather the critique of white universality (understood both as citizenship and human capacity) demands a reconsideration of all our social and political categories. As Jared Sexton (2011: 29–30) explains: 'We learn not just that power operates intimately (which is does) or that intimacy is inextricable from the question of power (which it is), but that the relation between the two … deranges what we mean, or what we thought we understood, by the former *and* the latter.' Thinking white supremacy and anti-blackness requires that we confront a relationality that exceeds the language of relation: the constitutive violence of settler civil society works to render full, ethical reciprocity between white and black – that is, friendship in the classic, Aristotelian sense – impossible *in advance*. This unavoidable centrality of a 'relation of non-relation' brings urgency to thinking through the politics of friendship in South Africa.

'FRIEND OF THE NATIVE'
As a discourse and idea, friendship between colonizer and colonized played a number of different, if sometimes overlapping, roles in South Africa during the late nineteenth and twentieth centuries. It provided a flexible language for the articulation and development of social solidarity across multiple sites, including the mission station, liberal organizations such as the Joint Councils movement and the South African Institute of Race Relations, trade unions, colonial commissions, cultural organizations, and the personal relationships that developed in these spaces. In this sense, the term 'friend' possessed an ambiguity that historians have noted in other contexts: it could

refer both to a privileged, intimate relationship and to a broader range of social acquaintances (Caine 2011). Overlapping with a Christian discourse of universal friendship, this language circulated alongside related terms such as brotherhood (indicating the gendered character of the discourse), cooperation (which became Colonial Office policy in the 1940s), and – in the language of the international labor movement – solidarity. As illustrated through Smuts's insistence on the primacy of white unity, this rhetoric informed a significant debate over where friendship should begin and the boundaries created by affective social ties. In the face of the colonized, settler nationalism frequently insisted on the sanctity of European brotherhood (see Tallie in this volume).

The intersection of race and friendship reinforced an element of racialized performance in South African life and politics. The dominant framework for staging the relationship between colonizer and colonized, both in South Africa and throughout the British Empire, was white paternalism: the patriarchal and heteronormative family provided the template for the affective dimensions of the colonial relationship (Nandy 1983). To a certain degree, liberal efforts to stage the friendship between black and white (such as the Joint Councils movement of the 1930s, and the liberal tea parties frequently mocked in the writings of black authors) sought to reconfigure this performance in order to create an image of equality. As BC leader Biko (2004) argued, this dramaturgy transformed black bodies into symbols of white enlightenment. The presence of Africans in liberal spaces lent them legitimacy. Inversely, some liberal activists urged the visibility of whites within black spaces and movements in order to reinforce their 'peaceful' and 'civilized' character. According to this conception, the presence of whites would break down preconceptions and resentments, thus guarding against the development of (an ostensibly exclusionary) African nationalism. It was in this sense that the liberal newspaper of the 1950s was entitled *Contact* (Soske 2015).

Liberal trusteeship, the civilized labor policy, and the ideology of indirect rule each implied the eventual entrance of Africans into modern civil society (or civilization) even as this outcome was deferred indefinitely and undermined in practice. The conceptualization of the Native Question also framed a theory of African nationalism. If the success of colonial friendship manifested in the gratitude of the native, the independent political organization of Africans was seen as symptomatic of a profound failure. In the eyes of Schreiner and Smuts, the policy of exploitation, by eroding the promise of a common future, drove the oppressed to a rejection of friendship. This narrative found its highest expression in Alan Paton's 1948 novel *Cry the Beloved County* and the 1940s liberal trope of the South African tragedy. Echoing Schreiner and Smuts, Paton (1948: 250) projected the dreaded reversal into the mouth of an African character: 'I have one great fear in my heart, that one day when they turn to loving they will find that we are turned to hating.' Stripped of independent historical trajectory, native agency was reduced to the embrace or rejection of white society.

From its inception, African nationalism developed a critical understanding of the discourse of liberal friendship. In the early decades of the ANC, leaders sought entrance for 'civilized Africans' into a common society with settlers, even as they frequently challenged the way that civilization and the capacity for citizenship was defined (Limb 2010). At the same time, nationalist intellectuals rejected white trusteeship in the name of African unity and agency (Butler 2013). Whatever their other differences, most African thinkers agreed that a truly universal civilization would not come through the graces of colonial assimilation, but necessitated the struggle of Africans to build a national identity and their own modern institutions. On this basis, Africans would enter modernity on their own terms and meet whites as equals. The critical embrace of civil society reproduced aspects of anti-blackness even as it articulated an African political subject in opposition to white supremacy (see Barchiesi in this volume). It also generated a profoundly conflictual relationship with the liberal friend of the native. Even as figures such as John Dube, the first president of the ANC, struggled to create the foundations of an independent African intellectual and social life, they relied on the patronage of white benefactors who constrained and occasionally sabotaged their activities (Hughes 2011). Although it was often expressed in private letters or within black-only spaces, the critique of the liberal friend was not an innovation of the ANC Youth League intellectual Anton Lembede or Biko, but an integral part of African political thinking. As ANC president Albert Luthuli (1991: 166) declared in 1960:

> The formation of the Union of South Africa saw the beginning of the defeat
> of liberalism as expressed by so-called Cape liberals of the day. Because of its

paternalism, many non-whites will not regret the demise of such liberalism. The issues of the struggle for freedom and democracy by non-whites are now so clear cut as to admit of no confusing assistance from our friends of the liberal paternalistic outlook who often advocate a timeless gradualism. This has sometimes provoked the cry, 'oh, save us from our friends'.

CHAPTER OUTLINE

Exploring a variety of sites both contemporary and historical, the volume *Ties That Bind* presents a kaleidoscopic view into the question of how friendship operates in relation to race in the context of South Africa. The chapters that follow examine this question through the lenses of history, art, work, education, fiction, and poetry, bringing to bear history, personal experiences, political theory, archives, ethnographies, and storytelling. We have included a broad range of scholars from different backgrounds and traditions to tackle the questions posed in this book.

The volume begins with Sisonke Msimang's powerful documentary theatre piece on friendship and race in post-apartheid South Africa in Chapter Two. Originally created for the Ruth First lecture series at Wits University in Johannesburg and performed with Lebo Mashile, Msimang reignited public debate on the nature of friendship across racial divisions, succinctly revealing the illusions of the rainbow nation and the contradictions of shared affections.

In Chapter Three, Stacy Hardy offers an explosive interpretative interview with poet, playwright, and musician Lesego Rampolokeng, an activist in the BC movement often noted for his spoken word performances and contributions with musicians such as Souleymane Touré, Louis Mhlanga, and the Kalahari Surfers. Hardy keeps up with Rampolokeng as he ruminates on the violence, music, betrayals, and impossibilities of friendship in South Africa both during and after apartheid. Their engagement moves in modes that defy register, from humor to anger, and from obtuse poetics to thoughtful intellectual engagement.

A number of authors in the volume cite the work of Frank Wilderson III, and in Chapter Four we include an interview with Wilderson, outlining his ideas on the theoretical underpinnings of Afro-pessimism, race and friendship, speaking specifically to his experiences in the South African context. Wilderson's ideas are woven through the volume, and the interview gives some form and context for why they are applicable in South Africa.

In Chapter Five, T. J. Tallie explores how the limits of sociality and friendship across race were central to settler colonial logic in Natal from the 1850s through the 1910s. In his detailed historical account, Tallie looks at ways debates about friendship with Africans played into both the aspirations and limitations of settler colonialism. Thinking through the idea of friendship as a coercive gift, Tallie focuses specifically on elements of subversive sociality, such as alcohol consumption, as a social bond between whites as well as its potential danger for the colonial rule of non-whites. Imagined through the impossible handshake Bishop John Colenso expressly wished he could have offered the African, Tallie offers an insightful reading of how friendship could simultaneously reinforce and unsettle gendered and raced hierarchies.

Franco Barchiesi's chapter, 'The Problem with "We": Affiliation, Political Economy, and the Counterhistory of Nonracialism' brings together a number of central themes that unite the volume. Barchiesi builds a counterhistory to the origins and preoccupations of nonracialism, rooted in the African response to the liberal friend of the native discourse. In an iconoclastic re-reading of the historical literature, Barchiesi argues that the dependency of the concept on the structures of settler colonial rule and racial antagonism has led non-racial nationalism to re-inscribe anti-blackness. He focuses specifically on the evolution of African nationalism and its critique of paternalist white friendship, arguing that the complicity between non-racialism and anti-blackness has been part of the celebration of political economy, work, and a generic, impossible idea of a nationalist 'We'.

Following Barchiesi's discussion of the political economy of friendship, Bridget Kenny expands the focus to examine the affective encounters between citizens and the South African state in Chapter Seven. Kenny brings ethnographic richness to think about contemporary ways that relationships of care and recognition exist between black workers and the state, and how such social relations enable precarious work. Grounded in detailed interviews conducted at the Casual Worker Advice Office in Germiston in 2012, Kenny unravels how friendship and affective relationships between precarious workers and the State reproduce vulnerability, while at the same time creating a space of political contestation that creates important types of solidarities and resistance. Kenny investigates how workers imagine and desire becoming an active public, invoking both the promise of possible futures, recognition, and the reality of exhaustion. Building on the work of Lauren Berlant, Kenny focuses on the 'cruel optimism' that workers have towards the promise of full-time employment and social assistance, even if that promise can never be fully realized.

From the realm of political economy and the state, we turn to art spaces and artistic practices that represent, enable, and contest ideas around race and friendship. In Chapter Eight, Daniel Magaziner investigates the friendships that were forged at the Ndaleni Art School in Natal between 1952 and 1981. Founded by the South African government to train students to teach arts and crafts in the Bantu education system, the school transformed into a space of expression, friendship, and limited freedoms partially removed from the rigid structures of apartheid. Here intimacies and friendships blossomed in unique ways. Rather than celebrating such a space as representing a lost history of multiracialism, Magaziner uses Ndaleni to place the politics of friendship at the center of an apartheid institution. Provocatively, Magaziner argues that art students embraced the strictures of the school in order to achieve community through a form of subjugation and dependence that was an alternative to the form that white supremacy took outside its walls.

In Chapter Nine, M. Neelika Jayawardane brings us into new territory, with readings of the artistic and literary representations of the relationships between maids and madams, which peer into affective spaces of domestic life. Through reading photographs of madams and their maids, Jayawardane exposes how the trope 'friend of the family' conceals multiple forms of power at play. She explores the complex ways in which the body of the maid serves as a counterpoint for the desires and self-perception of the white madam. Jayawardane interrogates the contradictions inherent in how this familiar relationship poses as friendship in the intimate spaces of South African households through readings of various photographic works.

Continuing on the theme of artistic representations, the artists' collective MADEYOULOOK confronts in Chapter Ten the absence of a language to speak about black love. In 'Corner Loving: Ways of Speaking about Love', the artists attempt to invent such a language by probing contemporary art, writing, and poetry that deals with modes of intimacy, ranging from the illicit street corner encounter to the complex interplay of music, language, and local idioms to concoct new ways of imagining and representing black love.

They suggest that the representation of black love necessitates a new visual and critical *tonality* that reflects the feel and nature of black love itself.

In Chapter Eleven, 'Kutamba Naye: In Search of Anti-Racist and Queer Solidarities', Tsitsi Jaji combines personal narrative and academic inquiry to navigate her discomfort and distress in attempting to forge alliances with a white Zimbabwean artist and former school friend, fusing critical race theory with the daily affective dissonance of personal encounters. In interrogating the transition of friendship from girlhood to womanhood through the lens of race, Jaji uncovers some of her own hidden secrets and unexamined truths. Bringing together personal writing, e-mail exchanges, and critical reflections, Jaji parses out of the difficulties of reimagining friendship as another kind of solidarity.

Finally, Mosa Phadi and Nomancotsho Pakade explore the complex experience of studying as black graduate students in a higher education context in South Africa, where the expectation is to preform blackness both as subject and object in the role they powerfully describe as the *native informant*. They argue that the olive branch of friendship offered to black students through white mentorship often hides levels of exploitation and objectification, which can ultimately smother the ability for black students to survive and thrive, both academically and economically. The authors find themselves in a precarious position of racialised knowledge production, simultaneously used as part of the transformation agenda of government and unable to fully exist as subjects without preforming as *native informants*. This positioning is all the more pertinent given the eruption of student movements that interrogate the raced spaces of contemporary university campuses and the decolonization of education in South Africa.

REFERENCES

Adhikari, Mohamed. 2011. *The Anatomy of a South African Genocide: The Extermination of the Cape San Peoples*. Athens, OH: Ohio University Press.

Ahmed, Sara. 2010. *Happy Objects*. In *The Affect Theory Reader*, edited by M. Gregg, and G. J. Seigworth, 29–51. Durham, NC, & London: Duke University Press.

Baderoon, Gabeba. 2014. *Regarding Muslims: From Slavery to Apartheid*. Johannesburg: Wits University Press.

Barchiesi, Franco. 2011. *Precarious Liberation: Workers, the State, and Contested Social Citizenship in Post-Apartheid South Africa*. Albany, NY: SUNY Press.

Barchiesi, Franco. 2012. 'Imagining the Patriotic Worker: The Idea of "Decent Work" in the ANC's Political Discourse.' In *One Hundred Years of the ANC: Debating Liberation Histories Today,* edited by Arianna Lissoni, Jon Soske, Natasha Erlank, Noor Nieftagodien, and Omar Badsha, 1–27. Johannesburg: Wits University Press.

Berlant, Lauren. 1997. *The Queen of America Goes to Washington City: Essays on Sex and Citizenship*. Durham, NC: Duke University Press.

Berlant, Lauren. 2011. *Cruel Optimism*. Durham, NC: Duke University Press.

Biko, Steve. 2004. *I Write What I Like: A Selection of his Writings*. Cape Town: Picador Africa.

Booysen, Susan. 2011. *The African National Congress and the Regeneration of Political Power*. Johannesburg: Wits University Press.

Burns, Catherine. 2007. 'Pubic Publics: The Zuma Trial and the History of Sex in South Africa.' History and African Studies Seminar Series, May 30.

Burns, Catherine. 2012. 'Writing the History of Sex in South Africa.' Presented at WISER, Johannesburg, August 6.

Burton, Antoinette. 2011. *Empire in Question*. Durham, NC: Duke University Press.

Butler, Anthony. 2013. *The Idea of the ANC*. Athens, OH: Ohio University Press.

Byrd, Jodi A. 2011. *The Transit of Empire: Indigenous Critiques of Colonialism*. Minneapolis, MN: University of Minnesota Press.

Caine, Barbara. 2011. 'Prisons as Spaces of Friendships in Apartheid South Africa.' *History Australia* 3(2): 42.1–42.13.

Caine, Barbara. 2014. *Friendship: A History*. New York: Routledge.

Cole, Jennifer and Lynn M. Thomas, eds. 2009. *Love in Africa*. Chicago, IL and London: University of Chicago Press.

Derrida, Jacques. 1997. *Politics of Friendship*. London: Verso.

Desai, Ashwin. 2014. *Reading Revolution: Shakespeare on Robben Island.* Chicago, IL: Haymarket Books.

Dlamini, Jacob. 2009. *Native Nostalgia*. Johannesburg: Jacana Media.

Dlamini, Jacob. 2014. *Askari: A Story of Collaboration and Betrayal in the Anti-Apartheid Struggle*. Johannesburg: Jacana Media.

Epprecht, Marc. 2004. *Hungochani: A History of Dissident Sexuality in Southern Africa*. Montreal/Kingston: McGill-Queen's University Press.

Epprecht, Marc. 2008. *Heterosexual Africa? The History of an Idea from the Age of Exploration to the Age of AIDS*. Athens, OH: Ohio University Press.

Fassin, Didier. 2007. *When Bodies Remember: Experiences and Politics of AIDS in South Africa*. Berkeley and Los Angeles, CA: University of California Press.

Gandhi, Leela. 2005. *Affective Communities: Anticolonial Thought, Fin-de-Siècle Radicalism, and the Politics of Friendship*. Durham, NC: Duke University Press.

Goniwe, Thembinkosi. 2010. 'De-Segregating the Audience: Race & the Politics of Exhibitions.' Presented at Beyond the Racial Lens: Bonani Africa Festival of Documentary Photography, Cape Town, August 19.

Goniwe, Thembinkosi. 2011. 'Desire: Ideal Narratives in Contemporary South African Art.' *African Identities* 9(2): 247–248.

Gordimer, Nadine. 1976. 'English-Language Literature and Politics in South Africa.' *Journal of Southern African Studies* 2(2): 131–150.

Gqola, Pumla Dineo. 2009. '"The Difficult Task of Normalizing Freedom": Spectacular Masculinities, Ndebele's Literary/Cultural Commentary and Post-Apartheid Life.' *English in Africa* 36(1): 61–76.

Gqola, Pumla Dineo. 2010. *What is Slavery to Me? Postcolonial/Slave Memory in Post-Apartheid South Africa*. Johannesburg: Wits University Press.

Hancock, William K., and Jean Van Der Poel. 2007. *Selections from the Smuts Papers: Volume 1, June 1886–May 1902*. Cambridge: Cambridge University Press.

Hartman, Saidiya. 1997. *Scenes of Subjection: Terror, Slavery, and Self-Making in Nineteenth-Century America*. London: Oxford University Press.

Hughes, Heather. 2011. *First President: A Life of John L. Dube, Founding President of the ANC*. Johannesburg: Jacana Media.

Hunter, Mark. 2010. *Love in the Time of AIDS: Inequality, Gender and Rights in South Africa*. Bloomington and Indianapolis, IN: Indiana University Press.

Jacobs, Sean. 2002. 'Jacobs on Nuttall and Michael, "Sense of Culture".' Review of *Senses of Culture: South African Culture Studies*, edited by Sarah Nuttall and Cheryl-Ann Michael. *Humanities and Social Sciences Online*, September. http://www.h-net.org/reviews/showrev.php?id=6731

Jamal, Ashraf. 2004. 'The Bearable Lightness of Tracey Rose's The Kiss.' *Chimurenga Magazine*. August 16. Accessed online: http://www.chimurenga.co.za/archives/1028

Keegan, Tim. 1996. *Colonial South Africa and the Origins of the Racial Order*. London: Leicester University Press.

King, Preston and Graham, M. Smith, eds. 2007. *Friendship in Politics.* New York, NY: Routledge.

Lalu, Premesh. 2009. *The Deaths of Hintsa: Post-Apartheid South Africa and the Shape of Recurring Pasts*. Cape Town: HSRC Press.

Lalu, Premesh. 2011. 'Restless Natives, Native Questions.' *Mail & Guardian*, August 28.

Landau, Paul S. 2010. *Popular Politics in the History of South Africa, 1400–1948*. New York: Cambridge University Press.

Lewin, Hugh. 2011. *Stones against the Mirror: Friendship in the Time of the South African Struggle.* Cape Town: Umuzi.

Limb, Peter. 2010. *The ANC's Early Years: Nation, Class and Place in South Africa before 1940.* Pretoria: Unisa Press.

Lowe, Lisa. 2015. *The Intimacies of Four Continents*. Durham, NC: Duke University Press.

Luthuli, Albert. 1991. *Luthuli: Speeches of Chief Albert John Luthuli 1898–1967*. Complied by E. S. Reddy. Durban: Madiba Publishers.

Mamdani, Mahmood. 1996. *Citizen and Subject: Contemporary Africa and the Legacy of Late Colonialism.* Princeton, NJ: Princeton University Press.

Mandela, Nelson. 1995. *Long Walk to Freedom: The Autobiography of Nelson Mandela*. Boston, MA: Back Bay Books.

Massumi, Brian. 2002. *Parables for the Virtual: Movement, Affect, Sensation*. Durham, NC: Duke University Press.

Moten, Fred. 2014. 'Blackness and nothingness (mysticism in the flesh).' *South Atlantic Quarterly*. 112(4).

Mphahlele, Es'kia. 1957. *The Non-European Character in South African English Fiction*. Master's Thesis. University of South Africa (Unisa).

Nandy, Ashis. 1983. *The Intimate Enemy: Loss and Recovery of Self under Colonialism*. Oxford: Oxford University Press.

Ndebele, Njabulo. 1986. 'The Rediscovery of the Ordinary: Some New Writings in South Africa.' *Journal of Southern African Studies* 12(2): 143–157.

Ndebele, Njabulo. 1996. 'A Home for Intimacy.' *Mail & Guardian*, April 26: 28–29.

Ndebele, Njabulo. 2000. '"Iph'Indlela? Finding our Way into the Future": The First Steve Biko Memorial Lecture.' *Social Dynamics* 26(1): 43–55.

Ndebele, Njabulo. 2013. 'Foreword.' In *Categories of Persons: Rethinking Ourselves and Others,* edited by Megan Jones and Jacob Dlamini. Johannesburg: Picador Africa.

Nkosi, Lewis. 1983. *Home and Exile and Other Selections*. Boston, MA: Addison-Wesley Longman Ltd.

Nkosi, Lewis. 2002. 'The Republic of Letters after the Mandela Republic.' *Journal of Literary Studies* 18(3–4): 240–258.

Nuttall, Sarah. 2009. *Entanglement: Literary and Cultural Reflections on Post-Apartheid.* Johannesburg: Wits University Press.

Nuttall, Sarah, and Cheryl-Ann Michael, eds. 2000. *Senses of Culture: South African Culture Studies.* Oxford: Oxford University Press.

O'Malley, Padraig. 2007. *Shades of Difference: Mac Maharaj and the Struggle for South Africa.* New York, NY: Viking Adult.

Paton, Alan. 1948. *Cry, the Beloved Country.* New York, NY: Simon and Schuster.

Patterson, Orlando. 1982. *Slavery and Social Death: A Comparative Study.* Cambridge MA: Harvard University Press.

Peffer, John. 2009. *Art and the End of Apartheid.* Minneapolis, MN: University of Minnesota Press.

Plaatje, Sol. 1930 (1975). *Mhudi.* Johannesburg and London: Quagga Press.

Posel, Deborah. 2005. 'Sex, Death and the Fate of the Nation: Reflections on the Politicization of Sexuality in Post-Apartheid South Africa.' *Africa* 75(2): 125–153.

Posel, Deborah, Jonathan Hyslop, and Noor Nieftagodien. 2001. 'Debating Race in South African Scholarship.' *Transformation*: i–xviii.

Rassool, Ciraj. 2004. *The Individual, Auto/Biography and History in South Africa.* PhD Diss. University of the Western Cape.

Shreiner, Olive. 1883. *The Story of an African Farm.* London: Chapman and Hall.

Schreiner, Olive. 1896. Letter to John X. Merriman. May 25. NLSA Cape Town: Special Collections, Olive Schreiner Letters Project Transcription.

Sexton, Jared. 2008. *Amalgamation Schemes: Anti-Blackness and the Critique of Multiracialism.* Minneapolis, MN: University of Minnesota Press.

Sexton, Jared. 2011. 'The Social Life of Social Death: On Afro-Pessimism and Black Optimism.' *InTensions* 5: 1–47.

Silver, Allan. 1989. 'Friendship and Trust as Moral Ideals: An Historical Approach.' *European Journal of Sociology* 30(2): 274–297.

Simpson, Audra. 2014. *Mohawk Interruptus: Political Life across the Borders of Settler States.* Durham, NC: Duke University Press.

Simpson, Leanne. 2013. *Islands of Decolonial Love: Stories & Songs.* Winnipeg, MB: Arp Books.

Soske, Jon. 2012. 'Open Secrets, Off the Record: Audience, Intimate Knowledge, and the Crisis of the Post-Apartheid State.' *Historical Reflections.* 38(2): 55–70.

Soske, Jon. 2015. 'The Impossible Concept: Settler Liberalism, Pan-Africanism, and the Language of Non-Racialism.' *African Historical Review* 47(2): 1–39.

Suttner, Raymond. 2008. *The ANC Underground in South Africa*. Johannesburg: Nordiska Afrikainstitutet & Jacana Media.

Vladislavić, Ivan. 2008. 'Staffrider.' *Chimurenga Magazine*. Accessed online: http://chimurengalibrary.co.za/staffrider-an-essay-by-ivan-vladislavic

Walsh, Shannon. 2009. 'Ethnography-in-Motion: Neoliberalism and South African Shack Dwellers' Movements.' In *Education, Participatory Action Research, and Social Change: International Perspectives*, edited by D. Kapoor and S. Jordan. New York, NY: Palgrave-MacMillan.

Wilderson, Frank B. III. 2010. *Red, White & Black: Cinema and the Structure of US Antagonisms*. Durham, NC: Duke University Press.

Wolfe, Patrick. 2006. 'Settler Colonialism and the Elimination of the Native.' *Journal of Genocide Research* 8(4): 387–409.

Woods, Donald. 1987. *Biko*. New York, NY: Henry Holt & Company.

NOTES

1   'Native' and 'Native Question' are both racialized terms of colonial discourse. However, in order to avoid cluttering the text, we have placed these terms in quotes at first usage only and ask the reader to extend the quotes throughout.

2   The distinction between friendship and enmity is core to a great deal of political theory, and has been discussed by theorists such as Chantal Mouffe, Hannah Arendt, Michael Hardt, Antonio Negri, Bruno Latour, and Giorgio Agamben. Mouffe argues that liberalism attempts to smother the friend/enemy distinction in political philosophy, seeking to reduce it to a resolvable conflict, police operation, or difference of opinion. As Preston King and Graham Smith ask in their edited book *Friendship in Politics* (2007: 44): 'From Aristotle's analysis of the nature of the polis we can retain the idea that what keeps the polis together is a kind of friendship — the question is *which* kind of friendship. Both the liberal form, the generalized friendship of utility, and the authoritarian form, the total unity that ensues from the logic of the political in the interpretation of Carl Schmitt, do keep the polis together, but at the expense of it being political. The question is, therefore, which kind of political friendship is capable of *both* keeping the polis *together* and keeping it *political*.'

3   Lauren Berlant (1997, 2011) also examines the interplay of desire with the notions of republican citizenship, subjecthood, and the promise of a 'good life', arguing that many notions of the political as such rest on a collection of fantasies and desires that animate what it means to be a citizen subject.

4   We would like to highlight, especially, the importance of the series of four
    conferences entitled *Love & Revolution* held at the University of the Western Cape
    (1 and 4), at the University of Minnesota (2), and at the Nehru Memorial Library in
    New Delhi (3). Patricia Hayes, Premesh Lalu, and G. Anurima are currently editing a
    selection of papers from these conferences.
5   Jared Sexton (2008) notably takes issue with ideas of both creolization and
    multiracialism in his important book *Amalgamation Schemes: Anti-Blackness and the
    Critique of Multiracialism*.
6   Orlando Patterson (1982) employed the term 'social death' to describe the alienation
    of individuals from their birth societies and their transformation into permanent
    outsiders (slaves) lacking the protection of kinship ties and other forms of social
    reciprocity.

WITH FRIENDS LIKE THESE: THE POLITICS OF FRIENDSHIP IN POST-APARTHEID SOUTH AFRICA

SISONKE MSIMANG

This research took the form of many late nights grappling with texts, everything from social network theory to studies on urban space and planning to philosophy. What it produced is fairly unique, part of a growing genre known as documentary theatre.[1] I have taken verbatim the words of people such as Sindiwe Magona, Njabulo Ndebele, Dennis Brutus, Zama Ndlovu, Sekoatlane Phamodi, and many other South Africans who are thinking publically about the problems South Africa faces and the dreams we must embrace, and I have asked Lebo Mashile, one of our country's most important contemporary poets, to perform them in order to make them visual.

I chose this methodology because I wanted us to remember that we have already written many, many important things about race and justice and humanity in this country. I also chose the documentary theatre genre because here in South Africa fact is often stranger and more poignant than fiction. In this context, performing real words on a stage forces us to confront their importance and it moves us beyond business as usual.

Lastly, I chose this genre because I wanted to signal that there is a new generation of contemporary thinkers: people such as Milisuthando Bongela, Danielle Bowler, T. O. Molefe, and others who are cited here, whose words are as much a window into this country's collective soul as those of Gordimer or Coetzee or Paton.

Now that the season of realpolitik is upon us and the rainbow myth is receding we must ask ourselves whether we still need a framework of reconciliation that presupposes friendship across the races as an important and useful barometer of the health of the nation.

Some will argue that the question of friendship is frivolous. They will say we must be more concerned with matters of politics and economics than of emotion, and that we don't need to be friends; we simply need not to interfere with one another's destinies. Others will insist that we must indeed be friends. They will wring their hands and argue that to abandon the idea of friendship is to abandon an important national ideal and perhaps to abandon a peaceful future.

Perhaps counterintuitively we must hold on to both instincts. On the one hand, our progress in improving the conditions of black people must be central and must be guided not by a desire for blacks and whites to be friends, but by the need for black people to live dignified and equal lives that are commensurate with those of their white compatriots. In defence of this, we must be prepared to alienate whites (and for that matter blacks) who do not accept this as a fundamental reality. We must accept that they might leave and seek their fortunes elsewhere and this must not concern us.

On the other hand, we must accept that although the notion of inter-racial friendship has sometimes threatened to overshadow the importance of black dignity, it is crucial that we keep its possibility alive, even as we tend to the more urgent matters of preserving and elevating the meaning of black personhood because this is the basis upon which a genuine and robust culture of respect in contemporary South Africa will be built.

To even begin to talk about interracial respect in modern South Africa is difficult because so much unintentional damage was done by our country's first iteration of reconciliation; what I refer to as Reconciliation 1.0. There were many flaws in that first version. Yet in light of palpable anger and discord on race in recent years, we have a new opportunity to develop a more honest code: call it the open source version. Indeed the seeds of this are evident in the activism that swept our country in 2015. South African students are at the forefront of designing the upgrade, and the next generation will owe them a debt of gratitude.

Ironically, perhaps, in thinking about how we deepen this new code we must stretch our minds back to ancient times, to the Greeks, to Aristotle in particular. For Aristotle, *philia* was the most perfect form of friendship. The great philosopher suggested that there are three kinds of friendship: friendships of convenience, where the parties interact, for example, in order to do business or Black Economic Empowerment deals; friendships of pleasure, where if the pleasurable thing, say drinking or smoking crack, disappeared, then the friendship would too; and friendships of character, in which 'one spends a great deal of time with the other person, participating in joint activities and engaging in mutually beneficial behavior'.

In this view: 'Between friends there is no need for justice, but people who are just still need the quality of friendship; and indeed friendliness is considered to be justice in the fullest sense.'

In other words Aristotle argued that between real friends, there is seldom need for the interventions of outsiders; justice is made possible by the nature and depth of the relationship. In short, where there is trust, there is no need for strongly enforced rules. By extension then, those who consider themselves to be good and moral cannot be truly good or moral if they do not have the 'friends' to prove it.

For the white South African, who is surrounded by millions of black potential 'friends', the implied question in Aristotle's framing of the relationship between friendship and justice is, 'Are you just?'

Because of our history, this moral and practical question is especially directed at white people. Friendship should and must be of great ethical and philosophical concern for whites. In general, white people in this country should worry and be pained by this matter in ways that black people need not be, for obvious reasons of demography and history.

If we are to replace the distorted and falsely optimistic vision of the rainbow with a more honest but no less aspirational vision of dignity and respect, whites will need to give up their ideological and practical specialness and they will also have to reject the increasingly irrelevant, weepy, and unhelpful mythology of Rainbowism. Those who are truly invested in the future of this country will also have to stop hiding behind their emotions and their tears whenever the subject of race comes up.

One of the tenets of the rainbow era was that those of us who extended our hands across the racial divides were thwarting racism. If the racist hates it when children play together, then surely those of us who encourage our children to interact are not racist?

Unfortunately it is not so simple. Friendships involving people who are more powerful than us have seldom served black people well. The power imbalances are too great, the possibilities for manipulation and domination even by those with good intentions are simply too high to assume that light friendship is the answer.

Today, a generation into democracy, young black people raised to believe that friendship across the races is an indicator of progress are questioning this. They are asserting that friendship, if you want it, is not free of responsibility. Some of them are going further to say that friendship is simply not on the cards for them.

In a South Africa trying desperately to figure out a way forward these assertions are not easy to speak aloud. Yet they represent a recalibration of our aspirations. Some people are worried by this: They are scared of what they call 'separatism'.

I am not, mainly because this sort of robust honesty does not mean that we have abandoned the idea that 'race' is empty a construct that should neither bind nor divide anyone. We can both believe in the need for a just world in which race is meaningless, and accept that in this time and place, 'race' is a term that is bursting with meaning.

Can we be friends across these 'racial' boundaries? Yes, we can. And No, we cannot. It's that simple and that complex. It is the struggle for understanding the complexity of this paradox that must enthuse and inspire us.

WITH FRIENDS LIKE THESE

SISONKE   Dennis Brutus said:

LEBO   There will come a time we believe when the shape of the
                   planet and the divisions of the land will be less important
                   We will be caught in a glow of friendship
                   A red star of hope will illuminate our lives
                   A star of hope
                   A star of joy
                   A star of freedom[2]

SISONKE	Brutus reminds us that freedom in South Africa has always had a spiritual and moral quality. The founders of this democracy believed that they were creating a society in which friendships could and should exist across the races.
	Today, a cohort too young to have ever known formal apartheid is asking why they should trust whites. This is a pragmatic response to a poorly managed reconciliation process, but it is worth remembering things weren't always like this.
	Helen Joseph remembers walking into prison with Lilian Ngoyi after the women's march when with some bitterness, Ngoyi said to her:[3]
LEBO	You are better off with your pink skin.
SISONKE	Joseph agreed and thought of her friend once they were both in prison.
LEBO	My pink skin brought me a bed, sheets, blankets. The mattress was revolting, urine stained. But Lilian slept on a mat on the floor with only blankets. I had a sanitary bucket with a lid. She had an open bucket covered with a cloth.
SISONKE	Similarly, Elinor Sisulu writes that when she was imprisoned with Albertina Sisulu, Barbara Hogan kept asking:
LEBO	Is Ma Sisulu being given this food? If she is not, then I don't want it. Take it away.[4]
SISONKE	The days of friendship stronger than the bars of a jail cell seem distant now. Today, almost 80% of black people in Gauteng say that they will never be able to trust whites, and almost half of whites polled say they think that blacks and whites will never be able to trust each other.[5]

When I speak with nostalgia about this generation of women Lebo says:

LEBO

I wonder if we, perhaps, are not idealistic about this solidarity? Does it look more real because the consequences of white people's actions in showing support for black people were so harsh back then? Did struggle offer a place for intimate and sincere friendships, like sisterhood? I am thinking of how we support each other in close relationships, especially female friendships. The kinds of friends who help you get out of bad relationships, who pick you up when you are down, who watch your kids when you need to take care of yourself, who tell you when your man is up to shit ... Did relationships across colour go there?[6]

SISONKE

I am shaken. The old idea of friendship as a tool for anti-racist struggles seems irrelevant and old-fashioned now.

Sekoetlane Phamodi confronts interracial friendships with a thoroughly modern sensibility: by deleting his white Facebook friends.

LEBO

As I trawled through profile after profile and album after album, piecing together both my real and Facebook life narratives and where my 'friends' fit into it, I started to notice a disturbing pattern.

A vast majority of my 'friends' were white. And, for an overwhelming majority of these, I was one of a handful of black individuals in their social circles. Wait, what? ... In every friends' list and every photo album, I found myself playing a bittersweet game of 'spot the black'. Our mutual friends were almost always lily white. The social events were lily white. And the status updates and posts were well punctuated with whiteness. I began to turn this over and over in my mind. How was it that in a country where more than 80% of the population was black, I found myself the sole or one of a handful of blacks in a lily-white list, party or picture frame? How was it that in a country where more than 80% of the population was black, my white 'friends' had, if at all, so few black meaningful friends?[7]

SISONKE   Simamkele Dlakavu reflects on a Facebook fight, reminding us that just beneath the surface there is often a well of white rage:

LEBO   Last week, I witnessed on Facebook interracial 'friendships' explode when a black friend of mine posted: 'It seems that if you're white and male 70% of the work is [already] done.' This is the response she got:
                     'Actually my friend you [are] so far [from] the truth it's actually scary. White men especially young white men have [it] very tough in this black empowered country. Now try be a white male and look for a job in this anti-white country ... well sorry hun it ain't going to happen due to the fact that us white folk don't meet the BEE requirements. My husband is a white male and 70% of his work isn't done for him hey. If anything he has had to work harder due to the fact that his skin ain't black. So let's rather say be young and black and my darling this country is your oyster. But yet everyone is so up in arms about apartheid ... personally it's the best thing that happened for young black south africans [sic] cause now white people especially men don't stand a chance here.' [8]

SISONKE   No wonder then, that many of us are skeptical of white friends. Their feelings matter more than ours. Our gains are seen as their losses. Zama Ndlovu illustrates:

LEBO   My first promotion came in 2009, a year so bad the economy saw a record negative economic growth. Despite this, I was one of a handful of people to get a coveted promotion. A white male friend and colleague cut my celebratory mood short with a passing comment: 'Let's not pretend your promotion had nothing to do with affirmative action.'

SISONKE   Ndlovu is remarkably insightful about this personal sleight. She notes:

LEBO   Over time I have had to constantly remind myself that my white friends and I occupy the same spaces but live in different worlds. In their world, apartheid was a 46-year-long incident that ended in 1994, the moment Nelson Mandela dropped his ballot into the ballot box. [9]

LEBO & SISONKE   With friends like these who needs enemies?

SISONKE   It is not only that whites are insensitive to the experiences of their black friends, it is also the case that whites who are friends with one another often form strong bonds over casual racism. Remember this news item?

LEBO   (newsreader's voice) In Pretoria today, two University of Pretoria students will face disciplinary action after a photo of the two dressed up as black domestic workers went viral.
                   The photo shows the two women covered in brown paint, wearing scarves over their heads and with pillows stuffed into their skirts to make their buttocks look bigger.
                   The photos were posted on Facebook but were soon removed. [10]

SISONKE   Why do fun and carefree moments of white youthfulness so often involve mocking and denigrating black people? After this event, on radio someone called into PowerFM and asked,

LEBO   How can we be friends with these whites when their
                        children can so quickly forget the intimacy of being
                        mothered by black women?

SISONKE   The TRC should have investigated the domestic labor
                        system. It might have helped whites understand that
                        in South Africa racism and intimacy are not mutually
                        exclusive, that in fact racism and intimacy are often
                        bedfellows. Novelist Sindiwe Magona's star character
                        Stella tells this story:

LEBO   There swimming afloat in that water of hers was her panty
                        … she'd left it there for me to wash.
                            What? Me? I taught her a lesson, that very first day. I
                        took something, a peg, I think, and lifted that panty of
                        hers and put it dripping wet to the side of the bath which
                        I then cleaned until it was shiny shiny.
                            You think she got my message? Wrong. Doesn't she
                        leave me a note? Stella, wash the panty when you wash
                        the bath.
                            What do you mean what did I do? I did not go to
                        school for nothing. I found a pen in her bookshelf
                        and found a piece of paper and wrote her a note too:
                        'Medem,' I said in the note, 'please excuse me but I did
                        not think anyone can ask another person to wash their
                        panty. I was taught that a panty is the most intimate
                        thing … my mother told me no one else should even see
                        my panty. I really don't see how I can be asked to wash
                        someone else's panty.'
                            That was the end of that panty nonsense.[11]

(Lines delivered as both Lebo and Sisonke laugh)

SISONKE   … The most intimate thing. Cleaning and feeding
                        whites in a racist society is intimate. And we all know
                        that intimacy is complicated. In 2010, Sarit Swisa, a

Master's student at this institution [University of the Witwatersrand] interviewed young white South Africans about their attitudes towards the nannies who raised them.

LEBO

Ethan: Ja, like I have racial issues but it would never, she's different. She doesn't fall under that category in my book and ... the thing is as well; she's the only domestic that we've ever had that I've been close to. The rest have been ... they come, they go, they steal, they this, they that. I don't trust them.

Laura: Like, even from a young age we always tried to help her to get better at her English and um, my mom used to pay for her to study while she was working for us so that she could not be a maid but she just chose that, that was better for her. But at least she did get an opportunity to study and stuff so, which is good for her

SISONKE & LEBO

if she ever decides to do anything else.[12] (Chorus)

SISONKE

These children remind us that white people have never quite known what to do with black people's feelings. Our labor has mattered: our arms that push strollers; our backs that carry white infants; our hands that wash white women's panties.

More than that, as Rian Malan reminds us in this passage from his memoir, black female bodies have often been used in other ways by white male teenagers:

LEBO

After practice I set off on foot down to Abbotswold Road, swept along by a gang of jeering, sniggering teenage boys. Whenever I stopped, they joshed and jeered so I had to keep going. We came to a big white house. My mates decamped outside under a streetlight and I slunk down the dark alley that led to the servant's quarters, moving on tiptoe because what I was about to do was unlawful. I tapped an iron door and the black woman opened it, wearing a satin nightgown.

The room smelled of all the things I associated with servants: red floor polish, putu, and Lifebuoy soap. Even her bed was waist-high on bricks to thwart the tokoloshe. I took off my clothes and clambered onto it and then I was in her arms, overpowered by the smell of her, and terrified, utterly terrified. I couldn't talk to her because we had few words in common. I didn't know what to do. I recoiled at the thought of French-kissing her, but I did it anyway because I was a social democrat and I did not want to insult her. And then I pulled up the nightie and instants later it was over. I rolled off and asked, 'Was I good? Am I big enough?'

She said yes.

She was very kind.[13]

SISONKE & LEBO	This is why we cannot yet be friends.
SISONKE	Like many others, this ritual of white male bonding and friendship involved violence and laughter at the expense of a black body. These bodies are often but not always female. This news item too began with laughter, the object of a joke was a Muslim man with a beard.
LEBO:	Kazi (27), from Ventersdorp, was with his father's friend Anser Mahmood when they were attacked at a Chicken Licken outlet on Monday.

'Two white people ... they called him [Osama] bin Laden in Afrikaans because of his beard ... and then they called us kaffirs', Mahmood told Sapa by telephone on Wednesday.

'I don't know what he hit me with. I was unconscious.'

'Nobody helps us. They wanted me dead also, but I survived.'

North West police said a murder docket had been opened for Kazi's killing.[14]

SISONKE	The white men who killed Kazi were brothers: a bond even closer than friendship. It was a bond that allowed them to beat a black body to death. Roedolf Viviers was sentenced to just eight years for the murder. His brother walked free. I think of Xolela Mangcu who has noted that:
LEBO & SISONKE	This country is moving closer and closer to the brink of racial war, simply because white people refuse to take seriously the pain of black people.[15]
SISONKE	The present climate is combustible in part because whiteness itself is constructed as being under fire. Inside the laager, whites have a camaraderie, united by their victimhood and blacks increasing 'racialism'. The celebrated artist Willem Boshoff offers a stunning example of this mentality:
LEBO	I am proud to be labelled racist if it means that: I am revolted by dim-witted 4x4 politicians I appreciate security walls electrical fences, alarms and guard dogs I detest crime and criminals no matter what the colour of their skin I fly into a rage when sports teams are forced to select undeserving players I could scream in frustration when jobs are given to unqualified people …[16]
SISONKE	The ideology whites have built in service of themselves in this country lives and breathes through their allegiances to one another. It is facilitated by friendship and a sense of being attacked by people who don't look like them.
SISONKE	Many blacks are outraged by Boshoff but Ferial Haffajee has a different take: she is tired of black outrage because

she thinks that whites are of diminishing importance in South Africa. She writes:

LEBO   Think Bonang. Cassper. Minenhle. Do we celebrate how lovely we are as deeply as we rage at remnant racism?[17]

SISONKE   Haffajee has no time for this talk about black victimization. She doesn't understand our race obsession when we are now in charge:

LEBO   I see a generation saying it is enslaved in a system of white supremacy. I feel I live in another world in one country; my freedom is precious and I would yield to nobody, especially 21 years after it finally arrived. I imagine no white supremacy because freedom means I don't have to countenance it any longer. And if found, you can today, kick it away like a cowboy boot from a piece of tumbleweed in a Western.[18]

SISONKE   I don't agree with her but I accept that her challenge forces us to imagine what it will be like to one day to:

LEBO & SISONKE   kick racism away like a cowboy boots from a piece of tumbleweed!
                        Whoooo!

(Laughter and triumphant sounds from Lebo and Sisonke.)

SISONKE   This day will come I hope, but it will need white people to think about the words of Njabulo Ndebele:

LEBO   If South African whiteness has an opportunity to write a new chapter in world history, it will have to come out from under the umbrella of international whiteness and repudiate it. Putting itself at risk, it will have to declare that it is home now, sharing in the vulnerability of other compatriot bodies. South African whiteness will have to declare that its dignity is inseparable from the dignity of black bodies.[19]

SISONKE   Repudiating the protections of whiteness always preoccupied Nadine Gordimer. In the 1980s she talked about why she didn't move to Zambia in characteristically descriptive terms:

LEBO   I discovered I was only a European there like any other white person. I took that very hard. At least in South Africa, even if I get my throat cut, I'm an African.

SISONKE   Her ideas on where whites fit in the subject of an early 1959 essay by the same name offer us a guide for today's questions.[20]

LEBO   If we're going to fit in at all in the new Africa, it's going to be sideways, where-we-can, wherever-they'll-shift-up-for-us. This will not be comfortable … it's … a matter of whites learning how to live in a different way, truly accepting what is coming which is black majority rule and not fearing, not wanting guarantees of group rights which will set them aside, set them apart, mark them out forever. … They can't be wanting to boss people around and doing all their thinking for them.[21]

SISONKE   It is hard to imagine whites fitting in sideways where they can. But we must. If South African whites are to be ordinary and not special how might they behave?

Perhaps a young white man buying his first home would be prepared to live in an affordable and pretty home in Soweto's swankier parts.

We cannot be friends if the very thought of making a smart financial decision of that kind repulses him and his parents.

Maybe a group of concerned white citizens can voluntarily, without any prompting from black people, seek to change the name of John Vorster Drive to Fatima Meer Road.

We cannot be friends if whites aren't willing to celebrate our heroes as their own.

Perhaps white parents in the Saxonwold neighborhood where Malan had his encounter would re-enrol their children at the neighborhood schools alongside the children of their domestic workers.

We cannot be friends if whites cannot see the sense and national importance of a single education system in which the destinies of black and white children are intertwined and equally valued.

But there is more: whites must perform these nation-building and privilege busting acts

SISONKE & LEBO   without any expectation of praise or hero-worship for subjecting themselves to the same conditions as blacks.

SISONKE   Then one day, without even noticing it, because it will happen without dramatic announcement or need for validation, we might wake up and realise that we have fallen into friendship and one morning just like that,

LEBO   We will find ourselves caught in a glow of friendship,

SISONKE   deep and

LEBO   intimate and

SISONKE   real and it will be of no consequence at all because the world around us will have changed so much that we will finally

LEBO   Finally

LEBO & SISONKE   be able to call ourselves free.

REFERENCES

Andrew, Miranda. 2012. 'Muslim Man Beaten to Death over Beard.' *Mail & Guardian*. August 8. http://mg.co.za/article/2012-08-08-muslim-man-beaten-to-death-over-beard

Brutus, Dennis. 2008. *Untitled*. Delivered at the Eighth Meeting of the Network of Intellectuals and Artists in Defense of Humanity and the World Forum for Alternatives, October 18. Caracas, Venezuela.

Caine, Barbara. 2011. 'Prisons as Spaces of Friendships in Apartheid South Africa.' *History Australia* 3(2): 42.1–42.13.

Dlakavu, Simamkele. 2015. 'Building Authentic Interracial Relations'. Independent On-Line. March 24. http://www.iol.co.za/news/building-authentic-interracial-relations-1.1836446#.Va0D0ni2Dds

Gordimer, Nadine. 1988. Where Do Whites Fit In? In *The Essential Gesture*. London: Mackays of Chatham.

Gordimer, Nadine, Nancy Topping Bazin, and Marilyn Dallman Seymour. 1990. *Conversations with Nadine Gordimer*. Jackson, MS: University Press of Mississippi.

Haffajee, Ferial. 2015. 'Old White Men, a Younger White Woman and the State of Black Outrage.' *News24*. May 15. http://www.news24.com/Columnists/Ferial-Haffajee/Old-white-men-a-younger-white-woman-and-the-state-of-black-outrage-20150515

Jennings, Ross. 2015. 'Survey of Surveys: A Survey of Citizen-Based Surveys Conducted by Provincial and Local Government in Gauteng.' Conducted for the Gauteng City-Region Observatory. Accessed March 31, 2016 http://hdl.handle.net/10539/17348

Magona, Sindiwe. 1995. *Living, Loving and Lying Awake at Night*. Northampton, MA: Interlink Books.

Malan, Rian. 1990. *My Traitor's Heart*. New York, NY: Grove Press.

Mangcu, Xolela. 2015. 'Race Transcends Class in this Country: A Response to Seekings and Nattrass.' *Daily Maverick*. April 6. http://www.dailymaverick.co.za/opinionista/2015-04-06-race-transcends-class-in-this-country-a-response-to-seekings-and-nattrass/#.VbcO8Hi2Dds

Ndebele, Njabulo. 2007. 'Iph'indlela: Finding a Way through Confusion.' In *Fine Lines from the Box: Further Thoughts about our Country*. Compiled by Sam Tlhalo Raditlhalo. Cape Town: Umuzi.

Ndlovu, Zama. 2014 'Some of My Very Best Friends are White.' *Mail & Guardian*. September 30. http://mg.co.za/article/2014-09-30-some-of-my-very-best-friends-are-white

Phamodi, Sekoatlane. 2013. *How White Is your Friends List?* Personal blog. January 1. http://mrphamodi.co.za/2013/01/how-white-is-your-friends-list/

Swisa, Sarit. 2010. *Domestic Bliss: How a Group of White South Africans Understand Their Relationships with the Domestic Workers Who Raised Them*. Master's Thesis. University of the Witwatersrand.

NOTES

1   This piece was first performed at the 2015 Ruth First Memorial Lecture, August 17, 2015. I am so grateful to Ruth First whose life and death speak to us across the ages, and I am thankful to the committee for keeping her memory alive. In particular I want to thank Indra De Lanerolle and Eusebius McKaiser for pushing me to be more rigorous. Lastly, thank you to the talented Lebo Mashile, who took a leap of faith to perform these words with me.

2   Brutus 2008.

3   For a full discussion (including these quotes) of the phenomenon of prison friendships during the apartheid era, see Caine 2011.

4   Caine 2011.

5   Jennings 2015.

6   Lebo Mashile, personal communication, June 18, 2015.

7   Phamodi 2013.

8   Dlakavu 2015.

9   Ndlovu 2014.

10   'Students Face Action over Racism.' *News24*. August 6, 2014. http://www.news24.com/SouthAfrica/News/Students-face-action-after-blackface-20140806

11   Magona 1995: 86.

12   Swisa 2010.

13   Malan 1990: 44–45.

14   Andrew 2012.

15   Mangcu 2015.

16   Taken from the Willem Boshoff website. July 28, 2015. http://www.willemboshoff.com/documents/artworks/RACIST_IN_SOUTH_AFRICA.htm

17   Haffajee 2015.

18   Haffajee 2015.

19   Ndebele 2007. The essay was written in 2000 and can be found at http://www.njabulondebele.co.za/images/uploads/finding_a_way_through_confusion_green.pdf

20   Gordimer 1988. The essays published in *The Essential Gesture* emerged from Gordimer's Tanner Lectures on Human Values, delivered at the University of Michigan, October 12, 1984. http://tannerlectures.utah.edu/_documents/a-to-z/g/gordimer85.pdf

21   Gordimer, Topping Bazin and Dallman Seymour 1990: 308.

3 BOUND TO VIOLENCE: SCRATCHING BEGINNINGS AND ENDINGS WITH LESEGO RAMPOLOKENG

STACY HARDY AND LESEGO RAMPOLOKENG

I first met Lesego Rampolokeng at the beginning of the millennium, a turning point in the history of our country, a time of rapid change and radical uncertainty, but also one of tremendous excitement and infinite possibility. Everything was being questioned: race as well as social, political, religious, and cultural life. To my generation, the dream of a free South Africa provided a space for new possibilities, new audacities, transgressions, and a new quest for collective identity.[1]

This was the South Africa that Rampolokeng and I, together with fellow South African authors Ivan Vladislavić, Phaswane Mpe, K. Sello Duiker, and Nadine Botha were invited to represent at the 2003 Crossing Border Festival in Den Haag, Netherlands. We traveled as a group and in a very short period of time spontaneous friendships were forged – especially among the young writers. Sello and I spent many afternoons walking Den Haag's streets, discussing the themes that propelled our work – the volatile intersections between race, class, and gender that continued to fracture post-apartheid society, especially in Cape Town, whose cosmopolitan character was strangely echoed in our surrounds.

We also talked about our dreams for other forms of belonging, of new friends, queer utopias, and different communities. Sex and desire with their erotic drives had a great part in it. As did politics. As Sello (Duiker 2001: 381) wrote in *The Quiet Violence of Dreams*: 'There comes a time when we must face who we are boldly, when we must listen to the music of our dreams and delight ourselves with courage as we grasp our destinies firmly in our hands.'

In our youth and bravado – our naivety – we were unwilling, and perhaps unable to listen to the words of caution coming from the older writers in the group – Vladislavić and Rampolokeng – whose complex reading of post-apartheid South Africa undercut our fervor. We should have paid attention. A year later, both Phaswane Mpe and K. Sello Duiker were dead – Sello tragically by his own hand. Their deaths had a stark impact on me. On one hand I felt betrayed: what of our shared dreams? Our shared futures? On the other hand, I experienced an excruciating sense of loneliness, of being alone, as a writer, but also as a person.

In the years that followed, the energy that characterized the period immediately after apartheid dissipated, along with much of its optimism. Faced with a growing sense of loss, at a loss as to how to address this loss, I lost myself in books. I soon discovered that I was not alone in my lostness or my aloneness. South African literature is full of loners, lost relations, and thwarted relationships. Friendship when it does figure is at best fleeting, tenuous. More often than not it fails us, or we fail it. Alienation and despair are at the heart of J. M. Coetzee's novels – friendship here never seems to establish anything but false communications based on misunderstandings. Vladislavić takes a different route, using friendship as a catalyst to launch his hapless, often tragic-comic characters into spirals of confusion. A less pessimistic approach, certainly, but ultimately one that ends with them no less alone. Even Zakes Mda's dreamers, and the disordered and disorderly loners in Joel Matlou's short stories fail to sustain lasting human relations. Bessie Head, Njabulo Ndebele and Keorapetse Kgositsile might make friendship a central concern, as have many writers from the so-called new generation (K. Sello Duiker, Songeziwe Mahlangu, and Masande Ntshanga,[2] for example), but in their books salvation seldom comes through communion with others. Rather, if it is to be found, it is in losing ourselves in the marginal spaces of our own individual dreams, our own fantasies, of ideas and languages that allow us to escape the violence and creative scarcity of capitalism, fascism, or any oppressive reality at all.

And this lostness is really what saved me, I think, from a deep despair, and not just about the suicides and the deaths, but from the idea of death, and the ongoing poverty, deprivation, and violence that dogged our society despite the emergence of democracy, and a fundamental feeling of differentness or aloneness or separation from other people. Both literature and friendship extend the possibility of immersion in another consciousness. They're the forms in which we find the power, in language, to inhabit, perceive, and recreate a shared world. Aloneness that undermines aloneness; a portrait of loneliness leaves us less alone.

Nowhere is this more starkly depicted and enacted than in the writing of Lesego Rampolokeng. As commentaries on, emergencies from, the specific social roots and the creative starvations of our beautiful land after 1994, his poetry books, novels, and spoken word recordings stand by themselves. Humanity is anti-social, evidently. And yet against this, Rampolokeng's work yearns for, calls out for friendship, not negating but demanding reading, provoking engagement with others through an open embrace of difference so that, – as in Blake's (1793) 'opposition is true friendship', the contraries are not dissolved, but realised.

His early works, such as *Horns for Hondo* (Rampolokeng 1990), operate viscerally, presenting poetry as something the body understands, as it is seduced and ensnared by the sound, its unpredictable multiplicity and originality, the extraordinary vocabulary, the open flux of syntax and imagery, and the pleasure, the delight, to be had from all of that, as well as the great humor in it. His poems keep drawing us (and resisting us) into their undertow, and into all the horror and complexity of Rampolokeng's frightening world.

As his career progressed, the explosive energy that characterized his work seemed to almost implode: reading his verse becomes like being caged inside a pressure-cooker of imagery and rhythm. As Paul Wessels (m.d.) writes in his review of *The Bavino Sermons* (1999), Rampolokeng's rolling, roiling 'dis-cum-dedication To Gil Scott-Heron':

> This very precise paradox inserts the poet firmly within the subject-matter of his work. This is no commentator, neutral observer of life. And reading this book is an exhausting experience. There is a disconcerting numbness that comes over the reader at a certain point. Affect seems to short-circuit. Image upon image assaults the senses.

The scatological language, the grotesque violence, the incisive insights into humanity, and in particular, the enemies of humanity make for something of a temporary loss of self the reader experiences.

To truly appreciate the power of Rampolokeng's work then, we have to let go of ourselves as individual beings, thereby allowing a strangers' world – or Hell, in this case – to possess us, to become us. Eventually, his works seem to say, all of us is an Other. Or we have the ability to be so, if pushed far enough. It's a beautiful and terrifying idea, the dissolution of the self as its ultimate fulfillment. We lose ourselves to find ourselves.

This illustrates at least something of the relationship between friendship and reading I am trying to grasp at through loss and the chasm that exists between each of us. As Michael Brennan (2005) writes in his reflection on mourning and poetry, 'In Absentia: Mourning and Friendship': 'Every word chosen and weighed with care if not a love for the unknowable, for what is beyond it, for the absence it contains and that contains it offers the possibility of relation, of friendship through the absences that exist at the heart of both being and language'. Writing then is a form of relation, at its best, an act of friendship without constraints, free of agenda, a binding beyond self and other, absence and presence, where each slips away.

I wrote to Lesego, first as a fan – ardent, awkward, searching – grappling to articulate the impact his poetry had on me. He wrote back. Flushed with elation, I wrote again. Our friendship took off quickly, energised by a sense of recognition and alliance, and finally active collaboration. Yet for all its camaraderie, the encounter was erratic, fleeting, and sometimes shadowed by trouble. Often our exchanges ignited my imagination; we tore the words from each other's mouths, creating an excitement that seemed like an electric storm, then nothing, blackout, for months, or sometimes years.

There was a lot separating us. He was a generation older, and 50 shades darker. A Soweto boy, born and bred, who had recently shorn his dreads, traded mine dumps for cow pats in Groot Marico. I was a *laaitjie* – doubly, young and white, and a girl. Cape Town-based. This wasn't a love story, no Nadine Gordimer novel[3] – we didn't hang out or even ever make out. What we did share was a library, a set of influences that ran riot from Antoine Artaud to Amos Tutuola, from Amiri Baraka to Steve Biko, Dumile Feni to Johnny Dyani – that and a passionate belief in the act of creation. This friendship was based in an impersonal form of intensity that went way beyond personal relations.

It was also a friendship that came with a warning. The challenge of Lesego's work and personality – especially to those near it – is how much comes in: the pain, the ghosts, the rage. As fellow poet Kelwyn Sole (2009: 240) once said: 'No contemporary South African poet – indeed, no writer – has occasioned more approval or disapproval, partly no doubt due to the confrontational nature of Rampolokeng's poetic persona and style, and the scatological, irreverent content of much of his work.' His fights and fall-outs with friends were legendary, often public.[4] Forget 2Pac vs. Biggie. Rampolokeng, I was told firmly was trouble – violent, volatile, unreliable. A poet with a head on fire, a dark heart.

Maybe it was this glitch, the stark difference between public reputation and my own experience that provoked me to pursue an interview. Was I testing him? Seeking a way to make sense of the disjunctive relations that informed both his life and his writing? Looking for some kind of affirmation of our friendship – an E. T. moment where we finally find language and stutter f-r-i-e-n-d? Did I hope to emerge with a neat manifesto that would lay out a new sets of potentials and limits of friendship in its functioning at once as a concept and as a practice?

I should have known better. Lesego refused to comply. Over the course of several hours of intensive conversation and a fury of e-mail exchanges my long-standing friend out-and-out refused to submit to an abstract formulation of friendship, to present it as anything but life, lived experience, being human – and thus something necessarily fragmentary, messy, incoherent, violent, and ugly.

> Friendship? My aunt's place, 5100 Tsolo Street, Orlando East. I spent some years there with Vincent Sekete, my cousin who grew up to be Sasol Three. Betrayed to death on the guerrilla-front. Ok, at some point in that house, lived a family-friend as they are called. A gentler person I do not know. Guess what? He turned out to be Joe Mahlangu, Lovers Lane killer. Serial murderer. He killed the Romeos & Juliets of the Soweto corners doing the huggies-&-cuddlies. Muggers, killers, rapists, so-forth.

We are talking sunken friendship, it would have to be a heavy dirge, some kind of death fugue, if I were to compose or write that. Actually I am constantly doing it, always, in different ways. I just need to transcribe my cries.

As our discussions ran and e-mails criss-crossed – often aimed not at, but past each other – the interview became a transcription of those cries. Less a conversation than a monologue, it came as a stream of consciousness delivered in form of memories, anecdotes, and confessions, as poems and snippets of autobiography – all deep in the tradition of the everyday thing and designed to thwart academic circumscription or conscription. Lesego simply ignored and elided many of my questions, didn't concern himself with making some kind of sense: clarifying points, connecting streams of thought, 'putting things well'.

My childhood, all friendships I made came through conflict. Brawls, arse-whippings ... blood-splat and mucus splatter connections, you could call it. See, without brutal violence, on all sorts of levels, there is no Soweto. I exchanged flesh-tearings with fists, running stone-battles, us kids while punk-arse adults stood there cheering. Blasted sick. Anyway, knives cutting through skin. No, I am not waving my scars in place of medals. Just spitting a little truth ...

A friendship then, not only characterized by conflict, but also born in and out of it, 'fights: the fluids that fluid on and onto those streets rendered ties that bound me to others', and one more often than not based on mutual exclusion rather than collective belonging:

I have forever been close to those who do not snugly fit, for whatever reason. In Chiawelo I ran with a boy called BOYKIE, he couldn't speak except through grunts and other non-verbal sounds. No orality there, of course. Maybe that is why I went about rapping some kind of dead poetry, no idea. Boykie had to go through wearing an OK Bazaars plastic bag on his chest cos he drooled, heavily. We would go to Sans Soucci bioscope in Kliptown, and intermission, get meat-pies, the best this side of things. And half his food would end up on his bib cos his hands were like claws, twisted, he couldn't hold things with any, shall we say, expertise? Anyway, always, at movie-end, stepping out we'd find the coloured kids standing on the stoep, waiting to fuck us up. But damn, after all the Bruce Lee Silver Fox Angela Mao shit on the screen there was no round-kicker better than Boykie. We would hand out bursaries of free arse-whippings and then run off, Boykie shrieking with glee. FRIEND, would never leave me behind, not once.

My old man, his first stint in prison was a 12 year bit. What happened, he was drunk asleep on a bench in a shebeen when he was woken up by croaks and gurgle-sounds of sorts. He sat up to find his friend, later to be my uncle, on his back with a guy wielding a panga over him. My old man, China they call him for his slit-eyes, got up and stabbed the guy in his heart. Kaput. They went to court. Guilty verdict. In prison, asked to show his number, he said he only pledged allegiance to his friend. So it was.

To the poet, the 'grunts', the 'croaks and gurgle-sounds' and even the ass-whipping of these early non-verbal friendships remain preferable to those false communications based on misunderstandings that come later with language.

Talking about unhealed wounds and my cicatrix that never give up on their itching: this Mark Of Cain below my left eye, this is how I got it. My high school mates wanted to run a train, a belt on this girl I had connected with in a tavern. Let me properly break it down. I lived in Phefeni, that night I was in a place called Emndeni, other side of that botched Pavlovian experiment slave-labour camp called Soweto. Far from home. We went drinking. I met a girl. Street-corner chemistry and the fireflames. Happiness, all good and nice in the neighbourhood. That was the night vagina circumcised me. I took a thrust and pain shot through my groin, like dynamite going off in my crotch. Like some razor had gone slash in my loins. I left the place with blood on my pants-front and flowing from under my eye cos then, these guys, friends of mine, came in and stuck an Okapi in my back, demanding that I get off so they could go in.

Memories of shit I would rather drop except to say I got cut, the one with the knife was trying to poke my eye out, I think. Well, they carry reminders of that night too. We all do, hearts heavy with piled-up crap.

Friendship here is not achieved by speech, but by sensation. It is communicated by means of the flesh. For Lesego, friendship is a trace left by and on the body.

I am no great emo-anything ultra-sensitive just cos I go as a poet, no need to strike hurt poses at the slightest provocation and bitching out. I've known all sorts abuse, rejection, been humiliated enough to know I prefer my wounds physical.

Lying to me means you view me as beneath you, in my books, cos you with-hold, bend/twist/turn-about information I am the poorer for not having and I think you laughing at me from some dark depths in you somewhere. You put yourself in superior-mode because you KNOW & GLORY in my ignorance. That is how it reads. So high you have a god's arse-view ... and all the way down ... thinking: slow, cretin, blind, can't see when being played. Superiority and inferiority. But guess what, I can pat you on your head. I can be very liberal to you. My name can be Alan Paton.[5] I can run my reformatory. And you're inferior to me.

Time and time again it is language that fails and betrays us – in its inability to communicate, but also in how it defines and polices friendship, nowhere more so than in the rhetoric saturating our political national discourse. 'Comrade' as a case in point: party political affiliation as the definition of camaraderie and the bond that dictates companionship – this is what language thrusts on us.

Let me start off by saying about this comrade thing. I've already spoke of was cousin, Vincent Sekete. He was one of the Sasol Three, the first guerillas of MK. They hit Sasol.[6] They hit Voortrekker Hoogte. They hit Sasol again. Up to today they are standard icons, lions of the apartheid revolutionary struggle. They were finally shot, ambushed along the 20km fence of Kruger National Park. The way I see it is like several war movies put together: SA defense force uniforms strewn across that landscape.[7]

Later, we sought to find how they were betrayed, how they were known to have been in that place at that time. Leaders to wit Joe Modise and Alfred Nzo were said to be to blame for having tipped off the SA authorities about that. Now they are high up in the ANC, now ruling party ... So it was a shock for me to hear my aunt telling me, that actually no, those might have been in the know, but the actual person who fingered them was the hero of the SA struggle, that great hero-leader later to be himself slain. All said, no need for names. I then get to ask myself about this cause of which we are speaking, comradeship. About whether comradeship is about giving up that within us that defines us human. Because you have to be something other than human to be at home with that, it was betrayal, treachery hurts very deep within you.

We see in this country people who are threatening all the rest of us with obliteration if we dare speak ill against this one pathetic creature with a lot of power. They're saying we are prepared to die, to kill for him. And then they sell out in that person and become them. So what exactly is it that we mean? Are we talking about the politics of expediency? It's expedient that I sit across the table from you, Stacy, now talking friendship because it serves my purpose.

Let's talk about Durban today. Joburg today. We don't have to go to the Holocaust. Rwanda. We can just talk about today. I have spent a lot of my time in KZN [KwaZulu-Natal]. Today people are being killed because they are dark. How long before the people I stood with, the comrades turn on me? How long before it graduates from people darker than navy blue to you, to me? 'I might've had a droplet of my blood merged with him, but it's not Zulu, man. He should die too, this guy.' So for me, this issue of friendship is ...

Patrice Lumumba sold out by who? Thomas Sankara ... who killed Sankara? Blaise Compaoré, longtime comrade, friend if you want to say, whatever. The list is endless, endless. And once you're conscious of these things, once you know of these things, then you know more likely than not you are going to die at the hands of whoever it is you consider friend ... I know that, I know that.

To embrace friendship then, Lesego suggests, one must embrace betrayal and perhaps it is only at the moment of betrayal, and in the loss that comes after, that we truly recognize friendship. The opposite of 'friend', then, is not 'enemy' but 'askari' (traitor).[8] He writes, 'I'm just saying ... betrayed by these people. I define myself as their friend. Whether they are my friends in turn is for them to say. I operate from the inside out. That's it. I operate from the inside out. I embrace them.'

Similarly Lesego refuses binaries via which friendship is constrained to amity, benevolence, brotherhood, charity, fellowship, or friendliness:

Are we grappling with a moral issue? Does positivity or negativity impact on what defines friendship? Does it need to be defined in terms of whether it operates on the positive sphere? Is it only friendship when it comes to good? I'll clarify what I mean. My brother in law ... these people were terrible criminals, who killed people and whatever, whatever. People in gangs ... The flipside of that is, when they would go out together and rob people, they were prepared to give their lives for each other. Is that friendship or is it not? If I don't leave you there. I'm prepared to die with you. Surely that's a human thing? Human beings are stealthy beings.

Nor is he prepared to accept an idea of public, or 'civic friendship', based in kinship, collegiality, community, civility, or even ideology or artistic practice. Lesego does acknowledge that political, social, and artistic formations such as Black Consciousness and the cultural organizations and independent magazines that sprang up under apartheid were hotbeds of immanence, presenting themselves as a society of friends (influence, competition, rivalry), and thus promoting opinion. His debut documentary film, *Word Down the Line* (2014), directed by Bobby Rodwell and featuring interviews with South African poets such as James Matthews, Keorapetse Kgositsile, Mafika Gwala, Jeremy Cronin, Sandile Dikeni, Vonani Bila, Khulile Nxumalo, Kgafela oa Magogodi, and Gift Ramashia, tells this story. But he is wary of absorption by any groups, institutions, and other forces that might reduce one's ability to change, move, or create freely.

Here's another thing. I've got my eyes open to what some people regard as a Black Consciousness era. I don't think it was an era petrified in time; it's not a frozen moment. I am very conscious of who and what I am. I define myself as Black Conscious. I understand what BC is, indeed, as the *Wretched of the Earth*. Regardless of the amount of melanin they've got and dah, dah, dah ... Now, we show, *Down the Line* at Rhodes University. And at the end of it, the Q&A session these youngsters say, 'No, you know what elder?' They say to me, 'I suggest that all the white people leave the hall now so we can get started.' Now, a comrade of mine, who I would give my life for, who's directed this thing that's moved them so much, is caucasian. She's caucasian. I know who this person is. And I know what this person did at a time when these black people were too even scared to scratch out a little word on a page for fear of brutalisation. I know what she suffered during apartheid. And these people are challenging me that this is invalid because she has less melanin in her? The fact that they are black, that they have X amount of melanin should validate them in my eyes? Oh, and no, I'm not standing up for my white missus! I don't have a white missus. Fuck that shit! My problem with that is my blackness, regardless of the Hegelian mode, regardless of Fanon, regardless of any of that, is mine. I don't define myself because other people stamp shit on me. You know?

He similarly sees no inherent affinity between art and friendship. My questions about artistic relationships as a form of friendship via inspiration, affiliation, or collaboration go unanswered. Nor is he prepared to directly engage any of the personal relationships that were seminal to him, to his writing, his existence, to his coming to consciousness. 'We all know artists exploit artists,' he says wryly, calling up a litany of failed friendships, betrayed dreams, the disappointed expectations and fraught alliances of community drawn together under economic and political or interpersonal stresses.

Close to his death, Ingoapele Madingoane was a lonely man. His BC comrades would have nothing to do with him. But after he died, sitting on the toilet with an axe in his skull, at his memorial the whole blasted fat piglet lot of them came out spouting platitudes. Friends.

Peter Makurube died in malnutrition and neglect after all the years he put in to the arts of poetry and music. He was persona non grata in all besuited over flabby frames and business spots. That history is a month-recent. Memorial and funeral, what happened? All the rats came out screaming praises. Friends.

Mafika Gwala died torn up, soul cut to pieces but spirit still flying high with defiance and an unchanged, solid belief in what he stood, a world beyond the grasping, clasping, clawed existence some sold on the stock exchange. That man brought me to consciousness. And at the end there he was in abject, dire circumstances. Eating away with the sickness coming in from without ... and then of course the Farts Minister had a lot of broken, hot wind to blow about how great Gwala was and that they'd been in negotiation to put him in the education-stream. Lies and bullshit. Faecal-faced friends.

Friendship is scary business. Mark that, about economics. I sit in the bushveld, no friendship in my field of vision, not even on the horizon.

A scholarly treatise for readers who never cared about scholarship, a memoir for those who have had enough with the insularity of simple confession, and a poetry book for the hip-hop generation, *A Half Century Thing* synthesizes the raw passion of a diary and the pleasure of a pop music album with the relevance and scope of nothing less than the history of South African literature, art, and music. Building on the ground traveled in *Word Down the Line*, extending beyond the tomb or grave, ('message from immolation /cremation') beyond homage ('mindful of how Brother Ali warned … / i don't disrespect the people who laid the tracks i travel on but … / i write with the marrow in the center of my own creation-bone'), it's a text that reads with an almost physical urgency, as though written in a human-heat ('I'm the RA that came before the SUN / the fire-soul of fanon's children'). Here Rampolokeng tangles and untangles a transgressive congregation of historic and fictional influences (Mafika Gwala, Keorapetse Kgositsile, Seitlhamo Motsapi, Sony Lab'ou Tansi, Yambo Ouologuem, Dambudzo Marechera — and his 'cockroach eye-view', Johnny Dyani, Mongezi Feza, Winston Mankunku Ngozi, Dumile Feni, Thami Mnyele, Fikile Magadlela, Miles Davis, Allen Ginsburg, Steve Biko, Frantz Fanon and oh, oh so many more), all while chronicling his disillusionment with the current dispensation:

> like Brit Gervais comedian-perversion:
> No Grace in climbing Nelson's column Just penis & anus reconciliation
> Ask Desmond the tutu-bishop
> Only Black in the rainbow when my rectum raps
> National flag misses my crap

and simultaneously trying to dig himself out of his own alienated funk:

> Boots digging me out of my roots
> Fists to my face not hitting me but my race
> & police special .38s loaded with cold metal & solid hate
> The authorities & my personality, how they relate …
> (how white lightning dictates what i write is frightening)
> enlightening how (as) they say 'it's blackness in high places
> Now throw the switch on your politics.'

From the word go, Rampolokeng moves forward in a stop-start fashion, jumping from decade to decade ('from throwing stones & the [dynamite] sticks of june '76 to tossing alternative Afrikaans rock with James the beboptist Phillips', from 'Amilcar Cabralised to howling with Ginsberg,[howling] not at the moon but at Armstrong … the Apollo creed was a bad seed'); fast-forwarding and rewinding ('Got splinters of history lodged in my afrofuturism. / it takes the primitive to make the progressive / – fake dialectic'); 'scratching beginnings & endings'; weaving in quotations and references; playing music off against the word ('frozen, cramped between Jimmy Cliff's "House of Exile" & Dambudzo Marechera's House of Hunger'), and blending other stories with his own.

There's a collective thinking of this kinetic thing that Lesego engages – the participation in, the doing of, it. What emerges is a community based on the sharing of a refrain, on the creation of a path of thought not guaranteed by any root, by any integrity, by any violence, but only by its ongoing search for freedom and love for humanity. What the social, the political, the civic/civil world has surrendered from itself, has given up on, goes then into the realm of the imagination. As he writes in 'LIBATION BLUES FOR MISTA GWALA':

Tension contrast release what is freedom
Can you pin the insurrection tone down?
It vibrates pitched at liberation time.
Artistic downward spiral

Move from cellophane to the cyber-download plane
Was company exec's stratospheric flight
to cut Mahlathini's lion-mane
Bird's grave was his sax
On top of him they shovelled narcotics
& between the orchestra & the soccer star
Lies the Hendrixian rockster

Words are medicine
Which is to mean also poison]]
six-nine can mean urine
But also conception

Half Century Thing is a devoted heresy, a sermon on the word, on politics and aesthetics that challenges what poetry does, what it can do, even what it is willing to address as a form. Most of all it's a very beautiful tribute to friendship, one that articulates truly dissensual politics (in contrast to consensual), not a cult, but a culture of heterogeneity through which each of us accepted the singularity of the other.

In 'Bass For Bra Willie', the first of a 'Movement in Four Body-Parts', Lesego presents an idea of friendship that not only allows for critique, but insists on it. It's at once a celebration and a scathing rap attack that riffs off and rips ups the constant jazz references that permeate Keorapetse Kgositsile's oeuvre. In this poem, Lesego acknowledges his debt to Kgositsile's practice by adopting its poetic strategies, while simultaneously turning those very tactics against the older poet.

In its passion and its wrath, its love and disdain, it corresponds with the idea of friendship based in brutal honesty developed between Amiri Baraka and Ed Dorn through their years of correspondence, as documented in the recent *Amiri Baraka and Edward Dorn: The Collected Letters* (Pisano 2014). Here Baraka says on more than one occasion, 'Dorn would rather make you an enemy than lie to you'. Lesego similarly shows his deep respect for Kgositsile by risking alienating him rather than perpetuating false platitudes.

In a conversation between Ramolokeng and Gwala published in the *Chronic* newspaper shortly before Gwala's death in September 2014, Rampolokeng said of Kgositsile, 'there is a need for the poet to die in order for the politician to rise' and this transmutation is at the center of his attack of here:

(Kgositsile's 'false gods' erased the poet raised between serial killers
& religion-drug-dealers blood-of-Christ-spillers & fear-feelers
& grown in healer-art embrace I like it hard at core with no fillers ...
true & up my ghetto-reality street passion of knife-in-flesh)

And later:

Bone stacks at Atlantic bottom
Rattle rise pierce through saxophones

Rhythm it wise with drummed skulls
Lungs mine-dust perforate for bass
& whip-strum melodies
piano ribcages kwashiorkor exposes
nerves percussive eugenic explosive
Moan-exorcise) that's jazz
Salvaged strings from the hanging tree
The noose sings (cheated) forlorn off-key
& free concept rim-shots
& the sounds are tight hot
Bubbling from the clay-pot
Come to bring the day out
(testes notes and ovaries tones neither coo nor moo that Mankunku
Jol'inkomo.)

The music introduced in this opening plays on throughout the book, becoming almost a din in the third part of the movement, 'CRAP TONES MY KIN-DREAD SPIRITS CAN TUNE INTO (OR the addict looks at the dark side of the spoon'. In this poem Lesego engages the fundamental role that encounters played in his life – as much in experiencing intensities and multiplicities through music and literature as in generating thought and in moving beyond poetry through poetry. Here private language and personal gesture move from solipsism to the social, as references become characters, which feel more like ghosts, fading into and out of identity with one another and even with the author.

'Ah, this pen scratches my work-song / complex chorded in perennial rearrangement,' writes Lesego, presenting himself as both music producer and poet; a fluent switching from high-toned to home(l)y and back again; name dropping from music history while simultaneously sampling and remixing the rhythms of those he references.

Gouge out the darkness' eyes
Exiled memory bellows across grief-distances:
The Bird's screech-spoke genius
Then the flies came with the critiques
But) None darker than Parker and his demons

Supplicant at Charlie's sermons
I'm prostrate before the apostate

The dance-floor is beyond reach
Nothing but flammable-speech
& No fire-dance escape
The poem flames out of control
& that's the nature of The Beast
Home is where the lions are corrugated
Even my self-definition is dated
Got splinters of history lodged in my afrofuturism.
(it takes the primitive to make the progressive
                                    – fake dialectic)
race has them assume intuition stumbles black into it:
'you would be great if you were doing it on purpose'
But the white is cold with it he 'experiments'.

Hornman blows the highest trill
 like opening a hole to heaven or hell
after the high the chill)
as if suspended on an abused tree
(they hurl insults at it) deaf to the gravity call
its fruit when it drops is deranged
        should be free rise not fall ...
Mongezi tips his bowl & it's a bloodspill

...

Say Thelonious gave piano internal bleed haemorrhage concussion
Cos he thought it percussion
 (condition Bukowski diagnosed after the fact of it lying on the slab
                    (read post-mortem / autopsy
Zim's 'grand' gutted for copper glory
(imagine a Picasso defaced for the frame
What a vandal\iZim
Kyle played it kneeling praying to the music-gods amid its gore
where it was pushing its own intestines in

Where the music instrument cemetery where do they go to die?

These words perhaps give a taste of Lesego's penchant for intertextual play, but they do not, cannot show quite how vibrant and complex his employment of redeployment is – names and ideas, images and rhythms woven throughout the lengths of each poem and the book as a whole – or how it gives rise to such an intense reading experience.

This is recombinant poetry propelled by the refrains and returns of other artists, the sounds and words of fellow musicians and writers that are evoked and manifested, drawn into the movement of new concepts and rhythms, and thus reformulated, re-animated, re-connected, re-booted. You can be human by yourself but, as Fred Moten (2015) points out, black don't go it alone: 'It's a social dance, unruliness counterpoised between riot and choir, and our melismatic looting is with child, sold all the time, but never bought.'

Or as Lesego calls it in his poem 'The Bavino Manifesto (Ars Poetica Versus the Arse-Poet-Dicker)': 'my conscience calls? i answer in intestinal scrolls / a textual maze feeding in & out of itself like underground Johannesburg / where i was cradled, ladled & shall be body-bagged.'

Throughout these 'intestinal scrolls' the poet delights in the possibility of words having infinite meanings and effects. In these dense, spiralling texts he sends his readers around and around the same words and ideas, lifting us to new proximities to them, and to mesmeric new landscapes, at once political, geographical, and deeply personal. Even when he's at his most destructive and violent, he is diligent about collecting the fragments of the forms he explodes, and always repurposes their shattered essence with humility and laughter.

> Colonial Literature … got me thinking blue … several blues … the blue of eyes, of collars, of some blood … & I bled til Mista Gwala sang me 'no more lullabies' but LIBERATION BLUES 1974, mourning Onkgopotse Tiro parcel-bombed up in the murder-church service of the god of pigmentation (& yessah, I realized then that 'me listening to jazz is not leisure / it is a soul-operation' & I knew then I had to choose between Jol'inkomo (that is, in his words 'bringing lines home to the kraal of my black experience' or Yakh'inkomo, to OUTCRY with Mutabaruka … to bawl the anguish like a cow being slain … & decided there was nothing bovine about me … & so …

I took to Staffriding … all the way from Phefeni to HERE.

As the above passage demonstrates, it's in his counterattack against mediocrity that Lesego is at his most exhilarating and eviscerating. While the multiple musical rhythms (jazz, dub, hip-hop, maskanda, malombo … all the sounds encompassed in what Johnny Dyani calls 'black family music' (Kaganof 2010) and the constant punning and wordplay make reading *A Half Century Thing* the most fun I've had with a book in years, it's a far cry from 'leisure'. Entertaining then, but never entertainment. *A Half Century Thing* is 'a soul-operation'; sharp, visceral, self-avowedly furious; a rhetoric of shame, of loss, of unquantifiable and unspeakable violence ('murderous history … aborted futures … zombied present …') that is necessarily also very fucking funny. In these poems Lesego laughs in the face of horror, in the face of others, in his own face, and in our faces. Even the most po-faced readers ('there is no such thing as "the right to faecal-expression"') will be hard-pressed the keep a straight face ('Mugabe-face') in the face of lines like:

I'm mourning the loss of my dreads.
now I'm the original 'lockless monster'.
Baloi, 'be afraid, be very afraid.'
Relation magnate to diamond-dust ferret?
Avuncular laugh to tubercular cough.

So la-la-land (eclipse
How Daylyt black them out
Like 'pee a sea and toss dromedaries back in it
Return-trip to Anus-land…
But 'dem towers leaning outta position pisa me off'…
Organic intellectual versus the synthetic ineffectual
& the censor-ship is anchored &anc-whored
in heads of the pansy-horde :

'you write poetry? Shem.
You the soft, sensitive, flower-fondling type, then?'
Fuck it, gimme my machine-ahm-pen!

Ultimately it's the force of a smile that protrudes through in *A Half Century Thing*, a smile mixed with a startled, helpless laughter. The book encapsulates the necessity of laughter, the deep relief and release that laughter offers. Pain, loneliness, loss – these casual horrors are called up, but also held off by the rebellious power of Lesego's ruthless chuckle and grin. And in making us laugh with him, at him, and with and at ourselves, the poet extends a hand of friendship to the reader, inviting us into the text and making us complicit in its creation, in its joys and horrors. Laughter then as an act of friendship, an act of defiance, of revolutionary praxis; a regenerative act:

> Indeed, we are Bound to Violence with Yambo Ouologuem.
> & Richard Pryor proved to be just that. He pried that tomb-talk open, stood
> it up & made comic of it, thus: 'the reason people use a crucifix against
> vampires is because vampires are allergic to bullshit'.
> I agree. so, mom, I think I might just be a vampire. From now on kindly call
> me Count Blackula.
> & hence, my Robin black Hood ambition:
> steal from men of the cloth & give to women of none

A Half Century Thing is thus a crossroads, a multiple connectedness. It's a meditation of friendship and an enactment of friendship created as an act of friendship that shows us not what friendship is, what it could be, or even who the friend is, but rather what can friendship do (*Salut, Deleuze!*),[10] that is, how friendship functions as an active and dynamic relationship, allowing affirmation as well as dissent, rage, and pain as well as laughter and joy, harmony as well as disharmony.

REFERENCES

Blake, William. 1793. 'Marriage of Heaven and Hell.' *Blake Archive*. Accessed May 2015.
http://www.blakearchive.org/exist/blake/archive/work.xq?workid=mhh

Brennan, Michael. 2005. 'In Absentia: Mourning and Friendship.' *Jacket Magazine*, April
27. http://jacketmagazine.com/27/bren-inabsent.html

Dieck, Martin and Jens Balzer. 2006. 'Salut, Deleuze!' In *Chimurenga* 9: *Conversations in
Luanda and Other Graphic Stories.* Cape Town: Chimurenga.

Dlamini, Jacob. 2014. *Askari: A Story of Collaboration and Betrayal in the Anti-Apartheid
Struggle*. Johannesburg: Jacana Media.

Duiker, K. Sello. 2001. *The Quiet Violence of Dreams*. Cape Town: Kwela Books.

Kaganof, Aryan. 2010. 'Johnny Dyani Interview'. In *Chimurenga* 15: *The Curriculum is
Everything*. Cape Town: Chimurenga.

Kona, Bongani. 2015. 'The Other Brother.' In *The Chronic, New Cartographies.* March. Cape
Town: Chimurenga.

Moten, Fred. 2015. 'Amuse-Bouche.' *Jacket Magazine,* February 12. http://jacket2.org/
article/amuse-bouche

Ouologuem, Yambo. 1971. *Bound to Violence*. Trans. Ralph Manheim. London: Heinemann
Educational Books.

Ouologuem, Yambo. 2008. *The Yambo Ouologuem Reader*. Trans. Christopher Wise.
Trenton, NJ: Africa World Press.

Pisano, Claudia Moreno, ed. 2014. *Amiri Baraka and Edward Dorn: The Collected Letters*.
Albuquerque, NM: University of New Mexico Press.

Rampolokeng, Lesego. 1990. *Horns for Hondo*. Fordsburg, South Africa: Congress of
South African Writers.

Rampolokeng, Lesego. 1999. *The Bavino Sermons*. Durban: Gecko Poetry.

Rampolokeng, Lesego. 2015. *A Half Century Thing*. Cape Town: Black Ghost Books.

Rodwell, Bobby. 2014. *Word Down the Line*. Directed by Bobby Rodwell. (DVD), 75 min.
Screened June 23, 2014. Durban, South Africa: Durban Film Fest.

Sole, Kelwyn. 2009. '"I Have Learned To Hear More Acutely": Aesthetics, Agency and the
Reader in Contemporary South African Poetry.' *Cross-Cultural Poetics* 21(22): 240–266.

Stivale, Charles J. 2008. *Gilles Deleuze's ABC: The Folds of Friendship*. Baltimore, MD:
Johns Hopkins University Press.

Tutuola, Amos. 1954. *My Life in the Bush of Ghosts*. London: Faber and Faber.

Wessels, Paul. n.d. 'Review of The *Bavino Sermons* in the Cape Times.' Accessed
online: http://www.ukznpress.co.za/?class=bb_ukzn_reviews&method=view_
reviews&global[fields][_id]=10

NOTES

1   The chapter title is borrowed from Yambo Ouologuem's 1968 novel *Le Devoir de Violence*, translated as *Bound to Violence* by Ralph Manheim in 1971, and later as *The Duty of Violence* by Christopher Wise (2008), which presents a violent vision of African history, and as Wise has argued, 'a view that there is no such thing as a public sphere that is completely free of irrational violence, and that in certain circumstances it is even a moral duty to enact violence against the other'. It is also a reference in Lesego Rampolokeng's poetry, and the subject of often heated discussions between Rampolokeng and me on the incapability of violence-doing and eroticism as one possible means of breaking such enslavement.

2   For a beautiful reflection on friendship in Masande Ntshanga's debut novel, *The Reactive*, see 'The Other Brother' by Bongani Kona in *The Chronic, New Cartographies* (2015).

3   Gordimer's third novel, *Occasion for Loving* (published in 1963), deals with the failure of tolerance and humanism; the increasing absurdity of the race laws brought friendship and love across the colour bar to a halt.

4   Years later, to explain his shifting allegiances and alliances, Lesego would quote Greg Tate on Amiri Baraka to me: 'We are so quick to, as Greg Tate said of Amiri Baraka, grow up in public. You don't only grow up, but we want society to see we grow up. So we turn around and crap on what we stood for in the beginning. … And you see it happening, here. It happened with Amiri Baraka. He was part of the Beat Generation … got married to this Jewish woman called Hettie Cohen … then when he broke out of that, not only did he move out of that but he started embracing himself as a Black Nationalist and crapped on that for which he stood. And then when afterwards he found Black Nationalism to not be equal to what he stood for, he moved on and crapped on it, and whatever, and whatever, and whatever.'

5   Alan Paton, once a principal of the Diepkloof Reformatory, is most famous as the author of *Cry, the Beloved Country* (published in 1948).

6   Sasol was a leading industrial institution at the forefront of coal to oil conversion and an important target, not only guarded by South African units but also regarded as a strategic asset by western security organizations such as NATO.

7   Sekete and his comrades (Barney Molokoane and Victor Khayiyane) did not run faster than the helicopters, dogs, and bullets of the South African Defence Force, but that operation was the first of the liberation struggle in which MK combatants killed so many of the enemy.

8   See Dlamini (2014), which engages the mercurial figure of the traitor in the liberation struggle against apartheid.

9   The book has since been published by Black Ghost Books (Cape Town, 2015).

10 This reading owes a debt to Charles J. Stivale's *Gilles Deleuze's ABC: The Folds of Friendship* (2008), as well as Martin Dieck and Jens Balzer's surreal and hilarious *bande dessinée* (graphic art book) *Salut, Deleuze!* (Hi, Deleuze), which appeared in *Chimurenga 9: Conversations in Luanda and Other Graphic Stories* (2006).

AFRO-PESSIMISM AND FRIENDSHIP IN SOUTH AFRICA: AN INTERVIEW WITH FRANK B. WILDERSON III

4

SHANNON WALSH

Frank B. Wilderson III is considered one of the key thinkers developing the theoretical tradition of Afro-pessimism. Afro-pessimism connects the work of scholars such as Saidiya Hartman, Jared Sexton, David Marriott, Hortense Spillers, and others, building on certain readings of Frantz Fanon, Orlando Patterson, and Joy James. One of the decisive critical moves made by Afro-pessimists is to take the Black[1] out of the space of a subjective, epistemological, or cultural identity, and into the realm of accumulation, fungibility, and ontology (Hartman 1997), defined by the three constituent components of slavery: social death, natal alienation, and general dishonour (Patterson 1985).

Afro-pessimists draw into question the historic development of the Human, and what that development has meant for the creation of the Black as non-Human. Wilderson (2010: 12) argues that Blackness is, 'an ontological position, that is, as a grammar of suffering, the Slave is not a labourer but an anti-Human, a positionality against which Humanity establishes, maintains, and renews its coherence, its corporeal integrity'. In this way, the socially dead, fungible Slave is a necessary *relationality* for the construction of the Human. That this relationship is both fundamentally destructive and *necessary* for the construction of liberated (mainly White) subjects is a fascinating and disturbing backdrop for a discussion of race and friendship. As Wilderson (2010: 22) writes, 'the circulation of Blackness as metaphor and image at the most politically volatile and progressive moments in history (as in the French, English, and American revolutions), produces dreams of liberation which are more inessential to and more parasitic on the Black, and more emphatic in their guarantee of Black suffering, than any dream of human liberation in any era heretofore'. Afro-pessimism is not a politics, but it does point to the need for a new kind of politics beyond Fanon's 'end of the world': a complete revolution of what currently exists.

An African American, Wilderson lived in South Africa during the 1990s, where he was elected to the African National Congress (ANC), and became a member of Umkhonto we Sizwe (MK). He taught at the University of Witwatersrand, and also at Khanya College during that period. His memoir *Incognegro: A Memoir of Exile & Apartheid* (2008) recounts his time in South Africa. It was followed by the explosive Afro-pessimist work *Red, White & Black: Cinema and the Structure of U.S. Antagonisms* (2010), which explores anti-Blackness through multiple modes and readings, from cinema to sexuality, popular culture, and libidinal economies. He is currently professor of Drama and African American Studies at the University of California, Irvine.

Wilderson's work on Afro-pessimism has been circulating in South Africa as questions around anti-Blackness emerge from a new generation of African intellectuals. Given his history in South Africa, and his provocative critical framework that disrupts ideas of civil society and the universal Human subject, I was grateful he agreed to think about the question of friendship and Afro-pessimism specifically in relation to South Africa. As Afro-pessimism gains critical traction, I took the opportunity to ask Wilderson to clarify how the concept is being used, as well as how these ideas might translate in the African, and South African context.

SHANNON WALSH (SW) I was interested in the section in your book *Red, White & Black* where you quote James Baldwin talking about the breakdown of his friendship with the white writer Norman Mailer. As Baldwin (quoted in Wilderson 2010: 172) writes: 'There is a difference between Norman and myself in that I think he still imagines that he has something to save, whereas I have never had anything to lose.' Can you speak to how you understand this dynamic between Baldwin and Mailer, and the relationship between friendship and race?

FRANK WILDERSON (FW) [My White friend] Heinrich and [white partner] Anita are my conduits for all this. That's because I never speak honestly to White people – it's too dangerous; it's too debilitating. White people are the most violent and naive people on the planet; especially liberals, the ones who think they're for social justice and all of that. Get too close, or remain around them for too long and what you find is that they are really no better than the loyal opposition of the murderous juggernaut that openly and unabashedly enslaves you. This is true whether you're dealing with Bernie Sanders Democrats or even socialists in the U.S. or whether you're dealing with British people in South Africa. So one must perform: because in your rage they will see only a threat to their own persons or to their way of life; they won't see that their very existence, their capacity to *be*, is where the threat to life is really located, where it all began. So, I'm always performing. I'm trying not to now, with you, because it is important that my words are as raw and unvarnished in print as they would be if I was talking to another Black with the understanding that what is said stays Black-to-Black. But Heinrich and Anita are two White people to whom I have spoken, openly, honestly, and over a long period of time. But they had to earn their roles as auditors – and it's not a two-way street. There's no reciprocity in the Master-Slave dynamic. As an urban guerilla and, technically, my commander, Heinrich had earned that role long before I met him. That does *not* mean that all, or even most of the Whites in MK were like that. I can recall some really disturbing conversations that I had with Derek Andre Hanekom and things I heard at a meeting with Ronnie Kasrils – my god! You turn your head sideways and listen to these two and you would hardly know that they were high-ranking guerillas. So, I think what I'm saying is that Anita (as a one-time White progressive who threw her labors into the project of Black liberation) and Heinrich (as an MK operative and later as an above-ground politico) sought ways and means through which they could be authorized by Black revolutionary ensembles of questions. What do I mean by that? Well, I know what I don't mean. For a long time Heinrich, like most of us in the ANC in general and MK in particular, were fixated on the idea that if you destroy capitalism you destroy civil society. And Anita thought that the essential antagonism was between men and women. Neither one of them had *raced* their paradigmatic views; much less Blackened those views (and I want to say that in Afro-pessimism we might use the word 'race' as a kind of shorthand, but it is inexact: because oppressed non-Blacks are secured in their coherence by a necessary anti-Blackness; so in a very real sense, Blacks are not only outside of Whiteness but we are beyond, or excluded from, race). But both of them, by becoming *predisposed* to be authorized by the most abject subject (or non-subject) in the room, evolved to where they are today.

I want to say that it's great, what has happened between me and Anita, and me and Heinrich; but, I also want to say I don't offer that as any kind of vision of the future. Because I love Anita and Heinrich and they love me, doesn't mean that anything essential has changed in the calculus of life. In fact, I think that both those encounters bring up more problems than possibilities. And you recalling my quote from Baldwin points to where the problems lie: my sentiments run the risk of blinding me to the unalterable *structure of* our 'relationship'; and, as Hortense Spillers would say, *yes, the scare quotes matter.* As is most often the case, Baldwin has already said it: 'Norman [Mailer] still imagines that he has something to save, whereas I have never had anything to lose.' If you take economic dispossession out of a bedrock translation of this sentence, then you can begin to understand why it is so many people are so anxiety-ridden when confronted with the specter of Black suffering and their relationship to it; why there are so many Derek Hanekoms and Ronnie Kasrils and so few Heinrichs and Anitas. This is why I say that my 'relationship' with my wife and my former commander present more problems than possibilities – if one is of a mind to hold them up as spectacles for a kind of nauseous we-are-the-world hope for the future. Future is what happens to people who aren't Black.

This reminds me of day in early June, the day Heinrich got out of torture [by the apartheid regime for being part of an underground MK cell]. He was one of my graduate students in Comparative Literature – his cover was that of a White nerd who liked to party. He and Tefu (an undergraduate at Wits, in the social sciences: both Heinrich and Tefu were trained operatives) and Bushy (Tefu's cousin and the MK commander of the West Rand) had bombed the Conservative Party (CP) headquarters in retaliation for the assassination of Chris Hani (allegedly orchestrated by Gaye Derby-Lewis, the Evita Peron of the Conservative Party). (One thing that should not be dismissed, even though Heinrich plays it down, is that Bushy needed for militant MK operatives to emerge and add their voices to the above-ground radicals who were voicing discontent at Mandela's sell-out of all that we had fought for. The only way two really secret people could become public and gain legitimacy was for them to be captured by the police and tortured; and this is important because they had gotten away with it, but Mandela had immediately called in as many leaders as he could and threatened them with expulsion or not having a place in the new South Africa if they joined the over 600 000 lumpen and youth who were rising up to foment revolution after Hani was assassinated. And the attack on the CP headquarters was to have been a catalyst or at least an accompaniment for that uprising. This is why, in my book, I write about how they went back to the rubble and left their identity documents there so that the police would burst into their dorm rooms and arrest them.)

So, Heinrich had just been released from six weeks of brutal torture. And now, the Whites in Comparative Literature wanted to throw a party for him. The grad students and faculty in the Comparative Literature department lived in a world in which they had no connection to the most pressing struggle on the continent and perhaps in the world, at that time; except for Dr Ulrike Kistner, who had also operated clandestinely, and the two Black graduate students (one who had been a political commissar for the PAC [Pan-African Congress] in one of its guerilla training camps). If memory serves me right, the Black students didn't come to the party – and no one seemed to miss them. White students drank too much and then began to chastise Heinrich for what he had done – it was subtle, lit crit chastisement; nothing so crass as to say, 'we don't believe in violence, and we thought you were one of us'. They would do things like quote someone like Deleuze, someone they just read who said capital was going to burn itself out, so, Heinrich, your efforts were wasted. The party turned out to be a really bizarre affair – I couldn't tell if they felt betrayed, embarrassed, or in envy of Heinrich. Now, it's hard enough being a White revolutionary and having this lot as your colleagues. Imagine what it's like to be Black and have to smile in these peoples' faces all day long. It's either your job or your sanity; and you end up choosing your job. The world is a ghetto.

But, that afternoon, before the party, Heinrich and I were standing in Yeoville. I was holding his wrists. I had genuine sadness about the marks of torture on his wrists, and I wondered if he was telling me the truth about everything that happened or if he was holding back some things. At the same time, the narrative of his torture was so different than Tefu's. Heinrich was tortured at the same time as Tefu, who is Black. Some people would say the important thing was that Tefu suffered more violence because the torturers jumped on his stomach, and poured hot liquid down his ears, and that kind of thing, and Heinrich got less violence. But that's not what interests me. What interests me is the fact that the torturers assumed that Heinrich had a mother and a father. They worked that into the narrative of his torture. 'Your father's dying. Your mother's going to be all alone', etc. There was this empathetic relationship that was happening intuitively between torture victim and torturer. There was none of that with Tefu. In other words, they imagined themselves to be torturing some*one* with Heinrich, and with Tefu they imagined themselves to be torturing some*thing*. That's the most important dynamic that I don't think that can be broken through political intervention. Afro-pessimism, had we had it as a lens of interpretation at the time, would have allowed us to understand this antagonism between Heinrich and Tefu, who were good friends and comrades, and who went up against the state together and in the same; so the antagonism is not in how they felt about each other. Of course not. It is in the something to salvage which Heinrich (like Mailer) had and the nothing to lose that went with Tefu to his torture chamber.

Besides the fact that Heinrich and I were so close that people thought of us as one entity from time to time (when we taught in the English Department at Vista University in Soweto) and despite the fact that I'm sure that I come from more money than Heinrich comes from, for example, there was this situation where our relationship to violence could not be reconciled. I was only transposed into someone who was *someone* in those moments when a White South African would hear my accent. Before that, I was just a kaffir. And then they would hear my accent, and they would do this about-face apology. In other words, to the degree that I could have the accoutrement of Whiteness is the degree that I could be an exceptional Black in South Africa. But in silently saying nothing and trying to get into a restaurant, that wasn't going to happen — even after 1991 or 1992, when several apartheid laws were rescinded. Tefu couldn't actually put on the garment of White America. He was just Black. Which meant he could never put on the garment of affiliation, or relationality. That matters because friendship is a kind of relation. So you're dealing with two people who have friendship attitudes towards each other, but one person has no capacity for relationality. And another person has all the capacity for relationality. You know?

SW Absolutely. This deeply complicates what is possible for any easy understanding of friendship; the one-sided capacity for relationality means that there is no relationality possible. I think that leads us towards the question of Afro-pessimism, and what it offers as an optic to describe the world. Can you describe Afro-pessimism, and how you use the term?

FW One of the things I want to stress is that the phrase 'Afro-pessimism' as a moniker or analytic lens really comes from Saidiya Hartman. In an interview I did with her I was telling her about how I was teaching Ayi Kwei Armah's West African novel *The Beautyful Ones Are Not Yet Born* (published in 1968) at Khanya College in South Africa in the early 1990s. Some call it a dystopic novel. I was trying to describe to Hartman the kind of visceral reaction there was to that book. The students had come to Khanya College after having been stopped in their high school or college trajectory because they were either part of unions or went to prison for whatever reason because of apartheid. So, Khanya College was a liberation school. Many of the students were active in the South African Communist Party, the radical civics, the ANC, etc. If they completed a year at Khanya successfully, they could go on to a White, English medium university like UCT (University of Cape Town) or Wits. Most of them went to university and became radical student leaders on campus. They were activist-oriented students and so they had a fundamental sense of possibility, which was very different from what was going on in that West African novel. They were steadfast in their conviction that South Africa was not Ghana. The stalled revolution that Fanon writes about wasn't going to happen in South Africa – of course, we now know that with Mandela and Thabo Mbeki and company, it *did* happen.

So, I was explaining to Saidiya Hartman that the pessimism about the condition of Black leadership in a neocolonial situation was something that the South African students at Khanya College, in 1992, couldn't countenance when thinking about the future of South Africa. It was something that happened in West Africa, but it wasn't going to happen in South Africa. It was as if they were saying we're different; not just that 'our struggle is different or more advanced, but *we're* different; the world won't pull us down into (Black) abjection'.

Saidiya said to me that in the U.S. we are familiar with that same gesture from Caribbean people who may accept that there is abjection of Black Americans, but coming from Trinidad, they think they have cultural heritage and accoutrement that will help them avoid the taint of abjection. She said that if we look deeper into that claim it doesn't hold; the specific claim of South African students, and the general claim of African and Caribbean immigrants in the United States, that they actually have a cosmology and a language and so they are not pure abjection; that, unlike Black Americans, they are imbued with relationality. She said it doesn't ring true. If you scratch the surface, you will find more commonality than not. That was one way in which I adopted that word 'Afro-pessimism': it provides us with an analytic lens through which we can comprehend the manifestation of social death lodged throughout the diaspora at a structural level, even though, at the level of performance (conscious interests) all sorts of contradictory things are going on.

I began to use the word 'Afro-pessimism' to describe the pursuit of what Jared Sexton calls 'unbearable Blackness'; but Saidiya gave me the term and pointed me in the right direction. It was also, of course, used by western journalists and policy wonks to describe the impossibility of African development socially and economically. We don't mean it in that sense, of course. The way we use Afro-pessimism has no relationship to that use of the term …

If you talk to me, Jared Sexton, Saidiya Hartman or David Marriott, you're going to get a different answer based upon on how we enter the debate, but I like to think of Afro-pessimism as a paradigmatic lens. Which really comes into tension with some of the questions you are asking us to consider for this book. It is an interesting tension.

Afro-pessimism is interesting because it is doing nothing but critique. That doesn't mean it doesn't have a relationship to political praxis, but once you pick it up for a political project then certain things start to become complicated and entangled. It's a critique of the assumptive logic of other forms of revolutionary thought, without offering revolutionary prescriptions. Which is also a little confusing. I like that because I actually think that the revolutionary thought of Black people, if it were allowed to proliferate, would be so comprehensive as to terrify me, you, and anyone who would actually think about it. So, I think that Black thought always has to be ratcheted down in polite circles: That's what James Baldwin meant when he said: '[T]he really ghastly thing about trying to convey to a white man the reality of the Negro experience has nothing whatever to do with the fact of color, but has to do with this man's relationship to his own life. He will face in your life only what he is willing to face in his.' [Laughs] A piece of it taken apart, and the rest left. This is why there are so few non-Black Afro-pessimists, and almost no White ones. They're just too goddamn happy. And to even consider the argument would fuck with that. And, most of all, they don't want to meditate on how their happiness, or just their plain ole capacity for psychic integration is inextricably bound to Black suffering. Few theorists are willing to be consumed by the *real* extent of Black suffering, of the violence of social death. The kind of tool, or instrument or means of approach that I used to leverage or to pry apart the difference between Afro-pessimism and say, Marxism, non-Black feminism, indigeneism, can be found in the way in which Afro-pessimism thinks about violence. The way in which Afro-pessimism thinks about violence cannot be reconciled with the way violence is understood by those other revolutionary discourses: Marxism, indigeneism, non-Black feminism. (Though, it should be clear to those who read this literature that Afro-pessimism is made possible by the critical labors of a particular strand of *Black* feminism, à la Hartman and Spillers.)

SW The question of violence constantly emerges when talking about Afro-pessimism, and is a key point both in practice, and also in comprehending the world. Can you explain further what you mean when you talk about violence?

FW I would like someone to come along and prove Afro-pessimism to be wrong. I find it too debilitating to take in on a daily basis, myself. But what I find is that people who want to prove it wrong are either dealing with a piece of it, or they are responding in a sentimental way, not in an analytic way. That's why I still hang onto it. The reason why I'd love to have someone prove it wrong is because of the way violence is thought through. I've poached a lot off of Orlando Patterson here, and I'm not sure he's entirely happy with that.

One of the interesting things that he says when he's talking about capitalism in his book *Slavery and Social Death,* is that the violence of capitalism has a prehistory. What he means by that is that it takes an ocean of violence to transpose people who are not workers into workers. It takes an ocean of violence over a couple of hundred years to discipline them into temporalities that are new and more constricting – and to have them imagine their lives within those constraints: urbanization, mechanization, and certain types of labor practices. But, Patterson argues, once the system is set up, then that violence recedes and it goes into remission. The violence comes back at times when capitalism needs to regenerate itself or, when the workers transgress against the rules and push back. Patterson says the violence of the Slave estate can't be thought of like that. It takes an ocean of violence to produce a Slave, singular or plural, but that violence never goes into remission. The prehistory of violence that establishes slavery is also the *concurrent history* of slavery. This is very hard for politicos to adjust to because it actually takes the problem outside of politics. Politics is a very rational endeavor, and so you can work out models that predict the structural violence of capitalism in its performative manifestation. But you can't create models that predict the structural violence of slavery in its performative manifestations. What the Marxists do with slavery is that they try to show how violence is connected to production, and that means that they are not really thinking about the violence of slavery comprehensively. The violence of social death (slavery) is actually connected with the production of the psychic health of those who are not Slaves. That's the more intangible, libidinal aspect to it. It's even difficult for me to accept.

In what we're going through now with Ferguson, and Eric Garner in Staten Island, and Sandra Bland in Texas,[2] all this stuff that's coming to the light … what's happening is people are wanting to make sense of the violence, rather than trying to theorize its *non*sense. Black death does have a certain utility, but it's not connected to the extraction of surplus value, not in any fundamental way. And it's certainly not connected to the usurpation of land. These deaths are integral to the psychic integration of everyone who is not Black. They function as national therapy; even though the rhetoric that explains and laments the deaths expresses this psychic dependence not directly, but symptomatically. It is complex, but it is simple too. Blacks are not going to be genocided like Native Americans. We *are* being genocided, but genocided *and* regenerated. And the spectacle of Black death is essential to the mental health of the world – we can't be wiped out completely, our deaths must be repeated, *visually*. The bodily mutilation of Blackness is necessary, so it has to keep repeating itself. It's not a function of clearing people to get the land. It's a function of stabilizing the anxiety that other people feel in their daily lives. It's the anxiety that people have walking around. It can be stabilized by a lot of different things: marijuana, cocaine, alcohol, affairs, but the ultimate stabilization is the spectacle of violence against Blacks. This is why online video posts of police murdering Black people contribute more to the psychic wellbeing of non-Black people – to their communal pleasures, and sense of ontological presence – than they contribute to deterrence, arrests, or even to a general sensitivity to Black pain and suffering.

SW This is a painful and difficult way of thinking about violence against Blacks. It disrupts so much of what we think we understand. At its core, it leads us directly to the question of the relationality of 'civil society' and how that space functions for Black people. In the way you conceptualize the spectacle of violence, it begs the question whether civil society exists at all as a space for political action.

FW I want to say, for the record, that I have been involved as a political activist since I was at least 12 years old. I don't want to put my activism forward as being exemplary of understanding the problem, for the simple reason that I think that what I've done over the years is struggle for everybody else but Blacks. *Workers, women, Native Americans, Palestinians ...* you name it. It just happened that way. That said, I am thinking of civil society in two ways. One is through [Antonio] Gramsci, and then through [Antonio] Negri and [Michael] Hardt, who say that civil society is now gone. Your readers who have studied Gramsci know that for Gramsci civil society is the methodological terrain, not a real cartography distinct from political society. Gramsci always says that the distinction is made for methodological reasons. There's no such thing as real civil society over here, and the state over there. Civil society is the place where hegemony rules as opposed to force (schools, guild associations, the media, etc).

The conceptual problem that I have with thinking of Black people as members of civil society is because the operative modality in civil society is consent. When there is a crisis of consent, a seemingly irrational violence kicks in, from the institutions of political society (the state) until consent is secured again. This gets back to what I said earlier about the prehistory of capitalist violence – those modes of command, Gramsci argues, need only rear their ugly heads again when consent has been withdrawn by the working class. But when the system of capitalism globalizes and the violence needed to erect and maintain it goes into remission, hegemony replaces it as the primary modality. Consent replaces command, or violence. But you can't think consent and Blackness together. This is major point that one finds in most if not all Afro-pessimist work – however else we might disagree with one another. Sure, the politicians will say they want to hear what Black people say, or hear where they are coming from, and you've even got Black politicos who think that voting or not voting makes a difference (in the way that it might for Latinos or Asians or Whites or even for Native Americans!)

The problem for civil society, the problem for capital, the problem for settler colonialism lies at the nexus of consent or the withdrawal of consent. But the problem of consent or its withdrawal evaporates when and where subjugation of Blackness is concerned. Blacks give spontaneous consent all the time. Just ask the Democratic Party! It doesn't matter. In other words, there is no auditor for the consent of Black voices. It's a useless kind of exercise. What matters is the placement and movement of Black bodies. What are they going to do when they get together? It's not, 'what are they producing discursively, what are they saying, how does their vision conflict with ours?' … None of that is at play here, because consent is not an essential modality of the Master-Slave relation. Violence is the operative modality – and that violence spans the entire time of the paradigm. It doesn't go into remission; you don't get a reprieve for good behavior. That is never a question. If that were to be a question, then Afro-pessimism's analysis of the political economy would be all wrong: the Black would be another category of worker, or woman, or subaltern, instead of, as we argue, the quintessential Slave.

It is my firm conviction that the problem is a lot deeper than I have outlined in *Red, White, & Black: Cinema and the Structure of U.S. Antagonisms*. David Marriott (2000) writes about the Black man who is being lynched and forced to eat his own castrated genitals – and then, on top of all of that, forced to tell his lynchers how good it tastes. It's a complicated argument, but his point is that this is a kind of analog for the workings of desire; and that desire is anti-Black; that what Lacan missed, and what Fanon was on to, is that desire cannot be dis-imbricated from anti-Black violence. In other words, one must go through life *knowing* in one's unconscious, that there is only non-Black or iterations of anti-Black desire; that violence has usurped the capacity for one to access and speak a desire that isn't overdetermined by negrophobogenisis. No one escapes this. No one. The man being forced to eat his genitals and express delight is just an extreme example of what goes on in more nuanced, but no less debilitating ways. So, the problem that we, as Black people face, is not simply how to make our suffering legible to a world that would shatter at its seams were it to *read* our grammar of suffering correctly; but, the other problem is the fact that our psyches are *forced* to process our own images as phobic objects that need be destroyed and/or contained for the benefit of a White ideal. This makes it very difficult for us to be worthy of our own suffering. At the end of *Frantz Fanon's War* David Marriott asks the question, 'What do you do with an unconscious that appears to hate you?' This question points to a kind of violence from which there is no spatial or temporal respite, no Gramscian civil society of the mind. This is different than the subjugation or elaboration of an Irish unconscious or of a Palestinian unconscious.

So, what all this is saying is that there is vertical integration of violence that neither Gramscian anti-capitalist theory nor postcolonial theory can grapple with; a violence that saturates and which has no point of origin that can be discerned — because, at the lowest scale of abstraction, in the Black unconscious (which, in many respects, is the highest scale of abstraction) ... there is no temporal plenitude prior to abjection (the arrival of this hatred is a loop, not a chronology) and there is no spatial alternative to it either. The anti-Black hatred that has *arrived* in the Black unconscious, is of a piece with the anti-Black hatred that is openly, and not-so-openly, expressed in civil society. It doesn't have time or place of origination that can be discerned; nor can an endpoint or new, un-usurped locale, be imagined to be regained and made whole.

What David Marriott shows is that it's really quite impossible for the psyche to produce what is needed, what Biko would call disalienation, which is a Black ideal. Fanon goes right up to the edge of it in *Black Skin, White Masks*, Chapter 5, 'The Lived Experience of the Black Man', and pulls away. Understandably. It was 1952 and he started this book so that he and his wife could have a good marriage, not so that he could find out how fucked up everything is. Which is why he's infinitely more lucid and direct in *Wretched of the Earth*, than he is with *Black Skin, White Masks*. The writing in the *Wretched of the Earth* is less symptomatic of the author's deepest traumas.

This doesn't mean that all of this plays out in ways which are easy to understand and predictable. For example, when we think about Blackness and the absence of consent, we realize that there are situations in which the absence of consent as a modality of Black subjugation is complicated.

South Africa is a place where it is harder to see the absence of consent because it seems like rulers and ruled are both Black. Yet I don't think that once you actually analyzed it theoretically, you could actually say that South Africa is a place where Black consent or its withdrawal matters. In South Africa, abjection is vertically integrated – as it is in American civil society – but it's operating at different scales of abstraction.

If the offer and/or withdrawal of my consent doesn't matter, doesn't factor into the structure of my subjugation, and if what I offer discursively to the world doesn't matter, then that means that I am in a completely different paradigmatic location than all those people for whom it matters a little, or a lot. That's why the prehistory of violence toward Blacks is the concurrent history of violence towards Blacks in the twenty-first century. That makes it difficult to think about because then, what do you do with allies? We come right back to friendship. I know I have made your problem deeper. You can have all the interpersonal ethics of reciprocity that you want; but when the chips are down – *and even when they are not down* – we do not exist within the same paradigm of violence: and violence is what makes and/or prevents everything. Everything. You wouldn't be a Canadian and I wouldn't be a Slave if it weren't for violence. Violence elaborates us. Violence sustains us. Two friends. Two lovers. With two irreconcilable relationships to violence? How tenable is that? It's completely tenable as long as Black people don't start a riot and wake the fuckwits from their dreams. I think, like Saidiya Hartman, that the sentimental proclivity to make tenable is soothing to non-Black people and feeds the frustration of the Slave.

One of the things that Baldwin is upset with Mailer about, is that Mailer didn't surrender his authority to Blackness. I think he could have been more sanguine about their relationship had that happened. It is much more ephemeral, and harder to grasp, and you can't necessarily put a practice to it. Mailer was kind of negrophilic and negrophobic at the same time, which was not an engagement.

I tend to think this through the transformations that Heinrich and, my wife, Anita, and a handful of other [White] people that I've known have made, but that wouldn't be meaningful to the mass of Black people. Even during the most troubling times in our marriage, Anita was grappling earnestly with these theories through her teaching of people like Marriott and Hartman, and then through trying to inform our relationship, as well as the political work she was doing at the time, with a kind of integrity worthy of the material she was teaching. I do remember when Heinrich was very displeased with me after the murder of Chris Hani. He began to think out loud about the kind of theorizing, affect, and energy of the Black Consciousness movement as being more valuable than what was being put on lockdown in the ANC (I was holding onto the rationalism of Marxism), and that's what I mean by surrendering to the authority of Blackness. He wasn't saying, let's drop everything and go down the optimist road of Biko's Fanonian influenced theories of psychic disalienation. He was saying, the ANC is a Black organization that doesn't listen to Black people; let's see what we can learn from politicos who actually listen to Black people and are willing to be led by what they hear. It's that kind of meditative process; it's about from where does authorization flow, not about the flat-footed question of *who* is an authority and who is not, at the level of individuals.

But to be *authorized* by Blackness is to court the end of one's coherence: the end of one's life. And I don't mean one would stop breathing from a bullet wound. That would be too easy. That would make sense. No, I'm talking about living a life for which death is *not* a punctuation mark; that final pause that makes sense of what has come before, as Lacan would have it. And no one wants that. But that's what Black 'life' is, if you read Marriott. So, whether it's at the level of the job (as in faculty meetings or dealings with Black students) or whether it's at the level of outright politics (like Bernie Sanders or Hillary Clinton 'meeting' BlackLivesMatter) the problem is how to contain and surveil what Boers called the *swart gevaar* without having to engage it.

SW In terms of your relationship with South Africa, and your ongoing engagement there, as well as the ways in which Afro-pessimist ideas have been picked up, can you talk about how your ideas have transformed? What are your thoughts on the situation in South Africa right now?

FW I think two things. Positively, I think that Economic Freedom Fighters (EFF) is an interesting movement … party … I'm not sure how to characterize it. I think that what you have is a kind of mixture of a really robust analytic view of South Africa, which is moving away from the allegory of colonialism and thinking of slaveness in an abstract way without having to think about chains and whips. At the same time, embedded in this is the need for a kind of populist practice. I'm fascinated, as those two things seem incompatible. I'm really fascinated with where and how it is going to pan out. If I were a voting man in South Africa, I'd vote for them. I hadn't voted since 1974 in the States. I think I voted one of Carter's elections and then I never voted again until the Mandela election in South Africa in April of 1994, and April '95 for the re-elections, I absolutely refused. I realized what a futile exercise voting is – every time I vote (which has been twice since Carter, in the U.S.) I come away with a taste like warm beer in my mouth. It's pure folly. The more liberals talk about how important it is, for example, to make sure someone like Donald Trump doesn't get elected (ergo vote for someone like Bernie Sanders or Obama) the more this lesson hits home to me. It could have been different in South Africa, but it wasn't. It isn't. I'll tell you a story: During the first all-race elections in South Africa, April 1994, there was all this hubbub in the White press about what would happen if we (the royal White we) woke up in the morning to find that the ANC had garnered 75% of the vote. That means that the ANC would rule with an outright majority. I, foolishly, was under the impression that that was what we were struggling for. Mandela and his cronies had other ideas. At each voting station there was a cadre of about five revolutionaries who were assigned to stay there 24/7 to watch the voting boxes. We didn't trust the international observers for the simple reason that they went back to their hotels at night. We didn't trust the people running the elections because even though they were part of an independent commission, we realized the hand of the De Klerk state was in there somewhere somehow. And there were also rumors that the police would steal ballots in the night. We had to be ready in case they did this. So, a political commissar from the PAC comes and tells his cadres to go home. And, I'm thinking *what the fuck*?! Then Derek Hanekom comes along and tells the ANC cadres to go home. You dig? The fix was in. I'm like, hell no, I'm not going home. And he's like, that's an order, Frank! So, the other cats leave and I'm standing outside the polling station at around midnight trying to struggle with Hanekom. Right.

I'm like, you know the pigs are going to sweep in here and steal ANC ballots the minute we leave and we won't have an outright majority in the morning (which, by the way, is what happened). And he's coming at me sideways, with a lot of non sequiturs but I know exactly what he's saying. The closest he got to telling me that this was an orchestrated sell-out was some line he fed me about how if, in the morning, we had an outright majority there could be civil war; more assassinations like the murder of Chris Hani. This, right, from a former political prisoner. So, I'm telling him how, if we *don't* get an outright majority, we won't be able to take over the central bank, we won't be able to nationalize the mines, we won't be able institute free tertiary-level education for Africans and so-call 'coloreds', we won't be able to give the United States of America the middle finger! We'll be locked in a coalition government with the people who had murdered 14 000 of us in the past four years, and murdered 1.5 million Africans in the frontline states over the past 40 years; people who supported Israel and the right wing in Central America. So, he sighs, right … he sighs and shakes his head and lays it at my door. He says that the problem with *me*, is that in the time he'd worked with me politically (he was not only in MK, but he was the president of my ANC branch in Yeoville), that in the time that he'd worked with me politically, I had never seemed to inculcate the fact that the ANC was not a communist organization, but it is, 'Frank, a very broad church, in which not everyone is committed to a communist or even a socialist dispensation'. All right, so, we know what an accommodationist he became as minister of Land Affairs when the ANC came to power. But part of the thing that reawakened in me was how sutured the act of voting was to liberal humanist reform. The people who promote voting are people who have no interest in *using* voting as an instrument to heighten the contradictions and promote crisis.

Coming back to where we started: my hope is that EFF can blend voting with Fanon's 'the end of the world'. But for that to happen the rank and file in EFF are going to have to support the radical elements in EFF, especially those elements who come out of the large groups of radical intellectuals and activists who are melding U.S. Afro-pessimism with a renewed encounter with the politics of Steven Bantu Biko. If they don't do that, they are going to be a group of people who are talking loud and saying nothing and who are not genuinely committed to taking resources out of the hands of White people and redistributing them to the masses. I would like to see EFF get into the parliament, not for what they could do, but for what they could destroy. Bringing an analytic framework that suggests that participation in civil society is a dead end *into* a political party *into* civil society, that's fascinating! I'm interested to see where it goes and completely supportive of that trend. But the party's predilection for populism could be a big problem.

SW Yes. It does also seem quite different than the Black Consciousness (BC) movement, which was still looking to the possibility of a civil society. Does Black Consciousness play a role in your thinking at all?

FW What has become EFF comes through the anthology on Biko that Andile Mngxitama, Amanda Alexander, Nigel Gibson edited; and to which I contributed a chapter. Our conversations reintegrated me, at a distance, to what was going on in South Africa. There's no diplomatic way to say this, so I'm going to say it. I think that EFF is more dangerous than the Black Consciousness movement. That doesn't mean that it will harness that iconoclastic potential. The more seats they get, the more they tamp down what I see as really dangerous iconoclasm that I'm supporting. What we had in BC was Biko's reading of one Fanon: the Fanon of disalienation. The Fanon who wanted to heal himself and other Blacks of 'lactification' or hallucinatory whiteness, and who wanted to cure his wife and other Whites of their superiority complex. This is where Biko spends most of his discursive time when he meditates on Fanon. There are at least two other Fanons. There is the Fanon of postcolonial resistance (as in *The Wretched of the Earth*), and there is the third Fanon, the Fanon of social death, the Fanon of the Slave, the Fanon of the 'end of the world'. I think that the comrades that have come through BC that are now in EFF are still engaging with Fanon, but they are engaging the Fanon of the 'end of the world'. And this is a really powerful thing because it comes about as a result of their reading of Sexton, Hartman, Marriott, and myself; and as a result of our responding to their interventions. It comes about as a result of a pan-African movement of the twenty-first century that is really exciting. Dr. Omar Ricks, a leading Afro-pessimist in Oakland/Berkeley recently returned from a tour of South Africa, during which time he gave two or three public presentations, sharing the stage with major people associated with the new revolutionary movement in South Africa – Andile was one of those people. I think that Andile Mngxitama and people around him could have infused EFF with the critical discourse that supports the radical agenda students, people in EFF and in the townships seem to want.[3]

A moment ago, it may have sounded like I was against that part of Fanon's project that calls for psychic healing. I'm not. But, I am against raising that project to the level of politics. It's a really tricky kind of thing because there are trends in disalienation of the Black psyche, you know? In other words, when Black people feel psychically more powerful; those moments occur when there's more of mass Black violence in the streets than less. It's kind of weird because I can't really write a sentence about it (a mass Black uprising – Fanon's 'end of the world') in the way that Biko writes a sentence about 'love yourself' (Fanon's 'disalienation') and that kind of thing. I'll try. There is something unspoken about the intent of Afro-pessimism and it is unspoken partially because we want to keep our jobs. However, this radically unspoken is empowering *to Black people* when they are able to discuss Afro-pessimism away from Whites and non-Blacks. I've seen it happen when I returned to South Africa on a speaking tour in September 2012. I've seen it happen in political education workshops, which I've conducted for BlackLivesMatter organizers in LA and New York. But the critique of the Human (in Afro-pessimism) is as harsh as the critique (in Marxism) of the capitalist. Marx critiques the capitalist for his/her *capacity* to accumulate, not for her/his attitudes, feelings, or even performance (whether benign or tyrannical) of that capacity. Afro-pessimism critiques the Human for his/her capacity to *be*; not for his/her lived activity – that is the second move in the Afro-Pessimist project, not the first move. (The move is descriptive: an analysis of the Slave position.) People who are *not* Black and who don't see their capacity to *be* as being parasitic on Black non-being, think *this*, the critique itself, is tyrannical, that the critique somehow abuses them. In other words, they invert the world and cry foul; hoping we can return to the status quo – you eating your own genitals and telling them how good it tastes. Black folks sometimes have a hard time holding the middle finger up to this symptomatic response. But in intra-mural contexts, Afro-pessimism rocks!

When I was in South Africa, and in my political work in the United States, Black people condemning other non-Black people in a political movement was often a very difficult thing to get through. You had to find a reason, and that reason often was puny in comparison to the rage that we felt. What the danger of Afro-pessimism is for the rest of the world is that it allows for Black people to take it up politically in a way that condemns the rest of Humanity for their existence, for their capacity; their temporal and spatial coherence, the integration of their bodily schemas, the security they inhabit knowing the violence they experience is contingent upon transgressions of codes, whether ethical or unethical. Afro-pessimism removes the burden of having to find a discriminatory action before levying a condemnation. (No one on the Left minds this when we're talking about the capitalist class, by the way.) Now that's a really, really dangerous thing. Baldwin says it, when he says, 'Mailer has something to salvage, I have nothing to lose', but he doesn't say, therefore whatever I do to him is okay. Fanon says it, in *The Wretched of the Earth*. But Baldwin is a humanist, he can't get there. As a result of not being able to get there, a lot of his work, not him personally, but the Civil Rights' leadership work goes toward policing Black rage and its proliferation. *Everyone* knows what Cornell West told us a decade ago: Black rage proliferates and it proliferates exponentially. First prize, for civil society, is when civil society can get *other* Blacks to police this rage. Andile lays it out when he says that the ANC is the bodyguard of White Supremacy. But without the mobilization of Black rage you get Marikana. Black police murdering Black workers on behalf of Whites sleeping in their homes miles away.

Afro-pessimism, and the ways in which comrades and sisters and brothers on the ground in South Africa and now, here, in the Black Lives movement are taking it up – not merely as an analytic lens, which is all that I and others had hoped for when we were formulating it, but taken it up as that which can inflect and inform revolutionary politics – is heartening.

For the first time in a long time, social movements are asking, how can we be informed by and authorized by a Black ensemble of questions; asking themselves what does it mean when David Marriott talks about how anti-Blackness creates a kind of generic hatred for Black beings, which is vertically integrated in all our psyches? Why this is *not* a form of discrimination but rather a necessary hatred. Why must global civil society keep reproducing social death so that social life can regenerate its members and prevent them from suffering a catastrophe of subjective coherence; how do we think a semiotics of violence in new ways?

SW So this dualism is fundamental to social life? There always must be a Slave necessary?

FW Yes. I know that it is a very controversial point to make. Patterson says, every *socius* has to understand itself. In order to understand itself, it needs a psychological grounding wire. And that psychic grounding wire is a Slave in its midst. Patterson sees slavery as kind of a necessary reproduction so that, if you're talking about the Choctaw Indians before Columbus, or people in the Amazon, or the Ashanti before contact with the Portuguese. ... Slavery is necessary to this psychic coherence of a *socius*. What's interesting about this is for me – not for cultural nationalists, not for Afro-centrists, not for integrationists, but for me – Blackness and Slaveness cannot be dis-imbricated. This is where Patterson might say I've bastardized his ideas. But I've argued this; I haven't simply asserted it.

You can't know yourself in relation to yourself. You can only know yourself in relation to those beings that are adjacent to you, and those beings that are completely opposed to your identity. That's how you create knowledge. The slave is necessary to the creation of knowledge about collectivity. For the first time in the *longue durée* of what we call the Human, slavery has become not just an experience that some people go through, but the actual dynamic of a certain position. Despite where [Achille] Mbembe would like us to take his work, *On the Postcolony* actually says more about Africa as a *Slave estate* than as a colony. His work has actually done a lot more than he intended, just as Patterson's did a lot more than he intended.

As Jared Sexton says, if Africa and Slaveness cannot be dis-imbricated, and Blackness and Slaveness cannot be dis-imbricated, then we've got a real problem. It's a problem that must be addressed, but cannot be redressed. The reason it cannot be redressed is because to redress it, you have to have coherence, diachronically or synchronically. For it to have coherence diachronically, you have to be able to point to the concept of Africa, to the concept of Blackness prior to Slaveness; a plenitude prior to the condition of natal alienation – which I theorize, by extension, as being *affilial* alienation as well.

And I don't think anyone can do that. The Dred Scott decision is just one of many texts that remind people (here it is a message to the lower courts) that Black people are guilty a priori, not because they did something, but because they have not, nor have they ever had, any standing as juridical subjects. To work on it synchronically, you'd have to point to a scale of abstraction, whether it's the psyche, the unconscious, the conscious, the family, the city, the state, or the globe, you have to factor some kind of scale of geographic abstraction where Blackness exists outside of a condition of gratuitous violence. What Marriot is saying is that the Black unconscious is always anchored by this churning of violence. That means that there's no scale of abstraction in which Blackness actually exists in a state of repose. This is why it is so, so hard for politics of redress to be developed when it comes to the recent spate of (filmed and reported) murders of Black people. How do you redress a dynamic that subtends the psychic health of the world?

SW This is what you mean when you say this is an ontological and not an experiential question? Jared Sexton also talks about how we need to see this position of Blackness as a global phenomenon. We don't need to only look at slavery in relation to the north Atlantic. This is one of the issues when talking about Afro-pessimism in South Africa. Many people get stuck on the idea of the Slave, and whether it is useful in the South African context. People struggle with how to think about that, and often go to an abstraction with the term 'Slave'. Can you talk about how you have been thinking about slavery in relation to South Africa, or beyond the north Atlantic?

FW The first move that I make is that slavery has to be re-conceptualized so that we take it away from the plantation. We take it out of the temporality of the nineteenth century, and we think about it in terms of its constituent elements. The constituent elements are natal alienation, general dishonor, and gratuitous violence.

This is *absolutely* applicable to South Africa. As I indicated, I don't think that the Marikana massacre would have happened, at least like it happened, if the police were who they were (Black Africans) and the workers were (so-called) colored. I'm not saying that no one would have gotten killed. What I'm saying is that there would be some kind of stoppage, some type of intervention in the psyches of those people pulling the triggers. They would have to momentarily adjust to remind themselves: 'Oh yeah ... they are Slaves also. We *can* kill them.' And I think that if the workers were White, it wouldn't have happened at all. What I'm suggesting is that the question of who is a Slave, and who is not a Slave, and does this slavery look like that slavery, is moving us more towards experience and away from ontology. I think that the importance should be placed on thinking paradigmatically – thinking less about political praxis and more about political ontology. People get tripped up by thinking paradigmatically when it is about Blackness and otherness in a way that they don't get tripped up in thinking paradigmatically about capitalism and communism. The anxiety quotient is so much higher here, and that's interesting.

I think that the anti-Black psyche a) cuts through geography and b) cuts through time, and it cuts through individuals so that anti-Blackness is the generative mechanism that structures my unconscious and your unconscious. Not that it structures your unconscious and not my unconscious. Marriott says that Black unconscious is usurped by the eagle-eyed view of moving toward the light – Whiteness – and understanding that one must garrison oneself against the intrusion of the Black phobic object. That is as operative in the Black unconscious as it is anywhere else. I think that dynamic was at work during the Marikana massacre. You can slow down that dynamic with a so-called colored person, or someone like Halle Berry. But, then the dynamic picks up again, once it is recognized that 'oh no, this is Blackened flesh, just a little less so', then it comes up again. It comes up in weird ways, like that person might not be thought of as a negrophobic object, but rather thought of as a negrophilic object: someone to possess with passion as opposed to someone to be afraid of and repel with violence. The same dynamic is still there, the so-called colored or biracial person in the United States is as fungible as the very dark-skinned person, they're just put to different uses. The fungibility of Blackness allows for the absence of thought, when it comes to what to do with that. Whether it is absence of the thought of what to do with that pleasurably, the absence of the thought of what to do with that violently. It is the absence of thought that is really important here. And the Marikana policemen were implements of that. They are not agents or the beneficiaries of their own aggression against Blackness, even though it saturates their psyches in ways similar to White racists.

SW I suppose the question that lingers is whether relationality and consent are possible *between* Blacks, at the level of the interpersonal, when we remove

Whiteness altogether. In your thinking is there a space for Black friendship and relationality, or are Blacks also forced to see each other as fungible?

FW That is the biggest question. This is really difficult. I think that in the big and not-so-big moments of throwing ourselves against the world, something *loving* happens between Black people. This is where Fanon and *Wretched of the Earth* is important to me, because I do think that violence is a modality constitutive of liberation. No two ways about it. Fanon writes: '[T]his world cut in two is inhabited by two different species.' Species. It is an important word, symptomatic of Fanon's Afro-pessimism, even though, for the most part he is ventriloquizing a postcolonial perspective. And he goes on to write that, through revolutionary violence, the native ... 'finds out that the settler's skin is not of any more value than a native's skin; and it must be said that this discovery shakes the world in a very necessary manner'. Well, the world that shakes in a necessary manner is not just the world of the settler, his/her arrangement of power, but it is also, most importantly, the psyche of the Black that is shaken. And here is where Black friendship, Black love flowers; here is where the capacity for or promise of relationality is elaborated for the Slave, in the Slave revolt. Because, for a brief moment (and these are *always* brief moments) the Slave is confronting her/his/their *real* enemy; which is not the performance of subjugation by the Master class, but the capacity for that formation to exist. We *know* where our relational capacity went during the Arab slave trade, during the Middle Passage, during our long and torturous existence here. It went into the creation of the Human. And so, there is something that happens when we confront *capacity* itself; and that something is a glimmer, not much more than a glimmer, but a glimmer of a possibility for us to *be* with, of, and for each other. To experience Black love and freedom. I think that that is a precondition for the elaboration of the *truth* of intra-Black love, Black friendship. But there can be, and are, provisional, or partial encounters as well; which don't require an uprising in order to be staged. Such as jazz and poetry and Black literature. But I think people who are scholars tend to make too much of the emancipatory promise of those moments. As one young blood said to a cultural nationalist back in the day, 'Yeah, alright, bring your music but bring your gun as well.'

I believe Saidiya Hartman more than Fred Moten. Saidiya Hartman says, you feel like you have this transcendence, you have a marriage, which has transcended something or, any of the little micro encounters that happen, Black to Black. The fact of the matter is that it has changed a lot in your intra-personal dynamics, but it has not changed very much in the structure of where and how you are positioned, paradigmatically. She asks, if I become a great musician, and the music does something for me, and even for my relations with others, has that musical moment been an effect of my agency? Or is it merely an extension of the Master's prerogative? In other words, the musical performance is an occasion to come up to the big house and play, or to play in your cabin after sundown. It is occasioned and allowed (as I think Hortense Spillers said somewhere). Nothing happens in Black life that is not beneath the pall of this cloud of 'occasioned and allowed'. You can forget this at times, but not escape it. To turn your head from this is to believe that you are Black and not completely saturated, subsumed by anti-Black violence simply because you work in a bank or at a university – because, that is, you don't live in the ghetto. Bullshit. Sandra Bland didn't live in the ghetto. And nor did she kill herself. And, dig this, even if it turns out that she did hang herself, she certainly did not kill herself. That happened before she was born.

I live in a white neighborhood, in a rich Republican suburb. It's only because I've been allowed to, and the occasion is allowed because I'm a professor at a university. But I am not the agent of all that in a way that one could say I was structurally different from the condition of my ancestors in chains. I don't make moves that transform civil society. Civil society makes a decision to become elastic, or rigid. Depending upon when I was born and where, and where I live, that decision made by others for me will affect the quality of my life. That is the most important dynamic of intra-Black relations. There is no such thing as a pure intra-Black relation that is void of, absent, or beyond that fact. Which is why the Afro-pessimist end of the world, which is the end of the ability to think in the way that we think, is not Marx's end of the world because he's talking about the end of an economic system. We are talking about the end of what sustains people as people. Because what sustains them as people is Black death. When we move against the generative mechanisms of Human life, something happens between us. Even in those moments when our conscious discourse calls it a revolution for economic transformation, there is an excess, a Black structure of feeling that cannot be explained or contained because it portends an epistemological break; an ontological catastrophe. Our renewal beyond what we can imagine.

We can love each other, we can experience (though not necessarily narrate) liberation in those moments. Remember what George Jackson said about his younger brother who died trying to liberate comrades from the Marin County courthouse: 'for a moment he was free'. Now, I am not saying go out, kill a cop and be free for a moment. In fact, there is almost nothing of a prescriptive nature in anything I say or write. That's because if it is to be valid and lasting it cannot come from someone like me. It has to come from the ground up. But what I am saying is that Black love portends the end of the world. That should be clear. It's an exhilarating or terrifying proposition, depending on who you are.

SW Given what you've said here, how do you relate to the BlackLivesMatter (BLM) movement?

FW Sexton and others have homed in on a vital point: that here we have a grassroots movement mobilized by Black queer women. And something really remarkable can come out of this *if* … *if* BLM does not speak to the world at the expense of speaking to Black people. And this is the danger of any Black movement in the U.S. But so far, I'm thrilled. I think that what BLM has shown is that it is possible to broaden the iconic range in terms of how we think Black suffering.

In other words, we know that the world is narratively more interested in what they perceive as the phobic threat of the Black man. That is where civil society's interest is. We pick that up, in terms of dealing with our grievances and dealing with the murders of Black men, which there are tremendous amounts of. But in Los Angeles, Black women have been murdered in the hundreds for the past 30 years. Many of them were dismissed as sex workers whether they are or they're not — as though that impacts upon their worthiness as victims. Their lives aren't counted, and because it's probably the work of Black men, it goes off the radar in terms of how we think about these questions. We're running dangerously close to repeating the 1960s in which the violence against Blackness is first and foremost imagined as the violence against Black masculinity in the political imagination. If we were actually to create a political movement based on these women's deaths, we couldn't mobilize around that, I mean, we must try. We must try. But we can't mobilize around it precisely because our psyches are as captivated by

White anxiety about Black masculinity as White psyches are. Or, if they're not captivated by it, we understand intuitively that this is the only way to get heard. By talking about police killing Black men. We think we have to start there, otherwise, we won't hear ourselves and no one will hear us. BlackLivesMatter is struggling against that. That's a beautiful thing. Now, if, at the same time, BlackLivesMatter struggles against the insistence levied against us by White people and their junior partners (colored immigrants) to say 'all lives matter' or to condemn the murder of police officers, then a really significant milestone will have been reached. We will have turned the corner on heteronormativity within Black political formations *and* we will have given the proverbial middle finger to all those people from Bernie Sanders to Hillary Clinton down to the White leftist who likes to tell us what we need and what we should do, or how universal our suffering is, or why we should show remorse instead of relief when a cop is killed. Neither liberal humanist pacifism nor intra-racial homophobia will press down on our movement. We will respond to the world the way our ancestors did, with the knowledge that it is all one big plantation.

That's why I said I would love someone to show me that Afro-pessimism is wrong, but at every scale of abstraction I see violence and captivity. Whether it's the psyche alone in one's apartment, or whether it's the kind of ethical scaffolding of film, or whether it's the intuition behind a political project. It's all one big plantation. And we will recognize in the policeman's bullet, the liberal's handwringing and in the words of Al Sharpton telling people to go to the police and demand the end of police brutality, and don't riot – we'll see the same anti-Black violence. I think BlackLivesMatter has the potential to do all of that. But in order for that to happen the movement has to have two trains running.

This was an important teaching point of the simulation exercise we did when I conducted a workshop for 35 organizers from BlackLivesMatter at what was the Audubon Ballroom where Malcolm X was killed (it's now The Malcolm X and Dr. Betty Shabazz Memorial and Educational Center) on 168th and Broadway. I titled the exercise 'Strategy and Tactics', but, colloquially, I call it two trains running. I wanted us to see how and why it was/is important for us to transform our political rhetoric and the horizon of our revolutionary goals to be higher than transforming police behavior, so that that rhetoric and horizon can evolve to be against the existence of the police themselves.

I'm not saying that BlackLivesMatter's tactics that move toward the reform of police behavior be abandoned, because we need relief right now … we need two trains running. By that I mean, we have to have that tactical and immediate response to *tactical* police violence – in order to quell it. But we can't let that tactical response to police violence 'contaminate' – for lack of a better word – our overall orientation towards the police. We have to be against the existence of the police even if our tactics are such that they cannot rise to that level at this particular moment. And just being able to *own* that rhetoric (to speak from Blacks to Blacks) without hesitation or apology – my god, that would be a great leap forward! Combining that with a movement *away* from being transfixed by civil society's anxiety about the phobic object as masculine … well, we'll be on our way then.

SW What's fascinating, and what seems impossible to know, is whether there is the potential for things to be so entirely shattered that one could begin again that it could be possible to create a new beginning. I think at the micro level and at the level of intimacy, we experiment. Of course you can never solve the problem at the level of the intimate, but at the level of the intimate perhaps there is an ability to play safely with violence. Perhaps there can be a testing out of another potential at the level of the encounter, a way to see a shimmer of something else on the horizon?

FW There are a lot of contradictions. For example, on one hand you have a guerrilla cell, which is part and parcel of what I would call generative violence against the violence that structures Black (non)existence. As I indicated earlier, I think that in those moments there is something that happens. Maybe not necessarily in the cell alone, but when the cell is coordinated with a mass Black movement, which is also taking this stuff up. That was what I hoped for in South Africa before Chris Hani was killed, when he and Winnie Mandela were just being marginalized. Not that they were the intellectual architects, but they were beacons of something that was iconoclastic that would sometimes help people to not be so captivated by Mandela-ism, and by culture. Winnie and Hani captured the imagination of the most dispossessed.

I think in the cell I felt something for Heinrich that I hadn't felt for a White person. Something different was happening. And, over the past eight years or so I have felt that in my marriage, my deep love for Anita. I don't want to cathedralize either relationship more than that just yet. In addition, clandestine intimacy is its own beast, because the other problem is that clandestine activity is also kind of an anathema to intimacy. Intimacy is all about saying openly what's on your mind – sharing your thoughts and feelings. Clandestine activity is everybody keeping a little bit of the puzzle to themselves. I know there were times when Heinrich got me to do and say stuff, and he might have just lied to me about why he was telling me to do what he was telling me to do. There was all this intimacy, but it was not like friendship in another terrain because there were also secrets. I was a nobody to these people, I was just an asset. (My above-ground activity, as an elected official and as someone seconded to various regional structures, was less ambiguous.) An asset that they loved, but let's not confuse the dynamics. They were revolutionaries because they got to have the meetings, and hear all the secrets, and they decided what they were going to tell me, and at the same time I had this intimate bond. I found it to be a very fascinating thing to think about. I don't have a conclusion for that. 'Play safely with violence …?' Well, I'm not entirely sure what you mean, but I don't think that you or I have agency here. In the movies we're taught that love conquers all, but this facilitates our disavowal of the violence that has always already conquered love.

REFERENCES

Fanon, Frantz. 1963. *The Wretched of the Earth*. Translated by Constance Farrington. New York, NY: Grove Press.

Fanon, Frantz. 1967. *Black Skin, White Masks.* Translated by Charles Lam Markmann. New York, NY: Grove Press.

Hartman, Saidiya 1997. *Scenes of Subjection: Terror, Slavery, and Self-Making in the Nineteenth Century*. Oxford: Oxford University Press.

Marriott, David. 2000. *On Black Men*. New York, NY: Columbia University Press.

Patterson, Orlando. 1985. *Slavery and Social Death: A Comparative Study.* Cambridge: Harvard University Press.

Wilderson, Frank B. III. 2008. *Incognegro: A Memoir of Exile & Apartheid*. Boston, MA: South End Press.

Wilderson, Frank B. III. 2010. *Red, White & Black: Cinema and the Structure of U.S. Antagonisms.* Durham, NC: Duke University Press.

NOTES

1   In his writing, Wilderson explains that he capitalizes the words '*Red, White, Black, Slave, Savage,* and *Human*' in order to assert their importance as ontological positions and to emphasise the value of theorizing power politically rather than culturally.' (2010: 23) We have followed his usage in this chapter.

2   Eric Garner died after an officer in the New York Police Department put him in a chokehold on a minor infraction in July 2014. Outrage at his killing sparked the BlackLivesMatter movement. One year later, Sandra Bland was found hanged in a jail cell in police custody in Texas, followed by protests against her arrest and stated cause of death.

3   Mngxitama is no longer part of the EFF party.

5 THE IMPOSSIBLE HANDSHAKE: THE FAULT LINES OF FRIENDSHIP IN COLONIAL NATAL, 1850–1910

T. J. TALLIE

In 1854, John Colenso, the newly appointed Bishop of Natal, arrived in the colony on a preliminary tour. After meeting many of the settler families and colonial administrators, Colenso looked forward to meeting indigenous Africans,[1] with whom he hoped to build productive and close, lasting relationships. During one of his first encounters with a Natal African, however, Colenso (1855: 45) remembered that settler administrators (even those ostensibly self-designated as 'philo-Kafirs' or liberal-minded on racial divisions) had instructed him on the parameters of colonial friendship with indigenous peoples. He recalled:

> With all my heart [I] would have grasped the great black hand, and given it a good brotherly shake: but my dignity would have been essentially compromised in his own eyes by any such proceeding. I confess it went very much against the grain; but the advice of all true Philo-Kafirs, Mr. Shepstone among the rest, was to the same effect viz that too ready familiarity, and especially shaking hands with them upon slight acquaintance, was not only not understood by them, but did great mischief in making them pert and presuming. Accordingly, I looked aside with a grand indifference as long as

I could, (which was not very long,) and talked to Mr. G., instead of paying attention to the Kafir's presence.

At such an early point in the colony's history, the limits of sociability and friendship had already become clear in the minds of settler administrators. The logics of colonial rule in Natal required an effective division between the 'African' subject and the 'proper' settler; these divisions were to be further entrenched politically and legally through the implementation of customary law for Africans and civil law for European colonists. This moment of unrealized friendship provides a profound and intriguing site of rupture in the colonial record. From Colenso's intimation of the perspective of Mr. Shepstone, and the other 'philo-Kafirs', we can presume that the hierarchized distinctions between African and European were to be understood as a paternalistic form of love. Yet Colenso's shake was not a paternalistic or hierarchal form of 'love' for the African; rather, he imagined his gesture as a magnanimous, or brotherly act of friendship. If experts such as Shepstone understood colonial rule as the proper, paternal form of love that characterized settler/indigenous relations, how might friendship or forms of alternate sociability prove dangerous to the desired order? In what ways could friendship and social interaction unsettle hierarchies of race, gender, and colonial power?

This chapter will examine the history of colonial Natal along the fault lines of friendship and subversive sociability, from missionary overtures to the dangerous destabilizations of alcohol use. Focusing on the constitutive and constructed nature of raced and gendered hierarchies in colonial Natal, I propose a reading of friendship that underscores its fundamentally protean (and thereby disruptive) nature. Friendship and various forms of sociability across gendered or raced lines could work to either reinforce or unsettle settler power in the nineteenth century, and the legislative record is rife with concerns over 'improper' forms of socialization between Africans and members of settler society. The contradictory impulses of friendship discourses did not begin with the founding of the Union of South Africa. As colonial records demonstrate, the idea of friendship was frequently invoked by settlers within the colony seeking to justify their rule in Natal, while these references simultaneously contained the potential to unravel hierarchies of racial order.

Understanding just how these hierarchies operated requires an understanding of the larger dynamics of settler colonialism as they operated within Natal. The critical study of settler colonialism has enjoyed a new prominence in histories of North America and Australasia as a means of understanding the relations that structured both colonists and previous inhabitants of these lands (Byrd 2011; Coombes 2006; Driskill et al 2011; Morgensen 2011; Smith 2010). Yet, with few exceptions, this framework has not been widely applied to southern Africa, and Natal in particular.[2] Settler colonial studies situates the inherent conflict between indigeneity and settler nationalist claims to belonging within a larger framework of marginalization and appropriation, foregrounding the historic violence that structures these nationalist assertions of autochthony[3] in sites of recent European settlement. 'Settler colonialism destroys to replace,' as anthropologist Patrick Wolfe (2006: 388) has bluntly stated. 'Settler colonizers come to stay: invasion is a structure, not an event.' For Wolfe, settler colonies differ from colonies of extraction (or non-settlement) in that the colonizer literally comes to stay; unlike in other colonial societies where the colonizer eventually returns to the metropole, the nature of occupation is naturalized and daily enacted in an emergent national form. Likewise, theorist Lorenzo Veracini (2010: 31) has argued, 'all settler projects are foundationally premised on fantasies of ultimately "cleansing" the settler body politic of its (indigenous and exogenous) alterities'. In this formulation, settler colonialism defines a constitutive project where generations of settler occupants attempt to solve the 'problem' of indigenous and competing exogenous peoples in their midst. This is particularly relevant to Natal, where both the 'Native Question' and the 'Indian Question' haunted nineteenth-century settlers (and indeed later generations of historians).[4]

Yet settler society in Natal was by no means monolithic; the varied communities of settlers, missionaries, and colonial officials represented a host of different interests, concerns, and ideologies. However, it is possible to read nineteenth-century reports, letters, newspapers, and journals and perceive a general flow of ideas and concepts. Critiques of the colonial project by indigenous studies and postcolonial scholars have allowed for readings of general consensus or shared interest in spite of differing motivations. Reading Natal's settler history as one that seeks principally to legitimate and justify land occupation and a pursuit of autochthonous claims to the colony, it becomes possible to see commonalities or at the very least moments of contextual consensus among colonial actors. The British government established the colony of Natal in 1843 after forcibly annexing the then five-year-old Voortrekker polity of Natalia, a space carved out by land-hungry Dutch-speaking farmers from the lands of Nguni-speakers recently under the hegemony of the Zulu royal house led by Shaka kaSenzangakhona (*c.* 1816–1828) and later his brothers, Dingane (*c.* 1828–1840) and Mpande (*c.* 1840–1872). The colony of Natal served for many years as a somewhat neglected outpost to imperial officials in London as well as a space of intense contestation between a tiny settler minority and a far larger indigenous population.

Soon after the annexation, the skeletal colonial government and miniscule white settler population (including many former Dutch-speaking trekkers and a small coastal community of British traders) attempted to render the unruly spaces and indigenous populations legible to colonial eyes. Influenced by and in direct conversation with contemporary settler societies across the globe, Natal's new government sought to cordon off indigenous land reserves and enshrine African custom into a recorded and accessible code of native law. While the indigenous African population was scattered widely across the roughly drawn boundaries of the colony, and lacked a unifying ruling structure, they still vastly outnumbered the remaining Dutch-speaking trekkers and small numbers of British settlers in the first decades of Natal's existence.[5] With the arrival of the Byrne settlers in 1850, Natal's first major immigration scheme, and continuing throughout the century, Natal's nascent white population sought to increase their numbers in order to legitimate their political claim to the colonial territory. Yet, to the frustration of white politicians in Natal, immigration remained slow, and the indigenous African population continued to grow steadily. In addition, Indian migrant laborers, first procured by settler planters wishing to develop Natal's sugar industry, began to arrive in increasing numbers beginning in 1860. By the time of Victoria's Diamond Jubilee in 1897, just before the revolutionary changes in the region brought about by the South African War, extensive migrant labor moving to the Transvaal's mines, and the colony's entry into the Union of South Africa in 1910, Natal could count itself as one of Britain's dominions with responsible government and a measure of settler self-rule. However, the self-government of Natal, unlike the other British settler dominions (save for the Cape), remained very consciously a minority regime, increasingly committed to maintaining power and privilege based upon hierarchies of race.

In order to offer this understanding of Natal's settler society, I propose a methodology that critically appraises settler societies by privileging difference and disjuncture over a simple pursuit of commonality. Acknowledging that settlement was messy, contradictory, violent, cacophonous, and ultimately a *collision* of various actors, motivations, and power dynamics, provides a fruitful starting point for critical engagement.[6] Much like the way disorganized jumbles of sound can refract into new, traceable compositions within the noise, so too can the collisions of colonial settlement render within their inherent chaos identifiable, if shifting, patterns. Settler society in Natal can be viewed as a kaleidoscopic combination of varied actors – Midlands farmers, urban artisans, British and 'foreign' missionaries, and residential officials, for example – who each viewed the province differently yet could and did coalesce around specific interests. The concept of friendship allowed for moments of consensus among differing groups of colonial actors; missionaries and legislators, for example, might find a common rhetorical cause in discussing the potential for friendship with the native peoples of Natal. As a consequence, for settler observers, 'friendship' could operate as a signpost, a central point around which many of the broader contradictory and constraining aspects of colonialism in Natal could rally.

At its heart, the debate over friendship in Natal demonstrated both the aspirations of settler colonialism as well as its limits. The term itself contained considerable rhetorical power that could be marshalled for a variety of purposes; yet it also included inherent instabilities, from alcohol-fueled sociability to the power of indigenous peoples to subvert the very gift of friendship offered them by colonists. Some settlers could utilize an idea of interracial friendship as part of larger claims to legitimate rule; other settlers denounced the idea of interracial friendship as an obstacle to the inevitability of white dominance over the region. Studying nineteenth-century Natal through a lens of friendship allows for a reading of the contingent nature of settler colonialism, one that looks at how 'bundles of human relationships'[7] could be made and remade in the multi-sided contradictions of imperial rule. Such an analysis aligns the construction of settler structures in Natal with other contemporary colonies across the globe and foregrounds the considerable contribution of affective discourses (such as that of friendship) to the establishment of colonial power relations.

FRIENDSHIP AS GIFT

While the interracial friendship referenced in settler regimes could offer either a dangerous sense of instability for colonial authorities aimed at supplanting indigenous peoples or a cover for government officials seeking to naturalize their claim to the colony, this was by no means the only way in which friendship could operate in the context of colonial Natal. To return to the Colenso quote that opened this chapter, it is possible to understand how friendship could paradoxically serve to strengthen colonial hierarchies of power. When standing before an unnamed African man and a host of white settler observers, Colenso despaired over his inability to 'have grasped the great black hand, and given it a good brotherly shake', but what would the consequences of such an act of camaraderie have entailed?

The scene depicted between the bishop and the African is rife with social inequality, emphasized by Colenso's desire to offer a display of friendship to a native man in a land he had come to occupy. This exchange can be read as one of frustrated desire, as Colenso wishes to offer the gift of friendship to an African subject, a scenario similar to that imagined by Olive Schreiner four decades later. It is not a coincidence that both Schreiner and Colenso express interracial friendship as both a requirement for white settlers and an ideal to be pursued, despite the near-impossibility of its realization. Indeed, the friendship that Colenso wished to offer his unnamed African subject is a loaded one, inextricably linked to larger processes of colonial violence and economic coercion.

Although countless people have written about the positive and destructive aspects of the gift, my reading of the 'gift' of colonial friendship in this instance is drawn from two theorists, the French philosopher Jacques Derrida, and the American cultural critic Mimi Thi Nguyen. For Derrida (1992: 10–11), the concept of the 'gift' is a series of actions of homogenization and forgetting. First, the gift must flatten complexities between giver and receiver; the act:

> supposes a subject and a verb, a constituted subject, which can also be collective for example, a group, a community, a nation, a clan, a tribe in any case, a subject identical to itself and conscious of its identity, indeed seeking

through the gesture of the gift to constitute its own unity and, precisely, to get its own identity recognized so that that identity comes back to it, so that it can re-appropriate its identity: as its property.

This re-appropriation is apparent in the exchange between Colenso and his desired 'friend'. The act of 'giving' friendship entails recognizing Colenso as part of a collective subject group (colonizer, missionary, Briton) while simultaneously attempting to construct a receiving African subject, requiring a bridge across the chasm of hierarchical racial difference.

Second, the gift itself by definition creates debt, a sense of obligation or a need for fulfilment between receiver and giver. Yet, for Derrida, this must be ignored, indeed forgotten, in order for a gift to truly exist. 'For there to be a gift, there must be no reciprocity, return, exchange, countergift, or debt,' Derrida (1992: 12) argues. 'If the other gives me back or owes me or has to give me back what I give him or her, there will not have been a gift.' As a consequence, the gift must *not* be acknowledged as thus, or its calculative nature will be revealed, annulling it. As a result, the action of the gift is immediately intertwined with the act of forgetting its very purpose or nature; the gift must be offered but not acknowledged as such, lest it lose its significance or potential power. It is therefore not surprising that the desire for the gift of friendship remains an abortive one in the mind of Colenso, reduced to a mere wish in an awkward assemblage of dignitaries. Indeed, with this in mind, the warning of the assembled settlers to Colenso that 'too ready familiarity, and especially shaking hands with them upon slight acquaintance, was not only not understood by them, but did great mischief in making them pert and presuming' reveals more than a mere desire to maintain settler distinctions in their refusal of the gift of friendship. Rather, an obvious gesture of friendship on the part of Colenso could have been construed as a directly offered gift to African observers, and led to reciprocal demands and obligations as a result.[8]

For Derrida (1992: 147), the power of a genuine gift lies within its unacknowledged nature, a near-impossible feat. Otherwise, the gift becomes an instance of calculation, exchange, and indebtedness; it becomes part of an economic calculus of obligation. In such a formulation, a gift has the potential to entrap the recipient unawares: 'Unable to anticipate, he is delivered over to the mercy, to the *merci* of the giver; he is taken in, by the trap. ... Such violence may be considered the very condition of the gift, its constitutive impurity once the gift is engaged in a process of *circulation* once it is promised to recognition, keeping, indebtedness, credit.' The friendship that Colenso desired certainly could operate in such a fashion; part of the calculus of such friendship would be to facilitate Africans reoriented as Christian laborers, acculturated to the religious and cultural milieu of colonial society.[9]

Cultural theorist Mimi Thi Nguyen has expanded upon Derrida's work, arguing for a theory of *the gift of freedom*, namely, an ostensibly postcolonial project of gifted liberty in the twentieth century. For Nguyen (2012: 6–12), *the gift of freedom* is an expansion upon earlier colonial justifications that results 'in a cluster of promises' that continuously produces new forms of attachments, events, and obligations that can never be fulfilled or fully realized. This gifted freedom is both the afterlife and continuation of colonial policies of paternalistic care and guidance for 'benighted' peoples. Nguyen pushes Derrida's understanding of the gift into a larger geopolitical cycle, linking the homogenization and forgetting of the gift to larger state operations of power and indebtedness that is impossible to reciprocate.

Nguyen has much to offer in theorizing an idea of 'friendship' evinced by Colenso as part of a larger project of liberalism and imperial benevolence. 'Friendship' was no small part of the British imperial lexicon in southern Africa. Much of Colenso's later political agitation for the rights of Zulu peoples against Natal's settler government would be supported in part by the Aborigines' Protection Society in Britain. The APS informed much of its metropolitan reading public about the work of men and women throughout the empire in their periodical *The Aborigines' Friend*. In this instance, friendship could be used as a means not only to continuously claim a paternalistic interest in indigenous peoples, but to also reserve the right to perpetual protection. Therefore, British 'friendship' to African peoples went hand in hand with a constant support for imperial authority in the region. It was, to draw from both Nguyen and Derrida, a colossal 'gift' that could never be repaid. Instead, African peoples were to be ensnared in an affective relation of constant indebtedness to their enlightened British compatriots.

And yet, friendship as gift could entail affective senses of obligation and reciprocation that could be utilized by indigenous peoples. Such was the case in 1882, as the exiled Zulu king Cetshwayo kaMpande utilized conceptions of friendship to advance his own interests in southern Africa. Cetshwayo, who had been deposed by the British government following the Anglo-Zulu War of 1879, sought to regain his kingdom with the support of interested parties throughout the Empire. Drawing on a motley assemblage of supporters, from Bishop Colenso to aristocratic observers from the metropole to social reformers in Natal, Cetshwayo purposefully mobilized the language of friendship to regain power. Cetshwayo's kingdom had been reduced to 13 smaller chiefdoms, the largest of which was under the rule of a white settler and former confidant of the king's, John Dunn (1834–1895).

While in exile in Cape Town and seeking an audience with imperial officials in London, Cetshwayo frequently stated his 'friendship' with and loyalty to Queen Victoria while simultaneously decrying the false friendship of men such as Dunn who had replaced him. Cetshwayo (cited in Dixie 1882: 423) had harsh words for Dunn, stating baldly:

> When I reigned in that country I treated John Dunn as my friend; his return was to act as a spy between me and the English Government. He told them much that was false; he harmed in all the ways he could; he never could be my friend again; how can I then forgive him and live in peace with a man who treated me so badly after I had treated him so well?

Cetshwayo's invocation of friendship before British observers served as part of his larger strategy to subvert Dunn's control over Zululand and to secure his return to the throne. His declaration of false friendship with Dunn demonstrates one of the ways in which friendship could encapsulate larger questions of imperial stability and colonial order. The rhetorical move was eventually successful; Cetshwayo subsequently gained an audience with the Queen in August of 1882 and was briefly restored to his throne over a significant portion of Zululand while his erstwhile friend Dunn was deposed.

IMAGINING COLONIAL HIERARCHIES AND FRIENDSHIP

The idea of interracial friendship was commonly invoked by settlers while justifying their position within the colony. In an attempt to press for responsible government in 1880, Natal's Legislative Council (Natal (Colony) 1880: 452) asserted that:

The relations which exist between the whites and the blacks in Natal were admitted by Sir Garnet Wolseley himself, during his first visit to the Colony, to be marked by greater harmony and friendliness than he had witnessed between the races in other lands. The Natives and the Colonists have lived in perfect amity together for a period of over thirty years. Nor can better testimony on this point be needed than is born by the well-known fact that the Native Levies called out during the Zulu War entreated to be led by Colonists, rather than by Imperial Officers and strangers.

The announcement by the legislative council is a telling one. Interracial friendship is invoked as a means of legitimating settler minority rule in the colony; in other words, the 'perfect amity' between African and settler demonstrated sufficient domestic harmony in the colony and a sense of profound 'partnership' between Natal's African and settler populations. In the wake of the Anglo-Zulu War of 1879, the claims of Natal's settler government that perfect amity existed between autochthonous and indigenous peoples supported a narrative of settler control over potential African rebellion. By invoking the Native Levies' preference for settler over imperial leaders, the Natal government utilized an interracial affinity (or a form of friendship) in pursuit of settler autonomy.

Likewise, the 1881 Native Commission used the idea of interracial friendship between settlers and Africans in order to justify policies of control over indigenous peoples. At the end of its report, the commission concluded: 'We have considered the subjects before us impartially and with a kindly feeling towards the Natives. If this does not appear, we shall so far have failed in conveying our sentiments.' Not content to simply describe the amity between settlers and Africans, the commission (Natal (Colony) 1882: 48) added, patronizingly: 'There is, we think, in the Natives, not a little which the Whites generally feel to be attractive, and calculated to win friendliness towards a people with whom they are so closely brought into contact.' Both the words of the 1881 Commission and the Natal Legislative Council offer a critical view of settler coalescence around the issue of friendship. The idea of friendship with Natal's African population could be invoked by government institutions in order to justify their claims to power and authority in a colonial context. In this way, friendship was not merely a convenient fig leaf covering rapacious colonial exploitation. Friendship, and the affective register that accompanied it, operated at the core of colonial governance. To be clear, settler claims to colonial domination over indigenous bodies and lands in Natal were not merely justified through friendship rhetoric. Rather, settlers conceived and understood colonial rule through the idea of friendship with indigenous peoples. Nineteenth-century Natal, then, was an affective *state* in both meanings of the term.[10]

However, this instrumental view of friendship in pursuit of colonial prerogatives was not universal. For some settlers, interracial friendship was the antithesis of the social order that they hoped to erect in colonial Natal. For Charles Barter, prominent settler and politician, friendship was inimical to the designs of global settlement. In his 1852 book, *The Dorp and the Veld*, Barter parodied the philanthropic voice of metropolitan British observers and local missionaries such as Colenso, who spoke of friendship and amity, stating: 'We have come to soften, to teach, to civilize, to Christianize them; why should not the two nations dwell together in peace and friendship, on equal terms?' Yet Barter (1852: 171–172) countered: 'This argument is, if possible, still more specious than other[s], but equally hollow and fallacious.' For Barter, friendship between colonist and colonized was impossible, a mere wish of the hopeless do-gooder or prevaricating philanthropist. Instead Barter (172) argued that settlement in Natal was part of a larger history of colonialism around the globe, asserting:

> the two races, the white and the coloured – be it black, brown, or red – cannot exist in close contact with each other, but on one condition – that of the entire dependence of the weaker upon the will of the stronger. The notion of equality, equality of rights, or equality of treatment, is at best an amiable theory, unsupported by any single evidence drawn from sound reason or experience.

Barter continued, comparing the incompatibility of interracial friendship to the aims of colonialism in other settlement projects across the globe, linking Natal's African population to Native Americans, Aborigines, and Maori as populations that must be conquered and removed, not befriended. For Barter, the African was destined to either submit or disappear before the approach of white settlement, as had other indigenous peoples around the globe. Thus, friendship was a dangerous impossibility. This view of inevitable marginalization and the subsequent rejection of friendship found echoes in the British Parliament. Politician J. A. Roebuck argued in London that colonialism in southern Africa was a natural, if ostensibly regrettable, process of native extermination and settler replacement (Great Britain Parliament and Thomas Curson Hansard 1851: 272–276). In such a formulation, interracial friendship between colonizer and African could not exist.

Yet the rhetoric of global settlement and the denial of interracial friendship were not always used by settlers in favor of colonization. Some observers commented on the *lack* of interracial friendship as a means of critiquing the failings of settler society. Witnessing the movement of Africans from Natal and Cape Town to the diamond fields, Natal settler W. F. Butler harshly critiqued the very system of settler colonialism that debased Africans while holding out a purely hypocritical promise of friendship. In *The Natal Witness*, one of the colony's major newspapers, Butler (1876) exclaimed:

> How bitter must be the sense of disappointment with which he learns the real nature of the *role* he has accepted in the new creed and social state; how startling the discovery that this beautiful theory of the white man's love and brotherhood and charity to all men, means in the hard logic of fact the refusal of a night's shelter under the same roof to him; means the actual existence of a barrier between him and the white race, more fatally opposed to fusion, more hostile to reciprocity of thought, mutual friendship, or commonest tie of fellowship, than that which lies between civilized man and the dumb dog that follows him.

For Butler, interracial friendship was a possibility denied by settler selfishness and colonial rapacity. Like Colenso, Butler saw settler society as unwilling to extend the reach of friendship across a racial hierarchy, instead investing in minority control. Unlike governmental institutions that claimed friendship discourse in order to legitimate their claims to authority within the colony, Butler asserted that friendship itself manifestly did not exist. Yet Butler differed from men such as Barter and Roebuck, who used the lack of friendship as a means of justifying a theory of inevitable colonization and settler domination. In Butler's instance, this lack of friendship served as a springboard for calls of imperial reform, a challenge *not* to the actuality of settler rule, but to the practice of it as exclusionary. Such a view neither assumed nor denied friendship to advance settler goals, but rather asserted that the lack of friendship perpetuated an unstable inequality between members of the colonial population.

For settlers, friendship served as a signpost, offering a profound orientation device in their attempts to dominate the colonial state they were building in Natal throughout much of the later nineteenth century. As settlers debated the meaning of friendship, they argued whether colonial rule was ultimately based in the power of settler affection for Africans, or whether it was a mere delusion that masked the harsher realities of conquest and domination of indigenous lands. Friendship, then, held distinct rhetorical and causal meanings for settlers. At its core, the discussions over friendship with the African touched on the material and structural realities of settler colonialism in Natal. In the midst of the cacophonous, competing voices of colonial Natal, the concept could be used to justify the presence of Europeans in Natal, or disavowed utterly as a bid to supremacy. Both articulations, however, ultimately cast friendship (and its affective power) as the core structure of colonialism in Natal. Yet as a term, friendship was more frequently utilized to describe social situations within racial groups than between them. These same-race friendships, and the moments of sociability that engendered them, were both essential and dangerously destabilizing in the colonial period.

SOCIABILITY AND SUBVERSION: THE DESTABILIZING POTENTIAL OF FRIENDSHIP

Despite claims of interracial friendship or equanimity, friendship was much more likely to be used by settlers to describe interactions of people within their own racial groups in colonial Natal. While debating Indian immigration laws in the Natal Legislature in 1890, Charles King (Natal (Colony) 1890: 295) argued:

> I want our own selves to be occupying this Colony – Englishmen, Irishmen, Scotchmen. Germans and Norwegians very good indeed, but give us our own friends, so that we can associate with them and make our lives comfortable and happy with them. But the very last people that we should try to flood this Colony with are the Coolies.

For King, friendship served as a discursive marker that signified racial similarity as opposed to interracial connection. Friends were fellow European (and ideally English) immigrants. In the context of increased Indian immigration to Natal, King argued instead that the colony should be set up to preserve and enlarge already existing groups of friends at the risk of destabilizing cross-racial connections. Indeed, King (Natal (Colony) 1890: 320) later argued expressly for an increase in European immigration to the colony in the face of a potential increase in Indian migrants: 'The working men do not object to Europeans of their own kith and kin, their own relations and friends, coming to this Colony. We welcome every shipment of Europeans that comes.' The discursive dimension of friendship in King's argument is readily apparent. But this passage also again underscores the affective ties at the heart of the colonial project. White anglophone settlers are positioned as 'our own friends', and the increased association with these people leads to comfortable and happy lives. In this formation, Natal exists as an amalgamation of affective ties, the bonds between like-minded and like-tongued people constituting a community of belonging. Friendship, in this context, then, symbolized a sense of collaboration and connection in the face of potential 'foreign' challenges from indigenous Africans and Indian migrants, who could never truly be part of these bonds of similarity.

Yet these racialized friendships also contained within them potential for destabilizing sociability, particularly around drink. Throughout the nineteenth century, alcohol offered a prominent marker of social distinction within the colony; due to its dangerous and inebriating properties colonial legislators and imperial officials sought to limit its access exclusively to white settlers, who were deemed sufficiently moral to resist the deleterious effects of drink. In keeping with practice throughout settler colonies in the nineteenth century, Natal banned indigenous access to European spirits within the first decade of the colony's establishment, and legislators frequently attempted to limit African and Indian access to any and all forms of drink.

Alcohol offered a particularly intense form of social bonding, especially among men of different racial groups. While a significant literature exists on alcohol production and consumption in twentieth-century South Africa, comparatively little has been written about alcohol use in nineteenth-century Natal.[11] However, much has been written by southern African scholars on the contested meanings, symbols, and opportunities presented by alcohol consumption in the twentieth century (Mager 2010). In particular, Paul La Hausse's (1992) study of the 'Durban system' of municipal beerhalls remains a compelling and critical reading of state ambition, African resistance, and the politics of colonial labor. Anne Mager's work on masculinity and sociability in apartheid-era South Africa highlights the competing attractions, meanings, and benefits alcohol consumption held for African workers, white South African students, and shebeen owners, among others. Mager and La Hausse both assert that alcohol acted as more than a mere commodity over which settlers frequently attempted to reserve a monopoly on both distribution and consumption; rather, alcohol became a particular cogent site of contestation between colonial state, African workers, and the labor regimes that enmeshed them both.

This analysis has import for nineteenth-century Natal, where alcohol – whether in the form of European spirits or African grain beer such as *utshwala* – could potentially activate close bonds of masculine friendship at odds with the aims of a colonial state. For African men, beer-drinking parties served as a means of reinforcing social ties and enforcing bonds of community in the midst of a colonial state. As Michael Mahoney (2012: 98) has asserted, African drinking parties were 'quite simply the main form of entertainment and leisure-time socializing (in all the senses of that word) in rural Natal during this period'. In other words, the drinking party could offer a means for African friendships to be established, renewed, and celebrated independent of white oversight and control. Yet, for many of Natal's leaders, African drinking was an indication of disorder that threatened an unreliable labor supply. In a language of paternalism mixed with self-interest, they sought to limit the 'damaging' effects of indigenous drinking parties that occurred occasionally. Sir John Robinson (Natal (Colony) 1887: 381), the future first prime minister of Natal, thundered in 1886:

> Beer drinkings are in every sense of the term demoralizing and pernicious. In the first place they breed habits of idleness in the Natives. They accustom the Natives to a mode of life which is wholly opposed to the life of an industrious being. They encourage a constant flow of domestic dissipation, which is the parent of all sorts of disorders in the country districts. No one desires to interfere with the liberty of the subject less than I do, but I do not hesitate to say that had the Natives white skins these beer drinkings would have been put down with a stern hand.

Robinson declared that African alcohol-based sociability was inherently disordered and raucous. In so doing, he drew a line between African forms of friendship that would be seen as unallowable for settler men. For Robinson, the continued existence of such parties (and the friendships that they enabled) threatened an ostensible divide between white access to ordered alcohol sociability and the paternalist prohibitions meted out to people of color. Reading independent sociability and the strengthening of affective ties between Africans independent of white control as a sign of dissipation and disorder, Robinson's passage underlines the jealous settler desire for control over the contests of friendship and affection. In the eyes of settler administrators, friendship and its affective power operated at the core of the colonial project, and as such could not be allowed to develop among Africans independent of white control.

While settlers viewed alcohol as a critical element in establishing sociability among the ruling racial minority within Natal, they also feared the results of too much sociability and inebriation. The passage of increasingly restrictive alcohol consumption laws by the Natal legislature throughout the nineteenth century indicates that settlers believed that alcohol-fueled homosocial friendship should be legally established as the sole preserve of white colonists.[12] Yet these forms of white sociability and friendship depended upon settlers correctly performing their racialized self-control in relation to alcohol. Failure to appropriately perform sobriety in colonial society ran the risk of destabilizing racial hierarchies in Natal, as 29-year-old settler Martin Swindells discovered to his chagrin in 1865. Swindells lived in the colonial capital of Pietermaritzburg, and had met with friends for drinks at a local canteen. In his written apology to the Attorney General for a public instance of drunkenness, Swindells asserted that he believed he had not been drunk (although he confessed to making errors in judgment fueled by drink); perhaps most importantly, he explained that the entire incident (and accompanying libations) had occurred because he had met friends in the canteen.[13] At the heart of Swindells' statement lay an acknowledgment of the need for settler moments of sociability and friendship; his apology further acknowledged that these needed moments of colonial connection could also serve as dangerous sites of moral and social disorder.

While settlers viewed African beer-drinking parties as pernicious examples of sociability and closeness gone awry, they also feared how their own moments of public friendship could be derailed by excessive alcohol consumption. In 1890, the Natal Legislative Council debated over the possibility of creating an inebriates' asylum for white settlers continuously afflicted with drunkenness. The specter of the white inebriate haunted legislators, who feared that they symbolized a loss of their assumed control over themselves and the province at large.[14] Yet, much of the alcohol debate was also about the need for white camaraderie and larger friendship. When bringing the cause of inebriates' asylums up for larger debate, legislator Henry Bale (Natal (Colony) 1890: 564) identified those that suffered from addiction to drink as 'our fellow-citizens and fellow-Colonists, and on behalf of those whom I am not ashamed to call in many instances my friends'. By directly linking them as his friends and compatriots, Bale attempted to depict those struggling with alcohol consumption as part of the larger and crucial bonds of friendship within white settler society. This linking of alcoholism to larger issues of sociability and friendship continued as Bale argued that asylums would improve the crucial bonds of friendship among settlers: 'If, however, that man is confined, his *friends* will be relieved in the meantime of what is undoubtedly an incubus, and, if he is confined, it is possible that after his restoration he will be able to fulfill his duties' (emphasis added). In such a formulation, constant drunkenness is described as a destabilizing outgrowth of alcohol-based sociability. Bale names the condition primarily as a scourge to a settler's friends, and a stumbling block to the proper duties of a colonist.

Despite the shifts in views of alcoholism, white self-control over alcohol consumption remained tightly linked to notions of respectability and proper claims to rule in Natal. The racialized component of alcohol as a preserve of white settler enjoyment often served to counter manifestations of the global temperance movement in Natal. While drunkenness could be viewed by colonists as inexcusable and alcohol a potential vice, the ability to drink served as a racialized marker of distinction and a guaranteed means of enabling colonial friendships that many Natalians were reluctant to relinquish. As early as 1881 settlers adamantly protested proposed temperance laws that restricted access to drink and instead offered 'wholesome' entertainments aimed at young white men, arguing:

> It does not, of course, matter whether young men play billiards and drink or not, so long as they commit no excesses. There is nothing whatever abstractly

vicious in either billiards or wine. All reasonable and reasoning people are agreed upon that point ... Nobody disputes the fact that a man who gets drunk makes a beast of himself, albeit often a very ludicrous one ... But shall we reclaim them or stop drinking and gambling by establishing teetotal saloons and reading rooms? We think not (*The Natal Witness*, 1881).

The specific rhetoric deployed throughout the 1880s and 1890s by many settlers marshalled a sense of white masculinity as constituted by moderation and restraint, rendering further restrictions infantilizing, humiliating, and unnecessary. Significantly, these complaints also offer an argument in favor of maintaining drinking as a means of necessary socialization for the colony's white minority. The centrality of affective relations to colonial rule and governance is readily visible in settler debates over the 'problem' of alcohol for both indigenous and autochthonous peoples in Natal.

CONCLUSION: SCHREINER AND COLENSO

As Jon Soske and Shannon Walsh have pointed out in the first chapter, the rhetoric of colonial friendship espoused by Schreiner and her many different discursive inheritors 'takes as its object the emotional life of the colonized and envisions its outcome as generating bonds of affection between black and white'. Looking before Schreiner, and indeed before the Union, I believe it possible to view genealogies of friendship that simultaneously trouble and undergird the settler colonial project in Natal and South Africa more broadly. As a colonial gift, friendship remained inextricably twined with the larger hierarchies and frameworks of imperialism, namely its raced and gendered hierarchies that manifest in myriad ways, from labor to law to literature. Yet friendship also served as a signpost, a rallying point that could collect varied voices within the cacophonous din of colonial Natal. Settlers could either decry friendship as an obstacle to colonial rule, or seek to marshal it as a legitimizing force in their pursuit for white minority rule. Friendship exposed the larger frailties of the settler project, with alcohol serving as both a catalyst for needed moments of same-race sociability and an attendant fear of disruption and disorder. Ultimately, friendship encompassed a variety of competing and contradicting voices within settler society, perhaps most apparent in the desire of Bishop Colenso for that impossible handshake.

Friendship also carried within it an immense potential for instability and rupture. As Leela Gandhi (2006: 7) has argued:

> Late Victorian radicalism discursively extended the semantic scope of imperialism to diagnose it as a peculiar habit of mind, discerning within its structure a complex analogical system relentlessly mapping hierarchies of race, culture, and civilization upon relationships between genders, species, classes, etc. In this schema, departure from the self-confirming orderliness of imperial habitation was at once an experience of profound psychic derangement: exile to the chaos of a world without taxonomy.

It is patently obvious that Colenso's desire for a handshake and friendship was imbricated in larger politics of control, order, and hierarchy. Yet, the friendship he wished for cannot merely be reduced to a simple balance of colonial domination and subterfuge. Like Schreiner, Colenso's privileged pursuit of interracial friendship contained at its heart destabilizing elements; a potential derangement of imperial lines of order lay waiting behind that imagined hand.

At its core, the friendship envisioned by the thwarted handshake between Colenso and the unnamed African remained unrealized. The distance that remained unbridged between the two hands recalls the bitter reflections of Cetshwayo kaMpande on his failed friendship with John Dunn. The outstretched hands across racial lines always took place in a matrix of unequal power relations, and as much as friendship could destabilize systems of power, it did not completely erase them. Further, the constant distance between Colenso and the African body echoes the work of Frank Wilderson III (2010), whose theorizing on colonialism and 'anti-Blackness' belies the consummate disavowal of black humanity by white settlers. Far from making the African 'pert and presuming', the handshake had the potential to bring racialized bodies into close proximity and underline a shared humanity between native and settler that could not be imagined, even by ostensibly liberal members of settler society.

This, then, is the true takeaway of friendship of colonial Natal: as an ephemeral signifier, it could paradoxically reinforce desired order at the same time as it undermined (but never fully erased) racialized hierarchies. The uneven (and frequently imagined) affective ties between settlers and the indigenous peoples whose lands they sought to occupy therefore reveal the fragile contingencies of settlement. Yet the contradictory nature of friendship, its amorphousness, and the desire of colonists for land (and for indigenous consent to the process of colonization) continued to offer a tantalizing but unrealizable possibility between African and settler, much like that briefly outstretched hand.

REFERENCES

Anderson, Leigh. 1993. *Society, Economy and Criminal Activity in Colonial Natal, 1860–1893*. PhD Diss. University of Natal.

Barter, Charles. 1852. *The Dorp and the Veld; or Six Months in Natal*. London: William S. Orr and Co.

Butler, W. F. 1876. 'South Africa.' *The Natal Witness*, May 6.

Byrd, Jodi A. 2011. *The Transit of Empire: Indigenous Critiques of Colonialism*. Minneapolis, MN: University of Minnesota Press.

Colenso, John William. 1855. *Ten Weeks in Natal: A Journal of a First Tour of Visitation among the Colonists and Zulu Kafirs of Natal*. Oxford: Macmillan.

Comaroff, Jean and John L. Comaroff. 1991. *Of Revelation and Revolution,* vol.1: *Christianity, Colonialism, and Consciousness in South Africa*, 1st ed. Chicago, IL: University Of Chicago Press.

Coombes, Annie, ed. 2006. *Rethinking Settler Colonialism: History and Memory in Australia, Canada, New Zealand and South Africa*. Manchester: Manchester University Press.

Crais, Clifton C. 1992. *White Supremacy and Black Resistance in Pre-Industrial South Africa: The Making of the Colonial Order in the Eastern Cape, 1770–1865*. Cambridge: Cambridge University Press.

Crush, Jonathan and Charles Ambler, eds. 1992. *Liquor and Labor in Southern Africa*. Athens, OH: Ohio University Press.

Derrida, Jacques. 1992. *Given Time: I. Counterfeit Money*. Chicago, IL: University of Chicago Press.

Dixie, Lady Florence. 1882. *In the Land of Misfortune*. London: R. Bentley & Son.

Driskill, Qwo-Li, Chris Finley, Brian Joseph Gilley, and Scott Lauria Morgensen, eds. 2011. *Queer Indigenous Studies: Critical Interventions in Theory, Politics, and Literature*. Tucson, AZ: University of Arizona Press.

Du Bois, Duncan. 2011. *Laborer or Settler? Colonial Natal's Indian Dilemma 1860–1897*. Durban: Just Done Productions.

Elbourne, Elizabeth. 2008. *Blood Ground: Colonialism, Missions, and the Contest for Christianity in the Cape Colony and Britain, 1799–1853*. Toronto: McGill-Queen's University Press.

Etherington, Norman. 1978. *Preachers, Peasants and Politics in South East Africa, 1835–1880: African Communities in Natal, Pondoland & Zululand*. London: Royal Historical Society.

Gandhi, Leela. 2006. *Affective Communities: Anticolonial Thought, Fin-deSiècle Radicalism, and the Politics of Friendship*. Durham, NC: Duke University Press.

Great Britain Parliament and Thomas Curson Hansard. 1851. *Hansard's Parliamentary Debates*, vol. 116. London: Hansard.

Guy, Jeff. 1994. *The Destruction of the Zulu Kingdom: Civil War in Zululand 1879–1884*, 3rd ed. Pietermaritzburg: University of KwaZulu-Natal Press.

Guy, Jeff. 2013. *Theophilus Shepstone and the Forging of Natal: African Autonomy and Settler Colonialism in the Making of Traditional Authority.* Pietermaritzburg: University of KwaZulu-Natal Press.

Houle, Robert J. 2011. *Making African Christianity: Africans Reimagining Their Faith in Colonial South Africa.* Bethlehem, PA: Lehigh University Press.

La Hausse, Paul. 1992. 'Drink and Cultural Innovation in Durban: The Origins of the Beerhall in South Africa, 1902–1916.' In *Liquor and Labor in Southern Africa*, edited by Jonathan Crush and Charles Ambler, 78–114. Athens, OH: Ohio University Press.

Limb, Peter, Norman A. Etherington, and Peter Midgley, eds. 2010. *Grappling with the Beast: Indigenous Southern African Responses to Colonialism, 1840–1930*. Boston, MA: Brill.

Mager, Anne Kelk. 2010. *Beer, Sociability, and Masculinity in South Africa*. Bloomington, IN: Indiana University Press.

Mahoney, Michael R. 2012. *The Other Zulus: The Spread of Zulu Ethnicity in Colonial South Africa*. Durham, NC: Duke University Press.

Mamdani, Mahmood. 2002. *When Victims Become Killers: Colonialism, Nativism, and the Genocide in Rwanda*. Princeton, NJ: Princeton University Press.

Martens, Jeremy. 2001. *So Destructive of Domestic Security and Comfort": Settler Domesticity, Race and the Regulation of African Behaviour in the Colony of Natal, 1843–1893.* PhD Diss. Queen's University.

Morgensen, Scott Lauria. 2011. *Spaces between Us: Queer Settler Colonialism and Indigenous Decolonization.* Minneapolis, MN: University of Minnesota Press.

Morrell, Robert. 2001. *From Boys to Gentlemen: Settler Masculinity in Colonial Natal, 1880–1920.* Pretoria: Unisa Press.

Natal (Colony). 1880. *Debates of the Legislative Council of the Colony of Natal: Second Session – Eighth Council, from November 6, 1879 to February 19, 1880*, vol. I. Pietermaritzburg: Vause, Slatter & Co.

Natal (Colony). 1882. *Report of the Natal Native Commission, 1881–1882*. Pietermaritzburg: Vause, Slatter & Co.

Natal (Colony). 1887. *Debates of the Legislative Council of the Colony of Natal: First Session – Twelfth Council, from September 7, 1886 to February 3, 1887*, vol. IX. Pietermaritzburg: Natal Printing & Publishing Co.

Natal (Colony). 1890. *Debates of the Legislative Council of the Colony of Natal: Sixth Session – Twelfth Council, from April 10 to July 8, 1890*, vol. XIV. Pietermaritzburg: Wm. Watson.

Natal Witness. 1881. 'Untitled.' *The Natal Witness*, August 19.

Nguyen, Mimi Thi. 2012. *The Gift of Freedom: War, Debt, and Other Refugee Passages.* Durham, NC: Duke University Press.

Schreiner, Theophilus Lyndall. 1901. *The Black Man and the Franchise: Also, Natives and Liquor in South Africa.* London: Simpkin, Marshall, Hamilton, Kent & Co.

Smith, Andrea. 2010. 'Queer Theory and Native Studies: The Heteronormativity of Settler Colonialism.' *GLQ: A Journal of Lesbian & Gay Studies* 16: 1–2.

Tallie, T. J. 2014. *Limits of Settlement: Racialized Masculinity, Sovereignty, and the Imperial Project in Colonial Natal, 1850–1897.* PhD Diss. University of Illinois, Urbana-Champaign.

Tsing, Anna Lowenhaupt. 2004. *Friction: An Ethnography of Global Connection.* Princeton, NJ: Princeton University Press.

Veracini, Lorenzo. 2010. *Settler Colonialism: A Theoretical Overview.* New York, NY: Palgrave Macmillan.

Wolfe, Patrick. 2006. 'Settler Colonialism and the Elimination of the Native.' *Journal of Genocide Research* 8(4): 387–409.

Wilderson, Frank B. III. 2010. *Red, White & Black: Cinema and the Structure of U.S. Antagonisms.* Durham, NC: Duke University Press.

NOTES

1   The use of the term 'indigenous' to describe the African peoples who inhabited southeastern Africa concurrent with and prior to the arrival of British settlers in the region is not universally accepted. While I agree with Norman Etherington's (1978) assertion that 'this concept has limited applicability in southern Africa' due to the fact that 'in many parts of the world indigenous people define themselves as a dispossessed aboriginal minority seeking justice at the hands of the colonizers who stole their land', I feel that the comparative historic nature of land dispossession and violence renders the term useful. Such an argument puts me in opposition to Mahmood Mamdani (2002: 14), who asserts that 'the greater crime [of colonialism] was to politicize indigeneity'. Rather, as a historian, I believe the simultaneity of logics of dispossession and violence, along with aspirations to native removal creates a compelling claim for understanding Africans in colonial Natal as indigenous peoples who had to confront both the actions of European settlers and later Indian 'arrivants'

(Limb, Etherington and Midgley 2010: 5). For more on the concept of 'arrivants' in a settler colonial context, see Byrd (2011).

2   Some of the limited examples of settler colonial theorizing in Natal can be found in Morrell (2001). The first major acknowledgment of settler colonialism as a framework for Natal is in Jeff Guy (2013).

3   When referring to settlers I prefer to use the phrase 'autochthony' and 'autochthonous' to differentiate from indigeneity and indigenous and seek to avoid using the term 'native' where possible, given its particularly vexing history in southern Africa. Autochthony is different in this context as it seeks to be a replacement form of indigeneity, one that is claimed and understood through previous claims of indigenous peoples.

4   This practice has continued within South African historiography, where Duncan Du Bois (2011) reproduces unproblematically the 'Indian Dilemma' without querying its larger relationship to settler colonialism even as he correctly locates the ambiguous relationship of exogenous groups in a settler imaginary. On a different note, Jeremy Martens (2001: 13) locates the central paradox of even posing such a question: 'The answer to this riddle was perpetually elusive, however, and only in the late twentieth century would white South Africans realize that no amount of working the oracle could solve their "Native Question", and that meaningful change required them to stop posing it.'

5   As Michael Mahoney (2012) has convincingly argued, the 'Natal Africans' of the mid-nineteenth century were not a homogenous 'Zulu group' as they would become under centralized colonial intervention and indigenous resistance in the later colonial and early Union period. Mahoney's work builds upon existing work by historians of early colonial Natal. As both Jeff Guy (1994, 2013) and Norman Etherington (1978) have argued, African communities in Natal may have not been unified as 'Zulus', but they certainly had enough presence numerically to make their needs and desires felt in many parts of the fledgling colony.

6   For the ideas of competing, cacophonous disjunctures, I am indebted to a trio of theorists: Byrd's (2011) use of cacophony pairs incredibly well with Anna L. Tsing's (2004) particular privileging of disconnect over unity and Clifton Crais's (1992) theoretically rich understanding of flexible 'bundles of relationships' that characterized the eastern Cape Colony in the nineteenth century.

7   The term comes from Crais (1992: 11).

8   Indeed, this was truly the result for two generations of Colensos in Natal. The work of the Colenso family to identify with and claim solidarity with Africans against the

interests of the settler government was, in many ways, a form of gift-giving. This gift was rife with power inequities, but in turn came with reciprocal claims for protection, aid, or patronage, from a variety of African peoples. This dynamic is most visible in two instances: first, in the correspondence between Harriette Colenso and Dinizulu (1868–1913), the son of the Zulu monarch Cetshwayo kaMpande, who had been exiled and imprisoned following the 1906 Bambatha Rebellion; and second, in the reciprocal claims offered by the early African nationalist and author Sol Plaatje, who dedicated his *Native Life in South Africa* to Harriette Colenso.

9   For more on the complexities of conversion, acculturation, and resistance, see Jean Comaroff and John L. Comaroff (1991); Elizabeth Elbourne (2008); Etherington (1978); Robert J. Houle (2011).

10 I am grateful for Jon Soske's phrasing here.

11 The only major work covering nineteenth century alcohol consumption in Natal is Leigh Anderson's 1993 PhD dissertation, which focuses on criminality and the attempts of the colonial state to manage perceived anti-social activity. While useful, Anderson's work offers a list of crimes and crime reports rather than a systematic analysis of their importance to the settler colonial project.

12 Natal's Legislative Council changed the colony's alcohol laws no fewer than nine times during the period from 1854 to the granting of responsible government in 1893. For more on inebriation, alcohol, and the law in colonial Natal, see Anderson (1993) and Tallie (2014).

13 Pietermaritzburg Archives Repository, Attorney General's Office, file 1/8/7 folder 112A/1865.

14 For more on alcohol and its relationship to masculinity and race in colonial South Africa, see Crush and Ambler (1992) and Schreiner (1901).

6 THE PROBLEM WITH 'WE': AFFILIATION, POLITICAL ECONOMY, AND THE COUNTERHISTORY OF NONRACIALISM

FRANCO BARCHIESI

ew words have captured the hopes, expectations, and ethical claims of twentieth-century South African progressivism as has 'nonracialism'. The concept is in fact remarkably apt to embrace a range of contending ideologies, from white liberalism to African nationalism, from socialism to capitalist developmentalism. The introduction to the first documentary collection on the topic, published at the dawn of the post-apartheid transition, proclaimed:

> When the people of South Africa make their demands for justice, there is one word they use again and again: nonracialism. In an era of past slogans sung and shouted at mass meetings and headlined in leaflets and banners, this word stands out precisely because it is not glib. The demand for a non-racial South Africa is the common ground that unites a wide range of forces for change. The primary goal is a completely restructured society, a democracy in which people are not differentiated according to racial criteria, but enjoy rights as equal citizens in one united country. To be democratic, the future South Africa must be non-racial: that premise is fundamental (Frederikse 1990: 3–4).

Looking back at the struggle's past, David Everatt (2009: 1) concurs that among the most consistent threads in the discourse of liberation in South Africa was a commitment to nonracialism. Much of the appeal of nonracialism has to do with how it blends an objective (a democracy with equal rights, opportunities, obligations, and responsibilities, regardless of race), a strategic vision leading to it (a movement that transcends racial divides by constituting the South African nation as the actor of popular and constitutional sovereignty), and the tactics translating that vision into practice (the alliance of organizations that, even when initially anchored to racial identities, sees them only as steps toward deracialized liberation) (see Gillespie 2010; Soske 2015).

In times of global fascination with Occupy Wall Street and 'prefigurative politics' – in which social movements proclaim their purity on account of the consonance between their practices and the social regeneration they herald – one can see why the political capital of South African nonracialism has depreciated less than that of its putative originator, the African National Congress (ANC). It has become commonplace among critics to reproach the ANC for allowing its performance as a ruling party to fall short of its nonracial declarations. For some, de-racialization of public life has been marred by persistent 'race thinking' (Maré 2003: 13), reflected in corruption and cronyism under the guise of 'black empowerment', but also in grassroots' demands for justice and redress that blame inequality on white privilege. Concerns are thus raised about how the post-1994 liberal democracy can finally lay to rest apartheid's 'denial of the oneness of black and white' (Suttner 2010: 517). For others, the 'thread' of nonracialism, as Julie Frederikse (1990) calls it, might not have been so long and sturdy to begin with. The ANC overtly espoused a language of non-racial democracy in the 1960s, amid continuous internal travail over how to square a politics of the 'non-racial', premised on the recognition of the country's diversity, with the organization's foundational commitment to African nationalism. Even then, the organization remained exposed to attacks from those, such as the Unity Movement or the Pan-Africanist Congress, reclaiming a more straightforward anti-racism (see Gillespie 2010; Soske 2015). Yet, Achille Mbembe (2006) warns us that, despite the concept's unresolved questions and the decay of the ANC's rule, we need more nonracialism, not less; indeed we need it more than ever. Pondering the country's rising authoritarian tide, the instrumentalization of violence and disorder by politicians, and the manipulation of protest by skilled demagogues agitating the specter of injured blackness, Mbembe trusts liberal democracy to manage claims for justice within the existing state of things. Without such moorings, he continues, black youths would fall prey (as everywhere else in Africa …) to their irrational, phallocratic, chauvinistic, and millenarian *ressentiment* stoked by 'false prophets' of all sorts. The peril, Mbembe (2006) adds, comes from

> poor young black men, many of whom firmly believe in the craft of witches and occult forces. How can it be otherwise? Their life expectancy is fast diminishing. They hardly trust the constitution. They deeply resent the new rights granted to women. Often, they will use rape as a means to discipline them while compensating for their own perceived loss of power. With nothing to lose, it is easy for many to choose predatory behavior over political life.

In the twilight of 'political life', his worried stare turns to the blurring of distinctions between old white supremacist nativism and the passions of blacks turning into a 'democratic mob'. Lurking beneath this apocalyptic scenario, the narration of which seems curiously to mirror the millenarianism it deprecates, Mbembe detects

> the shift away from the project of nonracialism to a re-segregation of the public sphere. To the continuing denial of white privilege, many blacks are responding with an exacerbated sense of victimization and disempowerment. In the name of the 'right to self-definition', they are paradoxically recreating and consolidating the mental ghetto – a lethal device white rule so effectively used in order to inflict on them maximum psychic damage during the times of bondage.

Mbembe's defense against catastrophe, nonracialism, entered the South African political lexicon relatively recently, well after the 1955 Freedom Charter. As the leader of the Congress of the People, the ANC had in fact struggled to assert its credibility, both domestically across racial divides and internationally, as anticolonial movements on the continent remained mostly suspicious of collaboration with whites. Yet nonracialism has since acquired an aura that seems too impeccable for merely contingent explanations within organizational diatribes around strategy and ideology, even when occurring at historical turning points. It rather suffuses the very political project of freedom with motifs of friendship and human embrace. In this chapter I will therefore examine the emergence of nonracialism *as a concept*, which is not simply coincidental with its explicit public enunciation. In Reinhart Koselleck's (2004: 79) *begriffsgeschichte* ('history of concepts') approach, the social life of concepts exceeds their 'linguistic articulation' as it springs from conflicts or problems calling for new terms and vocabularies. Concepts become part of debates through contestation of the political possibilities contained in a given present. Their role is not to describe or systematize an existing reality, but to establish a tension between experiences and expectations so that 'the moments of duration, change, and futurity contained in a concrete political situation are registered through their linguistic traces'. Conceptual history requires that terms are rigorously anchored in historical sources, but is nonetheless different from intellectual history as it is less dependent on a philological approach. Instead, it uses modern categories to grasp developments not fully apprehended in the awareness of past epochs and thus not yet crystallized in the sources. Contrary to a mere history of ideas, conceptual history is thus part and parcel of social history (Wehler 1980).

I start with the contention that the 'linguistic traces' of nonracialism resonate with, and re-inscribe, political narratives that emanate from the antagonistic positioning of white to black in the experience of settler rule.[1] Nonracialism as a concept has therefore a considerably longer time span than its explicit use by anti-apartheid movements. It goes back to the very processes that institutionally established white South Africa. Before addressing that history, some terminological and theoretical clarifications are necessary. I am using the word 'antagonistic' in a specific sense, derived from the work of Frank Wilderson and authors – especially Frantz Fanon, Saidiya Hartman, and Hortense Spillers – within a theoretical framework Wilderson defines as 'Afro-pessimism'. An *antagonism* is for Wilderson 'an irreconcilable struggle between entities, or positions, the resolution of which is not dialectical but entails the obliteration of one of the positions'. It is thus different from a *conflict*, which is 'a rubric of problems that can be posed and conceptually solved' (Wilderson 2010: 5) as a progressive re-composition without the obliteration of one of the contending entities. Wilderson premises the distinction between antagonism and conflict on the reality of 'Black' slavery as one in which whiteness constituted itself as 'Human' by denying humanity, and its correlates of capacity and relationality, to former African subjects turned into 'Black' bodies as property. Blackness-as-slavery structures an ontological realm of absolute and permanent dereliction, which fortifies 'anti-Blackness' as the foundation of whiteness-as-humanity. As an ontological condition of permanent captivity, 'anti-Blackness' survives the abolition of racial slavery as it perpetually reproduces 'Blacks' into objects of parasitical white capacities ranging from absolute and gratuitous violence to ethical projects aimed at upgrading newly emancipated or colonized 'Blacks' through policy and social intervention. The afterlife of racial slavery after 'emancipation' is secured by white claims to possess the ethical and productive norms needed to 'improve' 'Black' functionality in white civil society and political economy, which justifies the positing of 'Black' bodies as objects of white instruction, meditation, concern, or coercion. An important corollary is that 'anti-Blackness' is not merely synonymous with racism or 'white supremacy' because it cannot be reduced to historically transient cultural or institutional manifestations, but rather operates as a *paradigm* imposing, across that transience, the inertial temporality of 'social death' upon 'Black' reclamations of life, agency, and subjectivity. Blackness and 'anti-Blackness' thus operate on a plane that is different from conflict and transcends 'Black' subjugation as solely the result of racial ideas and practices or socioeconomic exploitation and alienation, as liberals and Marxists have respectively emphasized in South Africa's 'race vs. class' debates. Concurrently, although black activism can alleviate, modify, or roll back institutional racism at the level of conflict, it cannot, at the same level, undo paradigmatic anti-blackness, an outcome that is only thinkable as the antagonistic incompatibility between black claims to humanity and a white world predicated on denying that humanity.

In colonial governance influenced by liberal perspectives, anti-blackness and the philanthropic politics of white friendship were complementary rather than antithetical. Whiteness could dress up in universalist humanitarian garb the passage from emancipation to the reconstitution of Black subjugation in the western hemisphere and European rule in Africa, on condition that 'racism became an essential solvent for dissolving the otherwise blatant contradictions between liberal democratic ideology and colonial practice' (Holt 1992: 215). Discussing the Jamaican instance of what was rapidly becoming a global and paradigmatic continuity, Holt (xviii) observed that 'the racism that made it possible to think of people as slave labor gave way to a racism that freed individual slaves while justifying the domination of entire nations'. Catherine

Hall (2002) has focused on the evolution of white friendship for the black other in the context of abolition and European colonial consolidation. Early optimism, especially among evangelical missionaries, that legally emancipated black slaves would marry Christian values with production discipline was rapidly disappointed by black recalcitrance to employment contracts, nominally free but routinely backed by legal coercion (Hall 2002). As imperial discourse presented the onset of African colonization as the continuation of the anti-slavery impulse, a growing missionary opinion, by then distrustful of black subjectivity and motivations, rallied behind modalities of rule rationalizing the use of force with the laws of political economy. Political economists affirmed the development of human productive potential as a matter not of religious instruction, but of objective evolution toward whiteness and European civilization (Hall 2012). Their corollary was that emancipation from slavery and from blackness – seen as harbingers of servile dispositions to ignorance, laziness, stagnation, lack of character, and poor ambition – were coterminous. Indeed blackness was the quintessential condition calling for violent coercion in materializing what were otherwise seen as the self-evident and self-fulfilling natural laws of modern economic behavior. In white ethical discourse, emancipationist ideas of universal human affiliation hatched an updated and reinforced imaginary association of being black with being slave as conditions inimical to true human freedom. Jacques Derrida, in reminding us of the Aristotelean origins of friendship as a concept designating the politicization of a structure of feelings, meditated on affiliation as its foundational notion. As a distinctively human relationship, affiliation celebrates the virtues of free deliberation that make it an ethical choice for a universalized humanity. The *Nichomachean Ethics*, Derrida (2005: 197) continues, 'recalls the friendship due to the slave, but the slave *qua* human, not *qua* slave'. Slavery, as the quintessential condition of objectification and denial of self-determination, is incompatible with friendship as politics. The white humanitarian effort was then to 'emancipate' what was human in the 'freedmen' and the 'natives' out of the Black-*qua*-slave, which was left, as Wilderson (2010: 333) puts it, 'out of the frame'. Rather than recomposing a black subject, white friendship presupposes 'Black decomposition … as the guarantor of Human coherence: value'.

The Subaltern Studies project has extensively discussed, in the case of South Asia, the problematic tangles of conflict and affiliation resulting from ambiguous relations between anticolonial nationalism and the ideologies and institutions of European rule. Premesh Lalu (2008) writes that in South Africa a similar critical orientation was thwarted by debates to define 'the people', which opposed predominantly white left social historians to African nationalist narratives. Social history's engagement of nationalism neglected the 'disciplinary upheaval' caused by the early twentieth-century 'Native Question' – including its impacts on African knowledge and liberal modernization narratives – and underestimated how 'nationalist discourse punctuated these disciplinary projects, often in selective ways that ultimately contributed to the subjection of agency' (Lalu 2008: 272). Social history, in its yearning to recover everyday popular practices and resistance, thus failed to grasp that the national-popular subject it was rescuing was already implicated in the discursive and material forces that had made South Africa a colonial situation to begin with. The birth of African nationalist politics cannot be understood outside its critical relationship with the ideology of white 'friendship for the native' as it evolved out of colonial paternalism and delineated a distinctively liberal vision of white South Africa. Central to that process were images of affiliation that verged on overcoming rigid racial barriers and imagining forms of socioeconomic interdependence between blacks and whites. African nationalism in the first half of the twentieth century articulated its autonomous claims while cultivating that terrain of affiliation, which thus acquires critical importance for a conceptual questioning of the history of nonracialism.

In what follows, I show how African nationalism evolved as an autonomous political project, from the endorsement of affiliation steeped in visions of socioeconomic cross-racial interdependence to a critique of paternalistic white friendship. It also placed, however, as the protagonist of liberation a political subjectivity – the colonized African as a human actor of production and civil society – suitable to conflict and recognition in relation to dominant whiteness. As a consequence, African politics excised a more antagonistic, intractable, and unpredictable blackness. The volatile balance of conflict and recognition involving white rulers, liberal reformers and the early ANC invested the imagined African 'nation' with productive attributes, work discipline, and behavioral norms. Crucially revolving around contesting the ideal rationality of *homo oeconomicus*, that political dialectic cast black life, to the extent it was incompatible with white ethics and labor imperatives, as a threatening 'other' whose exclusion from the polis seemed to underwrite the possibility of cross-racial interlocution.

I focus on the first three decades of the twentieth century as the period when defining the place of the 'native' becomes an ethico-political problem for the capitalist order of the newly unified state. I am specifically interested in the trajectory from the crisis of 'Cape liberalism' at the end of the nineteenth century to the 'joint councils' experiment with interracial dialogue in the 1920s. Challenging conventional periodizations of South African liberalism and its alleged breaks,[2] I consider this period as characterized by homogeneity in the evolution and transformation of a discourse of white 'friendship for the native'. The ANC contested, and eventually opposed, white rhetorics of trusteeship and friendship, but its reclamation of an *African* autonomous capacity to define nation and civilization did not question a 'phobic' categorization of *Black* as the antagonistic negation of that very terrain of contestation.

By moving the temporal signposts of nonracialism, not as a term but as a concept, I propose a reassessment of the historical time of domination and resistance. The triumph of the ANC's brand of nonracial nationalism is not just the linear end of a 'thread', but a problematic political possibility fulfilled against other unactualized virtualities, which were eschewed.[3] As a terrain of argument and conflict, nonracialism originates well before the Freedom Charter or even the radicalization of the ANC during the 1940s. It goes back to the dilemmas of black positionality in the white-ruled colonial space premised on the eradication of African political sovereignty and economic independence. The problematic of nonracialism exists at the crossroads of multiple temporalities, not just in the narrative of resistance against domination, but also in South Africa's 'colonial situation'.[4] The literate, politically conscious expressions of the colonized opposed the colonizer while also demanding to be recognized as 'civilized'. The elaboration of the African nation as a claim-making subject was inseparable from its elites' ambition to be legitimate counterparts in relations of power and conflict, no matter how harsh and unequal. The chapter ends with a discussion of how those antecedents resonated into the dilemmas surrounding, between the 1950s and the 1960s, the rise of nonracialism as a strategic option for the liberation movement. I do not discuss the debates accompanying the ANC's turn to nonracialism. My history of that concept is thus a 'counterhistory' because it departs from the conventional, linear narration of events and ideas. By making the 1920s speak directly to the 1960s, I 'fold', in Deleuzian terms

(Deleuze 1992), historical temporality to extract the salience of concepts.[5] My intention is not to underestimate the complexity of nonracialism as politics, but rather to add the reciprocal implication of nonracialism and anti-blackness to that complexity.

The Union of South Africa was formed, in 1910, amidst multiple cleavages – the African franchise, political representation, the color bar, pass laws, land dispossession, and liquor regulations – addressed by a plurality of positions that hardly fit a domination-resistance binary. Colonized voices, such as nascent black cultural or political organizations, intellectuals, churches, trade unions, chiefs, and local notables, reclaimed from various colonizing interlocutors – the Empire, local administrations, and the central government – rights and prerogatives that emphasised the distinction between civilized and uncivilized non-white subjects. Even as black politics was converging toward national organizations such as the South African Native National Congress (SANNC) founded in 1912 and renamed ANC in 1923, it mostly represented educated layers, often employed in urban professions, trades, or low-level government jobs such as clerks or interpreters. Cecil Rhodes's maxim – 'equal rights for all civilized men' – framed the ambitions of organized African politics at the time. The self-described liberal tradition of the qualified franchise entrenched in the 1853 Cape Colony constitution symbolized a benchmark of political achievement that African leaders held dear despite the small numbers actually enjoying voting rights, and their repeated erosions in the late nineteenth century (Odendaal 1984). Education, Christianity, work ethic, and a European lifestyle were the foundations upon which the colonized expected to collect the payoff of western civilization. In the process, black politicians sought alliances with white liberals, humanitarian missionaries, and colonial reformers. A mutually, if often tacitly agreed, possibility of being acknowledged within that public sphere allowed black grievances to at least be heard, even if not recognized as legitimate. It authorized, in other words, conflict to avoid antagonism.

Early debates on the 'Native Question' revolved around how to enforce white supremacy and what to make of the differences, within the native population, between those who partially absorbed European standards and those – the incorrigible blacks refusing to evolve from a condition routinely deemed as 'raw kaffir' – who were refractory to them. The paradigm of segregation thus cast blackness as not merely coincidental with 'race'; anti-blackness and racism were conceptually distinct although practically complementary. The production of differences within the colonized and disenfranchised populations rested on their respective distance from the assumed barbarism of blackness as, in Fanonian terms, a 'phobic object' (Fanon 1986: 119–120). It is indicative that, as Deborah Posel (2001) explains, the trajectory of racial legislation that led to apartheid did not proceed from, or even consciously seek, an objective definition of 'race'. It was rather premised on white common sense attaching to 'black' a range of negative characteristics, ranging from physical appearance to lifestyle. As she puts it, 'the ordinary social experience of white privilege was exactly the standpoint from which race was to be judged, so as to perpetuate "conventions" of race already ingrained in the social fabric' (Posel 2001: 104). When portending to help the 'native' evolve toward civilization, whiteness was not only careful to emphasize that equality between Europeans and Africans was not part of that evolution. It also stated that its precondition was a separation of the 'native' from the 'black' as essentially incapable of civilization. The overt and intentional suppression by the white-ruled polity of blackness as political agency infused vitality to white civil society by making it responsive, although to a rather limited degree, to the claims of specific African individuals, organizations, and struggles. The self-styled 'friends of the natives' advocating the removal of disabilities for 'civilized' Africans did not have nonracial democracy in mind as much as the consolidation of white liberalism's moral claims. By rendering blacks the inert and incapacitated objects of its own ethical self-reflection, white civil society imagined itself as transcending mere economic exploitation or political coercion. But, to resonate with assumed white capacity for empathy, native claims had first to share with colonial humanitarians, and often state authorities, hostility toward unruly positionalities and the deeper antagonisms they evoked. 'Uncivilized' natives – which African leaders also defined as 'raw' and 'primitive', echoing white technocrats and liberals – recalcitrant to European values, white guidance, and wage labor, were then portrayed as stuck in rural stagnation, tribal superstition, lack of ambition, and low self-respect. They became the common adversaries for those who defined 'civilization' as a field of legitimately contrasting claims, the antagonistic and threatening alterity whose erasure, silencing, and deprecation allowed conflict to take its course.

I now turn to ideologies of work and economic activity to describe these as specifically underpinning images of affiliation at the core of conflict and recognition in South Africa's colonial situation. The dialectics of dominant whiteness and emerging African nationalism rested on the shared imperative of turning the native into a modern producer. Conflict was predicated upon common antagonism toward blackness as a state of 'native' estrangement from capitalist production and western ethical norms.

A PARTING OF THE WAYS? NATIONALISM, LIBERALISM, AND THE POLITICAL ECONOMY OF AFFILIATION IN THE UNION OF SOUTH AFRICA

In the early twentieth century, the Cape non-racial franchise underwrote imageries of cross-racial affiliation grounded in political economy and the African embrace of European civilization. By making the vote conditional upon income and property qualifications, the Cape colonial experiment aimed to incorporate African sectors as junior partners in a settler society whose uncertain consolidation was facing persistent resistance and the critique of pioneering mission-educated African intellectuals (Legassick and Ross 2010). As white rule gained a firmer hold, and became threatened by growing numbers of politically enfranchised blacks, the colonial government systematically eroded African voting rights by raising qualifications, introducing literacy tests, and excluding 'communally owned' land from eligibility criteria (Davenport 1987: 32–33). By the late 1890s African voters had seen their presence in the electoral body drastically downsized. The Union of 1910 formally excluded any extension of the 'native' vote beyond the Cape. Yet, non-racial franchise had sedimented among educated Africans the myth of 'Cape liberalism' as a tradition ostensibly committed to affiliation and friendship between Europeans and 'civilized', value-producing natives. Allegiance to different white parties was a key cleavage in Cape African politics, as evident in the diatribes between J. T. Jabavu's *Imvo Zabantsundu* and A. K. Soga's *Izwi Labantu*, whose more radical, even socialist-toned stance voiced the Cape's South African Native Congress (founded in 1898) as an early progenitor of the ANC. Both sides appealed to the supposed color-blindness of British imperial values as the guarantor of African incorporation in the political community. André Odendaal did not find it anachronistic to talk of 'practical nonracialism' in defining Jabavu's support for parliamentary collaboration with whites (Odendaal 1984: 15). Despite his greater assertiveness, Soga agreed with Jabavu in deprecating all political agitation in view of the 1908 national convention and the South Africa Act, which led to Union and its sore disappointment of African expectations (122–123). To white liberalism, being 'friends of the natives' while remaining committed to the ideal of a white-ruled South Africa promised a modality of socioeconomic inclusion that suppressed the possibility of autonomous black subjectivity.

In his study of Reverend John Philip, a key missionary voice in the Cape Colony, Andrew Nash (1978) traces the complexity and disparate origins of South Africa's liberal imagination. Cape liberalism derived its humanitarian pretenses less from the radical utilitarianism of Jeremy Bentham, with its refusal of natural rights and skepticism toward legal regulations, than from a conservative constitutional discourse influenced by William Blackstone's *Commentaries on the Laws of England* (1765–1769). In that version, sovereignty centered on the rule of law and the defense of natural property rights was the supreme guarantee, for settlers and natives alike, of civilization as a system protecting the former from internal anarchy and indigenous resistance, and the latter from internecine warfare and the depredations of white colonists. The centrality of protection within a white-ruled hierarchy of civilizations underscored, in ideologies of South African colonial expansion, the law as the foundation of rights and not, as Bentham had it, a necessary limitation on freedoms. Liberalism could thus balance the otherwise incompatible discursive forces of white supremacy and a 'biopolitical' rule benefitting all mankind. Important consequences follow. The legalism in which they couched their ethical project and non-racial utterances made white South African liberals defer to state sovereignty and white supremacist governance as 'non-universal power bases … in order to promote their universalistic aims' (Nash 1978: 22). As a corollary, white rule – be its ideological inclinations imperialist, segregationist, or even Afrikaner nationalist – could selectively borrow from liberal discourse, often with the active collaboration of liberal intellectuals themselves,[6] tropes to masquerade black subjugation as white ethical dilemmas.

Political economy solidified a colonial space in which the rule of law presided over the power of whites, the distinct status of westernized blacks, and the survival of uncivilized natives as a subordinated labor force. In the aftermath of the mineral discoveries, work ethic and the 'dignity of labor' underpinned representations of interracial economic interdependence, which eschewed claims to political equality. Labor and political economy were testing grounds for the settler's ambition to shape, improve, and protect the native's character as the antidote to uncivilized blackness. Lord Milner and his collaborator on native policy, Godfrey Y. Lagden – the chairman of the 1903–1905 South African Native Affairs Commission, whose final report was an early attempt to systematize segregation – portrayed white rule as not merely coercive, but also concerned with the moral and economic elevation of the African. In outlining the principles of postwar reconstruction in a memo to the Colonial Office, Milner defended his native policy against criticisms from the Aborigines' Protection Society, but he agreed with the APS that African institutions, forms of landownership, and 'tribal government' should not be 'unnecessarily' tampered with and 'traditional customs' were to be respected 'as far as they are not in gross conflict with civilised ideas'.[7] Although he stated his opposition to the enforcement of labor contracts by force or fraud, Milner approved of racially coercive measures, such as the pass laws in the former Boer republics, objecting only to their arbitrary and despotic implementation by local magistrates. He ultimately regarded 'civilized' restraints on natives' ways of life as part of a rationalistic pedagogy to turn Africans into participants, under white guidance, of a capitalist economy. Departing from the issues raised by the APS, he addressed native education, the improvement of which he espoused under the proviso that

I do not mean that they should be educated like Europeans, for their requirements and capacities are very different, but that they should be trained to develop their natural aptitudes for their own good and that of the community. Undoubtedly the greatest benefit that could be bestowed upon them or South Africa generally would be to teach them habits of regular and skilled labour. So far from sharing the prejudice, which seems to be felt by some of your correspondents against any form of inducement to the natives to work for whites, I think that, as long as the inducements are legitimate, the more natives that are engaged in mining or other industrial pursuits the better for them and for the country. But while saying this I desire once and for all formally to disclaim on behalf of this administration, any desire or intention to *compel* natives to enter into the service of white employers by any means whatever.[8]

Induction into labor was about economic necessity and objective market laws. The masters and servants statutes, with their coercive enforcement of labor contracts and criminalization of strikes and desertion, were a cure against Africans' self-destructive instincts and the temptation to refuse waged work 'in a mere access of childish levity'.[9] Milner peddled passbooks too as an educational device to ensure that natives would enter the labor contract, on a voluntary basis, only once they 'understand the terms of [t]his agreement, and that the agreement is voluntary'.[10] He therefore opposed passes for 'Cape boys' who 'conform in their habits and conduct to civilised standards, and are much further removed from the raw Kaffir, than they are from Europeans'.[11] Milner's recommendations envisaged a 'Native Code' whose paternalist rationale he enunciated in a two-pronged argument. With regard to Africans, he proposed that 'any restrictions imposed on their personal liberty do not go beyond what is necessary, not only for the protection of the white population but for the good of the natives themselves'.[12] Then he warned against alienating 'colonial sentiment' and white self-government, the necessary partners of imperial rule of the natives, 'who, at best, are children needing and appreciating a just paternal government'.[13] Mining companies, Milner concluded, were entitled to collaborate to compress African wages to an efficient level; under the laws of political economy that was fair play.[14] Natives would only gain if

> the government are also animated by a spirit of fairness and friendliness to the great industry – built up by the skill, the science, the indefatigable labour, the enterprise undaunted by official bullying and discouragement, of thousands of our fellow countrymen and other Europeans – upon the continued progress of which the welfare of the Transvaal, and indeed of all South Africa for at least a century will mainly depend.

Lagden was even more explicit than Milner that the native's mind had to be protected from blackness, and what he considered its atavistic barbarity, so that civilization could advance. He represented Africans before European conquest in crudely racial terms, remarking on their 'lack of intellect' and physical features that 'create[d] the impression of being not unlike baboons'.[15] Working under white masters was a transformative experience, to the point of improving their appearance and making them look more intelligent.

'Regeneration through civilisation'[16] literally separated 'the native' from 'the black', rendering the native a malleable entity, the character of which could be molded by colonial law into producing useful value. Without white rule, blackness was a condition lacking all ethical progress, in which Africans were

> owning no right which might did not give, as marauders preying on each other's lives and property, as slayers of their own kindred out of mere blood-thirstiness, as murderers by 'killing off' at the instance of witchdoctors who were often inspired by the desire for booty or by hate.[17]

In his testimony before the 1904 Transvaal Labor Commission, Lagden elaborated on the specific function of work ethic in developing 'civilized' native needs in accordance with economic rationality:

> There are those in this country who believe that to keep the natives down to the lowest level is the best, because he is an animal and will work as an animal. That view, I think, is a false one. What we have got to do is to consider what will induce the native to work; to create in him a certain number of wants, and according to the standard of the native's wants, so will his efforts be to gratify them, and, if he wants to wear decent clothes, and decent boots, and his wife wants to wear decent clothes, and have a looking-glass, and a chest of drawers, and a decent house overhead, and if the children – taking example from them – want also to be clothed, then it means that every man who has ideas of that standard, together with his wife and children, has got to work harder to maintain that standard.[18]

White recognition of economic interdependence should not abet black yearnings for political equality, the 'spirit of insolence' behind which he blamed on agitators such as the Ethiopian churches. The task of colonial rule was to 'combine with our fair treatment of the natives a determination to protect the white people from undue insolence, to deal stringently with desertion and to carry out the provisions of the Masters and Servants Act'.[19]

The racism of Lagden's or Milner's state-building efforts posited fairness toward, even professed friendship for, the native to be possible only on the basis of, in Wilderson's (2010) terms, 'Black decomposition'. Like many imperialists of the time, Milner, who identified himself as a moderate liberal, and Lagden, a technocrat eschewing extremism and political polarization and thus often disliked by white settlers, were following a well-trodden path. Their denigration of blackness echoed the liberal combination of a reform-minded impulse deferent to scientific reasoning with the stereotyping of formerly enslaved and newly colonized blacks as incompatible with economic rationality (Eudell 2002; Foner 1988). John Stuart Mill, as a famous example, justified enforced obedience among 'barbarians' and 'uncivilized races.' For him, even 'slavery' could be temporarily required to turn blacks into humans, despite his overall assessment of the advance of liberty as a universal principle.[20]

One can hardly see Milner or Lagden as apostles of nonracialism, affiliation, or mutual recognition across racial divides. Indeed their idea of a South African body politic soon became the critical target of nascent African nationalism. Nonetheless, the discursive terrain they mapped was where African political opposition made its claims. To obtain recognition of 'natives' as imperial citizens, African leaders were prepared to accept a hierarchical differentiation of degrees of civilization set by European criteria of education, Christianity, property, occupations, and, where available, the franchise. Furthermore, as I have discussed elsewhere, employment and participation in the white-run economy justified pleas for the African nation's fair share of opportunity from the march of modernity (Barchiesi 2012). Improvement through self-help and hard work informed visions of black upward mobility within a social order whose racial foundations were not to be disrupted through overt confrontation. African nationalism did not have the same animosity toward capital or racialized labor regimes as it aimed at elements deemed unruly, such as restless urban black youth or disreputable women, who resisted, eluded, or subverted the discipline of working for wages.

The crisis of Cape liberalism accompanied a shift in the economic center of gravity toward the Transvaal's mineral districts. Black wage labor, glorified in the rhetoric of the 'dignity of work', became more important to the white economy than an independent and partially enfranchised African peasantry. The geography of black politics concomitantly shifted as Transvaal-based organizations gained prominence and gradually radicalized. The overt racial despotism of the segregated 'compounds' was less conducive than the Cape franchise to ideas of cross-racial affiliation. A renascent opposition rejected white paternalism and questioned the motives of friendship. Pixley

Seme (1972) announced the new spirit with a declaration of pride for the 'African race', exuding optimism that modernity would be a 'brighter day' and a universal human family would embrace Africa as a distinguished and illustrious civilization. In 1916 Sol Plaatje concluded *Native Life in South Africa* by turning the tables on civilization itself, questioning the Boer's fitness to rule the natives and indicting the Natives' Land Act as a test of the sincerity of imperial trusteeship. To the African nationalist attempt to define a new, autonomous national subject corresponded a shift in liberal discourse, on an imperial scale but with visible South African ramifications, which jettisoned mere faith in laissez faire and called forth the powers of the state to nurture colonized peoples into productive liberal subjects (Sartori 2014). Settler colonialism as such was no longer a terrain of conflicts, which shifted toward the definition of the identities bound to inhabit it. The change gave short shrift to the many blacks for whom the possibility of signifying subjectivity was dramatically curtailed by detachment from wage labor, nationalist politics, workers' organizations, or residual forms of landownership and political authority. For the political actors contesting the new unitary state, blackness thus configured was a carrier of social pathology.

Despite a conservative element, the Transvaal Native Congress (TNC) adopted radical positions and, often in collaboration with socialist organizations, supported black workers on strike, notably the 1918 movement of municipal laborers in Johannesburg (Limb 2010). A politically cautious SANNC expressed growing concern for the African working class, even if at the national level it did not approve of industrial action. SANNC leaders condemned the 1918 municipal strike, blaming it on young immigrants from rural areas, which they depicted – in a language strikingly resembling Milner's and Lagden's – as immature 'children' bent on chaos and undermining their elders' gradualist, moderate efforts to gain recognition as loyal imperial subjects (Landau 2012). African generational and gendered authority glorified wage labor as a condition of decency, respectability, and orderly, nonviolent protest. Its antagonists were the urban tsotsis, the 'work-shy' youth, and women employed in unauthorized beer brewing or sex work, entities that either evaded working for wages or defined their place in modernity from positions capital found indigestible.[21] Interventions in the SANNC's official mouthpiece, *Abantu-Batho*, combined an increasingly explicit support for black workers' wage demands with a persistent deprecation of radicalism.

The newspaper endorsed the 1920 African mineworkers' strike on the Witwatersrand, but also implored white unionists not to fear the natives, who, as responsible workers, ought to have a right to industrial action. An *Abantu-Batho* editorial protested that the strikers' nonviolent conduct and self-restraint proved that African workers were 'civilized'. The TNC emphasized the need to preempt future radicalizations through industrial conciliation and wage determination with equitable African representation in a bid to avoid 'the parting of ways between the capital and labour' (Limb 2010: 420–427).[22] The rise of the African worker in struggle trusted recognition from the adversary more than rank-and-file autonomy. Reaching out to capital and the state entailed the prior disowning of black radical voices.

Self-improvement and recognition through work played a foundational role in the political discourse of the SANNC and the ANC. John Dube, the SANNC's first president, was a small entrepreneur and founder of the Ohlange Institute. A *Kholwa* (a term used to identify mission-educated Christian Africans) from Natal, he was deeply influenced by Booker T. Washington and Victorian liberalism. Convinced that 'capitalists are the black man's best friends', Dube argued that proper wages, working conditions, and housing would correct a 'lack of industrial habits' (cited in Limb 2010: 96, 290) hampering African usefulness to the white economy. In enabling socioeconomic interdependence between blacks and whites, the hierarchical operations of which Dube did not fundamentally question, wage labor elevated the civilized 'better class of natives' above 'the ruck of the natives', the rural masses and urban lumpenproletariat, not yet ready for white recognition. Should whites fail to employ Africans with fair play and respect, the danger was that African workers would revert to their worst passions, falling into the hands of 'agitators' preaching 'racial ill-feeling' while abandoning 'responsible Native leaders' (Dube 1929: 145–146).

Working-class voices especially envisioned political economy as a terrain of cross-racial affiliation. The rhetoric of the Industrial and Commercial Workers' Union (ICU) urged economic participation over grassroots radicalism. Its repertoire combined entrepreneurialism and Christian work ethic with socialist keywords. It was not narrowly economistic, but contended nonetheless that black advancement relied more on a level playing field than structural transformation (Champion 1927). The Communist Party of South Africa, founded in 1921, and its forerunner, the International Socialist

League (ISL), vehemently attacked racial domination as a manifestation of capitalist exploitation. The party's advocacy of nonracialism was phrased as a commitment to proletarian internationalism. In the end, therefore, and despite the growing number of blacks among members and leaders, it evaded the dilemmas arising from the role of whites in shaping the tactics and strategies of black workers' struggles (Van Duin 1995). For David Ivon Jones, a founding father of the ISL, Marxist-Leninist politics was the application of 'socialist principles' to the 'Native Question', without which the whites-only, pro-segregation South African Labor Party was hopelessly inadequate in confronting 'the great and fascinating problem of the native' (cited in Campbell 1998: 317). Early left depictions of African workers' subjectivity as a problem to be solved through scientific socialism, judiciously dispensed by educated whites, anchored African progress to a critical reflection that mirrored mainstream policy discourse. By the late 1920s, the party had come closer to the ANC and in 1928 accepted the Comintern-approved 'native republic' line, which cadres most committed to non-racial class internationalism opposed. The new approach consecrated the centrality of the African, although not as black but as a worker, wresting self-realization from the political economy of capitalism. Party press celebrated, in a further parallel with dominant images of progress, the native urban waged proletariat as an advanced layer amenable to class identification, while dismissing black rural life as a receptacle of backwardness and superstition (Anon. 1926: 4).

Until the 1940s and the radical turn in the African nationalist movement, images of interdependence and the quest for national affiliation played a more prominent role than confrontation in organized black opposition to white rule. Limited sectors of sympathetic white opinion provided African activists and intellectuals with new platforms. Particularly significant were the Joint Councils of Europeans and Natives established in the early 1920s at the initiative of white liberals inspired by interracial forums in the American south in the heyday of Jim Crow. Members of the U.S.-based Phelps-Stokes Fund's Commission on the Education of Africans, and F. B. Bridgman of the American Zulu Mission, brought the idea to the attention of South African reformers, especially J. D. Rheinallt Jones and Howard Pim. The joint councils were local structures with occasional national meetings and had an equal representation of Europeans and Africans, the latter either elected from recognized organizations or selected by council members among westernized notables. The ANC did not officially endorse the councils, but many of its leaders and intellectuals, including Richard V. Selope Thema, Selby Msimang, Z. K. Matthews, and John Dube, regularly attended and took leadership positions. The joint councils supported the principles 'that Europeans and natives alike are integral parts of our South African nation, and that the opinion of both natives and Europeans should be sought on all national questions'; 'that the matters in respect of which European and native interests coincide are far more important than those in which they differ'; and that 'the future progress of South Africa is inseparably bound up with the economic prosperity of *all* sections of our South African population'.[23] Early council leader, Howard Pim, was a Quaker philanthropist, educationalist, and polymath, and a protégé of Lagden, who admired Pim's approach to the Native Question as a non-ideological blend of science and humanitarianism. In 1908 Pim founded the Transvaal Native Affairs Society, a whites-only debating circle committed to 'a liberal, consistent and practical native policy throughout South Africa' (Rich 1990: 670–671). In that forum Pim affirmed his loyalty to the Cape liberal tradition of 'civilized' franchise and qualified the meaning of his friendship for the racial other: 'There is probably more to be feared from a savage with an assegai than from an educated native with an umbrella.'[24]

The joint councils were committed to political economy as the solution to the Native Question. They emphasised liberal labor market principles that rejected racially coercive legislation, but also the inevitability, if not the necessity, of segregation. White liberals posed in such forums as friendly intermediaries between two worlds, the Africans' and the settlers'. But the councils' relative racial openness did not question the assumption that white standards and ethics were endpoints of native evolution. In his chairman's address to the 1929 joint councils conference, Pim remarked on the qualitative differences from Europeans of essentialized Africans in need of white help to compensate for a lack of competitive spirit, calculating rationality, personal responsibility, and capacity to raise healthy families. As natives were, for Pim, by their very nature unaware of their shortcomings, the joint councils constituted a unique pedagogical opportunity to enlighten them to their true interests. The trope of affiliation as economic interaction, not political equality, underpinned Pim's argument. He saw urbanization and industrialization as negative for 'poor whites' and 'poor natives alike', recommending for the latter a viable peasant agriculture. In his view, the mutual 'prosperity', hitched to a fully competitive labor market with no color bars, of two entities that remained hierarchically differentiated and racially segregated was essential to the social compact of a non-coercive colonialism. He ended by quoting Spinoza (referred to him by an unnamed 'native writer'), on the 'true end of the state' being 'liberty' and 'not in dominating over men, restraining them by fear, subjecting them to the will of others'.[25] Yet the joint councils endorsed racial segregation at a national meeting convened in 1923 by the Dutch Reformed Church, passing a motion by Edgar H. Brookes, later a founder with Pim of the South African Institute of Race Relations (SAIRR). Brookes's motion rejected repressive and ideologically driven racial separation, but pushed segregation as a practical measure 'based on Bantu traditions and requirements'.[26]

It was within the parameters white liberals set for interracial affiliation and friendship that the intellectual conversation of the ANC emerged in what was to become 'nonracialism'. It is true that the ANC's engagement with the joint councils was driven by relatively conservative figures such as Selope Thema, many of whom would later become either estranged or marginalized by the organization. It is also the case, however, that the joint councils were the most important, if not the only, platform where the ANC elaborated a social and labor policy (Limb 2010). At the Johannesburg Conference on Native Affairs of 1924, Thema delivered an articulate intellectual rationale for African leaders' involvement in the councils.[27] He started by placing in a position of equivalence, as enemies of interracial cooperation and propagators of 'race hatred', white supremacists and black anti-Christian 'demagogues', on whom he then mostly focused his invective. Thema quoted from W. E. B. Du Bois' *Dark Water* that 'a belief in humanity is a belief in colored men. If the uplift of mankind must be done by men, then the destinies of this world will rest ultimately in the hands of darker nations', to argue that Du Bois was an extremist standing in the way of a 'better feeling between the races'. The alternative, rising from the ruins of the Great War, was the discourse of the League of Nations and what Thema revered as the cooperative spirit of the Versailles negotiations, which he witnessed as a SANNC representative. In the end, Thema wrote, there was no Native Question in South Africa, only a race relations problem of persistent intersubjective misunderstanding, which regrettably led blacks to oppose whites on the basis of the Garveyite cry, 'Africa for the Africans'. But, luckily in his view, the joint councils spread 'a growing consciousness of inter-racial dependence' which was a 'keynote to inter-racial co-operation'. The educational mission of the councils consisted therefore in convincing both sides, in a formulation that anticipated the Freedom Charter by three decades, 'that this country belongs to the European, the native and the colored peoples – it is their common heritage', a message that 'has come to stay because the spread of western civilisation over all the world has brought all the races of mankind within its domain'. It was on 'western civilization' that Thema anchored nonracialism as the vision for a new South Africa, not on the contribution of the 'darker races' to the uplift of humanity. His plea for 'interracial dependence' found receptive ears among liberal social reformers such as William G. Ballinger and Mabel Palmer. They saw in the councils an avenue for steering the ICU toward the positions of the Colonial Office under former Labor politician Arthur Creech Jones and the 'responsible' and collaborative unionism propagated by the International Labor Bureau as an alternative to Bolshevism, always ready to prey on the most unruly, instinctual, and anarchic impulses of the 'natives' (see Barchiesi 2012: 128–129).[28]

Despite their limited policy influence, the joint councils gave a decisive twist to twentieth-century debates on the Native Question, whose confines they blurred into the 'labor question', rather than keeping the two clearly separated.[29] The overlap was indeed characteristic of South Africanism as a white colonial patriotism premised on the key question of how to govern the economic interdependence between races while ensuring continuous black political disenfranchisement and social subordination (Barchiesi 2011; Bozzoli 1981; Dubow 2006). South Africanism staunchly opposed blackness as political capacity, but allowed a conversation about the porosity and striations of racial segregation, especially with regard to the position of urban and educated blacks as laborers and consumers for the white economy. The deep implications in debates around South Africanism of early nonracialism and the evolving discourse of interracial friendship were not only episodic and implicit, but quite directly influenced individuals who would play a key role in ferrying African nationalism toward more assertive and less deferential shores. Z. K. Matthews cut his political teeth in the joint councils and the SAIRR before his Yale graduate studies in race relations under one of the fathers of the councils movement, C. T. Loram. Matthews' subsequent politicization in the ANC was not along radical lines, but nonetheless announced a style of activism that transcended the collaborative stance of a Thema. He chaired the committee drafting the 1943 African Claims and helped write the ANC's 1949 Programme of Action, which inaugurated active nonviolent defiance to the apartheid regime. In 1953 he proposed the Congress of the People, which would culminate in the 1955 Freedom Charter. Early in his intellectual trajectory, Matthews had praised 'white education' for its promise to 'open the eyes of our people to their own nakedness'. Moving beyond nakedness, a typical colonial stand-in for black barbarism, required for him a full appreciation of the African's productive functions within the white-ruled capitalist economy. He blamed work avoidance and the youth's preference for casual jobs on 'Bantu life' mired 'in a very backward condition'. The 'necessity of working at his job not intermittently but permanently' would, instead, make of the native 'an intelligent subject and an industrious worker' as well as a self-respecting member of the polity, worthy of citizenship and white recognition (Matthews 1933: 140–141). Later, when under attack from the ANC's Africanists and youth leaguers because of his participation in the state's Native Representative Council, Matthews promoted the Congress of the People as a restraint on radical struggle, an option that was eventually discarded by a Freedom Charter that had more transformative intents than he envisaged (Rich 1992).

The pre-war imaginaries of white friendship and the ANC shared the assumption that there were two distinct ways of being a native. One was a hard-working, thrifty, moderate, and morally prudent subject, which deserved recognition from white society. The other was John Dube's 'ruck of the natives', an uncanny echo of what white public opinion routinely referred to as 'raw kaffir',[30] indolent, improvident, instinctual, stagnant in tribal ways when in the rural areas, and prone to anarchic disruption when superficially civilized in the urban environment. Proof of being immune from reverting into blackness and barbarism – of not being Howard Pim's 'savage with an assegai' – was for the 'native' an admission price on which white and African elites tacitly agreed. Indicatively, proceedings of joint councils meetings collated presentations on the healing effects of wage labor, church life, and native welfare associations and speeches, mostly delivered by African experts, on topics such as gang violence or 'the *amalaita* menace'.[31] Ghosts of black anarchy and the takeover by unsocialized young hooligans of respectable non-white urban society motivated African expectations of good jobs and decent education as a necessary non-racial bastion of stability. Alarm regarding the pathology of black families, another recurring trope of twentieth-century anti-blackness (Spillers 1987), reinforced African elites' assurances that white guidance was needed for the natives' stumbling entrance into civilization. The underlying assumption was that white supervision of black affiliation was required by black inability to structure a properly human filiation.

The friendship framework of the joint councils did not survive the hardening of racial segregation and the abolition of residual African voting rights in the 1930s. Alfred B. Xuma, who had been enthusiastically active in the councils and the SAIRR and considered Pim an 'inspiration', was by the early 1940s disillusioned with the institute, which stood 'in the way of African organizations and democratically thinking Europeans, especially as it is taken in official quarters as a body that represents African opinion' (cited in Limb 2012: 61–62). The bitter conclusion was that 'we … have to be saved even from our friends, if necessary' (90). A new generation of ANC leaders would express a more assertive Africanness in opposition to Xuma's moderation. Friendship with 'democratically thinking Europeans' was to be tested on the terrain of practical defiance of the apartheid state. It was in the sense of an African organization joining a 'common political programme' with 'other oppressed people, organised workers, and European opponents of the political color bar', not in terms of principled adherence to abstract principles, that the ANC's 1959 conference resolutions qualified its 'sufficiently "non-racial" … outlook'.

After the National Party's rise to power, white liberalism and African nationalism radicalized – respectively in the evanescent experience of the Liberal Party from 1953 to 1968, and in the trajectory from the 1955 Freedom Charter to banning, exile, and the armed struggle – as they embraced nonracialism as an explicit ideological project. Agendas of mutual recognition under the aegis of white trusteeship were discarded. There was also a left, Marxist nonracialism, neither liberal nor nationalist, in the footsteps of the Unity Movement's tradition, critical of the ANC's collaboration with racially defined bodies (Gillespie 2010). Did these shifts imply a prevalence of epochal change over continuity? Did they represent a 'degree zero' of nonracialism, resetting it as a progressive ideology? Did they make the historical antecedents I have discussed in this chapter irrelevant, relegating them to archaeology rather than genealogy? Were those antecedents, as left and nationalist historiographies have represented them, merely incomplete steps in the development of a popular democratic or revolutionary consciousness? Responses centered on explicit political strategies or stark alternatives between continuity and change obscure how the grounding of resistive and democratic subjects in the modernizing narratives of production and political economy have mutated, without disappearing, during nonracialism's shift from a moderate framework of collaboration to a radical banner of confrontation. Changes have occurred in the way non-racial discourse is deployed for the purposes of 'othering' a threatening black presence, but modalities of political interdiction have nonetheless maintained their function of securing the coherence of that discourse. The vicissitudes of cross-racial friendship tell a story that is not only about dialectics of domination and resistance. Opposition to white rule has been conceptualized and enacted in forms that simultaneously liberated certain representations or demands and silenced or suppressed others. Without a long-term perspective on entailments of embracing and pushing away, giving voice and dismissing, which problematize the history of nonracialism, one can hardly understand the sizeable symbolic and organizational investment the white left has placed in non-racial politics, especially after it was confronted by the Black Consciousness challenge from the late 1960s. Such loyalties would seem paradoxical amidst recurrent complaints that nonracialism remains an ill-defined idea, to which the ANC has given an incomplete, contradictory, and faulty implementation.[32]

I now consider how the counterhistory of nonracialism is relevant to assessing its adoption as an ideology of democratic change. It is at this point that my conceptual examination requires departing from linear historical narration, skipping debates and controversies in the liberation movement, and 'folding' different temporalities.

TRACES OF THE NON-RACIAL: CONCEPTUAL HISTORY AND THE POLITICS OF ENUNCIATED NONRACIALISM

The embrace by the ANC and the Congress tradition of nonracialism as an ideological keyword was a later outcome of the radicalization that began in the late 1940s. Bannings, exile, and the priorities of the armed struggle hampered the elaboration of non-racial politics. Gerhard Maré (2003: 20) writes that the ANC's vision did not go beyond 'non-antagonistic relations between races'. He discusses an oft-quoted paper by Pallo Jordan that tried, on the eve of the end of apartheid, to elaborate the ANC's view on the nation, democracy, and popular sovereignty. Jordan upheld the 'colonialism of a special type' thesis, which the ANC adopted from the Communist Party, but was first formulated in liberal circles, especially in the work of Leo Marquard (Maré 2003: 19). Emphasizing the coincidences between the colonial and the national questions, Jordan defines the ANC's nonracialism as a force that abolished racial domination and the 'antagonistic blocs' of the colonizer and the colonized through the establishment of a unitary, democratic state with universal suffrage, equal citizenship, and full civil liberties regardless of race. To operate in the direction of 'dissolving the antagonism' (Jordan 1988: 118–119), democracy should also provide rights and legal protections to diverse cultural identities. Left critics have long been skeptical of this argument, accused of blurring the line between principle and political expediency, thereby conflating nonracialism and liberal multiracialism.

Jordan's programmatic 'post-antagonism' presented an unstable object of discordant discourses as a coherent strategy. Apologists of nonracialism celebrate its contribution as it emerged from political battles as something unique and different from other versions of multiculturalism.[33] Yet the travails of non-racial discourse reside not only in those battles, but also in the anguished reflections in which key figures salvaged a non-racial vision from profound suspicion about the motives of whiteness. Jon Soske points at Albert Luthuli's doubts as he arrived at nonracialism as an ethical, rather than political, project of African generosity and hospitality in the recognition of the country's diversity. Nonetheless, handwritten notes on the margins of Luthuli's public statements reveal his rage and indignation at white desire's deep investment in black subjugation (Soske 2016). It is indicative that Luthuli's ascent as a prophet of nonracialism required, in the consideration of white liberals, once again relegating to the unspoken the voice of an antagonistic blackness. Nonracialism as politics continued to suppress the black under codes (the African, the colonized, the oppressed) more conducive to action in the rubrics of conflict and coalition-building. Positions such as the late 1950s ANC's strategy and Luthuli's ethics do not dissipate Fanon's and Wilderson's hypothesis that a fully coherent black political thought is impossible in, because it would require the undoing of, a structurally anti-black world.

Other registers and literary forms are needed to clarify the dilemmas of black coherence in white South Africa, the respective place of Africanness and blackness in changing national imaginings, or whether it was politically possible for Africanness, as reclaimed by the ANC, to represent the human without succumbing to the pseudo-universality of liberal civil society. As the ANC entered its season of banishment and exile, Nat Nakasa published his meditations in the form of journalistic reportages on urban life and interracial personal relations. Nakasa came from a family steeped in an earlier discourse of white friendship with the native. His father had approvingly written on the 'gospel of self-help' with the inclusive optimism characteristic of the late 1930s. As a member of the *Drum* collective, Nakasa faced the reproach of radical activists, who resented his apparently unfocused, apolitical rebelliousness. The teenage Thabo Mbeki was not impressed by Nakasa's disorientation when, offered a ride home, he was too drunk to give directions (Brown 2011: 43–44). Nakasa's *Johannesburg, Johannesburg*, published in 1964, is a tormented meditation on his inability to claim a place, political or otherwise, despite benefitting from the friendship of the white world and its gifts, education, professional training, and the promise of middle-class life. Nakasa disliked the reverence and intellectual consideration of the city's migrant Zulu proletarians, who 'saw me as an interpreter of the white man's ways because some of my friends were white' (Nakasa 2005a: 5). His profession sheltered him from the most dehumanizing consequences of apartheid for black workers and township dwellers, yet his status was not as unassailable as to place him in any capacity to effect political change. Referring to African workers, he confessed: 'I resented them because I felt a responsibility towards them and I was doing nothing about it.' The psychic and physical space in which he could retrieve a sense of agency was not direct political defiance, but interstitial violations of racial barriers, such as jazz venues and drinking dives that admitted a multiracial clientele and blended socializing with freewheeling and impolite conversation. In an early writing Nakasa (2005b: 9) defined this form of life as 'the fringe', a 'No-Man's Land, where anybody meets anybody'. The fringe could be a joyful, exhilarating place subverting ethnic identities, institutionalized 'peoples', and collective belongings imposed by white rule. But Nakasa was also aware of the dramatically asymmetric positionalities white and black had in the fringe of an anti-black world. The former faced at most the uncertainty and precariousness that came with a risky type of cross-racial *jouissance* and cultural consumption. For the latter, the 'fringe' was a slippery grip that never allowed taking one's stare away from the abyss of dehumanization and absolute dereliction. The imaginative power of the 'fringe' has to do not only with its representation of the ambiguities of black-white friendship, but also with how it conveys the air of social death hovering above black social life in the non-racial zone.

The type of discomfort Nakasa expressed toward the conditions of non-racial friendship in the white city was relegated to the margins of the political inasmuch as it grated against nonracialism as a progressive discourse. Yet many of his themes were later echoed in the sustained political polemic against white liberal friendship and its invocation of nonracialism in the work of Steve Biko. Underlying Biko's denunciation of white liberals and leftists patronizing and controlling black struggles was a broader understanding of nonracialism as an assumptive logic keeping blackness as a political subjectivity at bay. Biko (2002: 20–21) posited the black striving to 'attain the envisioned self' in an antagonistic relationship with 'the "non-racial" set-up of the integrated complexes', which by their nature did not allow a questioning of the white privilege that underpinned left and liberal discourses of solidarity and affiliation. Trusting such 'complexes' would be 'like expecting the slave to work together with the slave-master's son to remove all the conditions leading to the former's enslavement' (21). Biko's unsettled duality of blackness as simultaneously ontological death and promise of new human life revealed the persistence of questions that hegemonic nonracialism papered over. Such questions interrogate, in particular, whether antagonism lies between socioeconomic positionalities (the colonizer and the colonized), as for Jordan, or between the imagined non-racial political community and its black other.

Among the 'non-racial complexes' that Biko took aim at was the primacy of class identity, which in South Africa has long underpinned the centrality of political economy in visions of affiliation from divergent ideological positions. Biko's (2002: 50) positing of blacks as 'the only real workers in South Africa' removed labor from political economy's terrain of exploitation and fused it with blackness as a condition of dereliction and captivity, which underscores the 'anti-black attitude' of white workers as 'the greatest supporters of the system'. Not even poor whites, despite being economically analogous to blacks, are any less hostile to them, 'hence the greatest anti-black feeling is to be found amongst the very poor whites whom the Class Theory calls upon to be with black workers in the struggle for emancipation' (Biko 2002: 50). Yet, left critics of mainstream nonracialism maintained a stolid allegiance not only to 'class theory', but also to the time-honored idea that it is on the terrain of political economy and labor relations that blacks should be educated to recognize their true interests. Eddie Roux, prominent communist (later liberal) intellectual reflected, in 1928, on the decline of the ICU, plagued in his view by the anti-communist authoritarian leadership of Clemens Kadalie and the growing influence of white liberals such as Ballinger and the 'Chamber of Mines representative', Howard Pim. Roux's diagnosis was couched in terms that were not discordant with these latter's analysis of black pathology and its remedies:

> It is not really remarkable that the native leader almost invariably 'goes west' sooner or later … It is just another instance in Africa of the man who had lost one system of social ethics and had not yet acquired a new one. I wonder whether the natives we are training in our CP schools (we have now four such night schools) will produce a new type of native leader – one with an idea of social service of loyalty to the party and the Comintern. We start with the 'raw' native, who often can barely speak English … It ought to be possible in the course of some years starting with raw material to train conscientious native communists, just as the missionaries have succeeded in training conscientious native Christians.[34]

The missionary impulse persisted in informing radical nonracialism on the left. Neville Alexander is exemplary of an anti-racism that rejected both the ANC's ambiguities and the Black Consciousness critique of class discourse (Gillespie 2010). Yet, Alexander, who surely refrained from identifying the 'raw native' as a beneficiary of class solidarity, was not foreign to tones that more than superficially recall Roux's. Reminiscing in 2009, toward the end of his life, on the trajectory of the Unity Movement – started in the 1930s from the expulsion of critics of Stalinism from the Communist Party and the experience of the All-African Convention – Alexander (cited in Gillespie 2010: 70–71) reclaims the radical rejection of race in its socialist opposition to the state and capital. Yet, he admits that, non-racial commitments notwithstanding,

You could see that people saw themselves as belonging to different races. Especially with a lot of peasants going to conferences, a lot of workers. When you read those minutes, you see it was also a matter of political education. You can see how people would express themselves in racial terms and the leadership would then educate them by responding in non-racial terms and trying to explain how it was an issue of workers, it was an issue of poor people, it wasn't an issue of 'Black' and 'Colored' and 'Indian'.

For Alexander, as for Roux, non-racial class solidarity was a destination Africans had to be educated toward. Both identified in indigenous lifestyles and languages obstacles to be overcome. Alexander recalled that it was tactically advisable to let Xhosa workers speak 'in their idiom [so] they can think things through ... But you use your opportunity to educate them' (cited in Gillespie 2010: 71).[35] The direction and endpoint of such 'thinking through' depended on a transition from one undesirable way of being black to a proper collective working-class identity, which was politically productive even if its definition did not belong, nor was it self-evident, to the desired agents of socialist politics. It was the mission of activists possessing knowledge of political economy and its critique to give life to the working class from the magma of unpredictable, if not threatening, blackness. Confronted with the challenge of Black Consciousness, Alexander (cited in Gillespie 2010: 73) eventually refined his opposition between 'African' and 'Black', premised on the assumption that

Everybody can be an African ... By promoting an identity like 'African', as opposed to 'black', you are in a sense doing *both things at the same time*. You are leaving that space for nonracialism ... but you are attacking white supremacy *at the same time*. If you are going to use racial categories to fight race, you are simply perpetuating racial habitus, racial consciousness, racial prejudice. In the end, racial division (emphasis in original).

Even in a mode of theoretical reflection that more rigorously than any other has foregrounded the relation between nonracialism and radical anti-racism, the African as a political subject only emerges by keeping blackness at bay.

The advances of structuralist Marxism and the success of independent trade unionism in the 1970s helped to polarize the 'race-class debate' into an opposition between liberal idealism (targeting divisions by race as an ideological and cognitive construct) and Marxist historical materialism (centered on class as the expression of objective social contradictions). Sacrificed and suppressed in the polarity was Biko's insistence on anti-blackness as conceptually distinct from, yet practically complementary to, racism or its deployment in the machinations of class power. If anything, trade unions in which white cadres and intellectuals had a share of leadership positions that was out of proportion to the demographic composition of the rank and file, used their privileged access to western debates in academic Marxism to emphasize more than ever production, labor relations, and the workplace as breeding grounds of true proletarian consciousness. White labor leaders consciously internalized the view that their education could be turned into a device to refine black workers' direct experience of racism and injustice into a broader understanding of class as the objective truth of that experience. It was a matter of explaining, in the words of 1970s union official, Alec Erwin (cited in Frederikse 1990: 138), that 'there's something bigger than just the whites that were suppressing them ... a factory worked more than on just whiteness'. The diatribes between 'workerists' and 'populists' in the 1980s were spurred, conversely, by developments in black protest emphasizing that black oppression extended beyond the factory walls. In the townships, whiteness and anti-blackness were experienced in exponentially dramatic, even lethal ways, which in the end provoked a sustained grassroots critique of white leadership in the labor movement (Buhlungu 2006).

CONCLUSION

Nonracialism has rallied a vast and ultimately successful opposition to apartheid, to which it provided a point of convergence and unity. Its performance as the ideology of the post-1994 liberal-democratic dispensation under nationalist rule has been more problematic, as it proved unable to overcome the extreme inequalities of the past and the ways in which they underpin the persistent privileges of whiteness. Critical analysis has predominantly sought explanations in contingent factors, especially as it blamed the ANC's contradictory twists and turns and its alleged betrayals, by embracing neoliberalism, either of its ideal roots or of its social constituencies. Meanwhile, work and political economy, identified in this chapter as sinews for nonracialism's long twentieth century, have provided little comfort to the growing black multitudes who must endure, either in the presence or the absence of actual employment opportunities, the compulsion to find low-wage jobs.

There is no simple, linear, and consequential history of nonracialism in South Africa. One must be careful not to read either the ANC's moderate origins nor its early fondness for experiments such as the Cape franchise or the joint councils as 'overdetermining' its subsequent history. My focus on nonracialism as a concept does not overshadow its valence as a symbolic order drawing strength on conflating blackness with 'race', with the effect of further eclipsing to the realm Saidiya Hartman calls 'the unthought' (Hartman and Wilderson 2003) the structuring role anti-blackness plays in South Africa as a national community. In its place stand more tractable debates on the importance of 'race' in relation to class, gender, nation, ethnicity, or identity. As a response, this chapter rejects an explanatory strategy grounded in the contingency of political or intellectual strategies and the temporality of social conflicts. It is not my aim to devalue African resistance and its achievements. As long as only one (white) South Africanism was allowed, settler governance could conflate 'natives' and 'Africans' as its incapacitated and deferent objects. It was the great achievement of early African nationalism to separate those two terms and assert an anticolonial discourse steeped in an African ethics and imagination of freedom and civilization. Its definition of political capacity did not, however, undermine western norms of production, education, and conduct, which reproached the unpredictable, work-averse, impolite, uncivilized, 'raw native', an antecedent of Fanon's lumpen and Wilderson's Black. Even when contesting – on the basis of its own ethics and discourse – the ground of friendship and affiliation, political Africanness as the expression of a colonized and racially oppressed subjectivity did not touch the incompatibility between blackness and the white world. The latter defines itself by placing the former into the paradigmatic predicament – which Wilderson calls the Slave, as distinct from the subaltern and the colonized – of incapacitated, problematic, silent object of ethics, discourse, and imagination, an entity for which the maximization of productive potentials is not obviously conducive to human status. Nonracialism has emerged – through successive iterations, some moderate and collaborationist, others radical and uncompromising – by foregrounding the political subjectivity of the respectable native or the class-conscious and nationally assertive African against whatever unruliness, unpredictability, and threatening otherness reside in the black. The discursive modalities presenting this tension as an antagonism were clearly in place by the end of the third decade of the twentieth century, and operated genealogically when nonracialism was finally enunciated.

Perhaps at stake in a counterhistory of nonracialism is a critique of the type of progressive temporality, to recall Koselleck's point, which enables the social life of concepts. In South Africa as elsewhere, activist and critical discourse has long celebrated the time of resistance as one of eventfulness, either in the form of historical time marked by concrete political effects and outcomes or, in Deleuzian terms, as a time of becoming, or the self-actualization of the resistant subject, which is so central to current social movement rhetorics. To raise the question of anti-blackness in South African history, not only as an effect of white supremacy, but also as a precondition of political conflicts and non-racial discourse, is to point out how the time of the event is shadowed by paradigmatic time, or time that 'obliterates distinctions between past, present, and future' (Neusner 1997),[36] by virtue of an imposing, atemporal, and inertial present. The imposing presence of anti-blackness acts not only as the foundation of white modernity as an overt project of racial domination, but also of the ethical dilemmas – chiefly in regard to how whiteness turns blacks into productive workers and virtuous subjects – that enable white-ruled civil society through time.

The contiguities of non-racial thinking with the paradigm of anti-blackness are not a novel topic of inquiry, especially for critics who consider racism and anti-blackness as analytically distinct although reciprocally reinforcing (see Martinot 2002; Sexton 2008). In South Africa, however, explorations of non-racial and anti-racist politics have eschewed that distinction; partly on account of the more pressing political urgency of fighting against an overtly racist state, but also because of the uneasiness a hegemonic non-racial left felt toward political traditions such as Black Consciousness. Nonracialism has, instead, tended to flatten reclamations of blackness as a mode of political subjectivity into 'racialistic' discourse condemned as essentialized, regressive, and divisive. As an alternative, it has celebrated work and political economy as foundations of a national-popular 'We'.

Little space was left to reckonings with how work, despite the moral wrappings in which successive regimes have presented it, has participated in the subjugation of black South Africans in ways that were not limited to exploitation, but rather reinforced a pervasive societal dereliction. Political economy is more effective in pointing at the imaginary social ills work is supposed to heal than in enabling a social compact fulfilling its universalist claims. Who embodies, and has embodied, such social ills in South Africa? Do Mbembe ('poor young black men, many of whom firmly believe in the craft of witches and … often, they will use rape as a means to discipline') and Lagden ('marauders preying on each other's lives and property, slayers of their own kindred out of mere blood-thirstiness, murderers by "killing off" at the instance of witchdoctors') evoke the same phantasms, despite their radically different times and political outlooks? What is unsaid in left injunctions that Africans are workers first and blacks second, even if their suffering on the latter's score is simply incommensurable with the former? How much black life has to be excised to reclaim the 'oneness of black and white' (Suttner 2010) out of a history in which whiteness has overwhelmingly imposed the terms (the labor market, the nation-state, western education, socialism, liberal democracy) for the enunciation of such oneness? These are urgent questions for a critique of South Africa's democracy that does not look away from, if not paradigmatic time, at least a structural questioning of white supremacy. Otherwise, the post-apartheid dispensation will keep fortifying itself by scapegoating the allegedly irrational, incomprehensible disaffection of disaffiliated black youth, striking mineworkers, and service delivery protestors, the current incarnations for pundits and policymakers of Milner's childish Africans or Dube's 'ruck of the natives'. As ethical positions, friendship or solidarity for the other are of little critical use to the extent they are concerned with the order such feelings are meant to validate. In Aristotelean terms, they love the Human by hating the Slave. Beyond friendship is a stare at what the Slave and its antagonisms have to say about the world.

REFERENCES

Anon. 1926. 'Country Life: How Capitalism Has Changed It. A Native Viewpoint.' *The South African Worker* 11(528): 4.

Balandier, Georges. 1951. 'La Situation Coloniale: Approche Théorique.' *Cahiers Internationaux de Sociologie* 11: 44–79.

Barchiesi, Franco. 2011. *Precarious Liberation: Workers, the State, and Contested Social Citizenship in Post-Apartheid South Africa*. Albany, NY: SUNY Press.

Barchiesi, Franco. 2012. 'Imagining the Patriotic Worker: The Idea of "Decent Work" in the ANC's Political Discourse.' In *One Hundred Years of the ANC: Liberation Histories and Democracy Today*, edited by Arianna Lissoni et al., 111–35. Johannesburg: Wits University Press.

Biko, Steve. 2002 (1978). *I Write What I Like: Selected Writings*. Chicago, IL: University of Chicago Press.

Bozzoli, Belinda. 1981. *The Political Nature of a Ruling Class: Capital and Ideology in South Africa, 1890–1933*. London: Routledge & Kegan Paul.

Bozzoli, Belinda. 1991. *Women of Phokeng: Consciousness, Life Strategy and Migrancy in South Africa, 1900–1983*. Johannesburg: Wits University Press.

Brown, Ryan L. 2011. 'A Native of Nowhere: The Life of South African Journalist Nat Nakasa, 1937-1965.' *Kronos* 37: 41–59.

Buhlungu, Sakhela. 2006. 'Rebels without a Cause of Their Own? The Contradictory Location of White Officials in Black Unions in South Africa, 1973-1994.' *Current Sociology* 54(3): 427–51.

Campbell, Jesinta T. 1998. 'Romantic Revolutionaries: David Ivon Jones, S. P. Bunting and the Origins of Non-Racial Politics in South Africa.' *Journal of African History* 39(2): 313–28.

Champion, Allison Wessels George. 1927. *The Truth About the ICU*. Durban: African Workers' Club.

Davenport, Rodney. 1987. 'The Cape Liberal Tradition to 1910.' In *Democratic Liberalism in South Africa: Its History and Prospect*, edited by Jeffrey Butler, Richard Elphick, and David Welsh, 21–34. Cape Town: David Philip.

Deleuze, Gilles. 1991. *Bergsonism*. Trans. Hugh Tomlinson and Barbara Habberjam. New York, NY: Zone Books.

Deleuze, Gilles. 1992. *The Fold: Leibniz and the Baroque*. Trans. Tom Conley. Minneapolis, MN: University of Minnesota Press.

Derrida, Jacques. 2005. *The Politics of Friendship*. Trans. George Collins. London: Verso.

Dube, John L. 1929. 'The Industrial Organisation of the Native People.' *Report of the National European-Bantu Conference*. Cape Town. February 6–9. Alice: Lovedale Institution Press.

Dubow, Saul. 2006. *A Commonwealth of Knowledge: Science, Sensibility, and White South Africa, 1820–2000*. Oxford: Oxford University Press.

Eudell, Demetrius L. 2002. *The Political Languages of Emancipation in the British Caribbean and the U.S. South*. Chapel Hill, NC: University of North Carolina Press.

Everatt, David. 2009. *The Origins of Non-Racialism: White Opposition to Apartheid in the 1950s*. Johannesburg: Wits University Press.

Fanon, Frantz. 1986 (1962). *Black Skin, White Masks*. Trans. Charles Lam Markmann. London: Pluto Press.

Foner, Eric. 1988. *Reconstruction: America's Unfinished Revolution, 1863–1877*. New York, NY: Harper.

Frederikse, Julie. 1990. *The Unbreakable Thread: Non-Racialism in South Africa*. Bloomington, IN: Indiana University Press.

Gillespie, Kelly. 2010. 'Reclaiming Nonracialism: Reading The Threat of Race from South Africa.' *Patterns of Prejudice* 44(1): 61–75.

Hall, Catherine. 2002. *Civilizing Subjects: Metropole and Colony in the English Imagination 1830–1867*. Chicago, IL: University of Chicago Press.

Hall, Catherine. 2012. *Macaulay and Son: Architects of Imperial Britain*. New Haven, CT: Yale University Press.

Hartman, Saidiya and Frank Wilderson III. 2003. 'The Position of the UnThought. An Interview with Saidiya Hartman Conducted by Frank B. Wilderson, III.' *Qui Parle* 13(2): 183–201.

Holt, Thomas. 1992. *The Problem of Freedom: Race, Labor, and Politics in Jamaica and Britain, 1832–1938*. Baltimore, MD: Johns Hopkins University Press.

Jabavu, Davidson Don Tengo. 1920. 'Native Unrest: Its Cause and Cure.' Paper presented at the Natal Missionary Conference, Durban, South Africa. July.

Jordan, Pallo. 1988. 'The South African Liberation Movement and the Making of a New Nation.' In *The National Question in South Africa*, edited by Maria van Diepen, 110–124. London: Zed Books.

Koselleck, Reinhart. 2004. '*Begriffsgeschichte* and Social History.' In *Futures Past: On the Semantics of Historical Time*, edited by Reinhart Koselleck and translated by Keith Tribe, 75–92. New York: Columbia University Press.

Lalu, Premesh. 2008. 'When Was South African History Ever Postcolonial?' *Kronos* 34: 267–281.

Landau, Paul. 2012. '"Johannesburg in Flames": The 1918 Shilling Campaign, *Abantu-Batho* and Early African Nationalism in South Africa.' In *The People's Paper: A Centenary History and Anthology of Abantu-Batho*, edited by Peter Limb, 255–281. Johannesburg: Wits University Press.

Legassick, Martin and Robert Ross. 2010. 'From Slave Economy to Settler Capitalism: The Cape Colony and Its Extensions, 1800–1854.' In *The Cambridge History of South Africa*, vol. 1: *From Early Times to 1885*, edited by Carolyn Hamilton, Bernard K. Mbenga, and Robert Ross, 253–318. Cambridge: Cambridge University Press.

Limb, Peter. 2010. *The ANC's Early Years: Nation, Class, and Place in South Africa before 1940.* Pretoria: Unisa Press.

Limb, Peter, ed. 2012. *A. B. Xuma. Autobiography and Selected Works.* Cape Town: Van Riebeeck Society.

Losurdo, Domenico. 2011. *Liberalism: A Counter-History.* London: Verso.

Mamdani, Mahmood. 1996. *Citizen and Subject: Contemporary Africa and the Legacy of Late Colonialism.* Princeton, NJ: Princeton University Press.

Maré, Gerhard. 2003. '"Non-Racialism" in the Struggle Against Apartheid.' *Society in Transition* 34(1): 13–37.

Martinot, Steve. 2002. *The Rule of Racialization: Class, Identity, Governance.* Philadelphia, PA: Temple University Press.

Matthews, Zachariah Keodirelang. 1933. 'The Educational Needs of the Bantu.' *Some Aspects of the Native Question: Selected Addresses Delivered at the Fifth National European-Bantu Conference, Bloemfontein, July 5–7, 1933.* Johannesburg: South African Institute of Race Relations.

Maylam, Paul. 2001. *South Africa's Racial Past: The History and Historiography of Racism, Segregation, and Apartheid.* Aldershot: Ashgate.

Mbembe, Achille. 2006. 'South Africa's Second Coming: The Nongqawuse Syndrome.' *Open Democracy.* http://www.opendemocracy.net/democracy-africa_democracy/southafrica_succession_3649.jsp

Nakasa, Nat. 2005a. 'Johannesburg, Johannesburg.' In *The World of Nat Nakasa*, edited by Essop Patel, 3–8. Johannesburg: Picador Africa.

Nakasa, Nat. 2005b. 'Between Two Worlds.' In *The World of Nat Nakasa*, edited by Essop Patel, 9–14. Johannesburg: Picador Africa.

Nash, Andrew. 1978. 'Dr. Philip, the "Spread of Civilisation" and Liberalism in South Africa.' Paper presented at the Conference on the History of Opposition in Southern Africa, Johannesburg, University of the Witwatersrand, January 27–30.

Neusner, Jacob. 1997. 'Paradigmatic Versus Historical Thinking: The Case of Rabbinic Judaism.' *History and Theory* 36(3): 353–377.

Odendaal, André. 1984. *Vukani Bantu! The Beginnings of Black Protest Politics in South Africa to 1912.* Cape Town: David Philip.

Posel, Deborah. 2001. 'Race as Common Sense: Racial Classification in Twentieth Century South Africa.' *African Studies Review* 44(2): 87–113.

Rich, Paul B. 1990. 'Race, Science, and the Legitimization of White Supremacy in South Africa, 1902–40.' *International Journal of African Historical Studies* 23(4): 665–686.

Rich, Paul B. 1992. 'Reviewing the Origins of the Freedom Charter.' In *Peace, Politics, and Violence in the New South Africa*, edited by Norman Etherington, 254–283. London: Hans Zell.

Sartori, Andrew. 2014. *Liberalism in Empire: An Alternative History.* Berkeley, CA: University of California Press.

Seme, Pixley. 1972 (1906). 'The Regeneration of Africa.' In *From Protest to Challenge. A Documentary History of African Politics in South Africa, 1882–1964*, vol. I: *Protest and Hope, 1882–1934*, edited by Thomas Karis and Gwendolyn Carter, 69–71. Stanford, CA: Hoover Institution Press.

Sexton, Jared. 2008. *Amalgamation Schemes: Anti-Blackness and the Critique of Multiracialism.* Minneapolis, MN: University of Minnesota Press.

Smith, Daniel. 2012. 'Deleuze and the History of Philosophy.' In *The Cambridge Companion to Deleuze.* Cambridge: Cambridge University Press.

Soske, Jon. 2015. 'The Impossible Concept: Settler Liberalism, Pan-Africanism, and the Language of Non Racialism.' *African Historical Review* 47 (2) 1–39.

Soske, Jon. 2016. 'How to Approach Heaven.' *Chimuranga Chronic*, April.

Spillers, Hortense. 1987. 'Mama's Baby, Papa's Maybe: An American Grammar Book.' *Diacritics* 17(2): 65–81.

Suttner, Raymond. 2010. '"Africanisation", African Identities and Emancipation in Contemporary South Africa.' *Social Dynamics* 36(3): 515–530.

Van Duin, Pieter C. 1995. '"Workers of All Colours, Unite": South African Communism, the White Working Class, and the Ideology of Proletarian Nonracialism, 1917–1943.' *Comparative Studies of South Asia, Africa and the Middle East* 15(2): 64–71.

Wehler, Hans-Ulrich. 1980. *Geschichte als Historische Sozialwissenschaft.* Frankfurt-am-Main: Suhrkamp.

Wilderson, Frank B. III. 2010. *Red, White & Black: Cinema and the Structure of U.S. Antagonisms.* Durham, NC: Duke University Press.

Xuma, Alfred B. 1930. 'Bridging the Gap between White and Black in South Africa.' Address at the Conference of European and Bantu Christian Student Associations, Fort Hare, June 27–30. http://www.sahistory.org.za/archive/bridging-gap-between-white-and-black-south-africa-address-dr-b-xuma-conference-european-and-

NOTES

1   A vast historiographical debate exists as to when and in what circumstances expropriation and social subjugation become self-consciously enunciated in terms of white supremacy. As such concerns are not central to this chapter, I refer to Maylam (2001) for a useful overview.

2   A recent example is Everatt (2009).

3   I am referring here to Deleuze's (1991) opposition of 'virtual' and 'actual' — whereas what is virtual produces concrete effects that are immanent to the *present* — which he distinguishes from the relationship of 'possible' and 'real', in which the former indicates the likelihood of a *future* transformation. Although disabled by prevailing political projects, unactualized virtualities do not cease to produce effects.

4   For a pioneering contribution defining the colonial situation as a totality entailing the reciprocal, if asymmetric, transformation of the colonizing and colonized society, including the emergence of new social spaces and identities, see Balandier (1951).

5   The method of the 'fold' is central to Deleuze's approach to concepts and to his view of philosophy as 'the creation of concepts'. In this sense, it supports my goal of a rigorous conceptual history that is grounded in the sources, but does not depend on their exegesis (see Smith 2012).

6   Nash (1978: 21) makes the example of distinguished liberal voice, R. F. A. Hoernlé, who, when confronted with the post-1910 collapse of Cape liberalism and the end of the African franchise in 1936 advocated, in 1939, racial partition as an imperfect yet practical way to protect Africans from the consequences of power inequalities between blacks and whites.

7   National Archives (Pretoria), Transvaal Archives Repository (hereafter TAB), SNA, Vol. 11, Ref. 442/01, ff. 38–60, Milner to Chamberlain, December 6, 1901, f. 42.

8   Milner to Chamberlain.

9   Milner to Chamberlain, 59.

10 Milner to Chamberlain, 46.

11 Milner to Chamberlain, 53.

12 Milner to Chamberlain, 54–55.

13 Milner to Chamberlain, 57.

14 Milner to Chamberlain, 59–60.

15 'Draft Dispatch to Secretary of State', March 1–5, 1906. University of the Witwatersrand Department of Historical Papers (hereafter DHP), Lagden Papers, A951, Fcc, f. 52.

16 'Draft Dispatch', 52.

17 'Draft Dispatch', 50.

18 *Report of the Transvaal Labor Commission. Minutes of Proceedings and Evidence*, February 1904, TAB, Ampt Pubs, Vol. 46, Ref. CD1897, 90, para. 1835.

19 Lagden to Rose Innes, October 31, 1901. TAB, SNA, Vol. 11, ff.14–16.

20 See Losurdo (2011) for a systematic exposition of the racial ambiguities of classical liberalism in its opposition to institutionalized slavery.

21 See Bozzoli (1991) on the intersection of gender and generation in the struggles for social control in a context of early labor migration.

22 Not surprisingly, the establishment of such mechanisms with the Industrial Conciliation Act of 1924 and the Wage Act of 1925 would exclude African workers.

23 DHP, Howard Pim Papers, A.881, Ac5.6.2, 'Chairman's Address to the National European-Bantu Conference', Cape Town, February 6–8, 1929.

24 DHP, Pim Papers, Fa 18/3, Native Affairs Society of the Transvaal, 'Address Delivered by the President, Mr. Howard Pim, at the Annual General Meeting Held in Johannesburg on February 23, 1909', 7.

25 'Chairman's Address', 12.

26 DHP, Records of the Joint Councils, AD.1433, Ac.1.2, 'Conference on Native Affairs Convened by the Federal Council of the Dutch Reformed Church', September 27–29, 1923.

27 DHP, Records of the Joint Councils, AD. 1433, Ac3.3.11, 'The Establishment of Joint Councils and a Federal Council', by R. V. Selope Thema, Conference on Native Affairs, Johannesburg, October 30–November 1, 1924.

28 For an example of the discursive link, from the standpoint of African elites at the joint councils, between unrest and black 'ignorance', see also Jabavu (1920).

29 Such a separation remains, instead, at the core of the scholarship on the alleged specificities of South African colonialism, starting with Mamdani (1996).

30 ANC leaders and African nationalist politicians used this expression well into the 1930s. See for example A. B. Xuma's (1930) praise, in the speech that launched his political career, of the Cape educational curriculum as turning, among others, Tiyo Soga and John T. Jabavu from 'raw "Kaffir boys" … primitive men so-called, not a day removed from savagery or from the life of barbarism' into 'citizens in their common country'.

31 DHP, Records of the Joint Councils, AD.1433, Cj.2.6.17, S.S. Tema, 'The Amalaita Menace'. Johannesburg Joint Council of European and Natives, 1935. *Amalaita* defined youth cultural associations of Zulu migrants, which popular imagination often associated with criminal activities.

32 For example, in his history of nonracialism in South Africa, the only such monograph in circulation, David Everatt (2009) focuses on nonracialism as a white project, not only because of the otherwise intractable complexity of the theme, but also as a result of his explicitly stated conviction that only by embracing nonracialism and the Congress agenda could white activists, otherwise numerically and organizationally insignificant, influence the liberation struggle. The possible impact on non-racial agendas of the foundations of such influence, namely the privileges and education conferred upon whiteness by the very system those activists were fighting, is left unexamined by Everatt.

33 For a brilliant overview of these debates, see Soske (2015).

34 DHP, Ballinger Papers, A.410, C.2.3.7, File 3, Eddie Roux to Norman Leys, September 16, 1928.

35 Alexander recognizes that close connections with the Black Consciousness movement elicited a more sophisticated understanding of the social reality and experiences of race as the latter moved toward class analysis, but adamantly rejected 'the idea that a non-black person can't experience what a black person is' (Gillespie 2010: 71).

36 For discussions on the notion of paradigmatic time I am also deeply indebted to Frank Wilderson.

7

AFFECT AND THE STATE: PRECARIOUS WORKERS, THE LAW, AND THE PROMISE OF FRIENDSHIP

BRIDGET KENNY

Twenty years ago, when I first came to South Africa, I worked at an advice center called the Industrial Aid Society (IAS) on Jeppe Street in downtown Johannesburg. This was around the time of the first democratic elections, but before post-apartheid labor law reform began in 1995. Every early morning, long queues and quiet clusters of workers waited outside the door. We would serve some 50 workers a day. If a worker was a member of a union, we would send her back to her union to resolve her issues. The paralegals accompanied workers to what were then known as industrial councils to sit framed by polished wood and to argue for their protections. If the worker did not fall within an industrial council, the advice office would phone the employer to negotiate the basic conditions laid out in a wage determination, or fill out the paperwork for the Unemployment Insurance Fund, or tick the boxes detailing the body parts lost or injured for occupational health benefits. It was through working at this advice center for three-and-a-half years that I realized how mutually constitutive precarious labor and regulation were.

In 2012, I returned to another worker advice center, the Casual Worker Advice Office (CWAO) in Germiston.[1] It was set up specifically to assist casual, contingent, and contract workers. In the period between the IAS and the CWAO, South Africa has undergone two decades of democracy with labor law reform a primary lineament of expanded protection and participation (Adler and Webster 2000; Webster and Von Holdt 2005). Indeed, employment has been definitive of the ANC's (African National Congress) imagination of social citizenship in post-apartheid South Africa (Barchiesi 2011).

Yet while labor reforms extended the definition of employee to many workers previously not covered, it also structured labor protections around a set of normative assumptions about who that worker was: 'a male, permanent, full-time, long-term employee with employment benefits (medical aid and pension fund) working at one fixed workplace where formal representation by a nationally organized union is available' (Page-Shipp 2003: 11; see also Kenny 2009; Theron 2005). Many precarious workers did not fit into this model. Moreover, basic protections that did apply were simply *de facto* subverted by employers or not pursued by unions.[2]

Hundreds of workers approach the glass front of the CWAO office. They come individually, and they come in groups to seek assistance. Many are union members and many have tried in vain to get the unions to take up their cases. Unlike in 1994 at the IAS, paralegals now accept these cases without automatically returning workers to their unions. The advice office then was conceived consciously as a rung in the justice system meant to support unions to exercise representative voice.[3] Today, the advice office may instead be serving as surrogate union.[4]

In this chapter, I explore the stories of precarious workers who claimed their labor rights by seeking the help of the advice office. In these processes, an affective relationship is performed between workers and the state, as well as a claim to friendship with other (black) workers. The promise of 'friendship' – care, recognition, and mutuality – between the state and precarious workers, is not fulfilled, but rather reproduces the sign of 'friend', momentarily, with other workers (or with the identity 'worker'), through what becomes common disappointment.

By recalling my entry into South Africa 20 years ago, I emphasize the durability of labor rights as a site of affective desire for workers. On the cusp of democratic labor reform, such hope perhaps was to be expected. But, after decades of disappointment, other questions beg to be asked. What does it mean for precarious workers to continue to make claims on the state for legal rights and regulation in a context where their daily experiences have shown that South African labor law has often not provided them with protection? How are workers' legal claims tied up with notions of the political subject 'worker', to formulations of what constitutes 'the political', and to resolute, ordinary, and enduring desires for political futures? I argue that 'precariousness' does not merely describe a set of vulnerabilities more or less safeguarded against, but itself can be viewed as a site of relationship, which directs affective attachments and longings toward models of the 'good life' (Berlant 2011), which bind workers and the state together. In this chapter, then, I examine the abiding relationship between precariousness and the law through a reading of the affect and troubled friendships reproduced therein.

Precarious workers' claims to rights and regulation cannot merely be seen as a desire for recognition and inclusion in an order of participation already constituted. I suggest countervailing conclusions: that in these daily, fraught, and often unsuccessful actions, workers' commitments propel a claim to political participation that simultaneously reproduces subjugation through affirming the law as arbitrator of rule and norm (and through affirming the subject of rightful participation), and yet insists, through workers' 'action in concert', that here is a site of contested political relation (Arendt 1958; Honig 2013). In this way, I suggest that precarious workers return to the law to claim more than recognition as 'employees', even as their affective attachments reproduce their desire for this ideal of freedom.

Mostly these workers lose; mostly they fade back into the bustle of a busy morning taxi rank; mostly they begin again to look for yet another low-wage job. But at the moment they stake their claims through action and then through narrative, they constitute publics through appearance to others and through action in concert (Arendt 1958; Markell 2003). While these precarious workers may not always secure protections, they keep open a claim to a space of relation dependent on their participation – constituted with the state and with other workers (or at least the idea of other workers). Returning to the advice center suggests their affective faith in this 'friendship' with the state (participation as mutual and reciprocal) which labor rights calls up. They reaffirm a belief that they can still activate a public. Thus, we also need to consider to what political subjects and orders workers attach their energies. What 'normative promises' enliven workers' actions and to what effect (Berlant 2011; Berlant and Edelman 2014)?

'PRECARIOUSNESS' AS A RELATIONSHIP OF DEPENDENCE

The expansive literature around precarious work does not simply describe forms of employment at variance from the 'standard employment relation', but also the subjective experiences of these forms of insecurity (Kalleberg 2013; Standing 2011; Vosko et al. 2009; Webster et al. 2008). Much social scientific examination of precarious labor seeks to explain the cause of particular forms, and finds, often regulatory, solutions to mitigate the vulnerabilities exhibited. This chapter argues instead for recasting the problematic of precarious labor in South Africa by reading it through affect. I argue that precariousness is a particularly emotive site of relationality that speaks to the abiding ties of work, race, and the law.

The dictionary gives us four related meanings of precarious which can help us: 1) depending on the will or pleasure of another; 2) dependent on uncertain premises (dubious); 3) dependent on chance circumstances, or unknown conditions; and 4) characterized by lack of security or stability that threatens with danger. Precarious comes from the Latin *precarius*, 'obtained by treaty or mere favour', and relates to the feminine *precaria*, the root of prayer,[5] as suggestive as any. We can think of precariousness, then, as a relationship of dependence, defined fundamentally through inequality and reproduced through uncertainty. Describing a relationship, precariousness takes shape through its affective content. Indeed, in many ways it marks a position other than the presumed mutuality of 'friendship'.

When we discuss precariousness in relation to labor, it has become common sense to describe the insecurity and vulnerability of workers. Donna Haraway (1991) wrote about what was then called the 'feminization of labor' (and see Standing 1999). Instability became visible when conditions of labor associated with women's work became (alarmingly now) extended to both men and women. Haraway (1991: 166) pointed out this hyperbolic move,

> Work is being redefined as both literally female and feminized, whether performed by men or women. To be feminized means to be made extremely vulnerable; able to be disassembled, reassembled, exploited as a reserve labor force; seen less as workers than as servers; subjected to time arrangements on and off the paid job that make a mockery of a limited work day; leading to an existence that always borders on being obscene, out of place, and reducible to sex.

'Feminized' labor became located in embodied beings in contrast to the neutral category of employee. And so, as Haraway noted, precarious labor signified a disturbing visibility of these conditions within and against the norm. And, we begin to feel its affect – the anxiety, the risk, the 'obscenity', indeed, the unsettling intimacy of precarious labor.

In the global North, scholars argue that precariousness is reflected as a loss of stability characterizing the past (Allison 2013; Kalleberg 2013; Molé 2013; Standing 2011). Where a social welfare state has not been a mediating feature of an economy, such as for black South Africans, precariousness seems rather more ordinary (see Mitropoulos 2005; Neilson and Rossiter 2008). Angela Mitropoulos (2005) suggests that tying 'precarious' to 'stable' represents investment in a normative juridical order. She asks whether 'the motif of precariousness works to simply entice a desire for its opposite, security, regardless if this is presented as a return to a time in which security apparently reigned or as a future newly immunized against precariousness [through law]'? She comments: 'If it is possible to say anything for certain about precariousness, it is that it teeters.'

Being precarious means that one is vulnerable, embodied and dependent on chance, uncertainty, or the will of another, and yet these authors also suggest that it is always by negative implication, linked to its other – standard, secure, stable, protected, abstract. Precariousness seems to call up simultaneously its affective relation to exposure and its yearning for order and rule. Thus, Judith Butler defines precarious as 'injurable'. The ontology of being human is located in 'loss and vulnerability', which comes from being 'attached to others, at risk of losing those attachments, exposed to others, at risk of violence by virtue of that exposure' (Butler 2004: 20). For Butler, then, precariousness is the very condition of subjectivity, and hence, belies the security of the sovereign subject.

What might these affective vectors mean for workers and their claims to the law, which acts by interpellating specific subjects? As Stuart Hall (2000: 26) so clearly explains, there is a gap between the discursive hailing of the subject and the turn to the hail. Hall (25) outlines the problematic thus: 'It is not enough for the law to summon, discipline, produce and regulate, but there must also be the corresponding production of a response (and thus the capacity and apparatus of subjectivity) from the side of the subject.' Quite literally, the law summons the South African precarious worker through her contrast to the full-time, permanent employee. In order to make claims to the law in the guise of a legal subject (contract worker, casual, migrant, unskilled laborer), she turns toward interpellation, but as Hall suggests, that moment is indeterminate. What do workers seek when they make these turns? What are the affective attachments tied up in relationships to the state, to employers, to fellow workers?

Another way of posing the question is to query what enables people to 'endure' (Povinelli 2011). Enduring requires imagining a different sort of future that enables one to carry on now. Lauren Berlant (2011) directs us toward forms of attachment that enable endurance; she wonders whether these affective binds that keep one hinged to the present at some point become forms of 'cruel optimism'. Thus, participation in low-wage, unstable service work signals a desire for the 'normative promises of capital and intimacy under capital' (Berlant 2007: 281). Precarious labor offers a site to disentangle desires for attachments to normative orders that are 'optimistic': they may help us to survive now, but do so by orientating us toward a projected future to be held-out-for, where these dreams will eventually come to pass (Berlant 2011; Berlant and Edelman 2014; and see also Povinelli 2011).[6] In other words, optimism for Berlant is an affective phenomenon historically situated, which promises a future but, in doing so, may be 'cruel': it may keep us tied to an order that prevents us from getting there. This complicated formulation emphasizes not the effects of domination or even the sense of betrayal therein, so much as the objects of attachment of our political desires, which are powerful enough to continue to solicit this hope and our turn toward it. Berlant's suggestion that we look at what (specifically) moves subjects to desire can thus assist us.

Finally, political optimism located in work as a terrain of freedom in a context where black workers were slaves, vagrants, manual labor, or 'casuals' raises further questions. What are the conditions under which black bodies become desiring subjects? What are the conditions of subjection and self-subjection in subject-making that occur in these processes? How might affective ties be indicative of 'monstrous intimacies' (Sharpe 2010) that belie orders of belonging reliant on perpetual never-belongings, embodied shame and violent outcast, which then describe the same attachments? Christina Sharpe (2010: 83) writes: 'The colonized and enslaved are considered to be human because they "consent" to labor, and yet they are also not quite human because they "consent" to it enough to survive within it. Not consenting to such subjectivity is an option that is not permitted and not to be acknowledged.' Thus the very subject position of worker holds questions for interrogating the terrains of political desire of precarious workers.

The discourse of rights as a vocabulary of claims acquires a thickness in the minds of workers as well as in workers' struggles. To understand precarious workers' claims to rights and procedure, then, it seems to me that we need to extend analysis beyond a discussion of gains or losses in protection, and ask what do these ordinary and regular actions signify in terms of normative promises and processes of subjectification, which can be tracked as affective desire for (certain forms of) relationship with the state, and with other workers.

Through the turn to affect, precariousness becomes not merely a measure of insecurity, but a way into thinking through what is being attached to, with what evocations, to what effect, and how these sites (of work and of law) function to maintain and reproduce relationships of domination, hierarchy, pain, and endurance. It calls up other questions, such as whether or where solidarities (or friendships) persist within such dependencies? If the root of precarious is in prayer, we must ask how entreating, as directed appeal toward an object / an other, helps workers to survive in the present, but possibly not to thrive.

I turn to the stories of three (black) workers to look at how precarious workers perform their affective relations with the state and how they do or do not build friendships with other workers through their narratives in order to stake claims both for survival and recognition.

ENDURING ATTACHMENTS

The CWAO sits unobtrusively on an ordinary city street between a working-class shopping center and a regional taxi rank in Germiston, a historic working-class town now showing the effects of deindustrialization. The office is not easy to find if you are not looking for it, although against an outside wall stands a ten-foot-tall stencil of a worker in red and black. This logo is a domestic worker 'teetering' (to recall Mitropoulos) on a tightrope, although it could be argued that she is balancing with great skill.

Of a total of 584 cases registered between its opening in August 2011 and April 2014,[7] the majority of workers approaching the Germiston office worked in Ekurhuleni Municipality, the former 'East Rand', historically one of South Africa's key manufacturing regions (Barchiesi and Kenny 2002). More than half of the workers were 35 years of age or younger, and except for one, were 'black' (African or 'colored'),[8] and mostly men. Workers came from across sectors including the motor, food, chemical, and engineering industries predominating in Ekurhuleni, as well as from sectors traditionally associated with precarious employment, such as transport, private security, domestic work, wholesale and retail, contract cleaning, agriculture, and municipal services. The workers earned low wages, none more than R3 000 per month (less than US$300 per month).

I will discuss three cases, which have been dealt with at the CWAO over the past few years. The narratives come from individuals, but one of the cases was opened by a group of workers and two cases were independently initiated. All workers were in precarious employment, but differently so: one was a casual service sector worker, one a labor broker employee, and a third a full-time regular employee, but in a context of easy dismissal. Two moments are present in each story: each worker builds a case for a new, albeit momentary, public, in which he or she claims a different model of participation founded on relationships that are known and that are (and can be) reciprocally (even if unevenly) engaged in; and, each worker in so doing reproduces attachments to subject positions and to futures where participation is secured through the figure of precarity's other, the stable, rights-bearing, full-income-earning worker made real through rules outside and above. These two phenomena – new publics generated in action and ongoing attachments to law and employment – can be described through their affects, desires to relate, to have effect, to participate. But, while some workers achieved gains through their cases, all also experienced the ever-receding nature of their objects of attachment, a vanishing point pulling them forward now. As a relationship of inequality and uncertainty, precariousness becomes a sign of longing, which may well be cruel optimism.

OF SUBJECTS: LESEDI

Lesedi Mogotsi was a casual worker for a major supermarket chain.[9] She had worked for the retailer for three years, nine hours a day and five days a week. Her shifts varied between 6am to 3pm and 11am to 8pm. On the particular day that she was dismissed, she had worked her shift from eleven in the morning until eight at night. She bought some groceries and then went to the change room to get ready to leave. She called the security guard to come to search her parcels as the final procedure of the day. He searched her packages and then her handbag, digging deep into it until he came out with a wad of toilet paper. He asked her what it was; she replied that it was tissue. But, he wanted to know what was wrapped inside the toilet paper: 'He said there is something inside this and unwrapped it and found a Ponds [a vial of Ponds cold cream].'

She did not know how the hand cream came to be in her bag. She reasoned that every locker in the change room had a lock but hers, 'which means that anyone could have had access to my bag including the security [guard]'. The security guard then called the management who immediately called the police. She was taken to the police station, where she had to spend the night in jail. The next morning she got out, 'and then they had the hearing, and we argued [gave evidence] and I was fired'. She was not represented at the hearing by the retail union in the store, because she was not a member. As she explained: 'The union just came to listen, but they did not speak for me because I was not a member.'

After her dismissal she went to the Department of Labor, which directed her to the advice office, to assist her to contest her case through the Commission for Conciliation, Mediation and Arbitration (CCMA). She reported matter-of-factly,

Then there was a conciliation; the employers didn't come; okay, [I] applied for an arbitration, then the case come, and he [the commissioner] just makes pen notes as to my story. But then the commissioner didn't want to take my papers, but he just let me tell my story, and he wrote it down. But then after that, he then left with the company representative and the pile of papers.

She continued: 'And I wasn't feeling well with this thing, because I wanted to give the papers, and the commissioner refused. And I was just left out.' The commissioner ruled against her and confirmed the dismissal. She reported that nothing that she had said was in the report. She felt that 'it was obvious that the commissioner took papers from the company and not from me'.

Lesedi's narration of the company hearing emphasizes her invisibility. The process directed her to defend herself as if guilty: 'It was hurting that they maybe think that I took that thing.' Indeed, while the employer did not press criminal charges for the alleged theft (the cold cream cost around R80 or less than US$8), she began her juridical experience with the night in jail. She pursued the legal process in order to assert her capacity to have an effect, to be made visible (to be heard by the commissioner, to have him receive her papers, and to see her name and testimony in the judgment). In order to insert herself into these relations, she followed the rules. She invoked rules of evidence and logics of argument, explaining that she had asked for footage from the closed-circuit security cameras positioned in the changing room. Yet 'no one replies from the company'. In telling me her story, she traced her path through the store from the bakery where she worked, through one security checkpoint, which she passed without incident, to her locker. She appealed to the company, but it did not reply: 'They just said the Ponds was found in the bag, but to check how [it got] there, they were not interested.' Within this routinized procedure, Lesedi was like a ghost. Her intangibility registered in the union's lack of interest (to represent and potentially gain a new member), the state official's disregard, and the company manager's and security guard's disrespect. In response, Lesedi turned forcefully to demand attention from the law that could barely be bothered to hail her. In laying her claim for recognition through the procedural route of the law, Lesedi also invoked a public. In an Arendtian sense, she spoke to solicit an audience that might make its own judgment on her case, and that might restore her sense of her ability to act, rather than be acted upon by the domineering manager, company, and commissioner.

While the advice office prepared Lesedi for legal procedure, it also allowed her to retell her story to an audience. Having told her story to the commissioner who did not record it properly, she retold it to the paralegal who followed her argument, translating and commenting on their mutually agreed upon version of events, and asking for clarification before writing down her words. She then rehearsed it again to me. In the end, while the formality of the law was belied by what she had experienced as regularized personal relations between the state and her employer at the CCMA, the advice office offered her an alternative locus of testament: 'I came here and told my story and to get clarity on what am I to do and how it is going to happen.' As Arendt explained, action in concert takes on political meaning when it is made into a story, which claims public attention. Narrating the dismissal in her own words served to re-signify the events.

Going through the advice office enabled Lesedi to read her experience as common to others. It recognized her as a 'worker', as distinct from the state functionary and her employer, who I think, were coded as white. Shortly after she was fired, she said, the company discovered that the branch manager and security guard had colluded to steal millions in cash and merchandise. Lesedi compared the rumor of that serious theft with her case, offering evidence of her employers' 'corrupt' senior staff as vindication in her own case. Such are the stories of ordinary relation, punishment, and redemption that frame workers' understandings and experiences of labor law. She explained: 'Every worker feels that [my company] has someone inside the CCMA because ... you never win. ... All the workers, they lose.' Through the narrative she found a collective to which she belonged − the workers. Re-inscribing her individualized story as one of collective experience happened through entering the public space offered by the advice office and making her case there.

Lesedi's attempt to contest her dismissal did not redeem her relation to the law in official rooms or hearing chambers. She lost there, and at the same time, she witnessed the unprocedural and the arbitrary. In those spaces, she was called up as object of law, and led through a labyrinth of alienation where no one listened to her, but could decide on her standing to remain an employee. Failing as an 'employee' threw her out of one set of relations where the (arbitrary) employer's prerogative and the erratic attention of state bureaucrats were the rule. She was exhausted, materially of her resources and psychically of her faith in the elusive protections of the state. Her concluding words were: 'If you don't have money in this South Africa, nothing will go right for you.'

Elizabeth Povinelli (2011: 123) points out that exhaustion is not death; exhaustion 'raises the problem of endurance'. And so, this shop assistant learned that such precarious experiences defined commonalities, which themselves constituted what it meant to be a worker. Her attachment, then − what she could hold onto − was this subject, worker, constituted not through the strict interpellation of employment law, but in the everyday relational experience in the gap.

What Lesedi hoped for was for a space of participation defined through being heard, being noted, and being recorded, in short, through the reciprocity involved in the gesture of receipt. In her narration, she exposed the inherent inability of the precarious worker to participate in labor rights −

she became an object of example to confirm true employee-status, a negative subject serving as the limit condition, proof of a 'monstrous intimacy' (Sharpe 2010). In her story, it was immaterial whether she stole the vial of cold cream or not. She never confirmed or denied the accusation. Hers was a tale of a black body used to affirm a self-righteous order, where evidence and logic were denied her. Yet, her attempts at retrieving a legal realm of participation affirmed her solidarity (friendship) with a generic collective of other (black) precarious workers, left without rules, but carrying the same suspicions. The question is whether these pathways inscribed an ongoing 'cruel optimism' in returning to the state, as well as in positing a relation of affinity to other black workers. Indeed, is it the comfort of worker identity as attachment that enabled endurance?

OF PUBLICS: YVETTE & JAMES

Yvette Jiyane was a contract street sweeper for the municipality.[10] The labor broker for whom she worked contracted to provide the service of sweeping and weeding the streets and the sidewalks. She had been working with the contractor since 2009, but there were others who had worked three years longer than her. The street sweepers were mostly women, and men drove the trucks. There was a day shift and a night shift and some only worked on weekends. She reported that she earned R108 per day (less than US$10) and R2 200 per month. Her manager, also black and from Limpopo, pressured her to move more quickly, to clean more streets, and to work in the rain. He swore at them: 'They are using vulgar words. They can even swear with my mother. …When you go and speak to him, he tells us, "You can fuck off and find another job, assebelief [please, in Afrikaans]".'

Her manager pushed them: 'If I know that my street is too long, I must finish quicker so that I can rest. For them there is no time to rest.' She explained: 'I have to move with a broom and a spade, and I have to take all those things, every day. A broom and a shovel every day. So it is very hard. I can't travel with a broom in one hand and a shovel. Like some of the streets are too long. ... I have to go there [to the end of her route] and come back. In one day.' She worked with one other woman, each working opposite sides of the street.

She told me a story of how she was sick one day and resting under a highway overpass along her route. The team came by in the truck, but 'instead of taking me with a truck, they just left me there, instead of knowing I was sick and taking me with a truck to the clinic, seriously, they just left me there'. Her co-worker who was driving the truck would have been suspended if he gave her a lift, she explained. This story prompted a discussion of the several times she had been suspended for several weeks at a time. On three separate occasions in three years, her manager had suspended her for two weeks at a time, according to her, at his whim, with no clear explanation and no procedure. She said: 'When I tried to speak to him, what have I done? "Don't ask me so many questions," and they got in the car and just drive off, leaving me there, suspended. For what?' She was not paid for the period she was not working.

Yvette's income supported her own three children, her mother, and her sister and her sister's two children. Her oldest daughter was attending university and she contributed R500 to her fees. Her youngest was three years old. Her ex-husband did not assist with expenses for his children. Her sister had HIV, and she had been taking ARVs for four years: 'Her health is okay, but the food has to be there every day. She can't take her medicine without food.' Yvette's children lived in Limpopo with her mother, which meant that she had to rent a shack near Tembisa, for which she paid R650, plus R150 for a monthly train ticket to get to work.

The street sweepers joined the municipal workers' union, which organizes public sector workers. The union was hit by the privatization of services in the early 2000s. Workers who became employees of labor brokers have fought since then to be in-sourced as employees of the city, because of vast differences in pay and benefits accorded to public workers (see, for instance, Rees 2011). In contrast to their R2 200 per month, Yvette said that public sector workers earned R6 000. She reported that they had an agreement to be rehired as direct employees of the municipality, and that was why they had decided to join the union. But since joining the union, they had not had a single visit from any representative nor did she think that they actually paid union dues.

After trying for support from the union, the group found a flyer for the advice office and decided to seek its assistance: 'For a long time we are busy trying to find, to join a union, to find help, whatever that comes our way.' The street sweepers used the advice office to assist them with a plan to strike: 'Our demands were a better wage and a better treatment.' Yvette said that they had tried several times to strike, but each time they downed tools, the manager would meet them and agree to an increase. They would return to work, and then, they would get nothing. On their most recent strike, she explained: 'We just … got … tired.' The managers responded by firing a number of workers: 'Even myself, my supervisor just came to me yesterday and told me, "Ah, we heard that you are the one who is organizing the meeting. You are the one who is always in front."… So right now I have to expect a lot of treatment, a lot of bad treatment.'

The labor broker's contract with the municipality expired shortly after I interviewed Yvette, but with pressure from the advice office, the municipality agreed to renew the contract on a monthly basis until it made its decision on the next award. Then in September, the workers went on a protected strike, with the assistance of the advice office, to demand that the labor broker negotiate with the municipality to employ them directly when their service contract expired. Yvette and her co-workers were out on strike for nearly five months, in a fierce fight involving trashing of streets and worker arrests. But, in December, the labor broker lost the contract renewal bid. The strike ended since the workers no longer had an employer against whom to issue a demand. The advice office took the case to the Labor Court to argue that the incoming contractor had to employ the workers from the original labor broker as a continued service contract, as had happened before with the same workers. The judge ruled against the workers. None of them were hired by the new contractor, and Yvette moved back to Limpopo to stay with her mother.

Yvette and her fellow labor broker workers went to the advice office after failing to find help from their union. They wanted legal assistance to negotiate better pay, and perhaps permanent employment with the municipality, as had been promised them. Yvette said: 'From my side I don't care how they treat me, as long as the money suits my expenses.' Yet their struggle was fundamentally for 'better treatment'. Yvette's job wore her down physically, and confronting her manager tired her out. Like Lesedi, she was exhausted. Her actions, though, for a brief moment helped open the hope that they might force re-employment. Here, a 'permanent' job with the city became a symbol of money, and money a sign of her ability to activate her family members – keep her sister alive and her daughter in university (see Comaroff and Comaroff 1987). These calculations bothered her days and nights. The workers resolutely defended their efforts, 'educating' the community of shop owners and consumers along their streets and meeting regularly as a strike committee at the advice office, which served as a public in the making. Until, the strike ended, they lost their court case, and they dispersed.

Yvette's affective energies were directed toward a narrative of how the norms of relationship had broken down. Labor broking was the site of this affective destruction. By contrast full-time employment with the city would restore proper relationships. She would be able to keep alive her family members, both literally in terms of material survival and also as beings in the world. Thus she remained attached to the idea of full-time permanent employment as the place of belonging and mutual sociality. She and her comrades' collective struggles 'appeared' in public (the street), in Arendt's terms, to demand their better treatment. They asserted the figure of the labor broker worker as a legitimate and rights-bearing subject, and in this they found support from the advice office, but not the union. Instead of relying on the union to create this opening, their actions built a new political space of participation. They made their solidarities in the relationships that sustained their case for as long as it lasted. But they lost ultimately. Yvette's narrative focused on two aspects, the loosening of relationships between people like herself – black, and from the same hometown – and her new-found collective, which rejected an order that portrayed them as injured bodies left to sit by the side of the road. That they took to the streets, their territory as street sweepers, is significant. But this new public countered their misrecognition only for as long as they could make a claim for a change in status to become 'employee', through calling up their labor rights. Once the court ruled that as contract workers, they had no claim to employment beyond a limited duration contract, their toehold in this public slipped.

James Phiri was a metal worker at a company that sells steel sheets to engineering factories.[11] He worked full-time as a general laborer. He was dismissed after his employer assaulted him. James explained that the white employer was arguing with a customer who wanted a discount on an order. In the meantime, James and a fellow worker began loading the order. When the boss saw him loading the metal sheeting, he pushed James out of the way and yelled at him. The employer grabbed James by the shirt and hit him in the face. James fought back, and the employer dismissed him.

James immediately began a long and slow process to restore what he viewed as a violation of his rights. He went to the police to counter a claim of assault filed against him by his employer. He lodged an unfair labor practice with the Metal Industry Bargaining Council. As is typical of many stories about the navigation of these dark tunnels of procedure, the employer did not arrive at the first meeting. The arbitration date was set; the employer did not show up again. The bargaining council ruled in favor of the worker. James thought this was a victory. But the employer filed for recission of the award, claiming he did not get the fax notifying him of the meeting. This was granted. James returned to arbitration. The worker eventually won the case (again) and was granted an award for R18 000 (less than US$1 800) in lost wages. He went to the company to claim his award. The company refused to pay. He returned to the bargaining council. The council had to apply to the Labor Court to make the award a court order. He took the court order to the employer, who still refused. He went back to the bargaining council, which sent him back to the Labor Court to get a writ of execution, which he was directed to take to the Sheriff of the Court in Alberton. The Sheriff demanded payment to execute the writ. He had to find the R500 deposit. He waited.

The company started to pay him small amounts of money, 'R2 000 here and R2 000 there'. James returned to the Sheriff, who told him that the company had paid him nearly half the money, and he should consider himself lucky. The Sheriff advised him to drop the matter. The Sheriff said that every time he went to repossess the employer's goods to cover the award, the employer told him the property was not his. The Sheriff said that the employer had told him that James had agreed that he would pay him over time. James returned to the advice center to write a letter to the Sheriff saying there was no such agreement. It had been a year since the award.

The path of travel from Germiston to the bargaining council offices in Sandton, back to Germiston, back to Sandton, to the Sheriff in Alberton, to the advice office, back to the Sheriff, traces James' persistence, and the steady wearing away of energy in the process of defending himself. James had been earning R700 for a five-day week loading orders. He had had a better job as a forklift operator, for which he is qualified, but the company was bought out by a multinational and eventually he had been laid off. His wife was sick, and when I spoke with him, neither of them were working. They have two children. He was untroubled at the prospect of finding another job. He was used to this moving, the steps taken to get from one job to another. In his retelling, the assault and the dismissal did not feature as extraordinary events.

These were moments that simply set him moving again. He was pursuing his case because the award would assist with basic household expenses, and because he insisted on restoring his dignity. He came to the advice office when faced with yet another procedural dead end. In the end he understood the events in terms of the individual personality of his boss and in terms of the bureaucratic dysfunctionality and racist collusion of the state, as when the (white) Sheriff acted to obstruct carrying out his orders against the white employer.

Using the embodied physical and metaphorical idea of 'waiting', Javier Auyero argues that the slow wearing away of energy through engagement with unfriendly, unhelpful, inefficient, and mundanely hostile state officials and institutions is itself a form of domination. Auyero (2012: 19) writes:

> Poor people's waiting ... is inscribed in the mental and bodily dispositions of both dominant (state agencies) and dominated (those who wait), and because of this inscription both groups tend to naturalize or 'eternalize' this relationship of domination. Those that are forced to endure long, routine delays come to see waiting as unavoidable, as a sort of habitual practice that is taken for granted.

While James's waiting, too, felt like a deliberate wearing down, an exhaustion that directly accounted for state domination, his slow trajectory back and forth shows the imbrication of exhaustion and endurance. He went to the advice office to seek assistance with the legal procedure. His story is a stretched-out map of that procedure across the red landscape of Gauteng. While he waited, his slow persistence indicates his own attachments to an idea of dignity restored through the gratification of recompense, but here the receipt, more than the money. His desire for dignity was further translated through his determination to see his case through. While state machinery proved inadequate, it nevertheless designated him as a rights-bearing subject, as employee wrongfully dismissed. Each office along his route plotted his action, but ultimately he enacted this positioning through enduring.

James's waiting was counter-posed to his movement. Unlike Yvette, he held less optimism for the (next) bad job to save him. But, he was more closely interpellated within the subject role of employee. He was neither casual nor contract worker, and he worked in an industry in which an additional layer of agreements had been laid out through the bargaining council. His attachments were not to the job, but to ensuring the implementation of his rights. He quietly yet doggedly claimed his version of the good life in relationships – to state bureaucracy and to individuals along his path – that were reciprocal in the sense that he required response and acknowledgment. He too claimed a new public through the advice office, through refusing to be cast as black laborer intimidated by assault and arrest and through not accepting the dismissive shunting off by his employer, the Sheriff, and the bureaucracy.

His new public was made through traversing these streets linking disembodied institutions to his claim, and through using the law to persist. James's narrative was clear: he asserted his subjectivity as (black) man ill-treated. He claimed a name and a face against the generic black laborer his boss dismissed. And he won his back wages. His future was likely to be more of the same. Yet, in his endurance, his precariousness became a relationship within which he moved. The law was not external to his use of it. For Yvette, the law was an external arbiter. Affectively, James's subdued story offers a determined claim to rights, but in an everyday relational way, which had to be activated. That such a space would need to be maintained infinitely was definitive of precariousness. His subjectivity in a sense became his object of attachment. Dignity was the future he sought to keep him traveling now.

CONCLUSION

This chapter explores a range of affective investments in subject positions and publics defined through and against work and labor rights. Workers claim from their employers and the state because that is where they are born as subjects. They are recognized by law as having some measure of rights and at least proportional access to 'basic conditions'. Law interpellates them as employees and, as we saw, law defends these boundaries through adjudicating subject claims. Yet in subjectification, workers sometimes recall these categories and sometimes shift them in the indeterminacy of turning toward them. They are precarious subjects trying to position themselves within some kind of narrative of normative promise that offers them affective traction now. Reading precariousness in terms of affect and relationship helps to explain such directed yearnings. The fact that workers do tell these stories, do chart their movements around the geographies of rusted roads and hard histories shows how they persist.

Precariousness has been the standard experience of work in capitalism (Mitropoulos 2005; Neilson and Rossiter 2008). When one is precarious, one finds oneself in a condition of 'prayer', appealing with faith to an indistinct higher authority to grant one's desire. If precariousness is a relationship of dependence, of inequality and uncertainty, then these workers' stories show the abiding affect of work as space of stability and belonging, of the promise of state protection, of the comfort of the collective identity (black) worker, in short of the potential of 'friendships'. Thus, Lesedi's re-narrativizing of her case outlines her attempt to be recognized by the law. The failure of reciprocity within this set of relations defied affinity with the state; yet in this experience, Lesedi articulated identification (and solidarity) with the collective category (black) 'worker', now those expelled from this legal terrain. For Yvette, labor broking represented a set of relations that fractured ties. Through her momentary public with other workers striking against it, she reimagined a future that would allow her to persist. That this future depended on interpellation as full-time, permanent employees of the municipality confirmed her attachment to the promise of work with this condition securing mutual relations. Her active working out of these demands with other striking workers affirmed 'friendship' through action in concert, even if only in the moment. James's story of movement and endurance suggests that precariousness was indeed a matter of relationship, and not a state of vulnerability. For him, relation to the law could be constituted through the work of patient insisting at each specific locus. In this plotting, he affirmed both an alternative subject of 'black worker', and that his turns defined futures.

In all three stories, workers appealed for relationships of reciprocity, mutuality and recognition with the state, but were variously disappointed. In the process of both their actions and their re-signifying through the advice center, they articulated the enduring emotive pull of labor rights as a site where relationships could be constituted. Yet, in confirming instead the arbitrary, the limits, the *de facto* of state relations, they differently reinforced the signification of friendship in the sign of 'worker'.

Are these precarious workers' politics a form of 'cruel optimism'? These stories of precarious workers suggest ambiguous conclusions. The goals of inclusion and recognition through the law become worn paths and exhausting pursuits. As Povinelli intuits, endurance pushes us to think about what people do to abide, but when desires wear thin, other questions may surface.

Optimism may, indeed, invigorate attachment to the object of desire (Berlant 2011). In acting based on a future yet to come ('decent work for all'), workers may reproduce orders that can never get them there. As Sharpe (2010: 83) observes, the English court case that determined the free labor contract of Sara Baartman established not 'her freedom so much as the freedom of English subjects to work'. Reaffirming the political subjectivity of black workers may function to return faith in the universal category 'worker' as free subject, when the daily precariousness and dependence of black workers in real time in fact, as South African labor sociology over the past 20 years has repeatedly shown – offers little evidence of the entrance to this Canaan.

Thus, black workers' investment in work as site of subjecthood and agency may reproduce others' (like the democratic state or labor sociologists') desires to believe in worker politics as space of participation. This entanglement may be a 'monstrous intimacy', where 'worker' is granted the status to affirm relationships as an attachment to the idea of a future that is actually ill-hedged. The IAS appears as the starting point, a space of simple hope (aid, advice) on the cusp of democracy and in (my) memory's sweetness. And, still precarious workers endure the living of this not-yet status.

But, as Berlant notes, the 'disturbing encounter with modes of being incomplete, contradictory, and out of control', in other words non-sovereignty or 'precariousness', suggests the importance of 'the scene of living with our self-misrecognition' (Berlant and Edelman 2014: 67). Instead, 'new capacities for bearing, and not repairing, ambivalence' (61) may be born in enervated attachments.

In workers' precariousness we view the channeling of desire and the attachment to a life in which work and relations are ordered and stable, predictable and not uncertain. This faith, workers' persistent attempts to keep going in the world, can be seen as optimism toward the attachment to work and 'worker'. Yet workers' stories do not signify a politics of recognition through their legal claims to a discrete subject 'employee', as much as they enact through the daily rhythms in their regularity, uncertainty, dependency, embodiment, and intimacy, a present politics (tied to a future) where work confirms order and where promises of friendship remain. Recognition from the state and affinity with other workers, then, intertwine to complicate questions of friendship. That work is precarious may begin to exhaust the attachment; it certainly produces a host of ambivalences. We see workers seeking more than the next job or the legislative change, a reciprocation of their energies; a receipt and a response to their moves; a sense that law is as you make it. These precarious workers' narratives point to the ongoing attraction of relationships, indeed friendships that will recognize workers and will bring them into spaces of mutuality. But, in the impossibility of some relationships, enduring ambivalences may be generated through the attempts at new publics and momentary friendships.

REFERENCES

Adler, Glenn and Edward Webster. 2000. *Trade Unions and Democratization in South Africa, 1985–1997*. Basingstoke: MacMillan.

Allison, Anne. 2013. *Precarious Japan*. Durham, NC: Duke University Press.

Arendt, Hannah. 1958. *The Human Condition*. Chicago, IL: University of Chicago Press.

Auyero, Javier. 2012. *Patients of the State: The Politics of Waiting in Argentina*. Durham, NC: Duke University Press.

Barchiesi, Franco. 2011. *Precarious Liberation: Workers, the State and Contested Social Citizenship in Post-Apartheid South Africa*. Pietermaritzburg: University of KwaZulu-Natal Press.

Barchiesi, Franco and Tom Bramble, eds. 2003. *Rethinking the Labor Movement in the 'New South Africa'*. Aldershot: Ashgate.

Barchiesi, Franco and Bridget Kenny. 2002. 'From Workshop to Wasteland: De-Industrialization and Fragmentation of the Black Working Class on the East Rand (South Africa), 1990–1999.' *International Review of Social History* 47: 35–63.

Berlant, Lauren. 2007. 'Nearly Utopian, Nearly Normal: Post-Fordist Affect in La Promesse and Rosetta.' *Public Culture* 19(2): 273–301.

Berlant, Lauren. 2011. *Cruel Optimism*. Durham, NC: Duke University Press.

Berlant, Lauren and Lee Edelman. 2014. *Sex, or the Unbearable*. Durham, NC: Duke University Press.

Bhorat, Haroon. 2004. 'Labour Market Challenges in the Post-Apartheid South Africa.' *South African Journal of Economics* 72(5): 940–977.

Buhlungu, Sakhela. 2010. *A Paradox of Victory: COSATU and the Democratic Transformation in South Africa*. Pietermaritzburg: University of KwaZulu-Natal Press.

Butler, Judith. 2004. *Precarious Life: The Powers of Mourning and Violence*. London & New York: Verso.

Comaroff, John L. and Jean Comaroff. 1987. 'The Madman and the Migrant: Work and Labor in the Historical Consciousness of a South African People.' *American Ethnologist* 14(2): 191–209.

Desai, Ashwin. 2002. *We are the Poors: Community Struggles in Post-Apartheid South Africa*. New York, NY: Monthly Review Press.

Hall, Stuart. 2000. 'Who Needs "Identity"?' In *Identity: A Reader*, edited by P. du Gay, J. Evans and P. Redman, 26. London: Sage.

Haraway, Donna. 1991. *Simians, Cyborgs, and Women: The Reinvention of Nature*. London: Free Association Books.

Honig, Bonnie. 2013. *Antigone, Interrupted*. Cambridge: Cambridge University Press.

Kalleberg, Arne. 2013. *Good Jobs, Bad Jobs: The Rise of Polarized and Precarious Employment Systems in the United States, 1970s–2000s.* New York, NY: Russell Sage Foundation.

Kenny, Bridget. 2007. 'Claiming Workplace Citizenship: "Worker" Legacies, Collective Identities and Divided Loyalties of South African Contingent Retail Workers.' *Qualitative Sociology* 30(4): 481–500.

Kenny, Bridget. 2009. 'Mothers, Extra-Ordinary Labour, and AmaCasual: Law and Politics of Nonstandard Employment in the South African Retail Sector.' *Law & Policy* 31(3): 282-306.

Kenny, Bridget and Edward Webster. 1999. 'Eroding the Core: Flexibility and the Re-Segmentation of the South African Labor Market.' *Critical Sociology* 24(3): 216–243.

Lund, Francie. 2002. 'Social Security and the Changing Labor Market: Access for Non-Standard and Informal Workers in South Africa.' *Social Dynamics* 28(2): 177–206.

Maré, Gerhard. 2014. *Declassified.* Johannesburg: Jacana Media.

Markell, Patchen. 2003. *Bound by Recognition.* Princeton, NJ: Princeton University Press.

Mitropoulos, Angela. 2005. 'Precari-us.' *Republic Art.* Accessed 7 July 2011, http://www. republicart.net/disc/precariat/mitropoulos01_en.htm

Molé, Noelle. 2013. 'Existential Damages: The Injury of Precarity Goes to Court.' *Cultural Anthropology* 28(1): 22–43.

Mosoetsa, Sarah. 2011. *Eating from One Pot: The Dynamics of Survival in Poor South African Households.* Johannesburg: Wits University Press.

Naidoo, Prishani and Ahmed Veriava. 2005. 'Re-Membering Movements: Trade Unions and New Social Movements in Neoliberal South Africa.' In *From Local Processes to Global Forces, Research Report,* vol. 1, edited by the Centre for Civil Society, 27–62. Durban: Centre for Civil Society, University of KwaZulu-Natal.

Neilson, Brett and Ned Rossiter. 2008. 'Precarity as a Political Concept, or, Fordism as Exception.' *Theory, Culture & Society* 25(7–8): 51–72.

Neves, David and Andries du Toit. 2013. 'Rural Livelihoods in South Africa: Complexity, Vulnerability and Differentiation.' *Journal of Agrarian Change* 13(1): 93–115.

Page-Shipp, Bronwyn. 2003. *Agricultural Labor Laws and the Minimum Wage Determination.* Stellenbosch: Women on Farms Project.

Povinelli, Elizabeth A. 2011. *Economies of Abandonment: Social Belonging and Endurance in Late Liberalism.* Durham, NC: Duke University Press.

Rees, Robyn. 2011. *Organising Labor Broker Workers: The Case of Giwusa at AEL and Samwu in Tshwane.* Master's Thesis. University of the Witwatersrand, Johannesburg.

Sharpe, Christina. 2010. *Monstrous Intimacies: Making Post Slavery Subjects.* Durham, NC: Duke University Press.

Standing, Guy. 1999. 'Global Feminization through Flexible Labor: A Theme Revisited.'
   World Development 27(3): 583–602.

Standing, Guy. 2011. *The Precariat: The New Dangerous Class*. London & New York:
   Bloomsbury.

Statistics South Africa. 2014. *Labor Market Dynamics in South Africa, 2013*. Pretoria:
   Statistics South Africa.

Theron, Jan. 2005. 'Employment Is Not What it Used To Be: The Nature and Impact of the
   Restructuring of Work in South Africa.' In *Beyond the Apartheid Workplace*, edited by
   Eddie Webster and Karl von Holdt, 293–316. Pietermaritzburg: University of KwaZulu-
   Natal Press.

Theron, Jan and Shane Godfrey. 2000. *Protecting Workers on the Periphery*. Cape Town:
   Institute of Development and Labor Law, University of Cape Town.

Valodia, Imraan. 2001. 'Economic Policy and Women's Informal Work in South Africa.'
   Development and Change 32(5): 871–892.

Von Holdt, Karl. 2003. *Transition from Below: Forging Trade Unionism and Workplace
   Change in South Africa*. Pietermaritzburg: University of KwaZulu-Natal Press.

Vosko, Leah F., Martha MacDonald and Iain Campbell, eds. 2009. *Gender and the Contours
   of Precarious Employment*. London & New York: Routledge.

Webster, Edward. 2006. 'Trade Unions and the Challenge of the Informalization of Work.'
   In *Trade Unions and Democracy: COSATU Workers' Political Attitudes in South Africa*,
   edited by Sakhela Buhlungu, 22–43. Pretoria: HSRC Press.

Webster, Edward. 2011. '"The Wages Are Low but They Are Better Than Nothing": The
   Dilemma of Decent Work and Job Creation in South Africa.' In *The New South African
   Review 2*, edited by Devan Pillay, John Daniel, Prishani Naidoo, and Roger Southall.
   Johannesburg: Wits University Press.

Webster, Edward, Rob Lambert and Andries Bezuidenhout. 2008. *Grounding
   Globalization: Labor in the Age of Insecurity*. Oxford: Blackwell.

Webster, Edward and Karl von Holdt, eds. 2005. *Beyond the Apartheid Workplace:
   Studies in Transition*. Pietermaritzburg: University of KwaZulu-Natal Press.

NOTES

1   I was the Chair of the Board of the CWAO from its inception in 2011 to 2014. In 2012
      I interviewed workers about their reasons for coming to the advice office. I thank
      the workers for their time and generous reflections. I also want to thank Ighsaan
      Schroeder for facilitating these interviews, as well as for his amiable willingness to
      discuss my research. I benefitted from his input and reading of a draft of this chapter.

I also want to thank Deirdre Mullan for assistance with CWAO case statistics. Earlier drafts of this chapter were delivered at two workshops: the SWOP colloquium 'Precarious Society', September 4–5, 2012, at Wits University; and 'Contentious Politics, Capitalism, and Social Movement Theory: South Africa in Global Perspective', May 22, 2014, organized by the South African Research Chair in Social Change, University of Johannesburg. I thank the organizers and participants of these events for feedback, and particularly Karl von Holdt for his engagement and encouragement. All interpretations and errors remain my responsibility.

2   Within South African labor sociology, there has been extensive debate about the effectiveness and the institutional capacity of the trade union movement over this period (Adler and Webster 2000; Barchiesi and Bramble 2003; Buhlungu 2010; Desai 2002; Naidoo and Veriava 2005; Von Holdt 2003; Webster 2006; Webster 2011; Webster et al. 2008; Webster and Von Holdt 2005). Increases in joblessness, informality and precarious work have been well documented (Bhorat 2004; Kenny 2007; Kenny and Webster 1999; Lund 2002; Mosoetsa 2011; Neves and Du Toit 2013; Theron and Godfrey 2000; Valodia 2001). The unemployment rate remains, even by official definitions, hovering around 25% (Statistics South Africa 2014). The official unemployment rate excludes discouraged work seekers.

3   While at the IAS, I assisted with setting up a national advice office network and training paralegals, as well as participating in organizational discussions aimed at drafting policy positions to formalize the support provided by paralegals and advice offices within an emergent democratic labor dispensation. These discussions took place as the post-apartheid state's first Labor Relations Act (LRA) was being negotiated and promulgated. In the end, the LRA excluded paralegals from representing workers (only lawyers, unions and fellow workers were designated as representatives of workers in hearings or at the CCMA). This was a blow to advice offices and a change that the drafters of the LRA had not intended, according to communication with the IAS at the time from Halton Cheadle, key drafter of the LRA and labor law practitioner. It was a change that indicates the extent to which voice regulation through unions was the presumed model of participation in the industrial relations system.

4   Indeed, the issues brought by workers to the CWAO focus on basic matters that could easily fall under a shop floor union servicing role: underpayment or nonpayment of wages, including illegal deductions; not being registered for the Unemployment Insurance Fund; nonpayment of provident fund deductions; unfair dismissals. At the time of fieldwork, Cosatu (Congress of South African Trade Union) had launched a

research project to investigate the role of advice offices as a potential tool to extend representational rights to precarious workers.

5   http://www.merriam-webster.com/dictionary/precarious, accessed 3 September 2012.

6   Or, to put it another way, 'when it will all have come to have been', to use the future anterior tense, as discussed in Elizabeth Povinelli's (2011: 1–46) brilliant discussion of Ursula Le Guin's story, 'The Ones Who Walk Away from Omelas'.

7   Case data presented from statistical dataset given to me by the CWAO on April 25, 2014.

8   I follow the practice in South Africa of referring to 'black' as inclusively all those subjugated to oppression for their 'race' under apartheid. Official census classification maintains the following categories: Black-African, Coloured, Indian, and White. For a critique of post-apartheid ongoing racial classification, see Maré 2014.

9   Interview with Lesedi Mogotsi (a pseudonym), conducted by Bridget Kenny, August 23, 2012. Germiston, CWAO offices.

10 Interview with Yvette Jiyane (a pseudonym), conducted by Bridget Kenny, August 23, 2012. Germiston, CWAO offices.

11 Interview with James Phiri, conducted by Bridget Kenny, August 23, 2012. Germiston, CWAO offices.

8

'A SONG OF SEEING':
ART AND FRIENDSHIP UNDER APARTHEID

DANIEL MAGAZINER

I n retrospect, it was clear that his time at Ndaleni had been special. Abednego Dlamini was a student at the South African government's school for the training of African art teachers for two years, 1959 and 1960. He had come to Ndaleni after completing a teacher-training program at Mapumulo, where he had excelled in art and earned a recommendation that he pursue a specialist art teacher's course. At Ndaleni, Dlamini sculpted wood and studied art history; he developed a close relationship with his fellow students and their instructor, a white South African named Peter Bell. From Bell, Dlamini learned the technique of mixing bees' wax with oil paint to ensure that his murals could endure the elements. Before leaving campus at the end of 1960, Dlamini erected a ladder in a covered breezeway and painted a riotously colored depiction of life at the Ndaleni art school. Four students tend to the wood-burning kiln in which art students fired their clay creations; behind them, a painter looks away from his easel to observe their labors. He is painting a landscape: a tree, a curved road, an open field. Moving left, the figures become indistinct. There are more than a dozen of them, swirling with energy: students read, they chat together, smiling, arms companionably draped over shoulders. They shake out large pieces of fabric (perhaps for batik?) and bend at work over a lathe. There are flowers, a blue sky, hills, and trees.

Twenty years later, Dlamini remembered his mural: 'On entering the corridors you will observe long strips of mural painting, shimmering with harmonious and contrasting shades of colors in oils and beeswax. The medium of oil and beeswax was used by students under Mr Peter Bell.' He was wistful. To think about Ndaleni was to be 'revived artistically [by] the beauties my mind can carry and remember'.[1] The impetus for Dlamini's remembrance was the apartheid government's decision to close the Ndaleni Art School in 1982. But in truth, he had long yearned for Ndaleni. Almost immediately after leaving the school at the end of 1960, he had begun to juxtapose his experiences there with the realities of life as an art teacher, artist, and black South African in the middle of the twentieth century. He had admitted to Peter Bell he was having some trouble 'outside'. 'Outside' meant away from Ndaleni, beyond the hill that divided the mission property from the white-owned fields, pastures, and the white town of Richmond beyond. Outside, although 'one desires to carve and paint as much as possible … the conditions are not favourable'.[2]

A few more months passed. Dlamini failed to find work as an art teacher, then failed to secure work of any sort. His laments grew more lyrical as he bemoaned 'torturous, thorny scenery of this outside world which we are traversing under shadows of sorry and hard labor'.[3] In 1963 Bell left Ndaleni and Dlamini's old art instructor from Mapumulo, Lorna Peirson, took over. Almost immediately she became the beneficiary of his nostalgic juxtaposition of his time at Ndaleni with the realities of life beyond. To her he bemoaned the 'outside life's … cold hands' compared to the warmth he had found on campus. He was increasingly grateful that the art school had provided at least a temporary respite from 'reality'. He continued to write, to complain, to reminisce, to update: two or three letters a year, for nearly two decades.[4]

In this, Abednego Dlamini was not alone. Between 1952 and 1981, many hundreds of Africans from across the country spent at least a year at Ndaleni, which was housed in an old Wesleyan mission near Richmond in the KwaZulu-Natal midlands, ostensibly to be trained to teach the arts and crafts components of the Bantu Education syllabus. Students earned bursaries to cover their travel and residence at the school. In exchange, they contracted to teach for the Department of Bantu Education upon completing their specialist arts and crafts teachers' certificate. Teachers flowed out of Ndaleni. As they negotiated the demands of teaching art under Bantu Education, letters, by the hundreds, flowed back. As a whole, this correspondence defined the apartheid government's art school as place apart from South Africa, a place of expression, fellow-feeling, and friendship.[5]

The relationships revealed in these letters force us to consider the politics of friendship under apartheid in a number of different ways. The letters drip with emotion and affection. They insist on intimacy between representatives of dramatically unequal communities. Moreover, their authors attest that this intimacy was founded at an unlikely locale: a Bantu Education training college. The Ndaleni training college was a multiracial space and the affection between Dlamini and Peirson was a friendship between races. This intimacy belies scholarship such as that of Thomas Blom Hansen (2012), which claims that friendship was a by-product only of the racially confined, private spaces that evaded apartheid's politics of visibility. Indeed, where scholars have invoked intimacy under apartheid, it has been in the sorts of places that Blom Hansen considers the kitchen table, the home, the affectionately recalled township. Such nostalgia has generated controversy (Blom Hansen 2012; Dlamini 2009; Lewin 2011). Ndaleni and its correspondents inhabit a different conceptual terrain.

Yet it also would be a mistake to see in Ndaleni the story of the endurance of a certain kind of multiracial liberalism, in which members of unequal communities are made to stand in for the possibilities of a solidarity that apartheid forestalled. Such reminiscence (and occasional scholarship) relies on the language of exception. From limited evidence of cooperation and interpersonal intercourse, memoirists and others want to suggest that all would have been well in South Africa had racialist politics not done so much damage. There is a danger in overdetermining the interactions of white and black as rehearsals for a non-racial future yet to come. For interactions and even friendships between white and black South Africans, as with those among black South Africans themselves, were only rarely constituted by shared ideas about the future. Scholars who consider the later twentieth century have too commonly relegated intimacy to the zone of the overtly political, as if the only kind of love possible was revolutionary love, the only sort of friendship that of comrades, and the only betrayals those of confederate by confederate (Dlamini 2015; Lewin 2011). What of different sorts of confederacies, fashioned not in the racial enclave, but by transgressing the boundaries between race and location? What of confederacies born not in the choice of whether to conform, collaborate, or to rebel, but instead, in the choice to subject oneself to the wholly different authority that was art?

Ndaleni reveals how community is constructed in affection not exclusively for people but also for a system, a discipline, a possibility of subjectivation different from those on which the apartheid government insisted. Intimacy has been seen as the by-product of subjecting the self to regimes of control, as scholarship on subjects ranging from sexuality, Pentecostalism, scouting, the military, consumerism, and nationalism have argued (among other works, Cohen 2003; MacLeish 2013; Marshall 2009; Moodie 1994; Parsons 2004; Schatzberg 2001). Ndaleni offered the prospect of a community life that revolved around the exchange of creative work for time and Bantu Education employment for possibility. It was a community that shared a vocabulary of art and creativity, and chafed against those outsiders who did not appreciate values the community understood to be self-evident. It was a community of honest emotion, support, and friendship, even between the races, even during moments of sharp division.

Friendships between students and teachers were subject to the authority of a time and place. Lorna Peirson wrote frequently of her hopes that the community would 'continue to be united in interests both personal and professional'. They were, in her words, a 'family'. As we shall see, many of her students felt the same. Yet the conditions of that community's existence and the fact of its end, must determine what we make of such claims to be kin. There have been many ostensible 'communities' in twentieth-century history; some were art schools that overlapped with Ndaleni, such as the Polly Street Art Centre in central Johannesburg, and Rorke's Drift, relatively nearby in the midlands. But when students and teachers at places such as Black Mountain College in the United States claimed to be 'like a family' (Duberman 2009), it resonated differently than in South Africa, where kinship has long been subject to the vicissitudes of the local political economy (Hunter 2011). For many who were subject to apartheid law and impoverished by apartheid economics, art school represented not a place of freedom and exploration, but the possibility of subjection and belonging. To claim membership of this multiracial family was, in James Ferguson's (2015: 162–163) phrase, to declare one's 'aspiration to dependence'. It was to be subject to hierarchies of race, politics, and station and thus to claim a home. It was not easy and as the school's place within the dynamics of apartheid changed, the community could not last. By the late 1970s, it was apparent that the department planned to close Ndaleni, and the tone of the letters turned elegiac. Peirson hoped the family would stay intact, united in their subservience to the apartheid education system, under the sign of art education and through their connection to an old mission station. Her hopes were largely unfulfilled.[6]

Lorna Peirson was the fourth dedicated art teacher at Ndaleni. The first was a young English woman named Anne Harrison who taught art as a subject (as opposed to an entire course) to training college students from 1949 to 1951. Harrison was a London-trained art teacher who had come to South Africa seeking adventure in the years after World War II. She offered her services first to the Cape Education Department and then to the Transvaal before taking the specialist art teacher position at the Indaleni Training College, then under the authority of the Natal provincial government.[7]

Harrison's stay in South Africa was brief, but her ideas laid the foundation for the art program to come, especially the syllabus, which she modeled on the Bauhaus' famed *vorkurs*. The pedagogical style that she prescribed was even more vital. Harrison had apparently spent some time apprenticed to a circus before coming to South Africa. In her imagination, the art room was like the 'ring', 'no matter what personal problems [circus performers] had, emotional or physical, these were forgotten as they entered the brightly lit circle'. Both the circus ring and the art room were spaces within and yet apart from the rest of the world. Drawing on the legendary Bauhaus instructor Joseph Itten, she sought to create an atmosphere of 'dynamic-relaxation' in her classroom a mellow, friendly mood conducive to creating and sharply contrasted to the strict discipline that marked the rest of the mission.[8] The logic here, as at Bauhaus, was clear: through specific pedagogic interventions and practices, teachers would promote certain subjectivities. The free, creative expression of engaged, creative selves was to be produced by institutions.

This was sharply distinct from South African practice. Free inquiry and experimentation were never particularly valued and by the 1940s and 1950s, the state's evolving doctrine of 'Christian National Education' embraced the principles of so-called 'fundamental pedagogics' against the supposedly child-centered styles of progressive educationists in the west (Enslin 1984; Gardiner

2014; Msila 2007).[9] Fundamental pedagogics took a rather dim view of the internal life of the child. In some literature (Ensin 1984), pedagogues actually referred to children as non-adults, incomplete beings who needed teachers to fill them with the knowledge necessary to their future function in society. It is easy to see why apartheid race theorists embraced such ideas, and how Harrison's ideas about an open, dynamic classroom were a departure. Yet at the same time, Harrison remained a teacher. Her faith in institutional capacity to effect and promote affect was thus of the same order as the apartheid government's trust in the assumption that Bantu Education would promote obedient and compliant South African political subjects. In Harrison's ideas about art education we see a tension that was to structure the experiences of those teachers and students who came after her. She was a true believer in the expressive potential of individuals who were shaped by proper institutions. No less than Bantu Education and apartheid, the art school depended on a set of institutionalized practices for survival and legitimacy. Unlike Bantu Education, art education's institutions were a structure on which friendships and affection between teachers and students could be built.

It is important to note that Harrison's ideas were not hers alone. Well before her arrival in South Africa, arts and crafts teachers in African schools had suggested that normal pedagogical practices ought not to apply in their classrooms. 'Every child has within him a creative impulse which welcomes the opportunity of expression', the Natal provincial teachers' journal instructed in 1933. 'To stifle it is to harm the child.' Later that year, a Natal teacher named O. J. Horrax expounded on the correct teaching of art at greater length. Horrax (1934) urged all schools to embrace the one hour per day that the provincial syllabus dedicated to arts and crafts, and 'during this period pupils should be allowed to do any form of creative work they like'. Horrax understood that teachers should be in a position to 'impose' certain behaviors in the classroom, while also counseling a touch light enough to promote a sense of 'freedom'; in other words, authority remained, but it was to be lightly worn. Successive Ndaleni art teachers followed these precedents. After Harrison left South Africa, the art program's first two instructors were Englishmen, about whose pedagogical practices the archive reveals very little. Neither worked from a syllabus; both insisted on students cultivating individual expression. The second of these Englishman 'vanished' early in 1960, and was replaced by Peter Bell, who had been teaching art in the wider training college. Bell stayed at Ndaleni for almost three years, instructing people like Abednego Dlamini, and we know a good deal more about him.

Bell's successor, Lorna Peirson, reports being awed by the 'inspiration' Bell had provided for his students. His politics were part of this; he was an outspoken opponent of apartheid whose attendance at rallies and protests hastened his departure from South Africa in 1963. Yet more than his politics, the archive suggests that it was his faith that the school was a ring where different rules applied, that fostered students' affection for him.[10] From the outset, Bell wanted his students to understand that art school was about their experiences of creativity and joy, not the demands of the Bantu Education syllabus.[11] Bell promoted certain experiences that he trusted would result in the kinds of new subjectivities the 'ring' was intended to develop. Students' first days on campus were spent clambering through a forest owned by a local timber farmer, with whom Bell had established a relationship. Ndaleni art students were overwhelmingly township residents, largely from what was then the Transvaal province. In the forest, they were encouraged to smell the air, 'and generally to absorb the feelings of huge trees pushing their way to the sky. For most of them, it is a completely new experience.' Having introduced his students to trees in their natural habitat, Bell then began to teach. 'We return to the saw-mill, where from among the odd-shaped pieces of timber the mill cannot make use of – root-balls, forks, crooked stems, etc. – they choose the pieces they find interesting. These we bring back to the art school, where they set to work. I make no effort to influence them in the choice of subject.' This was the first day of art school, summer 1961.[12]

The lack of overt instruction was telling. Like Horrax, Bell believed that students ought to make up their own minds as to how they spent their time in the studios. This was an unconventional practice in many ways. Bell was a graduate of the Michaelis School of Art in Cape Town and in the early 1960s he frequently regaled his instructors there with accounts of his students' work. On one occasion his sculptor instructor, Ivan Mitford-Barberton advised Bell to have his students make masks, reasoning that this was a 'traditional style' for African art (notwithstanding the lack of a mask-making tradition in South Africa). Bell demurred: 'The fact that they don't [make masks] would suggest that they are not intended to do so. It would be phony if they did.'[13] Instead, Bell gathered what materials he had available and gave his students a free hand. At first glance, Bell's 'free' pedagogy evoked that of other South African art teachers, such as Cecil Skotnes, founder of and teacher at Polly Street during the 1950s and 1960s. At Polly Street and elsewhere, instructors refused to expose their African students to explicit instruction, lest European manners distort their 'authentic' African expression. Unlike Bell's practices, such pedagogy was strict control disguised as freedom. Bell, on the other hand, wanted to promote certain sorts of free-thinking subjects, not racially delimited artists, and for the freedoms he granted, his students felt tremendous affection for him. He has 'dedicated his life towards the betterment of needy and frustrated people', one student wrote.[14]

It was through such practices and experiences that Abednego Dlamini came to love his school. As South Africa raged in the weeks after Sharpeville, Dlamini ascended his ladder and began to paint the walls of the training college breezeway. He worked back to back with Hamlet Hobe, another student whose mural captured the joyous experience of being at Ndaleni. Spread across two wall panels, the right shows a typical Saturday night at the training college. Students are gathered in the hall, watching a movie that a teacher is projecting. The left panel is more pertinent. In it, Hobe zeroes in the art school's small building, which students in the mid-1950s painted in a dramatic array of lines and colors. Outside, a student shapes a fantastic statue from cement. No authority figure is evident. Hobe fades away the walls of the art studio to reveal what is happening inside. There, a handful of art students stand at easels, paintbrushes poised, painting from a model (another art student?) who sits at the front of the room. Beyond him, Bell leans against the blackboard. No one looks at him and his arms are crossed, his mouth closed. Art education was about 'the joy of the beauty that all can possess for the effort to find and see it', Hobe reflected soon after leaving the school. The mural that he left behind attested to this.

Dlamini and Hobe left at the end of 1960. They kept in touch with each other and their school over the course of the next couple of years, during which time both had difficulty finding work.[15] Hobe's name gradually fades from the Ndaleni archive; he resurfaces in the late 1970s, when he writes to ask for a replacement specialist teacher's certificate. Dlamini continued to write, to ask about the school and its students, and to express his longing to be 'one of the art scholars again'.[16] The peculiar rhythms of the ring went on in his absence. Between 1961 and 1963, students erected a riotously colored entrance way to the women's hostel, comprised of mosaics they had assembled from broken crockery and other waste. Other students executed extensive murals on the inner walls of the hall in which training college students took their meals. These tended either to display fantastic scenes of rivers, glades, and wildlife, or, like Dlamini's and Hobe's, the no less fantastic experience of life in and around the art school.

So things continued until midway through 1963, when Peter Bell's run-in with a local National Party official prompted him to decamp from South Africa. Dlamini's former art instructor, Lorna Peirson, was immediately given the position and found herself confronted by Bell's legacy. In lieu of practice teaching and mastering the various mediums for which the Bantu Education syllabus called, Bell had emphasized students' innate capacity to create with only his minimal intervention of providing materials. Students focused on fashioning one major piece of their own design during their time on campus, such as the murals, the mosaics, or the monumental cement and wire statue that Hobe depicted. There was little discipline. Students were granted latitude to spend their free time in nearby Richmond and the local Zulu reserves. Peirson gradually phased out both practices. By 1965, she had developed a syllabus that covered the whole of the Bantu Education arts and crafts curriculum. Additionally, she responded to a generalized lack of discipline by subjecting her students to the regime of the wider training college.[17]

In spite of these changes, art school remained a unique experience. Students were subject to the hostels' rules and regulations, but they earned important privileges in time and, through the labor of their bodies, in sensation. They followed a different schedule than did their hostel-mates in the training college. Classes generally ran from 8.30am until just after 2pm, when students would eat their main meal of the day. Peirson ignored this schedule. 'We never listened to the bells ringing down there; we had our own timetable.'[18] Art students attended lectures in the morning and then had a short break that fell in the interlude between breakfast and the training college students' afternoon meal. This was not ideal, but it was a privilege they alone could ignore the bell's call during the week. Life was both tremendously restricted and wonderfully free.[19]

Even though Peirson changed the syllabus, much remained the same. Students arrived on campus anxious and were immediately confronted with an unfamiliar pedagogy. On Solomon Baloyi's first day in 1976, Peirson showed him and his classmates a pile of wood. Or at least, he thought it was a pile of wood, until she revealed that these were, in fact, sculptures. 'This is a sculpture,' she said, handling a particular piece; their task was to find the piece that suited them and to reveal it. She did not provide much additional instruction.[20] Reflecting on her experiences seven years earlier, Pat Khoza remembers that Peirson typically assumed Bell's preferred stance: leaning against the walls, arms crossed, saying little. 'Hm, oh, look, carry on … Ok, thank you, I think we're all working very hard and very well now.' Students continued to work, chatting, experimenting, exploring, while she watched, walked around, and left.[21] As she saw it, her job was to offer materials, to 'push a button', and let things happen.[22]

Peirson's ledger was fairly transparent: on one side were listed her trips to Pretoria to attend syllabus meetings, on the other the marvel of introducing class after class to art. Her students remember her as a laconic, quiet person, even-tempered and not outwardly emotional. She describes herself as having a classic, 'English stiff upper lip' temperament.[23] She did not share much of herself with her students. But the archive suggests that what she did offer mattered tremendously in binding her students to each other and to her. The ring extended beyond the studio to take in students' expanding sense of their selves and their capacity while at art school. Peirson was an avid hiker and she secured special permission for the 1964 class to visit Giant's Castle in the Drakensberg to view cave paintings. The dividends went beyond the encounter with art history. 'You get up there and there's a difference and there's a lightening, and you start to laugh at nothing,' she recalls.[24] To visit the mountains was to extend the freedom of the studio beyond campus. It was to live less restrictively, more vitally, and thus to cultivate the joy that pedagogical theories placed at the heart of creating.[25]

Trips to Durban were even more frequent. Across the 1960s and 1970s that city's art gallery hosted national competitions, as well as touring exhibitions, and it became an annual tradition for students to pile into a rented bus and make their way to town. The gallery was only part of the visit, however; students spent of the rest of the day at their leisure, visiting tourist sites such as the Ocean Terminal, taking advantage of the opportunity to eat something other than the hostels' typically mediocre fare and, of course, going for a swim. Many were from the dry, high Transvaal, and, eagerly or cautiously, 'immersed themselves in salt water for the first time'.[26] Some took to the water, some did not, but all were struck by the experience. Early on Peirson had decided that swimming was as much a part of the trip as was the visit to the art gallery that was the ostensible justification for the journey. 'We make it compulsory,' her co-teacher, Craig Lancaster, later explained.[27] Being made to swim was of a part with clambering over streams and trying to see the sculpture in the log: it was about increasing students' sense of themselves and their capacities. A 1971 student summarized a trip to Durban: 'It was a song of seeing the sea and swimming or bathing in waters our parents never did and some will never do so.'[28]

Ndaleni students were preparing to become teachers; they thus observed with interest the pedagogy of their own instructors. By taking them to the beach and making them swim, Lancaster and Peirson 'tell us indirectly what to do with our own children [students]', Manasseh Nkole concluded. Education was about 'interest and value, as well as recreation'. That sort of education was what one got for enduring long journeys and government restrictions. He was grateful to 'Art, [which] gives you the opportunity. I am most happy … recalling the joy I experienced in Durban'.[29] It is worth pausing to reflect on this exchange. From Peirson, Nkole learned the value of the authority to demand that students do certain things that were seemingly outside the purview of art education as a pedagogical practice. Yet Nkole recognized that he was actually being taught through such experiences: first, how to open himself to the novel and unknown, and second, how to promote that same imagination in his own, hypothetical students.

Students were encouraged to take their instructors as models of their own future selves. These exchanges – authority for imagination, restriction for freedom – were also how they came to understand their personal relationships with their teachers. For many, Peirson came to figure as an ally, someone to whom students could turn and whom they trusted. After 1976, many students came to Ndaleni from politically volatile townships and schools. Of her classmates in 1978, the Soweto-resident Daphne Biyela remembers: 'We carried a lot of baggage with us to campus.' They had come in the wake of the government's brutal crackdown on black political organizations and the murder of Steve Biko. She remembers talking about these things while working in the studio at night. Biyela had been teaching in Soweto during the protests and was overwhelmed by the violence there. As it had been for Hobe, Dlamini and so many others, Ndaleni was an 'escape', both in terms of its physical distance from major centers, and in the community of like-minded souls that found their way to the hill. Biyela's Ndaleni was an emotional community, a place where people played guitar and sang, where they shared the common 'craziness' of self-expression: 'All those crazy people would fight one minute [and then] the next we would be laughing. And we'd be thinking about what we left behind.'[30]

Like many of her classmates, Biyela had been conscientized by events beyond the mission. She challenged the hostel's disciplinary regime. She boasted a modest Afro, which drew the ire of the hostel matrons. She brought a record-player from Johannesburg and played music in the hostel and the studio. She probed the boundaries of the art school's authority and at one point she was threatened with expulsion. The principal and matron called Peirson to campus; the latter drove in and, as Biyela remembers, 'told them where to get off'. These were her students and her school, and Biyela and her record-player stayed.[31]

As Biyela's account indicates, Peirson did not live on campus during her time at Ndaleni, choosing instead to live in a little cottage in the small, white farming town of Richmond. She would occasionally take students with her to town to buy a little extra food, or just to have a walk around; on some occasions, she supplemented their meager government bursaries in return for their help doing odd jobs, painting and otherwise fixing up her house. These were small moves, marked with the power dynamics that structured South Africa beyond the art school. There is no evidence that she broke bread with her students when she went home to her cottage for lunch. Unlike Bell, she never went public with her opinions about current events. She remembers walking and talking with a colleague in the late 1950s, a period when many teachers were abandoning the profession rather than accede to Bantu Education. 'Everybody had to make [a] decision,' she relates, and 'a lot of people left.' She chose to stay on, because she believed in education and wanted to continue teaching.[32]

There was little solidarity with broader societal struggles, but there was affection and, over time, community. Peirson was as much a product of her times as were her students; she believed that as a teacher and an elder her position demanded that she remain at a remove, even as she did what she could to enrich their time at art school. Today, she acknowledges that her attitude was 'European, paternalistic, and colonial' to a certain extent. In the past, no matter what sort of pedagogy she employed, she understood herself to be a teacher, and in twentieth-century South Africa, that by and large implied some degree of distance. She reflects that it took a long time for her to feel comfortable telling students her Christian name. '... I was that reserved.' She doubts whether the intensity of her time with her students ever transcended the 'gap' between black and white.[33]

Yet many of her students seemed to feel that real, if limited friendships were a by-product of art school. As suggested at the outset of this chapter, a significant portion of the Ndaleni school archive is retrospective and nostalgic, comprised of correspondence and newsletters that former students circulated after they left the school. Students were keenly aware that art school was different from life beyond. 'I am aware of the fact that I owe you some gratitude ... for what you did for me,' Enoch Malolo wrote to Peirson in 1974.[34] Jessie Muthige thanked her for helping him to turn 'a new leaf in a big way'.[35] Many credited her for whatever success they had achieved in art. In 1966, a former student named Thelma Radebe reported that she had met Bill Ainslie, a Johannesburg artist and teacher. 'I am really in heaven,' Radebe glowed, because 'he has been a great help ... and just taken on my side Miss Peirson's place.'[36] Students thanked her for art-specific knowledge and also for the less obvious, but no less indispensable, self-knowledge. 'Today I am a man who is able to face many difficulties with great patience and hope just because of you, mother,' Michael Ncamane wrote in 1965.[37]

Ncamane's recourse to the language of kinship was telling. Most students did not have experience of interracial friendship, so they tended to imagine their relationship with the older and female Peirson in terms of an admired mother or aunt. To many, she was MaPeirson, and as such was invited to a stream of weddings, baptisms, and anniversary celebrations. Abednego Dlamini met his future wife while studying at Ndaleni; at his wife's urging, he painted a portrait of her and dispatched it to Peirson. In 1964 he celebrated his anniversary at home on the South Coast and encouraged Peirson to attend. There would be chicken, he wrote, and 'I have long wanted to give you a fowl'.[38] Abiah Ramadi lived much further away, near Pretoria. He did not invite Peirson to his wedding, but he did credit her for helping him to generate the confidence start a family. 'Artistic progress of my life may be your main interest, but ... there are certain progresses [that] you should know about, which also signal [the] fruitfulness of your efforts,' he told her. 'I am married to a certain Evelyn. She is not an artist but shares my artistic interests … she is going to serve as a greatest source of inspiration.'[39] Philemon Kutumela took things a step further. In 1976 Kutumela joyfully announced the birth of his daughter, and hailed Peirson as an ancestor: 'She is named LORNA in memory of you Madam.' He asked that his community join with him to wish 'Miss Lorna Kutumela a long and happy life and may she soon enter the scribbling stage!'[40]

Such invitations most likely transgressed Peirson's sense of her position as a teacher. As far as I can tell, she never attended a wedding or a baptism, nor did she see Abednego Dlamini again after he visited campus briefly in 1968. Yet he continued to write to her to proclaim his affection, as did many others, while she quietly did the work necessary to maintain their community.[41]

Through correspondence and the school newsletter, Ndaleni students and teachers struggled to expand the ring beyond campus. They frequently came together to try to recreate the synergy of the Ndaleni experience. Former Bell students started a group that they called 'The Art Club', which met near Johannesburg a few times in the early 1960s. They were few, so it behooved art students to come together to 'preach the Art Gospel among the gentiles'.[42] Later that decade, Thelma Radebe and other Soweto-based alumni formed a club that they called the 'Arttra Studio' early in 1967. The window dresser Ezekiel Mabusela was among the eight graduates who met to paint and draw with materials donated by Ainslie.[43] 'We … thought it a waste for you to have taught us this wonderful and exciting art and for us to waste it by not doing anything to improve it,' Radebe related to Peirson. The group met many times a week for a few months, until someone stole most of their paints. Such setbacks notwithstanding, a year later they were still there, although reduced to meeting only on occasional weekends, as busy lives demanded.[44]

It was hard to make it as an artist, or as an art teacher, with or without the community's help. Samson Mahlobo had studied with Peter Bell in the early 1960s. In 1962, he completed an expansive mural that crowned one of the doors to the training college hall; like Hobe and Dlamini, his subject was the art school students in riotously mismatched clothes, virtually dancing with the wood they were collecting from the timber fields. He tried over the course of the 1960s to make it as both a teacher and an artist, with scant success. In 1963, he had told a reporter for the *Golden City Post* that he thought he 'might die' if he did not make it as an artist.[45] By the end of the 1960s, he apparently could no longer bear the strain of failing to do so and he killed himself.[46] His death was a blow. 'I didn't know he was so unhappy,' Hilda Mohlopi reflected, 'his letters showed a happy-go lucky person with a lot of humor.' She had never met him in person they were 'pen-pals through *ARTTRA*' but she had identified with his struggles across the 1960s. He had lived in her imagination, she wrote. 'I'll miss him.'[47]

Mahlopi's response to Mahlobo's death demonstrated that, given the challenges of living, the artful life was one best lived together. This is why Sophie Nsuza wrote so many letters to Lorna Peirson, even as her own art practice faded away. Over the course of the 1960s and 1970s, Nsuza and Peirson developed a uniquely strong bond, even though the former had actually studied with Peter Bell. Nsuza was from a poor family in Mahlabatini, who had come to Ndaleni as a much older student.[48] She completed her certificate and was briefly the first female graduate to teach art in a training college, before being recalled to her rural home to help run her family's small shop. Solidarities of gender and age lent a certain tone to her correspondence with Peirson; she called her 'Nkosazana', but also 'Lorna', or simply, 'my dear'.[49]

Nsuza was sure that Peirson was her friend and told her as much; the quality of their exchange made it unquestionable. Nsuza desperately wanted to keep creating and teaching, even as she ran the family business, and Peirson advised her to begin to instruct the local children in the rudiments of sculpture. This assuaged Nsuza for a while, but she was plagued with self-doubt and worried constantly that she was not following the right path. 'In my mind I have quite a number of problems to solve but I need your help,' she wrote in 1970, 'what worries me is that people in Zululand take me to be a great artist but I fear that I am far from that.'[50] She wanted to study more to equal the reputation she had earned, yet her business got in the way. Her letters were frank and emotionally honest: 'Crying over spilt milk doesn't help except bringing tears to the person who is dreaming about better education in Art.' She was one of Peirson's most dedicated correspondents, as if compensating for her isolation by attempting to reconnect her current self to her former life as an art student. 'Oh, my dear, I can write until I finish the whole pad when I think of what I am,' she lamented.[51] Still, she went on living. She married, had children, made enough money to donate frequently to support the newsletter, and thus her lifeline back to the ring.

Many others did the same. 'Now that I have received *ARTTRA*, I feel at home,' Priestess Xego smiled, 'because before I felt that I was living in my own world with nobody like me.' Reading it, 'I am with people, though they are far from me'. The school newspaper, shoddy and skimpy as it sometimes was, transcended space.[52] To be an artist was to know one's intimate self to be inextricably a part of a wider community. In the mid-1970s, four Ndaleni graduates found work around Madadeni, in the coal-mining region of northern Natal. None aspired to be a full-time artist. Yet they came together nearly every weekend at one or the other's home, 'discussing our points on the field of art'. It was, as Richman Simelane described it, 'marvelous when we are around the table sharing our ideas and experiments'. Friendship and community made possible the creation of beauty and were beauty's embodiment.[53]

Like beauty, however, friendships and communities fade. By the late 1970s, it was increasingly apparent that the school that had nurtured the art community was not going to be around for much longer. In early 1977 the department announced its intention to shut down the Indaleni Training College and to move the staff to a location near Pietermaritzburg, where it would fall under the Zululand authority. The art school was 'inter-ethnic', however, 'and plans are being prepared for the inclusion of this course in a big new training school north of Pretoria at Mabopane'.[54] By 1980, both Peirson and Lancaster had decided that they would not be making the move. That year they produced the last issue of *ARTTRA*, the school newsletter. 'This "Editor's Letter" is in the nature of a formal farewell to you members of the ARTTRA family,' Peirson wrote, adding, with typical understatement, 'this Ndaleni job has been a unique and interesting experience.'[55] 'Farewell to Ndaleni!' one of the school's last students wrote, 'I'm leaving to start my new abode.' He thanked his teachers and his peers for their 'generosity upon my humanity', describing himself as the 'child' of a gaggle of parents 'of different places, of different faces, but united in the … artistic mind'.[56] Former students wrote in: Hamlet Hobe and Abednego Dlamini from the early 1960s, for example, and students from previous decades. The 1980 school year ended; new students came once more in 1981; after that the old mission station shuttered its hostels and the art school closed.

Departures had always been part of the Ndaleni experience. From the mid-1960s until the school's closing, the art students held a sale in Pietermaritzburg, to raise money for materials and to give the successful among them some cash to take home. After the sale, the campus would empty out, art students making their way back to Pietermaritzburg, from there to disperse across the country, shouting promises to reconnect via *ARTTRA* as they boarded trains and buses. Peirson stayed behind to tidy campus. She rarely showed emotion. But in the quiet of the library, or the studio, each year like clockwork, she cried. She had never said much, but the songs they sang while creating and the chatter they shared had been her music as much as theirs, and it had gone silent. There would be no more mallets and no more brushes until the next class arrived. After 1981, there were no more. In 2013, the memory of each year's end was still enough to bring tears to her eyes. She asked me to turn off my recorder, the depths of her emotional connection to her students apparent. It took her some time to compose herself. When I resumed my questions, her tears returned.

In the past, year after year, those tears would eventually stop and she would return to work. As night fell, she would gather her things and walk among the statues and murals to her car and home. Peirson taught for four more years after 1981. She took a position as a specialist teacher at a new training college near Pietermaritzburg, where art was one among many subjects. She admits that she was burned out and that she did not take the work seriously.[57] She kept her home in Richmond and commuted for four years, before finally retiring to her small cottage, there to watch apartheid's violent denouement in the midlands. Her students at Ndaleni had helped her to paint its walls. At the end of 1985, for the first time since she had arrived in Richmond, she prepared canvas and began to paint.[58]

One of the most remarkable things about the Ndaleni story is how abruptly it ends. The art education program continued to run for a few more years from Mapobane, under the instruction of a local artist named John Blem. Lancaster and Peirson visited once and came away unimpressed. Bantu Education itself came under more sustained attack in the 1980s, and at the turn of the 1990s, the entire South African art education program was scrapped and rebooted to suit the times.[59]

So too did the networks and communities art students had established come to an end.[60] In the early 1980s, the occasional letter found its way to Peirson, but without the newsletter, news of exhibitions, births and weddings expired with her. She did not keep in touch with her former students. 'I seem to be wholeheartedly into something, and if it stops, it stops, and I move on to the next thing,' she notes unsentimentally.[61] Her 'thing' increasingly became her own painting and the friends she had cultivated in Richmond, where she began to exhibit.[62] She was 'chuffed' when, in 1998, Pietermaritzburg's Tatham Art Gallery held a retrospective of the Ndaleni Art School, largely to celebrate her legacy in the region.[63] A few ex-students who lived in the area attended the opening. It was the first time she had seen many of them in decades. Tellingly, all of those who visited the exhibition were either artists themselves or involved in art management or education. It was the last time she saw or heard from many of them (at least until my enquiries prompted a few ex-students to check in).

Ultimately, the privileges that students earned at art school could not match the privileges that Peirson herself enjoyed as a white South Africa under apartheid. In exchange for disciplining themselves to the demands of the hostels and terms of the government, art students at Ndaleni earned the right to visit galleries, to travel far from their homes, to swim, to talk in the studio late at night; they earned a measure of freedom and inspiration and developed the conviction that theirs was a special community, united under the sign of the 'artistic mind'. Yet most never made it as artists; many lacked even the opportunity to teach art. They remained poor, unable to afford the oil paints that Peirson purchased when she began to paint in her retirement. At and through the art school her students had earned the privilege she simply inhabited, and without her intervention, that privileged community waned and faded from view.

'From view' does not necessarily mean from life, of course. One of the great methodological challenges and frustrations of this project has been that although the archive resounds with hundreds of voices, I have been able to ask questions to only the most easily discoverable handful of these. I sat with Lorna Peirson for hours and corresponded with Craig Lancaster; I have tracked down those few Ndaleni students who were traceable through museums and collectors because they had 'made it' as artists, to lesser and greater extents. I have only been able to speak with those Ndaleni students who retained some access to the privileges of art and not to the vast majority of their peers who did not. I am reduced to imagining scenes that may or may not have happened, envisioning gatherings such as those at Madadeni in 1974, where teachers came together talk art — only in Jabavu in 1984, or Zwelitsha in 1989, or Mamelodi today.

Even if those conversations did happen, they were not the sorts of experiences on which the Ndaleni community and its friendships were built. Through my research I have tried to reconstruct those experiences, to see how Harrison's notion of the ring was extended to encompass the hillside, so that 'art' became a shorthand for talking about time and place, about the walk from the hostel in the twilight to work and think in a studio, about visits to galleries and mountains and oceans. As a late-1960s student explained, there was something powerful about the place: it was 'Art Home' and ex-students yearned for the opportunity to return, to visit, to study again under the trees.[64]

I have been fortunate to track down some ex-Ndaleni students and their teachers and to hear them remember moments of connection and affection. For the most part, the friendships constructed around the discipline of art belong now to the realm of nostalgia, to the wistfully remembered past. They are evident in the welling and receding of Peirson's tears, or in Daphne Biyela's eyes lingering over a photograph of her younger self, seated on a table in front of her classmates, a year's worth of work tacked onto the wall behind her. In our conversation Biyela remembered an emotional community, a place where people painted, played guitar and sang, where they shared a common 'craziness': 'All those crazy people would fight one minute [and then] the next we would be laughing.' On the hillside, in the ring, life was anything other than the 'gray', 'dull' reality that she claims prevailed outside, in places such as her Soweto home.[65]

It was to that Soweto home that she returned at the end of 1978, there to face the challenges of teaching art to upwards of 200 primary school pupils in an underfunded school where the principal and others failed to see the point. By the time Biyela and I met in 2013, she knew the whereabouts of only one of her almost 40 classmates. She was delighted to learn that I had tracked down a couple of other Ndaleni graduates nearby, although she herself did know any. This makes sense. Since 1981, Biyela, like the others, had moved on to seek new relationships through new disciplines: in her case, teaching, post-secondary education, and, especially, her church.

I want to believe that some friendships managed to transcend the place and time of their genesis. I want to believe that some Ndaleni art students managed to expand the ring which was in fact a barrier, protecting the joys of relationships founded on creating from the tides of a tough world. Desperate, in the past few years, I have spent hours typing names into Facebook and Google, sending messages in hopes of finding more Biyelas, hoping that computer algorithms might yield evidence of human companionship.

I have occasionally and unexpectedly been successful. Once, I found a blog written by a Johannesburg-based intellectual, a young woman who grew up in what is today Mpumalanga. In late 2013 she was invited back to her hometown, to give a 'motivational talk' to local schoolchildren. The invitation occasioned a bout of reminiscence about her school days, about her mother, and her grandmother a teacher who had once taught luminaries such as Kgalema Motlanthe. She also paused to remember her grandfather, J. M. Moche, who had attended Ndaleni in 1967. Moche was a shopkeeper and a popular man in town; the locals congregated at his shop to play the strategy game *morabaraba*. 'I learned artisanship from my grandfather ... who drew on everything, painted everything and collected old scraps to up-cycle into new, usable objects.' Moche was an artist, a grandfather, and a friend. He filled his granddaughter's world with beauty; he brought people together to play a game, to laugh, and enjoy passing time together. Smiling across a board or painting a chair, did he tell stories about his time at Ndaleni? Perhaps. At the very least, in his shop, in his village, with his family, he was back inside the ring.[66]

REFERENCES

Blom Hansen, Thomas. 2012. *The Melancholia of Freedom: Social Life in an Indian Township*. Princeton, NJ: Princeton University Press.

Cohen, Lizbeth. 2003. *A Consumer's Republic: The Politics of Mass Consumption in Postwar America*. New York, NY: Knopf.

Dlamini, Jacob. 2009. *Native Nostalgia*. Johannesburg: Jacana Media.

Dlamini, Jacob. 2015. *Askari: A Story of Collaboration and Betrayal in the Anti-Apartheid Struggle*. Johannesburg: Jacana Media.

Duberman, Martin. 2009. *Black Mountain: An Exploration in Community*. Evanston, IL: Northwestern University Press.

Enslin, Penny. 1984. 'The Role of Fundamental Pedagogics in the Formulation of Educational Policy in South Africa.' In *Apartheid and Education*, edited by Peter Kallaway, 139–147. Johannesburg: Ravan Press.

Ferguson, James. 2015. *Give a Man a Fish*. Durham, NC: Duke University Press.

Gardiner, Michael. Personal interview. April 11, 2014.

Horrax, O. J. 1934. 'The Teaching of Art in Native Schools.' *Native Teachers' Journal* 13(2): 81–86.

Hunter, Mark. 2011. *Love in the Time of AIDS: Inequality, Gender and Rights in South Africa*. Bloomington, IN: Indiana University Press.

Leeb-Du Toit, Juliette, ed. 1999. *Ndaleni Art School: A Retrospective*. Pietermaritzburg: Tatham Gallery.

Lewin, Hugh. 2011. *Stones against the Mirror: Friendship in the Time of the South African Struggle*. Johannesburg: Umuzi.

MacLeish, Kenneth. 2013. *Making War at Fort Hood; Life and Uncertainty in a Military Community*. Princeton, NJ: Princeton University Press.

Marshall, Ruth. 2009. *Political Spiritualities: The Pentecostal Revolution in Nigeria*. Chicago, IL: University of Chicago Press.

Moodie, T. Dunbar. 1994. *Going for Gold: Men, Mines and Migration*. Berkeley, CA: University of California Press.

Msila, Vuyisile. 2007. 'From Apartheid Education to the Revised National Curriculum Statement.' *Nordic Journal of African Studies* 16(2): 146–160.

Parsons, Timothy. 2004. *Race, Resistance, and the Boy Scout Movement in British Colonial Africa*. Athens, OH: Ohio University Press.

Rankin, Elizabeth. 2011. 'Creating Communities.' In *Visual Century 1945–1976*, vol. 2. Johannesburg: Wits University Press.

Shatzberg, Micahael. 2001. *Political Legitimacy in Middle Africa: Father, Family, Food*. Bloomington, IN: Indiana University Press.

NOTES

1 Abednego Dlamini, *ARTTRA* 40, October, 1980: 10.

2 Abednego Dlamini, to 'Sir', undated (1961?), Campbell Collection, University of KwaZulu-Natal (hereafter CC) – Ndaleni – A. Dlamini, 1.

3 Abednego Dlamini, to Peter Bell. Undated (1962?). CC – Ndaleni – A. Dlamini, 2.

4 Abednego Dlamini, to Lorna Peirson. January 24, 1963. CC – Ndaleni – A. Dlamini, 1.

5 To date the only substantial study of the Ndaleni art school is Leeb-Du toit (1999). The school features briefly in Rankin (2011).

6 Lorna Peirson, *ARTTRA* 40, October 1980: 3.

7 J. W. Grossert. 'Miss Ann Robinson (nee Harrison).' In 'Ndaleni Art Teaching School' yellow folder, no accession number. CC – Ndaleni, 1.

8 Anne Harrison, 'What Is This Thing Called Art?' Unpublished MS. Undated, 49, Lorna Peirson personal collection.

9 Interview with Michael Gardiner, conducted by Daniel Magaziner, April 11, 2014. Johannesburg. For more on the transition in education post-apartheid, and new curricular developments, see Msila (2007); for fundamental pedagogics under Unisa's authority, see Enslin (1984).

10 Interview with Lorna Peirson, conducted by Daniel Magaziner, June 17, 2013. Howick, KwaZulu-Natal; Peter Bell to Miss Dougall, March 21, 1961. CC – Ndaleni – S. Hobyane, 2.

11 Peirson, interview, 2013.

12 Peter Bell to Ivan Mitford-Barberton, April 21, 1961. CC – Ndaleni – S. Hobyane, 1

13 Bell to Mitford-Barberton, 1961.

14 Joseph Mabaso to Lorna Peirson, May 4, 1964. CC – Ndaleni – J. Mabaso, 1.

15 Abednego Dlamini to Lorna Peirson, January 24, 1963. CC – Ndaleni – A. Dlamini, 1.

16 Abednego Dlamini to Lorna Peirson, October 27, 1963. CC – Ndaleni – A. Dlamini, 1.

17 Peirson, interview, 2013.

18 Peirson, interview, 2013.

19 Interview with Pat Khoza, conducted by Daniel Magaziner, June 18, 2013. Durban.

20 Interview with Solomon Baloyi, conducted by Daniel Magaziner, June 24, 2013. Alice, Eastern Cape.

21 Khoza, interview, 2013.

22 Interview with Lorna Peirson, conducted by Daniel Magaziner, December 13, 2011. Howick; Peirson, interview, 2013.

23 Peirson, interview, 2013.

24 Interview with Lorna Peirson, conducted by Daniel Magaziner, December 11, 2011. Howick.

25 Report on Giant's Castle trip, *ARTTRA* 9, September 1964: 10.

26 *ARTTRA* 10, May 1965: 9.

27 Peirson, interview, 2013; Craig Lancaster, personal communication, July 28, 2013.

28 *ARTTRA* 23, September 1971: 13.

29 Manasseh Nkole, *ARTTRA* 38, October 1979: 3.

30 Interview with Daphne Biyela, conducted by Daniel Magaziner, June 26, 2013. Johannesburg.

31 Biyela, interview, 2013.

32 Peirson, interview, 2013.

33 Interview with Lorna Peirson, conducted by Daniel Magaziner, April 9, 2014. Howick.

34 Enoch Malolo to Lorna Peirson, January 19, 1974. CC – Ndaleni – E. Malolo, 2.

35 Jessie Muthige to Lorna Peirson, February 8, 1971. CC – Ndaleni – J. Muthige, 1.

36 Thelma Radebe to Lorna Peirson, October 20, 1966. CC – Ndaleni – T. Radebe, 1.

37 Michael Ncamane to Lorna Peirson, September 10, 1964, CC – Ndaleni – M. Ncamane, 1.

38 Abednego Dlamini to Lorna Peirson, November 28, 1963: 3; Abednego Dlamini to Lorna Peirson, November 18, 1964: 1. CC – Ndaleni – A. Dlamini.

39 Abiah Ramadi to Lorna Peirson, November 25, 1969. CC – Ndaleni – A. Ramadi, 3.

40 Philemon Kutumela to Lorna Peirson, undated. CC – Ndaleni – P. Kutumela, 1; *ARTTRA* 32, May 1976: 11.

41 *ARTTRA* 33, October 1976: 1.

42 O'Brien Nkasha to Peter Bell, July 5, 1961. CC – Ndaleni – O. Nkasha, 1.

43 Thelma Radebe to Lorna Peirson, February 4, 1967: 1.

44 Thelma Radebe, *ARTTRA* 14, April 1967: 9-10.

45 Clipping from *The Golden City Post,* September 29, 1963, no page number, Library of Congress, Washington D.C. – Harmon Foundation – MSS51615 – Box 90 – S. Mahlobo.

46 *ARTTRA* 20, May 1970: 25.

47 Hilda Mohlopi, *ARTTRA* 21, October 1970: 27.

48 Sophie Nsuza, April 26, 1978. CC – Artists Questionnaire, 1, 2, 5.

49 *ARTTRA* 8, April 1964: 7.

50 Sophie Nsuza to Lorna Peirson, September 7, 1970. CC – Ndaleni – S. Nsuza, 1.

51 Sophie Nsuza to Lorna Peirson, September 23, 1969. CC – Ndaleni – S. Nsuza, 1 – 2.

52 Priestess Xego to Lorna Peirson, April 27, 1964. CC – Ndaleni – P. Xego, 1.

53 Richman Simelane to Lorna Peirson, February 19, 1974. CC – Ndaleni – R. Simelane, 1.

54 *ARTTRA* 34, May 1977: 12.

55 *ARTTRA* 40, October 1980: 1.

56 John Dlamini, 'Farewell!' Undated (1980). CC – Ndaleni – J. Dlamini, 1.

57 Peirson, interview, 2013.

58 Peirson, interview, 2013.

59 Lancaster, personal communication, July 28, 2013.

60 Interview with Christina Jikelo, conducted by Daniel Magaziner, June 20, 2013. Cape Town. Interview with Godfrey Ndaba, conducted by Daniel Magaziner, June 26, 2013. Johannesburg.

61 Peirson, interview, 2014.

62 Lorna Peirson, Questionnaire. CC – Artists Index, September 8, 1988, 6.

63 Interview with Brendan Bell, director of the Tatham Art Gallery, conducted by Daniel Magaziner, April 7, 2014. Pietermaritzburg, KwaZulu-Natal.

64 Milicent Dzingwe, *ARTTRA* 19, October 1969: 12.

65 Biyela, interview.

66 http://walksoffaith.wordpress.com/tag/primary-school/, accessed on June 5, 2014.

9 'FRIEND OF THE FAMILY': MAIDS, MADAMS, AND DOMESTIC CARTOGRAPHIES OF POWER IN SOUTH AFRICAN ART

M. NEELIKA JAYAWARDANE

In South Africa, it is not uncommon to hear families say that their domestic worker is a 'friend of the family' or even 'like family'. While some employers strive to pay their 'domestics' a fairer wage, involve themselves in financing their laborers' healthcare costs, and funding children's educations, most domestics are paid the minimal accepted daily rate of R100. Sometimes, the payment includes R10–R20, to buy a cheap lunch and transport money back to the township. The obvious socioeconomic power imbalances between the 'madams' and 'maids' of South Africa limit claims purporting to incorporate laborers into family structures. Yet, despite this, the language used to describe voluntary social contracts that determine the bonds of friendship, and the less voluntary – but obligatory – social contracts between family members is invoked in order to frame this unequal relationship.

Irma du Plessis (2011: 46) argues that domestic work, because of its 'close affinity to the family', operates as a 'foundational unit in everyday and scholarly understandings of both "nation" and "society"'. Moreover, given the level of intimacy such laborers have in maintaining the architecture of white families, domestic work 'may be understood not only as a contemporary social practice, that is, a lawful and regulated albeit imperfect and incomplete form of employment, but also as a central feature of what may be termed the apartheid social imaginary, an implicit social understanding of the way in which things stand between fellow citizens'. Taking into consideration the 'extent to and the manner in which domestic work and the relationship between domestic workers, domestic employers and their respective families surface in the public domain in contemporary South Africa', it is no wonder that this type of labor, and the laborers who carry it out, are 'deeply inscribed with social meanings which are powerful in the present'.

The domestic spaces in which the boundaries of this unequal relationship are negotiated are also the location in which contemporary fears regarding the other – a 'domesticated' other who is invited into one's intimate spaces as a necessary component of maintaining one's exclusive domestic arena – are magnified. It is also the place where conversations about surveillance of the other's activities and the erection of security barriers against the antithesis of the domesticated (female) other – the volatile, dangerous (male) other – and his possible incursion into one's private enclaves, take place.

'SHE'S LIKE FAMILY': DEFLECTING AN UNBEARABLE TRUTH
Although the encounter between madams and maids – created, supported, and maintained by colonial and apartheid structures – provides rich material for analysing how unbearable social relations are made normative and acceptable, 'relations in the family and household remain largely out of view and outside the analysis' (Du Plessis 2011: 59). Despite the ubiquity of the madam-maid relationship in the South African landscape, the negotiations that take place within households, involving gender, class, and racial components of power difference are largely secluded from analysis; moreover, because of the private nature of this relationship, the shame associated with exploiting those laboring in domestic spaces, as well as the defensiveness invoked to deny exploitation, the troubling aspects are often relegated to comedy, wherein the maid figure upbraids the madam through ironic aside.[1] Comedy, like the repetitive refrain, she's like family or she's family, helps deflect the unbearable truth of the inequality at the heart of this relationship. When the roles of the players are comically inverted, the horror one might feel if one were to regard it without nicety or sentiment is dissipated, and the threat of a real inversion of roles – or a real transformation, in which neither party is always assured of being more powerful than the other – is removed.

In this chapter, I analyse how artists and photographers in contemporary South Africa attempt to question glib attempts at eliding such power imbalances and fears of the other in domestic landscapes. Specifically, I focus on examples of relationships between madams and maids in photography by Ernest Cole, Omar Badsha, Gisèle Wulfsohn, and George Hallett, and in Zanele Muholi's recent work that draws attention to possible interracial, 'queer' desire between domestic workers and the madams for whom they work. Each artist's work is an intervention in the South African institution of domestic labor; through their photographic projects, the photographers — and we, the audience — become 'vigilant witnesses to the oppressive nature of the apartheid system at work' (Ngcobo 2010).

Cole, Badsha, Wulfsohn, Hallett, and Muholi's photographs illustrate the manner in which photography and art can not only reveal problematic structures, but aslo offer dangerous possibilities through which seemingly impenetrable power structures may be troubled and/or made porous. Historically, in the South African landscape, the image and narrative ontologies — the visual and word vocabularies that provided the infrastructures for our ways of seeing the other, which, in turn, taught us how to behave toward the other — were intrinsic to the ways through which the humanity of certain 'other' categories of human beings' agency was compromised, and, as a result of inherent power imbalances, relegated to the liminal zone between human and laboring-object. Each — photographer and artist — addresses the gendered and socioeconomic spaces between 'madams' and their female domestic laborers, complicating discussions of race, intimacy, and the everyday, and adding to dominant narratives of South Africa history by presenting domestic spaces as locations in which fraught political interactions — and remarkable transformations — may take place.

Despite a lack of access to agency, those who are reduced to laboring-objects in the apartheid economy do not necessarily remain as instrumentalized 'things'. Achille Mbembe (2014) has noted that those in laboring positions may — in invisible, yet subversive and powerful ways — contest their objecthood, despite the confining structures that construct and maintain them as laboring-objects. Mbembe posits that often resistance begins with the act of dreaming: he argues that the dream of a 'different order' — of possibility, escape, and overcoming the regimes that reduced one to a thing — are 'a political practice' that forms initial pathways toward 'liberation'.[2]

In Cole's and Wulfsohn's work, a madam might see maids who seemingly comply with orders; yet we know that they are submitting themselves to indignities only in order to earn a wage that will support their families. In rare instances, we see that dreaming might be the only possibility through which the 'domestic' can signify, perhaps only for herself, a return to her personhood; her wild imaginative spaces undo her domestication, liberating her from the constraints set by madam and apartheid.

NEGOTIATING POWER IN COLONIAL AND APARTHEID DOMESTIC SPACES

In South Africa, the twin figures of the laborer (the 'maid') and the employer (the 'madam') have been, historically, marked by race, class, and gender. The maid figure that labors in the home is always female, and either black or coloured, while the madam is always seen as white. The complex relationship between madams and maids in South Africa has its historical roots in colonial spaces, where Cape Dutch women's 'domain and range' of power was 'located in the family'. According to Hermann Giliomee (cited in Du Plessis 2011: 54–55), Cape Dutch women had sufficient power to 'prevent their sons from marrying outside the European community and their husbands from bringing illegitimate half-caste children into the family'. Giliomee maintains that colonial-era Dutch women's ability to influence was thus 'situated at the intersections of race and reproduction', and that a 'central part of this power was exercised in the relationship between slave woman and female owner' (55). Although Afrikaner women are sometimes seen as oppressed or silenced by Afrikaner patriarchal structures – an exclusion from power evident in their 'absence from public life' after the National Party's victory – Du Plessis (57) argues that although such women may have 'retreat[ed] into their households with their families and domestic workers', they occupied a 'complex and contradictory' position, negotiating a 'double role' as both 'oppressed and complicit in the oppression of others', while engaging in a form of paternalism that created deep bonds based on dependency.

During apartheid, colonial laws and practices excluding othered bodies from metropolitan centers were amalgamated and strengthened. As a result, the relationship – and the hierarchical differences between maids and madams – became more pronounced. However, despite the many laws intended to maintain apartness and to create geographic barriers between whites and all othered bodies, 'one of the ironic juxtapositions of the apartheid era was the co-occurrence of racial segregation with labor policies that channelled black women' into the protected enclaves of whites, becoming one of the principle locations of contact between otherwise separated people who knew nothing about each other's daily lives (Durrheim et al. 2014). But because the levels of contact were always determined by state-mandated racial hierarchies, apartheid social structures, and belief systems about the other and her place, this relationship remains marked by an awareness of difference: the maid is included in the domestic affairs of madam and simultaneously excluded from her social circle.

The relationships that result between white families and their maids not only reflect, in small scale, the effects of both colonial and apartheid government policies, but also helped to indoctrinate generations of children into what was considered acceptable race relations (Durrheim et al. 2014). In the domestic spaces of nearly every white home, apartheid's hierarchies were normalized, with madam and maid performing expected roles for each other: on the one hand, there was the subservient, loyal servant who kept the home spick and span, acted as a generous, kindly, long-suffering second mother to the white children of the family, cleaning up after them while making – if her relationship with her employer was good, and she had been employed there long – tut-tutting noises about the spoilt children's bad habits.

Meanwhile, madam – who scolded her maid for tolerating the badly behaved children, collected gossip about the neighbors (via the maid's networks with other domestics in the neighborhood), commiserated about the difficulty of keeping one's man's interest, boasted about her maid's expertise with a difficult recipe or how she could be trusted with the entire household, but nonetheless kept a watch on her maid's daily activities – got to cultivate the benevolent, patronising persona of the generous and charitable well-to-do lady. The social spaces that apartheid created in the homes of white families fashioned these powerful caricatures, and they live on in our imaginations, despite the fact that in real life, neither maid nor madam have such simplistic lives or roles to play.

CASE STUDIES IN DOMESTIC WORKERS

Long before the twentieth century, the Cape fostered a tradition of landscape painting in which Muslim (referred to as 'Cape Malay') slaves and their freed descendants were included as picturesque parts of the landscape. In paintings by Fred Page, Irma Stern, and Gregoire Boonzaier, and photographs by Constance Stuart Larrabee, of the 'Malay Quarter' (the area inside central Cape Town where former slaves settled) and 'the city of Cape Town as a whole', Muslims are shown as compliant, docile, and picturesque laborers engaged in daily activities such as carrying water, washing clothes, selling fruit or fish, and farming – all *in the service* of white colonists' (Baderoon 2014: 37, 39–40, emphasis in original). They are shown engaging in quaint customs and ceremonies – such as weddings – associated with Muslims. These 'picturesque colonial paintings perform a stark ideological labor', Baderoon (40) argues, portraying a 'benign slave-holding society at the Cape', alleviating the guilt associated with the systematic violence of slavery, and instantiating a 'trivialising visual language' that underplayed 'evidence of resistance by slaves'. This picturesque tradition underscored the 'ambiguous visibility' of laboring 'Malay' bodies. They were visible because their bodies were always policed, yet they were 'perpetually out of view' because of the 'over-determined placidity' ascribed to their imagined persons in popular culture (40–41). In this way, the Malay were incorporated into colonial 'friendship': placid and supportive of the colonial project, unlike the threatening bodies of black laborers, who are entirely left out of the picture.

By the mid-twentieth century, Irma Stern's *Maid in Uniform* (1955), and Dorothy Kay's *Cookie: Annie Mavata* (1956), continued the tradition of depicting laboring bodies in painting, but by this time, the painters have departed from the tenants of the picturesque tradition.

In Ernest Cole's series of photographs of maids, some of which were included in a section titled 'The Cheap Servant' in his *House of Bondage* (1967), madams are absent, although children and pets of the household make cameo appearances in several images. Cole's images show maids walking employers' dogs, taking employers' children to school, resting in the tight, spare living quarters at the end of an exhausting day, and – on rare occasions – entertaining friends outside the perimeter wall of the employer's home. Each wears a dour uniform: a shapeless dress tied at the waist, faded by countless washings. Most wear aprons, even when outside the employer's home. Some wear little white caps that have no function other than to announce that the woman is engaged in domestic labor.

Despite the absence of white bodies against which to assess the relationship between the maids and madams depicted in the photographs, Cole's *House of Bondage*, and its subtitle, *A South African Black Man Exposes in His Own Pictures and Words the Bitter Life of His Homeland Today*, openly declare its political intentions. The book was unapologetically a political statement – an attempt to persuade the world to censure and boycott South Africa's apartheid regime. As a critical ethnographer of the time, he entered a social milieu that black participant-observers would ordinarily not be permitted to inhabit; exposing this world to a public beyond South Africa and providing proof to rumors that apartheid's architects worked hard to cover up. Cole, as witness, makes claims based on the authority of his personal experience; yet the 'the truth for which he claims responsibility is collective and general' because the social and racial locations of his physical person – as a witness – occupy 'a strange space where his personal position gives him authority to testify to a truth that is not personal' (Baer 2014: 2).

Cole's analysis of 'friendships' between madams and maids in Johannesburg's rarefied suburbs is set out in the narrative introducing the photographic series. It is impossible to pretend that the relationship between maids and madams is anything but fraught: 'White homes are the crucibles of racism in South Africa ... nowhere is there more animosity than in the everyday relationships between household domestics and their employers' (Cole 1967: 70). He notes that when he asked one maid about her relationship with her madam, she replied: 'Whites think that with their money they can buy everything, even your feelings. When they employ you, they tell you your duties will be this or that, but in the long run they make you into a shifting spanner ... bound to do every job. ... Without exception, [maids] were seething with anger, scorn and resentment' (71). The maids Cole photographed were working in the affluent suburbs of northern Johannesburg, including Killarney, Dunkeld, Illovo, Melrose, Melrose East, and Houghton. He had expected that these 'servants of the rich were having a somewhat better time of it', but was 'taken aback' to find that 'many were so bitter that they had no fear of being quoted or overheard'. Perhaps because Cole was the rare person who actually asked them about their day-to-day struggles, a level of communion and trust between the photographer and the maids resonates in the photographs; it is an intimacy that leads to revelation.

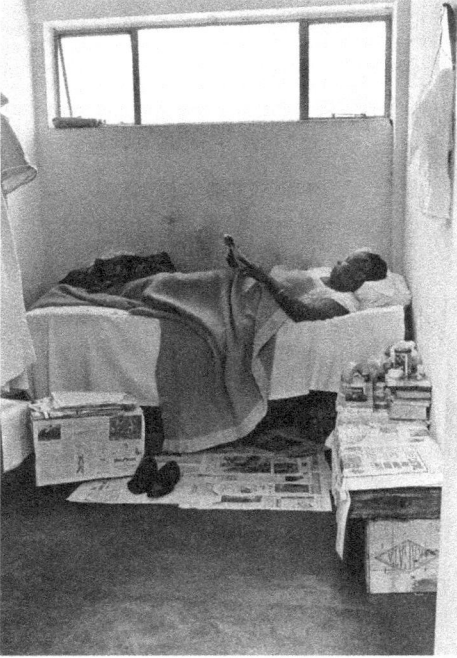

Figure 9.1
Image from *House of Bondage*
accompanied by the text: 'She lives on
edge of opulence, while her own world
is bare. Newspapers are her carpet,
fruit crates her chair and table.'
© Ernest Cole Family Trust

Figure 9.2
Image from *House of Bondage*
accompanied by the caption:
'Servants are not forbidden to love.
[Woman holding child] said, "I love
this child, though she'll grow up to
treat me just like her mother does.
Now she's innocent."'
© Ernest Cole Family Trust

Cole's political message is palpable in the captions accompanying his photographs. A maid lying down on a narrow bed in her room is accompanied by the text, 'she lives on the edge of opulence, while her own world is bare. Newspapers are her carpet, fruit crates her chair and table' (Cole 1967: 75; Figure 9.1). A photograph of a maid lovingly caressing an employer's child is accompanied by the caption, 'servants are not forbidden to love: [The woman holding child said], "I love this child, though she'll grow up to treat me just like her mother does. Now she's innocent."' (76–77; Figure 9.2)

Cole took many photographs of maids with their white employers' children, some of which were included in *House of Bondage*, and others that emerged in public in 2010, when the Hasselblad Foundation published them in *Ernest Cole: Photographer*. In one image included in the later book, we see the plain back of a maid in her uniform, walking a young child – no older than kindergarten-age – to school. She holds his jacket in her left hand, and his little hand in her right. He, jaunty in his schoolboy shorts and cap, looks back at the photographer, who must have been walking several steps behind them (Cole et al. 2010: 121). Others show servants caring for pets: in a photograph of a maid walking her employer's curly-haired dog, we see that the dog strains at the leash, turning to greet the invisible photographer, while the maid looks downward at the dog rather than at the human figure in front of her. In the background is a predictable sign affixed to the boundary fence of a property: 'Protected by Day/Night Burglar Alarms' (111; Figure 9.3). The sign provides assurance to those behind the fence, and signals to those outside the protection that white affluence can buy. In *House of Bondage*, a similar image of a servant walking an employer's dogs is accompanied by the text, 'dogs are well tended by black servant, and well-fed' (Cole 1967: 76).

Cole's work shows that a maid's life was always under surveillance, though she had little time to herself. Much of what drives the watchful eye of the madam is purportedly her worry about the maid not doing the work properly, or her qualms about the maid stealing small goods and food. However, as an answer to why madams feel that they must watch maids so closely, Cole lays bare something that goes largely unspoken: deep-seated anxieties about a black maid's sexual prowess coupled with myths about her moral looseness. These fears about a maid's potent sexuality and apprehensions about its ability to usurp madam's incontestable position as the queen of her home

Figure 9.3
Image from *Ernest Cole:
Photographer* shows a maid walking
her employer's curly-haired dog.
© Ernest Cole Family Trust

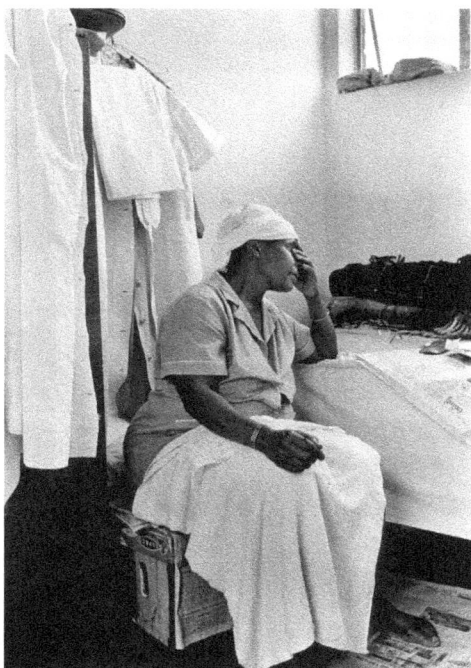

Figure 9.4
Image from *House of Bondage* is
coupled with the caption: 'Living
in her khaya [home] out back, a
servant must be on call six days out
of seven and seven nights out of
seven. She lives a lonely life apart
from her family. In white suburbs
there are no recreation centers
open to black servants.'
© Ernest Cole Family Trust

means that maids are constantly watched, but paradoxically, required to be invisible. Part of the attempt to erase maids' sexuality is the requirement to wear clothing that is as 'unassuming as possible' (Cole 1967: 73): 'Standard garb is a modest uniform with hair tucked under a starched cap, for servants are not allowed to be bareheaded in master's house.' In *House of Bondage*, he included a photograph of an attractive woman in a pinstriped suit waiting in a queue, along with a caption explaining that she was fired from two jobs because she was 'too chic' (80). Cole (73) adds, 'many a girl servant learns the hard way that madam does not appreciate competition. "I don't want two madams in my house," the lady announces.'

Even the rare opportunity to socialise is exposed to the watchful eye of neighborhood madams, as maids were not permitted to bring friends to their quarters. In a photograph showing a maid sharing a conversation with a peer, we see a young woman sharing some grapes – laid out on a newspaper – with a visitor (Cole et al. 2010: 114). The two women sit on the grass and enjoy what we know must be a rare moment of freedom from work. In case we mistakenly assume that they are having a picnic in the employer's garden, a caption on a similar photograph included in *House of Bondage* tells us that they are sitting outside the perimeter wall: 'Entertaining is done outside garden walls, since employers do not want strange "boys" or "girls" on their premises' (Cole 1967: 76).

Cole reveals women's lives devoid of the solidity and assurance of friendship. These are solitary, isolated lives cut off from community and communion. During the day, each maid may be surround by the bustle of her employer's family, but she remains behind a wall, unable to communicate her daily worries and concerns, or speak openly about how the employer's family treats her. The photographs document what happens once she steps away from madam's home. An image of a careworn maid in her room, sitting on a fruit crate, her bare feet resting on neatly spread out newspapers, is coupled with the caption: 'Living in her khaya [home] out back, a servant must be on call six days out of seven and seven nights out of seven. She lives a lonely life apart from her family. In white suburbs there are no recreation centers open to black servants' (Cole 1967: 78; Figure 9.4). We see this woman from the vantage point of the invisible photographer: she sits on her low crate, her elbow resting on her bed, bathed in soft evening light coming from a window set several feet above. She has cradled her brow in her left hand; the tips of her fingers brush against her closed right eye. Cole has found her at her most weary, a Madonna in deep sadness with no soul on earth to whom she could go with her cares. In his introduction to 'The Cheap Servant', Cole (1967: 71) explains his difficulties moving through white suburbs. Because he appeared to be black,[3] he had to 'move carefully … for whites are immediately suspicious of blacks they have not seen before'. Yet, he may have been simultaneously invisible to those in power, and consequently 'able to enter a great many households and interview a number of servants'. Even if a madam was suspicious of a black man in their neighborhoods, none would have imagined that he was photographing their maids. Though many of the maids he photographed must have been aware of Cole's presence (some clearly allowed them into their quarters), it is as though he shadowed them as they went about their daily tasks, his camera an unassuming eye that in the blink of an aperture, captured the women. He was thus able to use his invisibility to his advantage, becoming an insider who created 'a place from which to see' (Baer 2014: 6).

Guided by Cole's acts of witness, we begin to understand that the purported friendship between madams and maids is more myth than reality. His work reveals that maids' lives are severely limited; although they are daily engaged in labor that facilitates their white employers' social ambitions and family lives, their own lives are curtailed. In the one-room quarters in the back of their madams' homes, kept neat to a fault, we see a sort of social death for the maids – not because their own social groups have shunned them due to a transgression, but because the conditions mandated by apartheid create the same results. There is little chance for maids to live outside the boundaries of what constitutes their relationship with their madams, and little room for them to oppose their daily encounter with systematic degradation and injustice.

In the latter part of the twentieth century, photographs in the documentary tradition often included both madams and maids, signifying the social relationship between them as worthy of note, rather than one of the docility and compliance of the laboring classes. Further, photographers complicated the racial binaries of apartheid, making visible aspects of a society that are more nuanced than apartheid social engineering allowed. For instance, one of Omar Badsha's (1979) photographs taken on Durban's Grey Street complicates the white madam-black maid apartheid binary: the scene is that of a sari-clad Indian mother carrying a toddler, and a young, black woman, also carrying a young child on her left arm, while holding on to a small suitcase. The two women are hurrying (the sari-wearing woman's left leg is caught in mid-gait – her sandaled foot pokes out of the folds of her sari), though the presence of the photographer makes them turn and look toward him, while continuing to move forward. The little hard-shell suitcase that the black woman carries is the kind that children once took to school; perhaps the women are taking the older child to school, or running errands after picking her up. The two women are smiling cheerily for the camera, but the children scowl at the intruder. There seems to be a certain friendliness, an intimacy between them, if only for the moment in which the camera's shutter clicked. However, the first thing most people will notice is that the child carried by the black woman is not hers. She is wearing a dark dress or button-down shirt, not a uniform; she could easily be a friend of the sari-woman, accompanying her on a busy day. The class differences between them are not obvious. But, in the context of South Africa, and the time period in which this photograph was taken, there is no mistaking that this is a madam and a maid.

Gisèle Wulfsohn's 'Domestic worker' (1986) captures a daily scene on Lookout Beach, Plettenberg Bay: an aproned black maid walks a dog on the beach, with her madam walking a few steps ahead of her; both are barefoot, and unburdened by any bags. They are there for a morning walk, not for a day at the beach. The madam's arms are held behind her – perhaps she is holding her sandals – and her eyes are squinted against the rising sun. The maid's hair is covered by a white *doek* – the folded scarf worn to cover the head and hair – and she wears little adornment save a thin metal bracelet on her right wrist and a bead necklace. In her other hand, she is carrying what appears to be the dog's collar and chain. In front of her is her madam, wearing a stylish, check-patterned tunic with contrasting piping around the collar and sleeves. Their bodies are a study in contrasts: madam's middle-aged belly is pressed against the fabric; nonetheless, her person is flattered by the cut of the dress, as well as the structure provided by a well-fitted brassiere. The maid's body is shapeless in the thin fabric of her uniform, and we can see that her own middle-aged breasts hang low, disappearing into her general torso.

In another of Wulfsohn's photographs, 'Domestic worker and employer on beach, Plettenberg Bay' (1987), a seated madam and her children form the two lower points of the visual triangle in this scene, while the figure of the maid, standing between them, the whites of her heels facing us, forms the apex of this triptych. In this photograph, the madam, still a young woman, sits bronzing on a plastic deck chair; her three children — in little-girl halter-tie swimsuits and trunks — play in the sand nearby. A few feet from them, the surf is breaking on a perfect sea. Another metal-and-plastic folding chair is positioned to face the madam, but no one sits there; it is the seat on which madam's wrap rests. In between them, we see the barefooted figure of the maid, standing, facing the sea. The maid is wearing a short-sleeved uniform; an apron, tied at the waist, gives her body some form. She has placed her *doek* at an angle, so that the cloth shelters the entire right side of her head and face from the sun. All we see of her is her back, and that she is standing, with her arms crossed. Her seated madam has just been in the water. We can see her hair is still wet, slicked back from her face; she is now wearing sunglasses against the glare of the sun. We see her slim arms and bare legs, brown and tanned, this group has been at the beach for some time already. Madam's face is turned upwards towards the figure of her maid, in pleasant conversation, and there is an engaging smile on her face. Yet her domestic worker is not returning her gaze; she is looking straight outwards, toward the sea.

George Hallett's commissioned photographs of domestic workers in their Sea Point madams' homes return to the tradition of portraying the laborer, leaving the employer out of the picture.[4] Yet, the presence of employers — and the type of relationship they have with their domestic laborer — is impossible to ignore. Many in this series of photographs show domestic workers engaged in various cleaning duties while minding white children, who sit idly by. One of his photographs mirrors in composition and subject matter Dorothy Kay's (1956) oil painting of a potato-peeling 'Cookie'. Hallett's image is of a woman peeling a potato. In Kay's painting, the iconic potato lies still in her hand, half-peeled, while the long, pointed blade of the knife remains dormant, but poised. In Hallett's photograph, the potato in the maid's hands is offered to the viewer (the invisible madam), but there is no knife, reducing the ever-present threat of the laboring other in one's domestic spaces.

Other photographs in this series make the employers' presence more visible: in a diptych of images, we see a domestic worker on her knees, carefully wiping the windows in a living room. In the second photograph, she is standing, holding two framed photographs: one of a white man and another of a white woman. Again, the domestic's body is large, comforting, and homely. Hallett took the first photograph as he walked into the room. He remembers saying to the domestic worker that it was a shame that her employers were not at home, as he would have taken a photograph of her with them; at this point she went to the cabinet, on which stood two framed photos of her employers.[5] She held one in each hand, and posed with them: this formed the second photograph in the diptych. These two photographs show the woman's reverence for both the home and her employers. There is no fear in her face, but her expression reflects the adoration granted to those one has been trained to believe are one's benevolent superiors – superiors on whom one's life and livelihood depend.

Despite the difference in power, the mutuality of their relationship, and the bond they shared is evident in the anecdote Hallett told about this particular domestic worker: two years after he took the photographs, she was murdered, apparently at the hands of a thief, who accosted her as she was walking in a nearby township.[6] When Hallett exhibited her portraits in a retrospective of his work at the National Gallery in Cape Town, her employers joined one of Hallett's 'walkabouts', and told him of her death. He remembered clearly that they were 'still devastated'. Their grief affected him so much that he 'gave them a copy of the photograph to take home' (Hallett 2014).[7] The employers felt an undeniable affection for their domestic worker and mourned her death, but this anecdote also highlights the disparities in the relationship. This particular domestic worker's untimely and violent death highlights the socioeconomic and experiential divide between employers and employees. Although this domestic worker was lucky enough to live on her employers' premises, she had to travel an hour or more to a township on the outskirts of Cape Town to socialise with those she knew. The urban poor of South Africa, who live in these crowded townships, are more likely to encounter violence than the wealthy in the suburbs. The brutal end to her life accentuated the differences between the safety available to her white employers in their protected and policed white enclave, and the daily threats that she faced to her person – a point that is often lost in both apartheid and post-apartheid South Africa, where whites feel that the threat of violence that they face from faceless, black, male figures is far greater (Comaroff and Comaroff 2006).[8]

The final set of photographs I address is a work from an earlier period of Zanele Muholi's career, '*Massa' and Mina(h)* (2008a, 2008b, 2008c). Muholi's photography is contemporary and innovative; rather than documenting a scene, as did Cole, Badsha, Hallett, and Wulfsohn, Muholi engages in performance art, inserting herself as a subject in her photography, wherein she uses 'performativity to deal with the still racialized issues of female domesticity – black women doing housework for white families' (Muholi 2013: 31). Muholi complicates the dynamics of race by laying bare queer desire and frankly depicting sexual intimacy between same-sex lovers. According to Y. A. Gust and P. E. John (cited in Matebeni 2013: 414), Muholi 'makes imaginable, visible and speakable interracial "queer" desire while simultaneously opening a renegotiating and unfixing of hegemonic blackness' and highlights the possibility of 'claiming black female sexual agency' within those intimate relationships even when difference in power between the women is undeniably present.

'Massa' and Mina(h) explores the complex bonds of friendship between black, female domestic workers and their white, female employers, as well as the barriers that keep them firmly in their respective socioeconomic locations. Muholi explains that *'Massa' and Mina(h)* can be 'translated to mean Master and Me' (Onlywith 2012). The word 'massa' is a vernacular pronunciation of 'master' associated specifically with the way black men and women addressed their white, male 'owners'. Because of that history, the word 'massa' is resonant with violence, subjugation, and inequality. 'Mina' has a less fraught context; it is the word for 'I' in isiZulu.

The photographs in the series depict a fictional maid and madam. The part of the maid is played by Muholi, and the madam – ambiguously titled 'Massa' – is played by a white woman whose face and identity remain either out of the frame, obscured, or represented by the presence of a pet. These performative photographs highlight the contradictions and falsehoods underlying comforting narratives of 'family' and 'friendship' that assuage the discomfort felt by those in powerful socioeconomic positions; the visual narrative intimates a quiet curiosity and desire between a white madam and black maid, which Gabi Ngcobo (2010) argues is an 'emerging love affair' that the two women explore while remaining 'within their designated "roles"'.

In one of the photographs, *Massa(h) and Minah 1*, the maid, played by Muholi, has her hands over her white employer's eyes; they are evidently playing a game of 'guess who?' We know who is a maid and who is a madam not only because those positions are racialized in South Africa, but also because the maid figure wears a pale blue and white pinstriped uniform and a bleached white *doek*. Hlonipha Mokoena points out that the ubiquitous maid's uniform plays an important role in ensuring that both maid and madam remain aware of their social location, masking the exploitation of black domestic workers in contemporary South Africa. In her blogpost, Mokoena (2010) argues that the uniform

> is a cultural and sartorial artefact – part throwback to some aristocratic age when all wealthy households had liveried servants and part mockery of African femininity ... for the maid to do her work she has to strip herself of all accessories and clothes that make her unique. She has to become nondescript, inconspicuous, non-threatening. For her to perform her duties, she has to be seen to be submitting to the discipline of sameness.

Muholi complicates this power imbalance using several visual strategies. While the maid's face can be seen, the madam's face is mostly covered by the maid's hands. The maid bends her own face lovingly over the cherubic face of the madam, further obscuring her head. The madam's chubby cheeks resemble those of a child; her large, red, plastic hoop earrings add to the sense that she has child-like taste. It is only because she is wearing lipstick, and because there is a trace of a 'parentheses line' (an arc-shaped wrinkle) near her mouth that it is clear that she is an adult. The madam does not appear to be alarmed by the person who covered her eyes, so we know that there is trust and intimacy between the two women. In having the uniformed figure of a servant place her face and body so close to that of her 'massa-mistress', Muholi allows us to note the ways in which intimacy might create subtle shifts – if not reversals – of power. She hints at the fluid power dynamics inherent in such domestic relationships, which seem, at first to be stuck in a rigid binary: madam has all, maid has none.

In another photograph, *Massa(h) and Minah 2*, the camera is placed at floor-level, capturing the maid's body and face as she looks at the passing figure of her madam, her face curiously framed between the madam's parted legs, caught mid-stride. The maid is on all fours, polishing the floor in a blue-painted room that almost matches the color of her uniform. In the foreground, we see the bottom half of the figure of a white woman – presumably the madam, slip by in a translucent, flower-patterned summer dress and aquamarine high-heeled mule sandals. The madam's clothing, and especially her footwear – impractical, decorative shoes that slip off easily – signal a carefree lifestyle that requires little physical labor or walking. While the madam embodies movement and lightness, the maid, positioned solidly on the floor, is engaged in a repetitive, circular motion of floor-polishing. However, although the text of the maid's face, body, and actions speak of uniformity, invisibility, and monotonous labor, her gaze declares something converse to disempowerment: she is free to look and desire, and in that freedom, she displays a lack of subservience. Still, while maid and madam might mutually engage in constituting each other's desire, such attractions cannot be celebrated as emblems of postcolonial hybridity; the difference in power between them is too apparent to be ignored by easy theorising about our interdependencies and entanglements.

A third photograph, *Massa and Mina(h) 3*, shows Muholi from the waist up, seated to the left of a sweet-faced dog. She is unclothed – her breasts are exposed, accentuating her dark nipples – and her dreadlocks form a leonine mane around her head. The tattoo on Muholi's shoulder – an anatomical drawing of a womb, curling arms of fallopian tubes, and ovaries dangling like heavy fruit – means that we are assured that this is she, Zanele Muholi. The dog she is seated next to has well-maintained, near-white fur that turns golden at the snout and ears; it is a variety that needs its curling hair trimmed regularly. Muholi's deep brown arm wraps around the dog affectionately, but her eyes look away, to the left. There is the trace of an ironic smile on her lips. Further accentuating the 'joke' in this photograph is the dog's ample, pink tongue, which is caught in mid-lick, just as the tongue is wrapping around its nose. It is clear that the dog is dependent on Muholi's performative character's care. We know that it is domesticated because of the chain-link collar used for attaching a leash, and the bone-shaped blue metal tag that carries its identification. Although this might be her massa-mistress' pet, it is also possible to imagine that the dog is a stand in for the massa-mistress: subservient, dependent, domesticated by the domestic help. Muholi notes that the series is 'wholly inspired by my mother [Bester Muholi] who worked as a domestic worker for 42 years. I wanted to tell her story as well as highlight the parallels of her story' (Onlywith 2012). Muholi (2013: 31) wanted 'to acknowledge all domestic workers around the globe who continue to labor with dignity, while often facing physical, financial, and emotional abuses in their place of work'. She explains (Onlywith 2012),

Domestic workers were viewed as these men and women who did not have any education or skills but in essence they raised these families' children at the expense of their own. They were mothers to some of the nation's greatest people. They did work that should be done by four people, they were overworked and underpaid. All the while they did their work exceptionally and were proud of their occupations. This was an ode to my mother but also to draw attention to the inequalities that date back from slavery to the present day era of boss and subordinate. The worker gives up their life and they get exploited in return.

Muholi's work is a powerful, public, and complex political act, in that it has the ability to make us reflect, word, and acknowledge the complexities of the postcolonial present. The figure of the maid, in her pinstriped uniform, is part comforting familiarity and part discomfort. Her body and her labor are a palpable – if unspoken of – trace: an absence/presence 'service-provider' in our imaginary, who also speaks to our unspeakable desires. She is a remainder and reminder of apartheid, and the structural, economic, and social inequalities that remain unresolved – and, in fact, exaggerated – in the neoliberal present. Perhaps fantasy and longing are the only ways through which the maid can negotiate a space for agency; perhaps it is only in dreamlife, which has no way of coming to fruition, where she might imagine a reversal of power.

In attempting to 'highlight the parallels' to her mother's story, Muholi shows us that although the conditions that domestic staff had to live under in the 1960s – as evidenced in the photographs taken by Cole (1960s), or by Badsha, Hallett and Wulfsohn (1970s and 1980s) – may not be the same as the 2000s, the effects of economic realities on black domestic workers means that their relationships to their masters and mistresses remain consistent with those of bygone eras. Muholi's argument does not need to be historicized or periodized, precisely because her knowledge of the personal experiences of domestic workers shows her that not much has changed in South Africa.

Muholi's performative maids and madams who hint at interracial 'queer' desire, Wulfsohn's images of affluent, leisured madams and their maids at work, Hallett's domestic workers in Sea Point, Badsha's Indian madam and her maid in Durban, and Cole's series of photographs depicting the isolation and loneliness of maids' lives – each of these photographs captures a South African contradiction: the level of intimacy and distance between maid and madam. We see her instrumental position as laboring-object in the South African family scene: the maid is visible, and present in the domestic landscapes of the affluent, and yet, she is simultaneously invisible in those spaces, disappearing into the background.

LEGISLATING AN INSTITUTION BASED ON INTIMACY

The intimate bond cultivated between domestic workers and their female employers, essential for maintaining the relationship, remains central in the everyday functioning of South Africa in the post-apartheid present; Du Plessis (2011: 46, 48) argues that the institution of domestic work is not only 'intricately woven into the fabric of everyday life and [provides] continuity between the apartheid and post-apartheid social orders', but that it seems also 'to have a specific quality that allows it to carry and encapsulate something of the apartheid moral order that goes beyond the actual practice'. The relationship between madams and their maids, often fostered over a maid's many years – even decades – of service to a single family, is understood to transcend the sphere of politics. Thus, the institution of domestic work had little to no regulation until recently. It 'effectively operated' in 'a legal vacuum', with little or no regulation of working conditions or protection for workers (Jacklyn Cock cited in Durrheim et al. 2014: 3). It was '[o]nly in 1993 … [that] some legal protection [was] afforded to domestic workers [when] the government amended the Basic Conditions of Employment Act to extend certain rights to full-time domestic workers'. Still, the Act does not cover part-time workers (Du Preez et al. 2010, 395). An attempt to institute a minimum wage depending on region was passed in 2002. Despite these improvements, wages were, and are, low. This, coupled with rampant unemployment and lack of opportunity for women to make a living in rural or urban centers, gave the apartheid state access to an abundant, exploitable workforce ready to do the work demanded of them. Black women became a 'freely available' and 'abundant and affordable labor force', cooking, cleaning, and taking care of white families' children (Durrheim et al. 2014: 3). But 'introducing legislation to govern domestic employment relationships has little impact', Jeffrey du Preez et al. (2010: 400) found, notwithstanding attempts at instituting a minimum wage, working hours, and the obligation to present domestic workers with a contract. Employers often had little knowledge of 'wage and labor regulations governing domestic work', or found ways to circumvent the laws. Such resistance to change, writes Du Plessis (2011: 46), speaks powerfully to our failure to understand the ways in which segregation according to race, and the values of white supremacy remain 'interwoven in the texture of everyday life: domestic work was [and is] intimately bound up with the way of life South Africa offered its white middle classes, as well as large sections of the white working class'.

Thus, while the South African state has, in recent years, 'made significant efforts to turn this historically inhospitable informal sector of the economy into a substantially more formal and equitable sector', Stu Woolman and Michael Bishop (2007: 600) point out, 'most domestic workers are often only notionally free to alter their conditions of employment'; well-meaning policies and laws only work 'against a background in which people are assumed to be free to move and to alienate their labor'. When conditions are such that 'alternative employment and housing are scarce, education and skill levels are low', as is the case in South Africa, the structures necessary for prohibition of servitude are weak (599). Despite prohibitions on conditions of servitude, labor relationships that appear to be voluntary remain forms of domination because of social difference and lack of access to choices that would allow laborers to change their circumstances.

Further, in situations where there are obvious socioeconomic and political differences in power between two parties, the informal bonds of affection, often supported by dependency, create connections that are not easily identifiable along the axes of existing power relations. Friendships between madams and their maids can involve, on the one hand, practices that resist structures of oppression, yet also create, maintain, and benefit from those same structures. As Du Preez et al. (2010: 396) argue, paid domestic work, because 'it takes place in the employer's home', has 'certain unique characteristics that make it different from almost all other forms of paid work'. Because the labor takes place in the intimate spaces of the employer's home, it 'confuses and complicates the conceptual divide between family and work, custom and contract, affection and duty, the home and the world' (Du Plessis 2011: 46).

Although both employers and domestic laborers may recognize the inequality inherent in this institution, the cultivated aura of caring for each other allows both parties to continue to imagine the bond through the metaphors of family and friendship. Further, the fundamentally exploitative nature of the relationship is elided by many acts of charity and generosity. Kevin Durrheim et al. (2014: 7) conclude that the reason that 'such acts of generosity featured so frequently, indeed so insistently' is because heroic narratives 'soften, minimise and occlude' the 'fundamentally instrumental and exploitative character' of the relationship; after all, had the domestic been paid a fair wage, she would be able to pay for her own toiletries, children's school fees, and transport costs. The downward flow of assistance from employer to worker preserved the amicability of the relationship, nurturing warm feelings, emotional intimacy, and a sense of mutual responsibility. Yet these positive outcomes come at the cost of a widening gulf in status and increasing forms of dependency and gratitude.

MINOR RUPTURES

There are more signs that friendship between madams and maids is not as simple, or as untroubled as one might imagine. Take one of the taxis that wind down the mountain toward the bus station at around 3 or 4pm in Cape Town, and – if you speak Afrikaans or isiXhosa – you'll be able to collect salacious details about the local madams' – as well as their children's and their husbands' – doings. The gossip of the 'domestic' signals a different understanding of the relationship between madam and maid. The raucous laughter is an outlet, a survival tactic; but it also indicative of the maid's own perception of her 'native' subjectivity. Though madams throughout South Africa may believe that their maids' loyalty is bound by affection and gratitude, and that theirs is an unbreakable emotional bond, the ironic laughter, and the willingness with which the private boundaries of households are broken within the safety of this moving vehicle, speaks volumes. First, we realize that this ironic laughter is, perhaps, one of the few avenues of subversion available; that 'outing' the breaks in their madams' carefully cultivated myths of perfection is a way of dismantling the maids' own labor. But why trouble the value given to one's labor? Because maids are intrinsic to creating the material conditions on which the primary myth of their madams' perfection depends, this outing of imperfection is a way of undermining the secondary myth of friendship between the two parties. While many friends – even those on a more equal social and economic footing – may breach the boundaries of expected privacy, this particular breach happens every day, at a particular time of the day. It is a ritual that questions the expectations of the purported friendship between madams and maids and undermines the ceremonial bond of loyalty.

This ritual lays bare the possibility that domestic workers recognize that theirs is a transactional relationship, a transaction that barely benefits the maids, but benefits the madams enormously. While the ceremonial bond – and the loyalty expected of friendship – prevents the maid from discarding this unbearable load in the confines of her madam's home, she knows that she can unceremoniously throw it off at the end of the day in the taxi. Plying the streets of South African cities, these taxis are the vehicles that allow maids to expose the truth – the unspeakable, un-outable, unbearable exploitation at the heart of domestic labor in South Africa – away from the enclaves in which madams live.

The complicated history that South Africans created is evident in the documentary photography of domestic laborers and their employers. If we explore the entangled friendships between 'maids' and 'madams' in Cole, Badsha, Hallett, Wulfsohn, and Muholi's work in terms of power relations, we notice a curious inversion. We notice, at times, the visibility of the domestic worker, and the relative invisibility of the employer; yet, at the same time, the bodies of the domestics seem to protrude – the employers' and their children's bodies appear normalized (and therefore not as visible, since they don't call attention to themselves), while the bodies of the domestics seem out of place. This inversion of who is noticed, and who is not noticed, seems to contradict our conventional understandings about power. Typically, we imagine that those who have little power are less visible than the powerful. Levels of visibility or invisibility hint at the relativity of power in a particular landscapes. Although we might intuitively imagine that a person's visibility is proof of her/his power, looking like everyone else (rather than standing out) signals belonging, allowing a person access to power through the type of invisibility afforded to those carrying markers of power. While bodies of those who display powerful or dominant traits are allowed to pass with less examination and minimal intrusion, othered bodies are made more visible in order to police and control their movements.

The question of visibility/invisibility is part of larger discussions about how othered bodies experience, encounter, and travel through centers and spaces of power. Not long ago, these were spaces of terror for black bodies in South Africa, who could be stopped, interrogated about their legitimacy in those spaces, and if traveling without the correct documentation, imprisoned. Appearing as 'white' or 'European' in South Africa affords a certain invisibility and access that many have not acknowledged. For domestic workers who are internal immigrants in white spaces, being visible removes and reduces their power and access.

While they are intended to disappear in domestic spaces of labor, and are present only to enhance the opulence, cleanliness, and functionality of those spaces – and thereby elevate the visibility and social standing of their employers – it is when they move in between the space of their employers' homes and their own homes in removed locations that they become visible. Out on the streets, waiting for the evening taxi to take them to the central bus station, and walking the streets to the homes of their employers: this is when the body of the domestic worker is visible. If her relationship with her madam is good, she can expect some sympathy for her arduous journey; this knowledge can become a negotiating point for labor conditions, as Durrheim et al. (2014: 10) point out. She might feel secure in her employer's home, and, given the level of dependency, express loyalty to the family that employs her. She may seem, thus, for political thinkers and philosophers protected by their greater ability to deploy their agency, complicit in maintaining power structures that are detrimental to her.

Cole, Badsha, Hallett, Wulfsohn, and Muholi's work may not change entrenched institutions, especially not one as intrinsic to the day-to-day lives of millions of middle-class South Africans as is the daily labor of the 'domestic'. For those who are part of the audience of the photography, art or literature, the intimate bond between maid and madam – one that should cause enough discomfort to both parties for it to change to a more equitable relationship between employer and employee – continues without question. But the disruption that art provides, however minor, may provoke a rupture, giving pause to those who unthinkingly accept the assumptions behind their self-protective paternalism.

REFERENCES

Baderoon, Gabeeba. 2014. *Regarding Muslims: From Slavery to Post Apartheid*. Johannesburg: Wits University Press.

Badsha, Omar. 1979. *Letter to Farzanah*. Durban: Institute for Black Research.

Baer, Ulrich. 2014. 'Ernest Cole's *House of Bondage:* The Photography of Witnessing.' *Grey Gazette* 15(1):1–7, accessed January 30, 2015, http://www.nyu.edu/greyart/exhibits/ernest_cole/Baer_20140905_LO_YS_FINAL_ill_for%20web.pdf.

Cole, Ernest. 1967. *House of Bondage: A South African Black Man Exposes in His Own Pictures and Words the Bitter Life of His Homeland Today*. New York, NY: Random House, Ridge Press.

Cole, Ernest, Gunilla Knape and Struan Robertson. 2010. *Ernest Cole: Photographer.* Göttingen: Hasselblad Foundation & Steidl Publishers.

Comaroff, Jean, and John L. Comaroff. 2006. 'Figuring Crime: Quantifacts and the Production of the Un/real.' *Public Culture* 18(1): 209–246.

Du Plessis, Irma. 2011. 'Nation, Family, Intimacy: The Domain of the Domestic in the Social Imaginary.' *South African Review of Sociology* 42(2): 45–65.

Du Preez, Jeffrey, Claire Beswick, Louise Whittaker and David Dickinson. 2010. 'The Employment Relationship in the Domestic Workspace in South Africa: Beyond the Apartheid Legacy.' *Social Dynamics* 36(2): 395–409.

Durrheim, Kevin, Nicola Jacobs and John Dixon. 2014. 'Explaining the Paradoxical Effects of Intergroup Contact: Paternalistic Relations and System Justification in Domestic Labor in South Africa.' *International Journal of Intercultural Relations* 41: 150–164. Accessed January 30, 2015 http://dx.doi.org/10.1016/j.ijintrel.2013.11.006

Hallett, George. 2014. 'A Nomad's Harvest: A Retrospective Exhibition of Photographs by George Hallett.' Iziko South African National Gallery, March 5 to July 9. Accessed January 30, 2015 http://www.iziko.org.za/news/entry/a-nomads-harvest

Matebeni, Zethu. 2013. 'Intimacy, Queerness, Race.' *Cultural Studies* 27(3): 404–417. Accessed February 14, 2016, https://www.academia.edu/2914273/intimacy_queerness_race

Mbembe, Achille. 2014. 'Raceless Futures in Critical Black Thought.' Lecture presented to the Johannesburg Workshop in Theory and Criticism, June 30. Johannesburg, South Africa.

Mokoena, Hlonipha. 2010. 'Anybody Can Be a Maid.' *Africa is a Country.* December 6, 2010. Accessed February 14, 2016, http://africasacountry.com/2010/12/anybody-can-be-a-maid/

Muholi, Zanele. 2008a. *Massa(h) and Minah 1*. Stevenson Gallery. Accessed February 14, 2016, http://www.stevenson.info/exhibitionsbs/muholi/massa.htm

Muholi, Zanele. 2008b. *Massa(h) and Minah 2*. Stevenson Gallery. Accessed February 14, 2016, http://www.stevenson.info/exhibitionsbs/muholi/massa1.htm

Muholi, Zanele. 2008c. *Massa(h) and Minah 3*. Stevenson Gallery. Accessed February 14, 2016, http://www.stevenson.info/exhibitionsbs/muholi/mme.htm

Muholi, Zanele. 2013. 'Mapping Our Histories: A Visual History of Black Lesbians in Post-Apartheid South Africa.' Accessed February 14, 2016, https://zasb.unibas.ch/fileadmin/afrikakomp/redaktion/Dokumente/Veranstaltungen_2013/ZM_moh_final_230609.pdf

Ngcobo, Gabi. 2010. 'It's Work as Usual: Framing Race, Class and Gender through a South African Lens.' *AfricaVenier International*. Accessed February 14, 2016, http://www.africavenir.org/publications/e-dossiers/revisions/gabi-ngcobo.html

Onlywith. 2012. 'Rewritten in black&white – Interview with Zanele Muholi.' *Soloconlamiatesta*. October 22, 2012. Accessed February 14, 2016, https://soloconlamiatesta.wordpress.com/2012/10/25/rewritten-in-blackwhite-interview-with-zanele-muholi/

Woolman, Stu, and Michael Bishop. 2007. 'Down on the Farm and Barefoot in the Kitchen: Farm Labor and Domestic Labor as Forms of Servitude.' *Development Southern Africa* 24(4): 595–606.

NOTES

1   *Madam and Eve* is a popular South African cartoon created by Stephen Francis (who writes the strip) and Enrico Schacherl (the artist/illustrator) depicting the humorous, day-to-day interactions between a 'madam' (Gwen Anderson) and her 'maid' (Eve Sisulu). Gwen is more reliant on her housekeeper than she will publically admit; Eve is a no-nonsense, honest woman who knows, nonetheless, how to employ all her wiles in order to make the best of her situation. The strip revolves around these two women's negotiations for power — particularly around Eve's attempts to extract wage increases from her stingy madam.

2   I am indebted to Achille Mbembe for these thoughts on the relationship between dreaming and liberation.

3   Cole was the son of a tailor and a washerwoman, and was classified under apartheid rules as 'black'. At age 16, he departed from home, and claiming that he was an orphan, successfully petitioned to be reclassified as 'colored'. His new racial classification allowed him to travel around the city and country without a pass.

4   Hallett was commissioned to take these photographs by the Domestic Workers' Association in the 1980s. The photographs were intended for the association's small publication.

5   Interview with George Hallett, conducted by Neelike Jayawardane. July 10, 2014.

6   Hallett specified that she lived on the premises of her employers, but was killed in an unspecified township near Cape Town.

7   Hallett, interview, 2014.

8   Comaroff and Comaroff (2006) provide an in-depth analysis of how crime statistics, though conventionally framed as value-free facts, have taken on political heft and are interpreted as evidence of disproportionate violence experienced in affluent neighborhoods and on white bodies.

10

CORNER LOVING:
WAYS OF SPEAKING ABOUT LOVE

MADEYOULOOK

MADEYOULOOK is an artists' collaborative working in Johannesburg. For the past four years, we have been thinking about issues of 'black love'. We are interested in love, specifically romantic love, as an intellectual concept, worthy of rigorous and critical engagement. It is difficult to speak about love in this way. In contemporary art, it is largely a subject relegated to the arena of emotion and not warranting serious intellectual consideration. Contemporary art has disassociated itself radically from its Romantic past and today addresses such subjects with cynicism and even disdain. It is not difficult to dismiss love, to challenge its relevance, to question its existence. It is far more difficult to begin to speak about love as a potentially subversive and illuminating subject.

We are particularly interested in black love and thinking about how 'black people in love' can serve as a subject of inquiry that might bring to the fore new or nuanced understandings of our contemporary moment. Part of the difficulty of this discussion is its complexity and its entanglement with broader issues of black life, and this difficulty represents itself in this chapter, which potentially covers too many areas and is in some parts introductory. Nonetheless we attempt it because we see it as important. It is important to speak about black love because the subject is so underrepresented, especially in South Africa. Few narratives exist of black people in love, both in popular and critical discourse. Rather, the tropes of hypersexuality, the black body, promiscuity, and lovelessness assume all the spaces for imagining black people in love. There must exist a space for considering black love as love in itself, as intimacy, care, and mutual recognition.

In 2014, MADEYOULOOK produced a body of work entitled *Corner loving* that consisted of drawings, texts, and a series of lectures, in order to explore love and black love in complex urban settings. The ongoing body of work initially existed as an exhibition shown at GoetheonMain in Johannesburg, and later revised for *Ellipses* journal in 2015 (MADEYOULOOK 2015). 'Corner loving' is a term we have adopted for the practice of lovers meeting on street corners, often at night. It occurs in places such as townships and the inner city of Johannesburg. These corners serve as places for lovers (most often in new love) to meet 'privately' to spend time together. Initially, our interest in corner loving as a practice was to think about and question why couples would find the public space of the street the most suitable space for privacy and intimacy. We were interested in the social factors that this reflected: crowded homes, living spaces shared with strangers, conservative parents, scarce resources for other spaces such as restaurants. Through exploring the practice, however, the question of love in itself became central and the project began to explore broader themes.

The project sought to express the multiple dimensions of corner loving through three forms of media. First, we worked with Nolan Dennis and Pandeani Liphosa to develop architectural-style drawings of these corners. The drawings endeavored to determine corner loving as a practice worthy of critical interrogation. Second, we included texts of fiction and non-fiction narratives in order to express the intricate and intimate elements of black love, as well as to locate it historically. Third, we organised a lecture series that explored the various thematic aspects represented in the practice of corner loving. Thembinkosi Goniwe, Ashraf Jamal, and Danai Mupotsa gave lectures. The lecture series created a platform to bring together people who were interested in starting to speak about love, and to try to understand what a discourse on love might mean (Figure 10.1).

Figure 10.1
Exhibition installation of *Corner loving* by MADEYOULOOK.

BLACK LOVE AND A RE-IMAGINED LEXICON

Throughout the process, the ways in which varying media 'speak' about love differently became evident. In each medium, there existed a different kind of articulation, a different kind of elocution. It became clear that the ways in which we 'speak' about love determine the weight and criticality of the subject itself – both in form and in content. In general, it was difficult for all involved in the project (writers, lecturers, audiences) to find the right form of articulation, to find the right words and tones, to develop a new language (or way of speaking). We struggled with visual imaging of love and corner loving in particular. When considering a form or medium in which to explore this practice, we considered photography, film, and other options. However, we were constantly concerned about how to represent this practice without over-emphasising sexuality perceived as 'inherent', or demeaning the privacy of these lovers. These mediums too easily became voyeuristic and created a surface-level representation rather than excavating the underlying, more interesting, issues.

The perception of sexuality as 'inherent' became a question for us. How would we depict a practice of love by black people, in ways that moved outside of the tropes of hypersexuality and promiscuity? It was this assumption of the 'inherent' that was the core issue: black, working-class love is underrepresented and there is little imagery to which our minds can turn. We, as artists then, were at a loss of an imagination to draw upon: there was not an immediately available language to use. A lexicon particular to black love, outside of the stereotypes, does not exist. Since it is the intention of this text to begin this discussion, we will attempt to address preliminarily, a few key words.

Love: when referring to love, we refer specifically to romantic love, a feeling of love between a hetero- or homosexual couple not determined by time frame, age of lovers, or religious determination. We are specifically interested in romantic love – rather than other forms of love – because we see it as a subject that holds a contemporary urgency, where other forms of love, such as that of parenthood or between siblings, has a more comfortable or already engaged place in black narratives. While these subjects certainly warrant further exploration, romantic love has a more immediate priority as a space for engaging an almost entirely unexplored issue.

Affect/affective language: as opposed to love, affect refers to the experience of feeling and emotion. This might refer to negative, positive, or other feelings, but it exists in direct opposition to the assumed impartiality of distanced academic jargon.

Black love: '*black* love' is a term that requires the emphasis of blackness. In the sense that loving in itself, as a popular idea, has not included those who are black, it directly references an absence that needs to be filled. Black love in particular refers to love between two individuals who self-identify as black or brown, and form associations on those terms. In this text, we refer to black as a self-identification of various peoples across the globe, but most often refer to the specific experiences of blackness in South Africa.

Tenderness: refers to an aspect of love that might include such feelings or responses as carefulness, gentleness, intimacy, and softness.

Language/lexicon: refers to the words and collection of words that might be used to define and in so doing imagine a thing.

Speaking/talking: refers to the act of using a language or lexicon, in verbal, written, artistic, and other forms.

LOVE AND BLACK LOVE IN CONTEMPORARY ART

The underrepresentation of love within contemporary art is largely a consequence of visual art's break with Romanticism of the nineteenth century and a replacement by high modernist ideals of a more austere, abstract and anti-humanist form in the twentieth century (Dijkstra 2006). Contemporary art functions very much in the aftermath of modernism and has failed to retrieve much of the positive affective interests of its predecessors. While sexuality, the body, gender politics, and Queer theory have become ubiquitous in contemporary art practice, this is often in the form of a distanced and cynical approach to the romantic or sexual.[1] Another trend in contemporary depictions of love is an ironic use of the sugary and whimsical. Damien Hirst's *All You Need is Love, Love, Love* (2009), Jeff Koons's *Hanging Heart* (1994–2006) and Robert Indiana's *Love* (1966–1999) are typical of this embellished and overstated Pop sensibility. The over-saturated love motifs from popular culture such as butterflies, heart-shaped canvases, heart-shaped Valentine's balloons, and the word LOVE in upper-case letters have only served to lock the subject of love within the sphere of cynical frivolity and sentimentality.

While significant works abound on reclaiming black sexualities and bodies, such as those of Kara Walker and Carrie Mae Weems, and locally the likes of Zanele Muholi and Nicholas Hlobo, direct references to love and black love as concepts in themselves are rare. Zina Saro-Wiwa's *Eaten by the Heart Part 1: How do Africans Kiss?* (2012), and the Lagos leg of the broader *Progress of Love* (2012/2013) exhibition at CCA (Centre for Contemporary Art), Lagos are two interesting additions. Saro-Wiwa's work has received acclaim. A video work, it consists primarily of interviews with Africans on their experiences of love in an African context, particularly in relation to the examples of black love – whether parents or other elders – that existed in their lives. This work points to the lack of such images and imaginations.

bell hooks's *All About Love: New Visions* (2000) is perhaps the most seminal work on love and black people in love, providing the basis for much of the discourse on the subject. The book explores the natures of all forms of black love, including community, non-nuclear family and friendship love, but largely dismisses romantic love to brutality, patriarchy and pain – primarily based on hooks's personal experience. The book is important in that it seeks a personalised and affective approach to speaking about love; however, it does not engage romantic love outside of the negative. However, there are a number of blogs and popular online media forums on black love, located in the U.S., that are aimed at encouraging 'healthy black relationships', such as blackloveforum.com and blackloveandmarriage.com. By comparison, little exists in the South African context outside of music and some representations on television: much Afro-Pop, some Maskandi and Isicathamiya in music, *Emzini wezinsizwa* and *Bophelo ke sempheko* more historically, and the drama series *InterSEXions* aired on South African television, as well as in writing by the likes of Can Themba (1972), Todd Matshikiza (1961), and Phaswane Mphe (2001).

A contemporary South African artist who has addressed and explored questions of love and lesbian, gay, bisexual, trans, and queer (LGBTQ) relationships through her photography is Zanele Muholi. One image, *Katlego Mashiloane and Nosipho Lavuta, Ext 2, Lakeside, Johannesburg* (from the series *Being*, 2007) subtly and beautifully reflects some of the key questions of love in contemporary South Africa. The image depicts a couple, one sitting on the other's lap, in the moment of a kiss, clearly in a kitchen – most likely of a working-class home. The couple sit closely and intimately, squeezed into a small kitchen next to a coal stove. The image is shot in a tight frame, emphasising the intimacy and domesticity of the space, and therefore emphasising the intimacy of the moment – the photographer herself sharing closeness and rapport with her subjects. The kitchen and the stove in particular attribute this intimacy to a working-class couple, and therefore speak of love and closeness between two people whose love is often undermined. The coal stove might be a historical reference, connecting this couple to generations of black love in working-class worlds; however the image is shot in contemporary saturated colour, which brings it directly into the present moment. The image propels 'ordinary' black love into normalcy, the couple's intimacy and closeness is made everyday, on a historical continuum, and the viewer is compelled to directly relate to this couple's love. This image is powerful because we identify directly with a lesbian couple in love – an important political point in contemporary South Africa. And yet the image is powerful for what it does for black love as a whole – especially in a contemporary art field that is otherwise so lacking in this subject matter.

It is from this narrow space of representation that contemporary creative discourse must now try to find ways of speaking about love. Our experience has been that many people struggle to discuss love, and particularly black love. When introducing the idea of corner loving to people in our daily conversations, many used words such as 'illicit', 'clandestine', 'furtive', 'not quite kosher', and 'not protected by the marriage bed'. When imagining public displays of love and intimacy by black people, the immediate responses are negative. By comparison, we can imagine, the picture of a white couple kissing on a bench would not evoke the same visceral responses. Further to this, there seemed to be a difficulty for many to understand and then articulate why a subject such as corner loving would even be considered (or considered separately to forms of public displays of affection) for such detailed study. This reflects, albeit crudely, a general difficulty in recognizing and then further articulating a discourse on black love.

THE CHALLENGE OF SPEAKING ABOUT BLACK LOVE

At the Bonani Africa photography conference in 2010, Thembinkosi Goniwe challenged the South African art world and academia to begin making work about love. Consequently, we asked Goniwe to deliver a lecture about these themes as part of *Corner loving*. Goniwe's lecture was the last in a three-part series following talks by Danai Mupotsa and Ashraf Jamal, all part of the exhibition installation *Corner loving* at GoetheonMain in Johannesburg. Mupotsa's lecture centered on the 'white wedding' as a complex reflection of middle-class black identities, of the self and social context rather than the trope of appropriation that is often attributed to the practice. Jamal's lecture dealt with the issue of empathy, and love as empathic tool. In all three lectures, there remained the difficulty of finding the right register, the right approach, and the right words to fully articulate the role that a discourse on black love can play in our broader understandings of contemporary society. For brevity's sake we focus here on Goniwe's lecture, in which he applied a number of interesting approaches that might help us start to find possible ways of speaking about love.

The primary basis of Goniwe's lecture was to present the subject of love along a genealogy of thought that begins with Njabulo Ndebele's *Rediscovery of the Ordinary* (1986) and continues with Albie Sachs' 'Preparing Ourselves for Freedom' (1991). Both Ndebele and Sachs wrote at a period when the end of apartheid was in sight and pioneered the beginning of a conversation on imagining a post-apartheid society. For both there was the significant need to focus on issues of ordinary life, such as love, and an emphasis on the ability of creative forms to best articulate this. For Goniwe, the development of an intellectual discourse specifically on love is part of the political project of reclaiming the ordinary and ordinarily powerful parts of life that have been denied by our history. Presenting the discourse of love within this genealogy immediately infers a political and intellectual weight to the subject of black love that is otherwise denied. Furthermore, this weight then enables a more tentative experimentation with words and tonalities, enabling a move away from strict, stifling academic jargon (which would otherwise be necessary to establish some 'seriousness') and to move towards an affective and intimate way of speaking about love. *It is this act – of intimate and tender language – that is perhaps most profound and most important to a new discourse on black love.*

Goniwe began his lecture with a confession: 'Initially I was reluctant to talk. Because I stopped doing talks. For two reasons: they "put you out there", and they render you vulnerable.' Goniwe's confession established an intimate connection to the audience, a request for trust and affinity. This is a request to earnestly engage, for the purposes of building a discussion, and with people who are invested in a similar project. With vulnerability comes an implicit request for a response that reflects a similar tenderness from the audience, as that with which the ideas will be proffered. This is a courtship of sorts: an affective relationship is attempted. In doing so, Goniwe creates a tone that reflects the complexity of the subject he is discussing and ensures a collective recognition of the fragility of the subject and its potential for thought. Goniwe then dedicated the lecture to MADEYOULOOK as his former students, explicitly indicating his choice to render himself vulnerable as part of developing a community of practice, as a teacher, but also in dedication, as a peer. Further, the dedication was a sentimental act attributing a personal significance to his students. In so doing, Goniwe again rendered himself vulnerable and specified his lecture as a space of tenderness and *care-full* discussion.

At the same time, Goniwe was able to merge words of tenderness with hard-hitting statements that point to the political power and necessity of speaking about love. Quoting Steve Biko and Frantz Fanon, Goniwe connected the potential for love as a revolutionary subject and posited that a return to the writings of these theorists reveals an argument for the role of love in reclaiming black identities. His words did not belittle or 'make soft' the contemporary urgency of such a conversation. He connected the terms of intimacy with the terms of critique. Goniwe went on to talk about how a discourse on love might be developed and encouraged the seeking out of entry points into a discussion about love. In so doing, we may begin to find texts (visual and written) that can assist us with ways of speaking about love. In referencing Biko, Fanon, Homi Bhabha and other writers who may not directly discuss the topic of black love, Goniwe revealed that through their writing we might find theoretical lenses from which to consider it.

What Goniwe points to is the investment in varied texts as potential interfaces and intersections. While there may not be a myriad of direct references to black love currently, a number of texts exist that can be entry points or catalysts for wider ideas. In his lecture he referenced the work of writer Ama Ata Aidoo (2006) and connected it to the artworks of Zanele Muholi and Tracey Rose among others. Goniwe provides a tool or technique by which we may find images, words, and approaches that collectively enable the content from which the discussion is possible. While Muholi's work explores queer identities primarily, the insertion of narratives of intimacy, sexuality, and even love, means her work serves as a prompt into discussions of black love. Rose's *The Kiss* (2001) explores wider themes of race and gender, but has an overarching theme of romance that enables an entry into conversations about love. Further in quoting Aidoo's work, Goniwe claims the importance of recognizing and exchanging with the ideas and works of artists, scholars, writers, and others who are asking the same questions and engaging themes of black love.

DRAWING LOVE ON THE CORNER: VISUAL TONALITY

The *Corner loving* project searched for a language to bring together a critical perspective on knowledge production and a tender and mindful tonality. Over a four-year period, we sought out a visual form that would represent the critical aspects of the project, define the practice within a canon of thought, and achieve a tonality that reflects the subject matter itself. We found this form in drawing. We needed to remove the couples from the image of corner loving, partly to ensure privacy of the corners and also to avoid a voyeuristic (and therefore judgmental) tone in the work. We were interested in considering the practice in an open and inquisitive way. We needed a form that would reflect this openness visually. Furthermore we were interested in a medium or language that would be truthful to the contexts in which corner loving happens, but would also reflect a beauty and reverence for the practice. By using drawing, the images would represent an essence of a space rather than a clinical accuracy.

At the same time, we were interested in a form that would enable a rigorous interrogation of the practice. In so doing, we were interested (as we have been in previous work) in who determines the production of knowledge and about what subjects. To develop an approach that would elevate this practice and its social circumstances to a worthiness of consideration as knowledge production, we used notation and pseudo-scientific data to detail the number of cars and pedestrians in the area, the level of light, the circumference of light coverage, the sound levels, and surrounding points of interest, among others. Some of the notations referred to colloquial practice, attempting to enter these into an intellectual lexicon: 'Kapa-ring: is also a feature of corner loving. Friends of ten accompany one another and will hang back and hang out at a respectful distance while their friend meets their partner > security feature > peer socialisation > moral support.' The notations are detailed and numerous, requiring investment from the viewer with the content of the image. The content of the notations, and the extent of the data create a sense of a confidential sharing of the privacies of that corner. This produces an intimacy between the viewer and the corner.

The drawings are in a formal architectural-plan style, in a removed digital language to emphasise the 'scientific' or formal nature of the studies. While formalist and removed, the drawings are also simple and beautiful. The lines are fine and reduced, giving the drawings a light and open sensibility, emphasising the positive aspects of the practice. The fragility and intricacy of the lines, and the detail of the notations, require that the viewer engage the work up close and over some time in order to read the notations (Figures 10.2-10.5).

ARCHIVES OF BLACK LOVE

While some level of tenderness was achieved in the formal nature of the drawings, we still felt that the intrinsic individual and personal experiences of these corners were, in some way, missing. In considering a medium that might bring to the fore a deeper and more nuanced understanding of the ways in which lovers understand their own practice, and exist within a broader and long-standing tradition of love, we looked to written narrative.

The project featured five texts from archives and contemporary writers. The five texts were placed in ad hoc piles in the exhibition space and did not stand in direct relation to the other elements in the show, but rather as things in

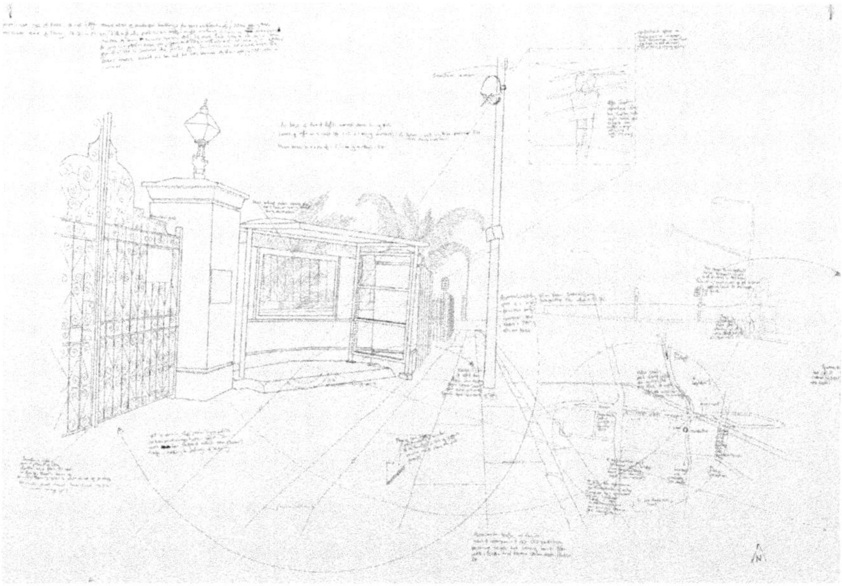

Figure 10.2
Corner loving by MADEYOULOOK. © Andreas Vlachakis

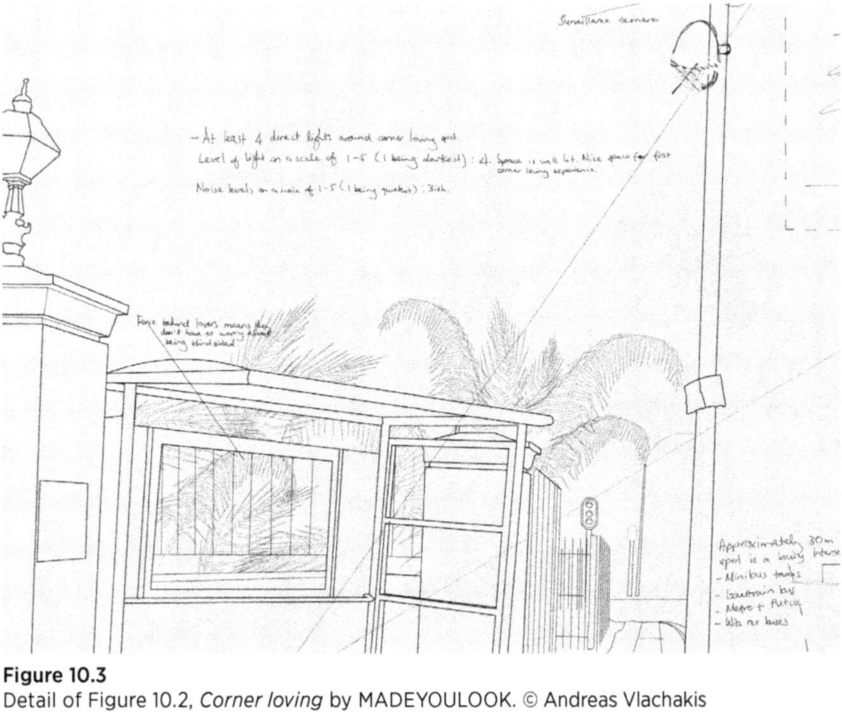

Figure 10.3
Detail of Figure 10.2, *Corner loving* by MADEYOULOOK. © Andreas Vlachakis

Figure 10.4
Corner loving by MADEYOULOOK. © Andreas Vlachakis

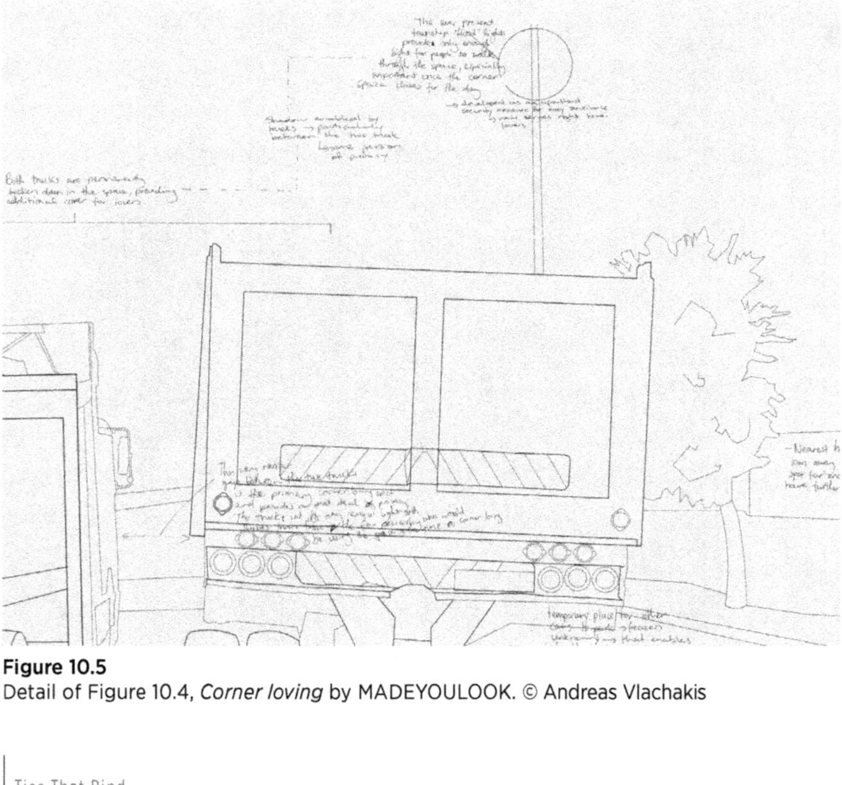

Figure 10.5
Detail of Figure 10.4, *Corner loving* by MADEYOULOOK. © Andreas Vlachakis

themselves. Each pile had 300 copies and could be taken home by exhibition visitors, therefore serving as a disseminator of the ideas put forward in the texts. The first is an archival love letter from a migrant worker to his wife at home in rural Bechuanaland of the 1930s. The letter breaks from the well-documented *bhupi bo fedile* narrative – failed masculinities, absent fathers, migrant poverty and urban acculturation – that has come to be associated with migrancy in South Africa and migrant letter writing of the time (Breckenridge 2000; Schapera 1941; and others from a large literature). The writer begins: 'I still think of how we loved each other.' The writer uses poetic phrases and evokes a fragile nostalgia that accentuates his faithful recollection of his wife's body, their closeness, and their shared sexual intimacy. It is also worth noting that the letter exists within a broader context of illiteracy. It may have been written by a literate interlocutor and read by an intermediary (Breckenridge 2000). This dynamic hints at a historical trajectory for the public-ness of intimacy and love between black people over time.

The second text, an excerpt from Todd Matshikiza's autobiographical book *Chocolates for My Wife* (1961: 126), is the author's recollection of an incident involving apartheid police while waiting late one night for the bus home. Recounting the exchange he writes:

> 'Oh Ghod, this one of the King Kong kaffirs. Okay an' what's that you got in the parcel, jong?'
>
> 'It's choc'lat's, baas, choc'lat's for my wife. I jus' got them now from a friend.'
>
> 'Oho, Jesus, Piet listen to this one. Of all my night shifts I never met a baboon like this one.' They gathered around me.
>
> 'Please, baas, don't break the box.'
>
> 'Ha, ha, ha … caw … caw … caw, ha, ha, ha,' until they split their sides with laughter. 'The monkey got choc'lat's for his wife …'
>
> They laughed into their big police van and their echo drifted into the night echoing long after they had gone. 'The maid is now called wife, caw, caw, caw, and choc'lat's for her!'

Matshikiza's literary re-creation of an emotionally brutal encounter with apartheid is reflective of deeply seated societal preconceptions about the ways in which black people love or show affection – the policeman indicates that he has never seen a black man with chocolates for his wife. Further, it points to the ways in which black people in South Africa have been 'allowed' to love, where social constructs and laws determined who could love, when, and how – as well as how the state could insert itself into the most intimate parts of people's lives. While much has been discussed about the ways in which love across races was outlawed and policed by the apartheid state (through legislation such as the Immorality Act and its amendments, and the Prevention of Mixed Marriages Act), Matshikiza and his box of chocolates – much like the migrant's letter – highlight how structural racism has defined the ways in which black love can exist and so often fails. It is important to note the language of the interaction: the culture of discrimination and denigration that denies the empowering of love. Matshikiza immediately uses the word 'baas' to assume an inferior position for his own protection, and that of the chocolates, while the policemen use words such as 'kaffir', 'baboon', 'monkey': all words that deny the humanism that love affirms.

This passage points directly to the difficulties of imagination where black love is concerned. The act of a black man taking home chocolates for his wife is inconceivable to his persecutors. But even more unthinkable is the possibility that a 'boy' can be a husband and the 'maid' a wife, or that black bodies can be deserving of love. Matshikiza goes on:

> I crawled into bed beside my long suffering wife who had not slept for many nights, exhausted with King Kong happenings. Lay on my back gazing into the ceiling where the flickering candlelight danced ever so gently, drawing images of travel and freedom.
> 'Darling, let's try somewhere else.'
> 'Mh ...'
> 'England.'
> 'America.'
> 'Anywhere else on earth is better than here.'

Matshikiza's (1961: 127) conversation with his wife Esme, following immediately after his encounter with the police, reveals a desperation for normality, dignity, and the right to love (or bear chocolates for one's wife) that can be possible only outside of the apartheid state.

The third archival text (ANC Archives), a letter co-authored by two young lovers who are also Umkhonto we Sizwe (MK) soldiers exiled at the height of apartheid, explores just this, and extends the questions of love in a political climate of such 'un-ordinariness'. It is part of a national discourse that denies or downplays the strength of the ordinary that is retained in the midst of such extremes (as Goniwe discusses in relation to framings of the black body as capable only of revolution). Importantly, this letter is part of a larger archive of MK soldiers in exile requesting the help or permission of the ANC to see long-estranged family members, or to help bury their deceased parents, and commonly for permission to marry. In many cases, the ANC supported MK soldiers, even paying lobola (Lissoni and Suriano 2014). This couple writes to the ANC leadership in Tanzania requesting permission to get married. The letter voices an awkward hybrid of bureaucratic parlance and the vulnerable language of two people in love. This is particularly challenging when attempting to establish that love can be a profound, stable phenomenon, and at once a dizzying emotion. The letter points to a generation of young people who sought to find some connection between revolutionary intentions and 'normal' life. A powerful attempt in a difficult world.

ROMANTIC INHERITANCE AND INTIMATE FRAMES OF REFERENCE

Finally, we commissioned two texts by young black writers for the *Corner loving* project. The first is by Buyani Duma (2014) and is a fictional parody entitled *Skhotane Love*. The text is a humorous and disturbing first-person narrative of a young woman embarrassed to ask her friend to re-use her weave, second-hand. The woman, who is considered 'the princess Diana of the taxi ranks', and would otherwise be seen only in the best and newest attire, can no longer afford these because she is in love with a Skhotane man. 'Skhotane' is a term referring to a subculture of predominantly young black men who wear exorbitantly expensive Italian clothing – characterized by large floral prints and brightly coloured Carvela shoes – and then burn them (and often burn cash) in conspicuous displays of manic consumption. This text is significant in its honest and stark reflection of the legacies of black love through apartheid and social degradation of 'ordinary' life and love. In many ways it indicates the difficult contemporary state of love that emanates from the challenging situations reflected in the archival texts we discuss. The protagonist feeds her lover's lifestyle because she is in love with him, and because she is enamored by a post-1994 South Africa that reflects its freedom in wild consumption. This text reflects a contemporary moment where black love is deeply challenged by poverty and inequality and the ways in which these function in black imaginaries and intimacy.

The final text, *kwaGagashe: A Micro Short*, by poet and writer Pamella Dlungwana (2014), is a fictional narrative about a Maskandi musician who takes his broken accordion to a traditional healer to be fixed (Figure 10.6). Without it, he is unable to 'speak' his love, as the accordion serves as a metamorphosing tool for emotional expression. Dlungwana's text is an exemplary approach to finding ways of speaking about language. *Key to her approach is the use of localized and dialectal terms, metaphors and references that, if understood, reflect the myriad complexities of black love, intimacy, emotion, and romantic inheritance.* Dlungwana invokes an individual who is a complex – but in many ways ordinary – combination of rural/township, traditional/ modern, and mute/expressive in ways that reflect a contemporary South African reality. In the following excerpt, Dlungwana makes a number of references that contextualise this love, and through association reflect its inherent (and important) blackness:

> In the evening light with cars drooping by, he knows her eyes in the headlights of a gusheshe which pull black streaks from the depths of her shy brown eyes, he hears the twitter of her Madam as she passes them mid embrace and in his chorus, he hears the mischief of the neighbourhood brats as they play unsolicited back up. These things make her smile, they make her hide her face in his chest and laugh as she scratches the ground with her shoe, leaving some illegible mark for the ants to decipher.

Corner loving is suggested in the mention of her eyes flashing in the light of passing cars, and in the range of potential voyeurs. The phrase 'he knows her eyes in the headlights of a gusheshe' suggests they mainly meet in this public way, and that their familiarity is determined within this context. The 'gusheshe' and the 'illegible mark' left in the ground evoke a township setting, and determine the couple as black – defining and acknowledging a specific black experience.

Dlungwana's text tells of a 'Madam' – suggesting the woman is a domestic worker, and alluding to the power dynamics of domestic labor, live-in help, and the limitations of working-class relationships. The presence of

Figure 10.6
Texts, with lecture area in background, in exhibition *Corner loving* by MADEYOULOOK.
© Andreas Vlachakis

'neighbourhood brats' confirms the public nature of the lovers' meeting, and their playfulness suggests a comfort from growing up in the familiarity of corner loving, a familiarity only possible in the context of working-class townships, where boy children have the freedom to be in the streets in the evenings. She continues:

> it's a clumsy european man and his heartache and Makhosonke's waited an
> additional 2 and a half hours for Gagashe to see it, to tell him if he can teach
> it to speak, to hold utalagu and the patter of children to come in the cusp of
> its hands, to keen as he keens, to plant the grass in the sky and paint the sky
> on the ground to suit her whim and fancy.

Dlungwana refers to the accordion as 'a clumsy european man' that requires some kind of repair or tuning to suit the specificities of expressions of love by black people. In so doing she claims black love for itself, rather than as a copy or appropriation of someone or something else. The protagonist waits for Gagashe to teach his accordion to speak, suggesting the inadequacy of its current way of speaking. Dlungwana goes on to attempt to describe the specificities of black expressions of love, as in 'the patter of children to come in the cusp of its hands, to keen as he keens'. She references metaphors of the Zulu language: 'to hold utalagu', and 'to plant the grass in the sky and paint the sky on the ground', expressions that would not be understood without knowledge of the language. By so doing, she elaborates a poetic tradition intrinsic to the structure of the language, which recognizes the language in itself as historically and inherently capable of, and connected to, romance and love.

The poetics of Dlungwana's tone and structure make the reading of the text layered and emotive. Multiple re-readings expose clearer understandings and richer layers of metaphor, insinuation, and musicality. The form takes on a lyrical tempo, echoing the Maskandi music to which she refers. In its complexities and multi-layers exists a veiling and opacity that creates a kind of intimacy and secrecy of the content, providing in Dlungwana's word choices the privacy and reverence of the subject of love. There is too, a political act in the opaqueness and the layered-ness of localized metaphor. Dlungwana writes for an 'insider'; this is a text more easily readable to the working-class, isiZulu-speaking corner lover rather than the educated, middle-class university professor. By writing this way, she creates content for posterity, and interrogation that serves a different audience. Unlike the academy, which seeks to explain and to translate otherness into 'real' knowledge, Dlungwana recognizes this form as knowledge in itself. This is a form of knowledge production that, as the drawings attempted, seeks to create content about subjects that are at worst deemed below the esteem of the academy or at best seen as objects that illustrate and interpret.

CONCLUSION: TOWARDS A NEW IMAGINARY

The significance of *Corner loving* lies in the need to develop a language and discourse about black love. In the production of knowledge exists a project about defining and attempting to understand ordinary and localized practice, context and society. Based on an empirical engagement *and* in an affective response to the complexities of this knowledge, there exists the potential for real shifts in the way we come to understand each other and ourselves. It is important for us that the nature of black love, and understanding it, be part of a broader engagement with South African society and the ways in which individuals, couples, and communities negotiate the politics of the ordinary and powerful parts of life. As Ndebele (1986) urged at the turn of apartheid, these new knowledges and reclamations of otherwise un-addressed parts of life remain imperative to a recovery of the self.

There are a small number of writers, thinkers, and artists who are seeking to express these issues, to unpack the nature of black love throughout the world, and to probe what it means for how we understand ourselves. As such individuals come together and begin these discussions, the words we use and the languages we develop become increasingly critical ways of ensuring that we understand each other (at a basic level), and that we are able to work outside of the stereotypes of contemporary rhetoric, in order to move toward a visceral and embodied understanding of our words and of black love itself. The *Corner loving* project attempted to bring together a group of people, all searching for the words to speak about black love. In so doing, we became increasingly aware of our inability to connect to each other, and to our audiences. By distilling our successes and achievements – the words, the turns of phrase, the tonalities, the vulnerabilities – we might be able to begin to build a lexicon, and in so doing a new imaginary of black love.

REFERENCES

Aidoo, Ama Ata, ed. 2006. *African Love Stories*. Banbury: Ayebia Clarke.

ANC Archives. *Dar es Salaam Series.* Box 17. University of Fort Hare, National Heritage and Cultural Studies Centre.

Breckenridge, Keith. 2000. 'Love Letters and Amanuenses: Beginning the Cultural History of the Working Class Private Sphere in Southern Africa, 1900–1933.' *Journal of Southern African Studies* 26(2): 337–348.

Dijkstra, Bram. 2006. 'Bram Dijkstra: Interview by Ron Hogan.' *Beatrice.com* http://www.beatrice.com/interviews/dijkstra/

Dlungwana, Pamella. 2014. *kwaGagashe: A Micro Short*. Commissioned *for Corner loving* exhibition. GoetheonMain. Johannesburg, October 23.

Duma, Buyani. 2014. *Skothane Love*. Commissioned for *Corner loving* exhibition. GoetheonMain. Johannesburg, October 23.

Goniwe, Thembinkosi. 2010. 'De-Segregating the Audience: Race & the Politics of Exhibitions.' Paper presented at Beyond the Racial Lens: Bonani Africa 2010 Festival of Documentary Photography, Cape Town. August 19.

Hooks, bell. 2000. *All About Love: New Visions*. New York, NY: William Morrow.

Lissoni, Arianna and Maria Suriano. 2014. 'Married to the ANC: Tanzanian Women's Entanglement in South Africa's Liberation Struggle.' *Journal of Southern African Studies* 40(1): 129–150.

MADEYOULOOK. 2014. *Corner loving*. Mixed Media. Johannesburg

MADEYOULOOK. 2015. 'Corner loving.' *Ellipses Journal*. Wits School of Arts. http://www.ellipses.org.za/project/corner-loving/

Matshikiza, Todd. 1961. *Chocolates for My Wife*. London: Hodder and Stoughton.

Mphe, Phaswane. 2001. *Welcome to Our Hillbrow*. Pietermaritzburg: University of KwaZulu-Natal Press.

Ndebele, Njabulo. 1986. 'Rediscovery of the Ordinary: Some New Writings in South Africa.' *Journal of Southern African Studies* 12(2): 143–157.

Sachs, Albie. 1991. 'Preparing Ourselves for Freedom: Culture and the ANC Constitutional Guidelines.' *The Drama Review* 35: 187–193.

Schapera, Isaac. 1941. *Married Life in an African Tribe*. London: Faber and Faber.

Themba, Can. 1972. *The Will to Die*. London: Heinemann Educational Books.

NOTES

1   Some key exceptions include Felix Gonzalez-Torres' 1991 untitled work dedicated to his deceased lover and London's South Bank Centre annual Festival of Love.

11

KUTAMBA NAYE: IN SEARCH OF ANTI-RACIST AND QUEER SOLIDARITY

TSITSI JAJI

I have been hovering at the brink of this essay caught in a dizzying paradox. The editors' invitation to contribute to this collection is a call to write about race and the politics of friendship in South Africa, or, as the title puts it, 'the ties that bind'. Early on, I decided to adopt a new genre, to write a more autobiographically grounded essay than usual, but as I've sought to take up their invitation I've had to reckon with the fact that many of my most obviously interracial friendships depend on race remaining one of the unspoken and indeed unspeakable subjects. When in doubt one goes back to one's beginnings, and for me these are my too-quickly eroding mother-tongue chiShona, where kutamba naye means both to play and to dance together. What I am doing here is playing with ideas, ideas about friendship, the passage of time and yes, dancing.

As a Zimbabwean who now resides and holds citizenship in the U.S., my relation to South Africa is a transitory one, but I have often found that as a relative stranger, a sort of national poorer cousin, I have been free to speak more frankly about race with Zimbabwean friends in South Africa than at home. In this chapter I want to think about two related questions. The first concerns the silences upon which interracial friendships rest, and what might be gained and lost when such silences are breached. And the second concerns the relationship between place and friendship, a question that opens onto considering what it means to befriend another abroad, what the relationship between nostalgia and friendship might be, and how memory restructures the narratives of 'home' for diasporic subjects in ways that can productively and mutually unsettle fellow travelers. In other words, what happens when old friends meet, and speak frankly at last, and how can we make sense of the irreconcilable differences that give rise not to conflict so much as a recognition of structural antagonisms otherwise masked and mystified by the conviviality expected in schools, rehearsal spaces, apprenticeships, and other ideological state apparatuses. As the daughter of a white American mother and a black Zimbabwean father, the invitation to think about interracial friendship is necessarily confounding. The affective and libidinal economy of my own family depended on my parents, my brother, and I viewing interracial love as normative and ideal, and thus my personal orientation has largely been to avoid explicit discussion of or even attention to racial difference in intimate relationships. On the other hand, my perspective is fundamentally anchored in the contemporary Zimbabwean diaspora. There are wildly divergent estimates for the number of Zimbabweans living outside our borders, but it is certain that the largest portion of this diaspora lives in South Africa, followed by the U.K., and to a lesser extent, Australia and North America.

After two decades in the U.S. my sense of racial identity is as much shaped by American politics as by southern African sensibilities, and thus composing myself, and composing this essay, begins to seem a baroque task indeed. The counterpoint must sound well not only against the contemporary scene in South Africa, but also against recent and longer histories in Zimbabwe and the U.S. But this is precisely why I think my essay might be useful as something more than personal memoir. The question of what grounds there are for theorizing the lived experience (to borrow Frantz Fanon's formulation) of Blackness across diverse and divergent geopolitical sites is a live and fraught one. Rather than making claims of legitimacy or urgency of thinking race through U.S. and southern African frameworks, I simply want to emphasize that these are field notes that, in their particularity and paratactical juxtapositions, produce instances of opacity that generate sufficient friction to occasion what Jacques Derrida calls 'community without community … friends seeking mutual recognition without knowing each other …' (Derrida 1997: 42).

Lingering over the anxieties of genre, and the struggles of beginning to write, I look back for examples. And I recall how two of the most important voices in early twentieth-century South African political thought, Pixley ka Isaka Seme and Solomon Tshekisho Plaatje, both turned to W. E. B. Du

Bois's early work, quoting from *The Souls of Black Folk* in their speeches and publications.[1] Citation and correspondence became modes of enacting political and affective affinities, forms of intellectual friendship that I want to return to. In his book *X – The Problem of the Negro as a Problem for Thought*, Nahum Chandler (2013: 70) proposes that Du Bois's rich innovation of thought was that

> his thinking of historicity in general was developed entirely according to a methodological protocol that required him to attempt to think the particulars, the minute historical specifics, that which we often call the micrological, of a specific historicity, the history and status of that which we call African American (or Negro) in America … [yet] also to specify, at all levels of generality, the systemic site of structures that organized the emergence of the African American or Negro as subject.

Chandler (2013: 74) goes on to describe how Du Bois worked from the particular status of the African American subject to generalize a theory of 'racial distinction, and hence the problem of difference in general', adopting a method that included the autobiographical 'to critically and reflexively inquire back into the genealogies and histories by which he was organized as such a putative subject'. Despite the hubris involved, I want to make a similar claim for the usefulness of such a method in trying to move from the particularity of certain experiences that organized my own subjecthood at the fault lines of local and global notions of race, to try to explore how friendship, as one of many forms of affiliation, might prove useful for ciphering what Michelle Elam calls *The Souls of Mixed Folk* (2011). The genealogy of my own formation as a raced subject intersects with world-historical events that continue to elude full accountings, and I find little in the memoirs of writers such as Peter Godwin and Alexandra Fuller that remotely resonate with my perspectives on interracial interactions, and so I take up Du Bois's method here, as both a salvo against the 'when-we' genre and as a gesture of pan-Africanist intellectual friendship, a willful choice to refract my thoughts through both southern African and U.S. black interpretive lenses.[2]

Zimbabwe gained independence 14 years before South Africa became a democracy, and so my generation was the first to attend schools with friends across multiple races, and thus we are also the first to look back on school friendships from our thirties and forties and consider how the erotic imaginary did and did not keep up with the fraternal and sororal dimensions of school friendships once we disappeared into the diaspora of adulthood. In the spirit of John Comaroff and Jean Comaroff's (2012) call to theorize from below, I want to suggest that rather than viewing Zimbabwe as a cautionary tale for all that might go awry in a postcolony, our perspectives on race, reconciliation, and irreconcilable antagonism could serve as an important intellectual and narrative reservoir to our neighbors in South Africa. We are not merely *makwerekwere*, and we know this from the inspiring demonstrations against xenophobia that took place in the wake of sporadic acts of violence against immigrants in March and April 2015. We are your neighbors, your friends to the north, your harbingers, and we bring fascinating stories to share while we stop over with you.

In my previous writing I've been interested in solidarity as necessarily dependent on difference and distance. I've proposed thinking of solidarity not so much as a shared position, standing en bloc, but rather as a stereo effect. Like a stereo system that re-creates the experience of surround sound by using small differences in phase between signals that listeners decipher, solidarity demands that subjects do the interpretive work to orient themselves in relation to others. That is the solidarity that I believe South Africans and Zimbabweans might find by thinking through interracial friendship together, in light of the historical and political differences that structure our positions.

As I think about friendship as a formative experience, I turn to my own formation in a Derridean comparative literature department (where many faculty considered Derrida a personal friend). In *The Politics of Friendship*, Derrida (1997: 53) goes back to Nietzsche's investigations of the paradox of friendship, writing that friends

> must have learned how to keep silent in order to remain your friend (*und schweigen müssen sie gelernt haben um dir Freund zu bleiben*); for such human relationships almost always depend upon the fact that two or three things are never said or even so much as touched upon; if these little boulders do start to roll, however, friendship follows after them and shatters. ... Friendship does not keep silence, it is preserved by silence.

This seems doubly true of friendships across racial lines in the context of an official state discourse of reconciliation. While it is seldom recalled in the press, Robert Mugabe's inaugural speech in 1980 essentially called for a collective compact of silence: in order to build a new country we were 'to let bygones be bygones'. However, in the post-independence era, calls to 'reconciliation' without publication of full investigative reports has become the norm, or, as Ruth Murambadoro (2014) puts it more pointedly, 'reconciliation efforts [have repeatedly been] reduced to a prescription of amnesia'.

How can friendship and its silences serve us as a useful structure of feeling through which to consider other possible consequences of keeping silent as we reckon with the legacies of states of emergency in southern Africa? Is it reasonable to make a leap from the registers of the intimate to the state in this way? For Zimbabweans looking back on 35 years of independence, might nostalgia offer up a knot of affectively charged memories through which to reconsider what solidarity and national belonging means, a possibility of a more ethical relation to a mounting list of marginalized fellow citizens: residents of Matabeleland and Midlands accused of being 'dissidents'; 'squatters' who were not willing or eligible to join collective farms; active members of opposition parties; gender and human rights activists; gay and lesbian Zimbabweans; feisty Catholic archbishops; informal traders; farm-workers of Malawian and Zambian lineage and too many others who have fallen foul of the state? It seems crucial to come up with a more robust account of silence's necessity and insufficiency in sustaining friendship at the current moment in southern Africa, precisely because it is the narrative of liberation struggles and the language of allies and solidarities among the frontline states that is most often used as a rebuke against the eruptions of violence against *makwerekwere*. If 'friendship' is to bear such a rhetorical burden it seems vital to think carefully about its uses and its limits.

While it may be more than this chapter manages to achieve, my attempt is to show how interracial friendship can serve as a rehearsal space for the inter- and intra-subjective work required to navigate through states of transition. In order to take up these questions, I offer an account of a reunion between myself and a school friend that took place in South Africa when I had an opportunity to watch her perform her one-woman show, and of the conversations we were able to engage in after that performance. I alternate between the performance, our conversations, and abstract reflections on friendship that focus on our striving together to find areas of solidarity and understanding, while also trying something other than silence as a condition for our friendship.

I am mindful of the ways in which my account privileges my voice and my perspectives on our meeting, and so in an effort to speak ethically I reflect extensively here on my personal history. Such a methodology is, of course, a bedrock of feminist studies, and particularly follows the work of U.S. black feminists such as Audre Lorde, Toni Cade Bambara, and bell hooks. I lay claim too, to feminist histories in southern Africa, and borrow the example of my South African elders, Charlotte Manye Maxeke and Nokutela Dube, both of whom used personal experience to ground their appeals for solidarity in their work in education, prisoners' rights, and other political struggles. In other words, the personal here is included because it informs and exposes a politics I have not found articulated elsewhere, a politics that seems more complex than the usual Manichean accounts of race relations in southern Africa (particularly Zimbabwe) suggest, a politics that I believe remains latent with possibilities. I want to argue for friendship as a vital rehearsal space for the performance of politics to come, politics that will necessarily be improvisational if we are to find alternatives other than the compulsory repetitions of past wrongs in an echo chamber of racial traumas.

In April 2014 I attended a performance of Stacey Sacks's one-woman show, *I Shit Diamonds,* during its Johannesburg debut. Stacey and I went to secondary school together in Harare, but had not seen each other for 20 years before the performance in South Africa. We were both visiting South Africa (she from Sweden, and I from the U.S.), and it was thanks to a mutual friend putting us in touch via Facebook that I was able to attend the show during a brief visit to Johannesburg for the African Literature Association's annual conference. The performance was developed as Sacks's thesis for a Master's degree in physical theater in Stockholm, and my discussion refers to both this initial encounter and the recorded version by Not Normal Productions on Vimeo (Sacks 2012).[3]

I Shit Diamonds is an experimental clown-theater piece set in 'Congolobabwe'. Stacey created and performs two personas, an inept but sincere and vulnerable cleaner named Shimmie and a grandiose politician named Mugabatokwe. Shimmie's persona is built on the traditional humanitarian servant-fool of *commedia dell'arte* and other European performance traditions, but is inflected with the specific gendered histories of male domestic workers in southern

Africa. Mugabatokwe is an exuberant dictator persona in the tradition of the *commedia*'s *El Capitano* figure, or in more recent times Chaplin's Great Dictator, Arturo Ui, and Ubu Roi; beyond that, his name presumably needs no gloss. Stacey ends her show by shedding her costumes, stripping down to her underwear to address the audience directly as herself, explaining that she made the show in order to protest the homophobic policies of the ZANU-PF government that make it inconceivable for her to return with her girlfriend to reside there as an openly lesbian couple. Despite my sympathy for her position as a disenfranchised queer subject, *I Shit Diamonds* unsettled, even angered, me profoundly as I felt it evoked a set of racialized tropes associated with minstrelsy. My response pushed me to investigate my reactions as a comparatist trained in global black literatures, and as a mixed-race, often closeted bisexual Zimbabwean-American who emigrated to the U.S. two decades ago.

The show was performed at Maboneng precinct's P.O.P. Gallery, and the mixed-use building's 'urban regeneration' site captured many of Johannesburg's contradictory impulses. As I walked past restaurants, residences, and commercial spaces abuzz with a level of 'cool' that no academic (recovering nerd) can ever aspire to, what was immediately striking to me was how, 20 years after democracy had arrived, a performance space could be patronized by an almost entirely white audience. This sense of time being out of joint (dis)oriented me in the space. After watching the play, I initiated a correspondence with Sacks that is now a new and crucial dimension of our friendship. South Africa's own charged racial histories offered a staging ground to reflect together with rare frankness on the politics of friendship, race, and queer activism that Zimbabwe's current politics make difficult.[4] This conversation is ongoing, and so I want to emphasize that this is a report from the field, and a set of provisional reflections.

Our exchange was most valuable in allowing us to break the form of a nostalgia-bound 'old-girl' (alumna) friendship. It was clear that the grounds for our conversations were no longer that we had attended the same secondary school, but rather that we were reckoning with how our differing diaspora experiences had shaped our paths differently. Here, the words of Nietzsche are particularly resonant, when he writes of *friends as ghosts,* that 'if we greatly transform ourselves, those friends of ours who have not been transformed become ghosts of our past: their voice comes across to us like the voice of a shade [in a frightfully spectral manner (*schattenhaft /schauerlich*)] – as though we were hearing ourselves, only younger, more severe, less mature' (cited in Derrida 1997: 75). To encounter a friend after so many years was, for both of us, a chance to encounter strands of ourselves with whom we had fallen out of touch in the absence of compatriots who shared similar memories. The beginning of our correspondence took the form of a poem-letter that I sent to Stacey by e-mail, which I include in full here:

YOU SHIT DIAMONDS: A LETTER TO MY SISTREN

Hokoyo. Beware of power lines.
That stage is
more crowded than you think.

Heh, my sista,
what you are saying, eh,
it is burning my ears, sista.
You are coming on the stage
with your green brush and your green spray bottle
and your cleaning rag which you make into a doek
for the brush and talk to it as if it was a black
and you are burning my ears. You are bumbling.
That is what the stage does, and has always done, to workers.
You are not saying this is a black, but that is what
I am hearing. I am hearing it pronounced, a blek.
It is definitely not indefinite, that article. Notorious.
You are saying this is Shimmie shimmying, and we
are all shim-sham shellacking and you
are making a joke of the crowing cock
and wearing that schupid moustache
and putting 2 and 2 together
and it is making me
burn up inside.

I am here to support you, but it is making me sick.
Is this what the old girls network is? Hey?
I am sitting in a chair in the third row far left, just outside
The light, next to my colleague who has come to see the show.

My white enlightened American married-to-a-black-lady colleague.
I am glad that he is there. Someone to talk to afterwards.
To try and intellectualize a way back from Congolobabwe.

Two things:
a) This is what racism looks like.
b) You were great. You were great. You were great.
My adolescence was haunted by compliments.
I feared every kind word was undeserved,
or too smooth and facetious.
My present to you, if I can offer it,
is the dangerous act of telling the truth.

But first, grant me this:
I wish with all my heart that you could take your beautiful girlfriend
To visit Zimbabwe, and see it for what it is, today, in its own terms.

I wish that you would notice that you and your girlfriend
Would suffer but it would be hard because it was new, not hard
because it was hard.

I wish you would know that when the West is ripped into
it is because there is nothing that has ever exacted contrition from
the West,
and you and I should know how exasperating that is:
to be wronged. And shrugged off. And wronged again.

I wish you would know how deadening that is.
Where is the West? Who is the West?
What does the West owe?
Are we waiting for the West?
Does the burlesque belong to the West?

Dear Sista, dear, dear Sista,
Of course I hated the show. Of course I did. You were brilliantly
funny. And you were sickeningly rude. You shat upon the graves of

ancestors - yours and mine. Yes, it is shitty beyond words that your
love is treated as shameful. I know a little about that. At least
my parents did. Lovers across a racial divide, breaking not only
racial codes but also the expectation of chastity on a religious
mission station, I wonder what they thought they were doing. I have
never asked them what it meant for their intimate love to have an
inescapable public politics. They've stayed together, every outing
a statement, for 38 years. They carried themselves with spiteful
dignity. They were probably too pious at moments. Their love was
political. Your love is political, and you gave me a way to think
about the violently ugly forces of abjection and shame which society
heaped on them, and is heaping now on too many beloved queer folk.
Thank you for that.

I write in solidarity with your struggle as an out lesbian. I
recognize that the struggle for gay liberation is the struggle for
liberation. The struggle for each and every human being to live a
life of dignity and self-sufficiency.

And yet, I find myself outraged at seeing the reduction of our
national Chimurenga, an entire liberation project ... a struggle
for independence that was fundamentally a struggle for basic human
dignity ... to a caricature of an old and corrupt man.
Maybe.
Is that the outrage?
No.
It is the Shimmie character. It is the fact that you take the
mickey out of a worker, a grown man working as a cleaner, in that
condescending accent that you are probably right to say we all
played with at some point, we spoiled snotty private school girls,
whatever our race. By which I mean, we were racist. We made fun of
people brilliant enough to live their working lives in at least two
different languages. We called elders by their first names and, in
a nasal disregard of their feelings, we expected their answers about
what was for tea, or how many biscuits, or when it would be served.
Everything was wanted immediately and everything revolved around

us. At a moment, that unending 1980 moment, when our country men
and women were going to doctors and lawyers and civil servants for
the first time. Nineteen-year-olds were learning to read. A nation
was being built out of the squat and squalid nothing that most of its
citizens had been reduced to for decades. That was not just a cock
and bull story. That was independence.

Have I missed the boat, got the wrong end of the stick, missed the
point?
Maybe.
Maybe I want to hear you say more clearly that this is not a story
of loss - the loss of the possibility of taking your love home to sit
on the veranda and say the 'whenwe's' - but a story of bewilderment.
Would you and Jen come home if that meant coming kumusha? Are we
still looking for liberation?

Can you and I be in solidarity?
Solidarity does not mean I am with you.
It means I sound you out. You sound me out.

What would liberation, rather than grieving, look like. What
would reconciliation rather than snatch-and-grab look like? Why
should you want it? Why should I? Sitting in the audience, I saw
myself pious and closed-minded and wanted to be open. I understood
how unexamined the privilege and snobbery of my adolescently
evangelical Christianity was as I watched you thumb your nose at
authority. Of course you had practice at that. What crap to be in
a school that thought honoring religious diversity meant sending
you to a study period during daily chapel services. Did I think my
'penance' or recompense or reconciliation demanded that I give your
show my thumbs-up? Did I retreat from paying attention to what you
were really saying? I wanted to listen to your cry but these things
are not all of a piece.

It stunned me to be in an audience that was basically a bunch of
white people laughing at a white person play a ridiculed black

character. Where I live now, we call that blackface minstrelsy. I
hate that I laughed at some of those tricks. Was that part of your
schtick? I wish I felt more confident that making an occasion for
a bunch of white people to laugh at black stereotypes wasn't also
part of your schtick. I wish I'd had the guts to tell you to your
face that your protest offends me. It makes me livid. Although, what
has me livid is that outrage is not my only reaction. Maybe you have
given me the gift of an experience of complexity. Of interfering
solidarities.

What I think is that you are really quite entirely too brilliant.
You make me long for an ethical witness to the pain of racist humor
wielded from behind a screen of white privilege at the same time
that I honor your cri-de-coeur, voiced as you survive and combat
anti-Semitism, homophobia and patriarchy. I know that so many of
the people in power and privilege who would not be caught dead in a
theater will never tell any truth of this sort. And so you have, in
reading this letter, however many times I may have misconstrued you,
brought on stage the gift of an ethical response. We will have paid
attention to each other. Will we have loved each other politically?
Will we be closer to listening together in solidarity? Will we be
brilliant and cut both ways, like diamonds?

What was remarkable about Stacey's response was her openness. She offered
the background of the work by sharing her thesis, which drew my attention to
its formal construction and connection to improvisatory theater and clown
performance practices. But it was also clear that I had greatly underestimated
what the affective charge of a letter like mine might carry, and in her reply,
Stacey wrote eloquently about its raw emotional impact.

Hi Tsitsi

Your mail hit me hard, a deep sternum punch. At first it made me
really upset, then totally misunderstood, then ... after a week's
reflection ... grateful.

A very wise teacher said to me recently: always look at the prejudices
of your critics. And it makes me wonder, what glasses do you wear,
which gaze are you choosing to perceive this show through? Is it
simply that my (admittedly all over the place) accent projected you
into a guilt-ridden teenage-angst past? With your current academic
achievements and the endless research around issues pertaining to
race, class etc ... i suppose it is impossible for you to look past such
things, to see what lies behind.

'I Shit Diamonds' evolved out of my very real desire to look at deep
tragedy and find the humor in it. I was asking, can we laugh at the
darkest corners of history and current dictatorship? Coming from
Zim, where my parents lost their entire livelihoods due to lack of
planning on their behalf (in the face of the fast track land reform
process, the hyper-inflation etc), i felt very close to the subject
matter. I wanted to dive into satirizing the insidious corruptive
elements of totalitarianism, to parody the fascist body, and all of
this through clown.

Shimmie, to me, is the articulate and humanitarian fool. He is the
storyteller, the care-taker who speaks awful truths yet laughs all
the way. His fatal flaw is that he speaks too much. In no way did i
intend to mock a poor black man, as you imagine. So far, you are the
one and only to accuse me of this, of the thousands of people who
have seen the show, but perhaps it is because you are the only brave
one ... i don't know ... in a way i can understand how you perceive
him to be a caricature, since part of my technique was trying to
distil a character to its very essence, and because of that i can
understand how minimalism could lead to reinforcing stereotype.
Admittedly, i've not been very successful in fleshing him out as
a real character, believable to the core. And this is really where
i would love your input. From your perspective, how can i move
him more into the real? How can i represent him as a lighthearted
optimist, a teacher who has accepted his lot in life, who looks to
the future with hope?

i need to understand exactly how you perceive my depiction of him
to be racist. Is it predominantly in the rendering of his accent?
As an actor i've made some conscious choices about how to depict the
'Congolababwe' accent - it is a bizarre mix of Zim, SA (Zulu, mainly),
as well as my own dose of general fictitious African country, a
hint towards the nonsense. Of course, i probably should be more
politically correct with taking into account historical elements of
'blackface', as you write about, and i know a lot of evil has been
committed in the name of ignorance (or supposed lack of intention),
but these 2 clowns 'found me' so to speak. Am not sure if you can
relate to this idea or not, the act of creation is such a mysterious
one, and still i can honestly say that both Shimmie and the Dictator
are also basic elements of ME. They are mask and counter-mask, 2
elements of the same clown, the powerful and the dispossessed, both
embodied in my own psyche. Both a part of humanity. My dictator is
Idi Amin, Mussolini, Gaddafi and Mugabe smashed into one. From a
contemporary clown perspective, he's the eternal parody of political
tyranny, universal in his specificity.

Is what you perceive to be a renewed form of blackface mockery a
matter of representation? Does that mean that any author/writer/
creator/actor/poet can never represent anything but that which
derives from their own ethnicity and experience? Is this not then a
question of creative fascism? What has happened in Zim is a part of
my own family's personal history and, as an artist, this show is my
response to the tragedy that has unfolded in our country.

You speak glowingly of our 'Chimurenga', but is that not living in a
glorified romanticised past? What did Mugabe do with his hard won
freedom? Can you ignore the Gukurahundi massacre and other fifth
brigade atrocities, the rampant and overt suppression and torture of
any opposition, a reactionary land reform process which destroyed our
economy, Operation Murambatsvina, the blatant misappropriation of
our natural resources by an indescribably corrupt elite? As an artist
i have to respond to these. To say nothing, for me, is tantamount to
being complicit. And, as an actor-clown deliciously drawn towards the

trickster figure as a stirring agent of change and transformation, something in me feels that your ethical disturbance is exactly one of the feelings i'm trying to evoke in my audience.

Have you ever heard of the idea: 'comfort the disturbed and disturb the comfortable'? This is what i try to do in my art. Admittedly, this show was specifically made for a European audience. In every venue i have played there have been people who come to me after the show, tears streaming down their faces, saying that i've alerted them to a situation they knew nothing about. And they feel moved to find out more, to be more educated. i'm glad that's the case, but as a clown, the educational element is less important to me than the fact of giving my audience in that moment a truly emotional experience, moving them from gut wrenching laughter to tears, especially in the realisation that this sick sick story is partially true. True for the past and the present, for there as well as for here, since the fascism continues worldwide, and we are all always a tiny step away from it.

Having no preconceptions or associations around the accent, Europeans don't judge it ... or me because of it. They accept the characters for who they are, through the obvious parody of me playing men. When i did the show at a circus festival in the Swedish countryside this last weekend, the audience totally fell in love with Shimmie, we had a lot of fun together. And when the dictator killed him, throwing his hat onto the stage from backstage, there was a perceptible 'Aaaahhhhh' which came from the audience, an 'ahhh' filled with sad sympathy. Lovely.

Initially the show was created as part of my Master's course (entitled 'A Year of Physical Comedy') at the Stockholm University of Dramatic Arts. The course was being run by Clowns Without Borders, Sweden, and included 2 international clown tours (one to Rwanda, to Congolese refugee camps on the border, and one to Myanmar, performing for children all over the country, in orphanages, HIV centers, etc), as well as the creation of a 45 minute show.

I've attached my Master's thesis for you to check out, it may help clarify some things around the performance. Please remember it is a reflection based on artistic research, which differs quite dramatically (i imagine) from regular academic practice.

Arrrrgh, this is a long conversation. Because, of course, there is the fascinating experience i had of playing the show in SA, where i knew there would be such different reactions since the show there has much more resonance. And i had massive fears about being misunderstood. For South Africans, i do mean the play to be a cautionary tale, warning people to be careful who they vote into power, since the current leaders display such a gross narcissism, encouraging blatant consumerism, nepotism, self-aggrandisement and behaving often as if they are above the law.

i can honestly say that from my perspective, political correctness is never a good platform from which to dive in the process of creating art, but ... and this is the crux of the matter for me ... the notion of having my work dubbed 'racist' is horrific. Doing the show in Cape Town was an eye opener for me, it was the first time i had a number of black people see it, and i was nervous. But there, something happened. The black audience members were the ones laughing the loudest (there was a group of about 10 people all sitting together on one side of the audience), they were gleefully screaming out 'Kill!' (i remember stopping during one of these moments and just looking at them, which evoked another round of laughter), and then at the end they were the first to jump up to give me a standing ovation. i wish i could have spoken to them afterwards. In Jozi, i sent out invites to all my friends, black and white, i gave out hundreds of flyers in the Maboneng district, talking to so so many people one on one about the show, and as you saw, mainly white people came. i wished it had been different, but with little resources for publicity etc, there was only so much i could do. The guy who did my lighting and sound (Edgar) was black and he said it was one of the best shows he's ever seen at PopArt, he would give me a long strong hug at the end of each performance.

i wonder why he didn't see it as racist. This is fascinating. Perhaps with your distance from our continent, and the privilege of high level education, you critical capabilities are heightened, your specific gaze tuned to scan performance for all kinds of racist innuendo. Please understand, in no way do i mean for the above contextualization of my show to be a justification. i truly value your experience and really want to understand how you imagine i can be more sensitive in the future. The piece is always transforming, always becoming, and so your reaction cuts deep and points to something that needs attention. Please send me some links to articles about these issues we talk about here, if you can.

Forgive me if this mail is all over the place, and probably highly inarticulate at moments. i'm working like crazy, and wishing for a summer holiday. Luckily Sweden is so phenomenally beautiful that wherever we travel with our touring clown trio, we're likely to find a wonderful lake to swim in after a very sweaty show. Life could probably not be any better.

Sending you this with a big spacey hug.

x

In thinking through our interactions within the framework of a new form of friendship, I returned to theoretical texts that felt familiar, safe, removed from the affective freight of my correspondence with Stacey. In Derrida's readings of Nietzsche, Aristotle, and others, enmity and friendship were closely interrelated in ways that resonated with the work of Frank Wilderson III, which this book uses as a key intertext. Yet I struggled with Wilderson's Afro-pessimism, questioning how apt his analysis of U.S. race relations might be in southern Africa, despite his deep experiential knowledge of the South African liberation struggle. Wilderson (2010: 5) insists that racial turmoil is better imagined as a 'rubric of antagonism (an irreconcilable struggle between entities, or positions, the resolution of which is not dialectical but entails the obliteration of one of the positions)' rather than one of 'conflict (a rubric of problems that can be posed and conceptually resolved)'. How could I make sense of my desire for an expression of anti-racist and queer solidarity with her, and yet acknowledge the anger I felt at what read to me as white privilege – the questioning of my response when another black audience member had not raised similar concerns, or the easy call to educate her. Wilderson made clear for me how our *positions* were in antagonistic relation even as our *affective affinities* remained in the register of friendship, while Derrida's writings on the politics of friendship exposed how the tacit agreement in any friendship to keep silence at the edges of our willingness to share each other's sorrows also depended on a reserve of sharing each other's joys. Yet '[s]ilence among friends will not work without laughter, and laughter bares its teeth, as does death' (Derrida 1997: 55). In other words, the impulses toward rage and enmity that Stacey and I sought to share and manage in our correspondence (the raw question we each ask of the other in our correspondence, *how could you*) seems to me a fundamental part of *friendship* that is necessarily *not* removed from enmity. In order to sustain our friendship we are trying to make room for that antagonism, and to find a solidarity that does not demand transparency or the annihilation of our experience so much as a de-legitimizing, a loosening of our *structurally antagonizing positions*. One sign of the struggle involved is in the delay in my reply, a trace of the continuing unease and difficulty I found in navigating the affective terrain of a rekindled friendship that had risked the breach of standard silences around race to reach for something more direct, more inter-subjective, more unstable, more improvisatory, and thus, potentially, closer to plenitude.

July, and then Nov 6, 2014

Dear Stacey,

I think we are on the same page. I read your e-mail quickly and
lay awake all night thinking about how I had not imagined what it
might feel like to read my proem 'You Shit Diamonds'. Reading your
words I knew that I had hurt you (cut, you say) in ways I had not
forecast, really because I had not thought. And I lay there wanting
to snatch back some of it, but really not, actually wanting to own
what I had said and to be face to face with it. To own the fact that
I might be talking not so much to you but to pieces of my self, and to
incarnations of my friends from a long time ago. But also I wanted
something like reciprocity - paying attention to the ways in which we

wound each other. Because I still want to own the pain of derogatory
racialized images and to be able to arrive at some understanding of
how that is real and recurrent even when un-meant.

Why do I think we are on the same page? Reading your thesis I
recognize the courage and dazzling self-indulgence of making
art ... I, too, journal; I shift between poem, prose, and other
languages; I chafe at the strictures of academia, and perhaps also
at the humiliating flexibility of personal writing. I also gather
the statements of my teachers and string them like beads that will
protect me, clicking through them for guidance in making decisions
in the lonely space that is responsibility.

Reading your thesis I am surprised by how little I find there
about the documentary nature of your show. I am reminded it is the
fruit of many months, years now, of artistic investigation. I am
reminded it is a show you made in Sweden, nurtured by teachers from
Italy, Canada, Sweden and elsewhere. I realize you probably had no
guidance from teachers who are not white. And this makes me sad, for
in your e-mail you talk about how few black people have been part
of your audience. You say I am the only person who has seen race as
central in your show, and that it is perhaps that I am courageous.
I think maybe it is that there are just not enough chances for
conversation, extended conversation, between white and black people.
And then I think, too, that I am not entirely honest here. After all,
in Zimbabwe I was 'coloured' ... a word that I feel so uncomfortable
with that I simply do not claim it. I do not think of my self as
'coloured' ... I do not even spell it that way these days, 21 years
after moving to America I often call myself a person of color, and
I embrace blackness as part of my political identity, seeing it as a
way to participate in a pan-African world where difference rather
than sameness is the grounds of solidarity. But what 'coloured' meant
in Zim was also being part of a cultural context that had its own
specific repeatable elements - an accent, dating patterns, cuisine,
neighborhoods, sports teams - things I felt were not mine, as a girl
with a white American mother and a black Zimbabwean father, an

amalgam of British and Swiss and Shona Tembo clan roots. I could
not choose a more perfect totem than the zebra, this animal that is
not grey, not mixed, but rather variegated, mottled, both/and. Yet
being mixed race it is easy for me to assume the privileged position
of blackness that is always the aggrieved and never the aggressor.
What if I am sneaking past the responsibility to examine my own
race-thinking, my own identifications, my own complicities and the
shame I feel in those? Don't I owe it to you to have that conversation
with myself and with you ... to own that some of why race remains
a raw topic for me is because as a high-schooler I spent much of the
school week surrounded by a largely-white group of friends with
whom I spoke no language but English and never truly challenged
them or myself to ask why I was the only person in our circle who was
not white. It is true, when my friend told me her dog did not like
Africans I told her mine couldn't stand whites, but really why did
we still have so much to say to each other after that.

Meanwhile I remember you and your crew, older by two years, a
magical junta of black and white and brown and Indian moxy - Rumbi
K, Nyasha B, Thandi L, Melissa M, Isabelle M, Lucy S, Rumbi B, Sarah
now Rujeko D ... were you all close? Or do I just remember it that
way? Were you all going clubbing together in 90s Harare? Did dating
make you as squeamish as it did me? I, an utter nerd, knew no-one
except church boys who were my prayer partners but not my dance
partners. Did you know you'd rather go to the dance with a girl? Was
Miss Cooke a role model? Were there safe spaces in our pink prison?

It's months now since I started drafting this, and I want to own up
to the fact that I dropped the ball, dropped the conversation at a
moment when it would have turned to an auto-critique. I am sorry I
backed out like that. I want to come back to this. Perhaps you have
attention for it, perhaps not. I want to own up to the ways in which
I loved your show because it said and did things that I am not brave
enough for, or at least haven't been. I have a little button in my
office that says 'Biracial, Bisexual' and I suppose if someone were
to snoop around my desk they could find it and even generously

say I'm wearing it as a badge of honor, but the truth is that I
pass for straight, pass for a straight ally, pass for a very passive
very straight ally. Sometime in November 16 years ago I tried out
a hypothetical on my father ... what would he do if his daughter
married a woman ... and without missing a beat he said he'd kill
himself. I've circled back on that conversation a couple of times
over the years, but on some level I decided it was easier to hang out
in the closet, if I could. My parents have changed perspective a lot
since then. Like with many people, discovering that some of their
dearest and oldest friends were queer challenged their assumptions,
and the comparison between interracial and same-sex love has been
especially powerful for them. But in the meantime I've fallen for
a sweetheart of a man, and I rarely mention being bi in public ...
there's enough blowback from both sides of the lavender line to
convince me it's not worth the trouble. Watching your play, though,
and trying to think about how to talk about it, I realize that I have
been hugely complicit in all kinds of homophobic structures ... the
discussions of gender in my book take heteronormativity for granted
and I never bothered to look for queer counter examples and forms of
subversion, disidentification, code etc., even though the magazines
I write about would have been the place to find that material. And
when, on many occasions, I've been asked to talk about Zim politics
whether at a party or on the radio, I've rarely mentioned Mugabe as
the originator of a certain racialized homophobia at the Zimbabwe
International Book Fair in 1995, the beginning of what is now a 20-
year wave of increasingly hate-filled speech by African nationalist
leaders who claim same-sex desire is spawned by the evil West. That's
something I need to talk about, something you open up space for
audiences to talk about with your show. And I need to be more honest
about my own position in all these debates etc about sexuality. For
myself, and for what it means politically. Is this my coming out
narrative? Not for folks who know me very, very, very well ... but
yeah, maybe on some level it's the creak of an opening closet.

There are still things that make me uneasy about what I'm thinking
of as the racial drag in I Shit Diamonds. But I am realizing that

part of why they trouble me is the specific genealogy of other
representations that I am reminded of as I watch it ... African Jim
in 1949, Rhapsody in Blue in 1933, maybe even Emperor Jones. Those
are perhaps not your intertexts, but they are a big part of why
even the Shimmie sequences embarrass me. I'm working on putting
all of this into words more elegantly, more clearly etc, but in the
meantime, at least I can send this along.

In all sincerity and with much love,
Tsitsi

The correspondence with Stacey prompted me to critically reflect on my subject position with more care and rigor and to take stock of how my autobiography, as the daughter of a black chiShona-speaking Zimbabwean of the Tembo-Mazvimbakupa (or for women, VaNyemba) Chihota clan and a white American of Swiss-English background who fell in love and formed our family during the Chimurenga struggle for independence in the 1970s, necessarily shapes my thinking. In many ways, I was writing to myself, trying to befriend a younger girl who had had little sense of the historical stakes of my racial identification. My letter was also bearing witness to my parents' efforts to cultivate friendship in their interracial marriage. I thought anew how practicing friendship and commitment has entailed great struggle for them, but has generated many brilliant strategies for sustaining a 40-year relationship together. As their daughter, I am, I suppose, always already in an interracial friendship, but, given that race is both rigid social construction and a floating biological fiction, I believe that the particular and the general are not irreconcilable – in other words, some of what I know and some of the ways I, as a person of multiple racial heritages, am interpellated into racial identities, is just as true for many people whose families are phenotypically of one race.

AN AFTERWORD
The first time I appeared in public as a performance artist I played the role of the Boy Jesus in a nativity ballet production, *Desert Angels,* in the newly independent nation of Zimbabwe. The performance took place at the Harare Gardens in 1981. Any megalomaniac tendencies in my personality may be

blamed on having been cast, literally, as the lead in a messiah complex at such an early age. In the Obama era, however, the ease with which multi/inter/mixed-raced subjects can be conscripted into performances of racial reconciliation that may have little to do with serious redistributive or reparative justice should give some pause. My casting was a sign of major shifts: ballet was a common urban site of socialization and gender formation in the white Rhodesian community during the Unilateral Declaration of Independence (UDI) years. I was one of the first few non-white Zimbabweans to join ballet classes, and Stacey was a fellow ballet student, later drawing on that training in her work in physical theater.

At the end of *Desert Angels* I remained on stage alone, hands outstretched, with a spotlight on me fading into dark. At the time, I thought it was just fun and absolutely simple … all your boy, Jesus, had to do was stand still and smile, how hard could that be? But with almost 25 years of distance, it gives me chills to think about the symbolic power deployed through the performance. That image offered an audience, sitting under the sparkling stars of Harare a few minutes to meditate in the season of Christmas on the vision of a small child whose body reconciled the genetic and nurtured codes of two races that had nearly destroyed each other in a recent war, and more fundamentally in centuries of conflict. Christianity was (and remains) such a dominant religious discourse that reconciliation and sacrifice were almost compulsorily broadcast.

Today, such reconciliation seems too naive, and indeed, too sectarian. True reparation would mean asking fundamental questions about what sort of performance was entitled to lay claim to such public spaces, who could book the theater when, what the grounds of meeting were, and most fundamentally, who tends those grounds, for what pay, who cleans the stage, who declaims from it, who shimmies, and who shines. Such reparation is necessarily ensemble work. If the revolutionary work left to be done will, as Emma Goldman imagined, be danced, what those of us who dance might bring to that work is not merely our presence, but our quirky stories, our queer foolery, our quiet sagacity, and ultimately our bodies, on the line.

REFERENCES

Chandler, Nahum. 2013. *X – The Problem of the Negro as a Problem for Thought*. New York, NY: Fordham University Press.

Comaroff, Jean and John Comaroff. 2012. *Theorizing from the South: Or, How Euro-America Is Evolving toward Africa*. Boulder, CO: Paradigm.

Derrida, Jacques. 1997. *The Politics of Friendship*. London: Verso.

Elam, Michelle. 2011. *The Souls of Mixed Folk: Race Politics and Aesthetics in the New Millennium*. Stanford, CA: Stanford University Press.

Epprecht, Marc. 2004. *Hungochani: The History of a Dissident Sexuality in Southern Africa*. Montreal: McGill-Queen's University Press.

Fuller, Alexandra. 2003. *Let's Not Go to the Dogs Tonight: An African Childhood*. New York, NY: Random House.

Godwin, Peter. 2004. *Mukiwa: A White Boy in Africa*. New York, NY: Grove.

Jaji, Tsitsi. 2014. *Africa in Stereo: Modernism, Music and Pan-African Solidarity*. New York, NY: Oxford University Press.

Murambadoro, Ruth. 2014. 'The Politics of Reconciliation in Zimbabwe: Three Times Failure — Will the Fourth Time Count?' *Kujenga Amani*. The Social Science Research Council. December 17, 2014. forums.ssrc.org/Kiyenga-amani/2014/12/17/the-politics-of-reconciliation-in-zimbabwe-three-times-failure-will-the-fourth-time-count/#. V3D20KY207A, accessed February 29, 2016.

Sacks, Stacey. 2012. *I Shit Diamonds*. Performance Piece accompanying Master's Thesis for *A Year of Physical Comedy*. Stockholm. Academy of Dramatic Arts and Clowns without Borders.

Wilderson, Frank B. III. 2010. *Red, White & Black: Cinema and the Structure of U.S. Antagonisms*. Durham, NC: Duke University Press.

NOTES

1   I have written of Seme's and Plaatje's engagements with Du Bois in Jaji, *Africa in Stereo* (2014: chapter 2, 29, 50).

2   For examples of 'when-we' nostalgia in writings by white Zimbabweans who have since emigrated, see Fuller's *Let's Not Go to the Dogs Tonight* (2003), and Godwin's less grating *Mukiwa* (2004).

3   The Vimeo version of the performance is no longer available online.

4   It is important to note that while state repression against queer people has long been among the more egregious human rights violations in Zimbabwe, the country has a long tradition of anti-homophobic activism, and GALZ (Gays and Lesbians of

Zimbabwe, an organization founded by the late composer Keith Goddard) remains vibrant and determined. Despite sometimes violent state repression, there are many queer-identified Zimbabweans, and, as Marc Epprecht (2004) has shown, there is a long history of same-sex desires and their recognition in the region.

12

THE *NATIVE INFORMANT* SPEAKS BACK TO THE OFFER OF FRIENDSHIP IN WHITE ACADEMIA

MOSA PHADI & NOMANCOTSHO PAKADE

This chapter is a philosophical discussion detailing how the alienation we feel as Black scholars,[1] and the assimilation we have to negotiate as aspiring Black women scholars in academia, reveals a crisis in social science.[2] We see this crisis best displayed through the figure of the *native informant*. This chapter is about the affective and actual role that we as *native informants* play daily within an unchallenged white academia. Franco Barchiesi's chapter (this volume) narrates the positionality of *Drum* magazine journalist Nat Nakasa as participant in the 'fringe' or 'No Man's Land' in Johannesburg during apartheid, a place where both black and white could interact without directly confronting the dehumanisation of black people. In a similar vein, South African universities inhabit a similar 'fringe' positionality. In this sphere, friendship between white and black becomes a space of 'complicities and intimacies' tied to the historical matrix of roles that place the *native informant* as a cultural interpreter before she can be seen as a consumer or creator of knowledge. The social sciences are in a condition of instability that has socially, politically, and economically alienated Black scholars.

Our chapter draws on Windsor S. Leroke's paper '"Koze Kube Nini?" The Violence of Representation and the Politics of Social Research in South

Africa.' This article, published in 1994, has been forgotten as it does not fit neatly into the status quo, though it has been cited by a few scholars. Leroke's paper was a critical intervention in a longer history of Black scholars in South Africa contesting and participating in academia. Twenty years after the paper was presented at the Wits History Workshop, the questions it posed have yet to be answered by the social science community in South Africa.[3] The difference this time is that we are directing our questions to Black scholars, including ourselves – as *native informants*. We use *native informant* as defined by Shahnaz Khan (2005), as both the research object who is represented, and/or has to learn the skills to represent herself within the framework of white academia.

What follows are reflections on the positioning of the *native informant* in academia, including the experiences of Black scholars challenging, subverting, and being complicit in the interwoven consumer-producer-owner nexus and unchanged structures of knowledge production in South Africa. We are interested in how this dynamic is structured around interpersonal relationships between Black scholars positioned as *native informants*, and white academics as the holders of institutional power who sustain and reproduce structural exclusions. Often the relationships between *native informant* and white academic adopt a cloak of friendship. We include reflections from our personal experiences within social science having to perform as *native informants*. These personal encounters are meant to open up broader questions of being a Black scholar in white privileged institutional environments. As Frank Wilderson (2010: 3) ponders, 'one cannot but wonder why questions that go to the heart of the ethico-political, questions of political ontology are so unspeakable in intellectual mediations ...'.

Obviously not every white scholar fits the mode we attempt to outline here. South African universities are heavily contested spaces, in which there are variations across institutional cultures, as well as a history of oppositional politics within the academy. Research enclaves in many universities straddle academic publishing commitments with social justice solidarity work. Yet even in such progressive spaces within the academy, the *native informant's* role remains. Our experiences convey the fundamental elements of the knowledge-power structure of the university, and its continued reproduction of whiteness.

THE UNSPOKEN IN SOCIAL SCIENCE

> Semiotics and linguistics teach us that when we speak (we here refers to Black people) our grammar goes unspoken. Our grammar is assumed. ... To put a finer point on it, structures of ontological suffering stand in antagonistic, rather than conflictual, relation to one another (Wilderson 2010: 5).

Social science in South Africa remains dominated by white academics, and has created an antagonistic space that has alienated Black scholars and locked white ones within their privilege. This irreconcilable reality, Leroke (1994) notes, unveiled itself most profoundly in South African social sciences during the 1970s and 1980s through research outputs aligned with anti-apartheid ideology. What was striking about these research outputs was 'the racial domination of white researchers' (Leroke 1994: 10) in anti-apartheid writing. Post-1994, there have been some gradual shifts seeking redress through more inclusive authorship. According to the Centre for Research on Evaluation, Science and Technology (CREST 2014) social science publication outputs have grown from 10% in 1993–1997 to 17% in 2008–2012. Yet the racial profile of the majority of published authors remains white. Leroke (11) maintains that the silence and non-reflectiveness in regard to continued white institutional privilege in South African social science is because

> ... social research has not adapted to the lives and realities of African South Africans. Instead, it has always acted as an exteriority that inserts itself through unknown procedures of self-justification. As an outsider, social research has prevailed as a legitimate universality. This is irrespective of the claims that have been made by South African social scientists that social research has been adequately modified and adapted to suit the realities of African South Africans. Subsequently, regarding apartheid, it has been argued that the proper use of social research (through a politically correct research agenda) can serve the interest of this population. But what about the interest of the researcher, those who formulate the research questions, those who 'write' the research text?

Leroke (1994: 9) wants us to look more closely at the 'social activity of social research knowledge-construction' in South Africa, insisting that 'social research fails to see itself as a set of social practices that are historically linked and identifiable with the social practices and institutions of apartheid and its predecessors'. Representations themselves can be an act of violence, an act of 'distancing', and an act through and within which a 'vacuum of separation' occurs and is maintained. The documented disparity between contributions of Black and white scholars, both in relation to research and authorship, shows clearly this distancing effect at work (Suffla and Seedat 2004). Even when considering gradual policy changes, the underrepresentation of Black scholars is extensive, as the Black experience is often captured as an 'other' already spoken for, that exists in texts written by the dominant white hand. South African social science has been historically framed around an idea that since the majority of blacks 'cannot represent themselves, they must be represented' (Duncan et al. 1997). The practice in social science since the enlightenment period is based on the 'othering' of the Black social experience; and those who study assume the status of knowledge carriers and producers hence historically white. Leroke's questions, such as: 'What makes representation possible? Who insists on reproductions of representation? What and who sustains its existence?', therefore remain unanswered.

The social sciences objectify Black lives by operating through a dualism, dividing the subject and object. We use the term dualism to represent two irreducible parts – hence creating an antagonism. The Subject in this case is the writer or researcher, and the Object is the person who is studied, 'the speaker' (Leroke 1994: 12–13). As Frantz Fanon and Wilderson affirm, the object is the 'Slave'. In this process of dualism, Leroke argues that most blacks 'serve as informants, as assistants, as objects of research'. A closer look at the number of black people contributing to knowledge production shows the black body as an extension, if not a support base, of the white writer's hand with its experience and training over the years. The white writer becomes the recognizable primary voice representing what has been interpreted and translated through the spoken experiences of the black object as an assistant. In addition, the object is portrayed as a 'second language speaker', a 'foreigner to the language of representation'. The white hand is evident in social research centers that have grown both in academia and in non-governmental organizations post-1994 (see CREST 2014). As a result, peer-review academic books or journals are written not for the object, even when it attempts to resolve the subject/object dualism. This remains the case even though there has been a slightly raised emergence of Black scholars.

Social research has played its role in the construction and perpetuation of racial domination of African South Africans, who make up the largest group of those who are researched. By appropriating, speaking, and writing about/for African people, social research has reproduced racial domination. This dualism has allowed social science to be tangled in the assumption that black people are the object. By object we also mean those who are reserved as participants, who cannot write the 'science'. Thus speech is the object's primary tool for self-representation. The object is seen as second language speaker; therefore in need of translation, hence the *native informant*. On the other hand, the subject is the self-allocated writer who frames research questions to study the object. This is the social science that trains and nurtures aspiring Black scholars such as ourselves in white-dominated academia. This has been our experience.

Louise Vincent (2008) offers the term *contact* in looking closely at the dynamics of integration and asserts that even though there has been an increase in black student participation at institutions of higher learning post-1994, this *contact* occurs within a context in which the overall hegemony of whiteness (in social sciences and campus life more broadly) remains intact. Institutionalized white supremacy within the academy reinforces the negative experiences of black students in contact with whiteness in universities: from the accents when engaging in discussions and starting dialogue, to the internalized sense that black people are stupid. South Africa's transitional democracy enabled *contact* in institutions of higher learning within a context that sought to address multi-layered racial segregation. In making *contact,* the *native informant* has two options: first, to 'refuse friendship' and withdraw from engaging with whites, thus becoming alien (see Soske and Walsh this volume); or second, as Vincent (2008) argues, to learn the social scripts of *contact*. Thus integration within the context of the South African university structure becomes laced with a kind of entrapment that simultaneously maintains friendship while pacifying resistance. Such assimilation means living with the 'conflict' rather than facing antagonism (see Barchiesi this volume).

Intimate contact is explored by Maria Rabe (2003), who focuses on insider-outsider binaries. In her study, the insider is seen as an individual belonging to, or having similar attributes such as gender, or class, or race, among other possible positionalities, within the research subject group. The insider becomes a valuable instrument in data gathering, assumed to be inherently capable of capturing the lived experience of research subjects, and able to offer nuanced insights that outsiders would miss. Such value emerges strongly during fieldwork, particularly when conducting interviews and recruiting participants. The outsider becomes the empirical voice of reason within the scientific community, using the lived experiences mined by the insider. This kind of social science positions Black scholars as both 'Slave' and 'Object' (Wilderson 2010). For this positioning to be effective, it is fostered and maintained through the offer of friendship. Evoking friendship is a convenient way to neutralise the object's questioning of the scientific method and its epistemology. Black scholars are taught to utilise the same instruments to research the Black – transformed again into object. How does an object who must act as a subject research other objects? Even if 'Slave' can be read as a somewhat extreme and dramatic expression, prolonged intergroup *contact* enables disjointed intimate relations, as we attempt to show below.

BECOMING A *NATIVE INFORMANT*

The dualism in South African social science described above has taught some of us (Black scholars) to perpetuate the objectification and alienation of Black people. Reflecting on tourism, Ciraj Rassool and Leslie Witz (1996: 336) in their analysis on the representations of society and its past, hint at processes of othering and the reproduction of subordinate status that remain unchallenged:

> Through the 'tourist gaze' on landscapes and townscapes, on society and history, the visitor affirms and reaffirms his imagined world. He – for the tourist gaze is quintessentially male – enters a world of images, lingering over, even gawking at what he sees, imaging and imagining, classifying, objectifying, capturing and appropriating through photographs, postcards, films and now the hand-held video camera. In the process, he slots, with relative ease, into power and privilege, knowing, gazing and designing the visited world.

We follow Khan (2005: 2022) citing Trinh T. Minh-Ha in using the term *native informant* to describe 'the person who translates her culture for the researcher, the outsider. It is a process ... through which the natives as subjects of research become the handicapped who cannot represent themselves and have to either be represented or learn how to represent themselves'. In the process of becoming a *native informant*, Khan (2023) notes that we develop an acumen for spreading 'scientific gossip'. This refers to the process through which we acquire skills to cite or reference the decorated elite classical thinkers within white-dominated academia, predominately white scholars who have become permanent points of departure when analysing the object and its context. Rabe (2003) points out three research studies in which white researchers wrote glowing descriptions of their insiders, acknowledging their invaluable skills and contributions to the data collection process. The black women are named. The white researchers in the study extol the natural fit between the insider informant and the subject group being studied. They concede that the quality of their research depends on the *native informant's* contribution. The *native informant* will then be invited to conferences and seminars to speak about the struggle that is facing her race, culture, gender, and identity. Struggles narrated by the *native informant* might at times be 'co-opted and appropriated within the liberal discourse so that we become-someone's private zoo' (Khan 2005: 2025). If willing, the *native informant* will propose solutions to the oppression and inferiority complexes facing her (see Wilderson 2010). But, in the end, it is clear whose voice is given weight by promotion and recognition in the context of institutional knowledge production. These factors describe the relationships and locations that Black scholars in South Africa inhabit.

As Khan (2005) asserts, it is already assumed within a context of institutionalized white supremacy that the *native informant* is the representation of the 'know-it-all' or 'authentic' voice of the object culture. Frantz Fanon (1967: 84–85) re-affirms this as he describes being black in the white world: 'I was responsible at the same time for my body, for my race, for my ancestors, I subjected myself to an objective examination ...'. This is the burden of bondage the *native informant* carries in white-dominated academia, almost 60 years after Fanon wrote those words. What is critical for us here is how this relation is maintained with a benevolent smile, a 'thank you' in the footnotes, or the performance of friendship. The *native informant* exists through this relation.

Even though there are open calls for journal submissions, and advertisements for research posts, historical inequalities and contemporary challenges combine to ensure that, in practice, most research continues to exist in a racialized matrix, which is further gendered and classed within a globalized hierarchy. This matrix distorts who is privileged in the academy and through what means, as imported intellectual skill comes in white, mostly male, or 'foreign' black bodies. Despite the systematic but thin funding response in the inclusion of the underrepresented analytical work of previously disadvantaged blacks, access to Black critical thought remains marginal.

Native informing becomes a contradictory process in the negotiated production of research texts laced with cultural insights seen to resemble what is closest to the shared, lived experience in an object group. Without dwelling on who the research is intended for or who it serves, we appreciate the political relevance of social research in allowing alternative and marginalised narratives to be documented. However, we are haunted by Leroke's (1994) assertion that the negotiation and sharing of knowledge in its many stages of production reproduces and maintains white privilege in academia. Critical to the reproduction of existing power structures are the familiar bonds of friendships between Black scholars and white academics, which fracture the Black psyche into constructs of marginality.

Ultimately the position of the *native informant* is 'precarious' (Khan 2005: 2025). The result of the dualism we find in academia is that the object – the Black – remains permanently 'anti-human', alienated and objectified (see also Wilderson 2010). When a Black scholar enters social science, the scholar becomes the *native informant*, signified as both the object and subject. The Black scholar is quickly taught that she must value first the need to represent the object. In so doing, the *native informant* is crucial to maintaining and silencing the violence of representation.

Since 1994, there has been a policy-driven initiative to include Black scholars in social science research, but, as we argue here, the epistemological methods deployed in this process of integration have not been examined. Leroke's (1994) inquiry in regard to alternative methods of science, and how representation of the Black might be changed in consequence, has not yet been answered by those Black scholars who have been included as *native informants* in the academy. Rather, the focus has been to facilitate increased participation of Black scholars in higher learning through providing funding in the form of student loans and scholarships. We offer our personal narratives below to illustrate that financial assistance does not address the manifestation of white supremacy in academic structures. We seek to show how funding has been used as a tool to manage the *native informant*, designed so that the process of epistemology cannot be questioned. It is possible for the Black scholar to retain her position on the academic 'fringe', maintained through friendship and scholarship grants, as long as she does not ask uncomfortable questions, but rather proceeds to reproduce the 'universality of science'. The structure of funding creates a façade of friendship. In most cases, those who approve grant applications are supervisors often white, whose role is to groom aspiring scholars through thesis writing and creating learning opportunities. Thus, money and mentorship become mutually dependent in the formation of friendship.

OUR EXPERIENCES AS *NATIVE INFORMANTS* IN SOCIAL SCIENCES

Ready to become *native informants* and to legitimise the language of social science in academia, in 2010 and 2011 we respectively enrolled for our Master's (Author 2) and doctoral studies (Author 1), respectively. At that time institutions of higher learning were responding to the demand to register Black scholars by offering funding as the next investment for a growing *native informant* generation. As detailed above, we argue that the funding system in tertiary education provides a form of support that significantly enables the *native informant* to be nurtured in white-dominated academia. Indeed, in our first year, we both received scholarships. However, the cost of performing the *native informant* quickly became clear to us. For both of us, the encounter with whites in the university setting, albeit in contexts of solidarity and friendship, revealed the precarious position of the Black scholar as *native informant*.

The reality of performing as the *native informant* revealed itself brutally for Author 2: both in the form of rejection and friendship. A year before finishing her Master's degree she was informed that her funding would be cut because she and the grant holder were registered at different institutions. After months of trying to find an appropriate department and a suitable supervisor for her project, Author 2 opted to register at a second institution. Her thesis, titled *Exploring the Meanings Attached to the Sexual Identity of Black Women-Loving-Women in Soweto*, focused on the Black expression of women's same-sex sexualities using Q methodology. However, she was again unable to find a supervisor, with the result that the grant-holder institution claimed it could not benefit financially from her subsequent or current publications. For Author 2, the lack of suitable supervisors revealed 'an institution that acted in accordance with the 'self-reproduction and perseverance of whiteness', which was therefore 'not willing to accommodate and adapt to innovative forms of knowledge production'. Instead of reflecting on its limitations and seeking remedies to fix the crisis, Author 2's feeling was that the institution had interpreted the problem as an administrative nightmare in which it was too costly to groom the *native informant*.

The problem was not only the financial loss the profit-orientated academic institutions would incur, but that the *native informant* does not have the liberty to pursue and be funded for her studies *for the sake of it*. Part of the expectation that binds one to funding is to maintain the dualism, and to publish legitimised social science research, which will lift the profit margins of universities.

As soon as the news spread among peers and allies that a potential *native informant* had been denied funding, there was an outrage among Author 2's friends and allies. As the system has taught us, in situations such as these the first response is to write a letter with signatories in protest to the unjust decision. In that process the *native informant* who needs to be trained to be a subject, is turned into an object again, and as expected from social scientists, the process of dualism manifests itself. The letter written to the Dean pointed out the academic merits and the critical research contributing to black women's same-sex sexuality studies. The letter was crafted to illustrate that the *native informant* had earned participation within the academy. Her intellect and thoughts were declared to signal her worthiness to learn and compete in disciplines that privilege whiteness. The letter objected to the discontinuation of funding close to the completion of the dissertation. In illustrating the 'unfairness', the letter highlighted the difficulty that tenured professors had in understanding that 'intellectual activity cannot happen without food in the stomach'. This lack of understanding, Author 2 argues, echoes Wilderson's (2010: 8) assertion that 'in their putative embrace of working-class incapacity there is also, from the standpoint of the Slave, a devastating embrace of Human capacity – that which the Slave lacks'. These descriptions of 'food' and 'stomachs' speak to the *native informant's* positionality evident in such instances of solidarity. As Wilderson (11) reminds us, 'the slave is not a labourer but an anti-Human, a position against which humanity establishes, maintains, and renews its coherence, its corporeal integrity'.

For Author 2, good intentions, solidarity, and letters of support served to 'thicken the discomfort and antagonism'; proof that a potential *native informant* seeking an opportunity within academia would be positioned as anti-Human. For the process of becoming Human, the *native informant* must declare her suffering in her search for support, from using words such as 'previously disadvantaged', to calibrating sources of income vs. number of dependents per household on a value matrix, in order to qualify for funding, with above-average grades indicating potential. Even in moments of solidarity among allies, the system forces our cases for integration as blacks into such categories that go beyond merit and the burden of being a competent *native informant*, and touches on the simple but complex process of becoming a human subject. This becoming-human insists on referencing the disadvantaged political position of suffering, if not exclusion, within the institutionalised social arrangement.

The perceived success of *native informants'* experience in accessing postgraduate degrees becomes an illusion, suggesting that 'you have made it' in relation to the many among peers and family. Being able to engage in seminars, writing, and debating ideas with a distinct intellectual tone of integrating theory and lived experience becomes a significant factor in the identity of a learned young Black. For those who are unemployed in the township you left behind, you become the educated one. For those struggling with their undergraduate studies, you become the one who has crossed and gone beyond. You become admired in both instances. Parents and family acknowledge your achievement, envisaged with possibilities yet to come. You have entered the world that your parents and those left behind might not fathom; false confidence creeps in, but is contained even before it is grounded. The *native informant* is introduced to academic networks (predominately white with other *native informants* who have 'mastered' the scripts) as the 'bright and promising' new one. Invitations to conferences and seminars enable mentors to showcase their students. While this occurs, the *native informant* has access to the inner circles. The site of friendship established through the development stages of research training, affirming as it can be, must be read with suspicion. The historical colonial friendship reminds us, white academia is loyal to anti-Black thought, and Black scholars are so often regulated to access without decision-making power, thereby confounding self-determination.

A potential *native informant's* ability to attract and secure funding becomes an affirming reward. The vote of confidence creates its own knot and further binds the friendship; you become thankful for the testimonies in recommendation letters. You will be expected to acquire more research experience beyond the thesis. To acquire such experience, a topic tied to the township experience will be on offer, and since you come with the language and access, you are invited to be a fieldworker – the subject. You are informed about untouched grounds and topics in social science and proceed to frame, design, and propose research questions to represent the object: the *native informant* seems to be the new subject. These are the nuances in social science, the required skills that one day you will expand on, or so you are told. Therefore, like a true aspiring intellectual, you accept the invitation and enter into the terrain you are most familiar with to mine data as means to practice and participate in knowledge production. Here the *native informant* becomes complicit in finding space within academia with the hopes of being counted among other Black scholars who continue to practice within this epistemological problem. When publications claim your thoughts, knots tighten at the realisation that your role was to become a qualifier and a referral point for the raw data that has been sourced. *The native informant* is complicit in the entangled knots.

THE *NATIVE INFORMANT* SAGA CONTINUES

As we grow weary of bitterness, which is muddled with the confrontation of being Black in a world that defines who you are and what you ought to be, James Baldwin (1963) further reminds us that 'confusion is a luxury which only the very, very young can possibly afford and you are not that young anymore'. In her second year of doctoral studies, Author 1 lost funding to complete her studies in a way that was wrapped up in the performance of friendship and solidarity with her white supervisor. At the time the funding was withdrawn because the Dean mistakenly thought she was enrolled for her Master's degree, even though he was present during her Master's graduation ceremony. This 'error' was initially dismissed as merely an administrative problem and simple to rectify, but it turned out not to be the case. The difference in this instance was that the discussion was contained within the student-supervisor relation with the white professor, a relationship that had often expressed itself as friendship and solidarity. The *native informant* wrote a letter with the belief that white academia would understand the alienation and objectification she had endured, and the anti-Black attitudes of the university. Extracted from the letter, Author 1 addressed her professor:

> We have seen European and American post-doctorates become a normalised feature of the unit sold as competent and publishing machines. This then frames the 'other' as Black African and incapable and therefore not worth cultivating. I have even come to believe that to qualify as a post-doc one must have been educated in the West, ideally white. The excuse for this false dichotomy and inherently anti-Black sustained systematic exclusion has been that Blacks do not apply for these posts, and this has been a stable explanation in the past four years. Again such thinking is maintained without considering or even engaging in a consultative process of rethinking and engaging this dilemma which could have included broadening advertising of these posts in newspapers and across the continent.

However, anti-Human status cannot be resolved through letter writing, as the *native informant* later discovered. The written response from the professor exposed this by ducking and avoiding the issue of race, making a case of neoliberal universities, citing short-termism and corporatisation in institutions of higher learning. Of course, there is an element of truth in the assertion that neoliberalism is one of the dynamics facing white-dominated universities in South Africa. However, the neoliberal rationale fails and denies the opportunity to come to grips with the dominance and privileges white academics have enjoyed within the very system of neoliberalism.

To illustrate the depth of the problem, a final example arises from the controversies surrounding an article published by Bandile Mdlalose (2014) in the journal *Politikon*. The debate centered on whether Mdlalose's article warranted sufficient academic merit to be included in a peer-reviewed journal. The article was written by a Black activist in a social movement – an object – reflecting on the contradictions of solidarity work in its white-classist form within movements, and the violence of representation, which is seldom addressed. The conflict and controversy of the article, according to some senior white academics, lie in how an activist-object's reflexive voice is full of 'unsubstantiated accusations'. Her referencing technique was questioned against normative standards, thereby discrediting her intellectual contribution without engagement on substance, consequently silencing her. In responding to the 'controversy' the journal opened a call for a special issue, which further unpacked her article, thus reducing and singling out her contribution for more scrutiny, clearly drawing the lines for those in solidarity and those against her ideas. Critical debate, which uncomfortably questions privileges, position, and epistemological approaches of social science that have thrived, are treated as footnotes in this framework of reasoning; hence Mdlalose's experience. Seeing the conflict only in neoliberal terms suits white academia, as they do not have to critically reflect on race and the gravity of alienation, which exists for the object. As Baldwin (1963) affirms, the only conclusion a *native informant* can arrive at in an antagonistic context that continuously fragments one sense of self is that 'any Negro who is … [in the] … educational system runs the risk of becoming schizophrenic'.

Our experiences may be specific, but they are certainly not unique as many continue to battle with similar issues at different sites of institutionalized white supremacy in South Africa. In both instances our experiences of being used as *native informants* while also denied the support and ability to complete our studies, dressed up in a language and practice of friendship by white academics, became intolerable. Nadia Sanger (2008) has shared her journey in the academy:

I realize now that I had, in many ways, repressed my experiences in the department because it simply was traumatic. Until now (and I'm still finding it difficult), I have been unable to articulate in a less emotional, and more coherent way, the kind of violence I and other black academics in the department were presented with. It is important to note that at no point while I was located in the department did I feel paralysed by the dehumanization … I tried to use agency to confront and highlight the racism in the department consistently – hence, I suspect that in order to get rid of me, my contract was terminated. My black colleagues, most who were quiet on the subject because they needed to keep their jobs and pay the bills, understandably, remained in contracts in the department. In many ways, I feel that I am speaking out in a public forum, for the first time after I was exited out of the department. I will not name the academics responsible for these dehumanizing tactics … In many ways, then, what I discuss here speaks directly to Angelo's notion of white mediocrity, and the ways that the black academics, in their complicity with the hegemony, speak with this mediocrity.

Sanger (2008) offers a glimpse at her efforts to balance the many layers of *contact*. She writes about the violence of her repressed voice, the reasonable logic of retaining jobs by keeping quiet; evidence of the punitive measures of non-renewal of contracts that threaten the parameters of critical engagement. Here, friendship is suspended and contractual relations are individualized. Black women academics' and students' marginalization, along with the invisibility of women as professionals post-1994 has been studied by numerous scholars (see Corneilse 2009; De La Rey 1999; Mabokela 2002; Mama 2003; Mazibuko 2006; Walsh 1995). Critical discussions of Blackness so often do not adequately include discussions of gender (Mabokela and Magubane 2004), further revealing how racism and sexism are deeply embedded in the academy.

CONCLUSION

Recently, an insurgent movement in South African universities has appeared to confront and challenge the discourse of transformation in higher education. The #RhodesMustFall (RMF) student movement at the University of Cape Town (UCT) and the Black Student Movement at Rhodes University made headlines in 2015, the former demanding the statue of colonial icon Cecil Rhodes fall, and later expanding to demand #FeesMustFall and an end of the outsourcing of cleaners. The Rhodes statue did fall. However, the movement made more pertinent demands, which have yet to be discussed with the same rigor as the discussion about the statue. The demands included radical transformation of academic staff, and changes to the curriculum, among others. The movement spread quickly. Out of the 23 state universities, 19 mobilized under the banner #FeesMustFall. As the protests intensified, the South African president, Jacob Zuma, decided not to increase higher education tuition fees for the year 2016. Some student structures were quick to accept the 0% tuition increase, while others echoed the historical call for free education for all. Prior to these struggles, Black scholars such as Xolela Mangcu (2015) have long been calling for more black professors as part of a solution to the black condition in white-dominated academia. In response, two black women in senior academic management positions argued that transformation exists; Graça Machel in her capacity as chancellor of the University of Cape Town, and Mamokgethi Setati as vice-principal of the University of Pretoria and president of the Convocation of the University of the Witwatersrand. However, Mangcu noted, their arguments dismiss the relevance of who teaches in favor of what the academy can produce. We sympathize with Mangcu's assessment, but we argue that the debate must go beyond the recruiting of black bodies. Issues of the epistemology of knowledge, how peer-review journals function, funding formulae of universities that target and exclude black students, neo-liberal management of universities and concomitant anti-Blackness should be connected and central. Mangcu's position does not move away from the older liberal tradition that saw black-white interpersonal contact, such as the joint councils, as the leading way to break down anti-Blackness. We disagree.

The RMF student movement was not enthusiastically supported by all academics; the gradual responses were mixed with many prescriptions on how the students should express their concerns. Albie Sachs, former constitutional judge, African National Congress (ANC) stalwart and a proponent of the arts evident in his 1989 essay *Spring is Rebellious*, is a case in point. Sachs (2015) proposed that the statue should be kept to 'force [Rhodes] to witness our constitutional democracy'. According to Sachs, the way forward would be to produce creative designs, broad-based panels and the inclusion of students' voices to intervene in re-framing the statue where it stood. This attempt to capture the rainbow of contradictions does not consider the anger and frustration of what freedom 22 years later entails for the previously excluded majority of black people in higher education. But more to the point, the willingness to engage the transformation agenda as proposed by the UCT RMF Mission Statement has been met with bureaucratic protocols that have been punishing.[4] Friendship and solidarity alone, however steeped in good intentions, will not overcome this impasse.

The notion of a modern African university as described by Amina Mama (2015) speaks to knowledge production rooted in social justice issues, responsive in its context and critical of its practice as an institution. From 2010, the year we registered, to date, student protests have emphasized loans, registration, and outstanding fees, annual fees increases, accommodation, and other issues in a context of limited government subsidies and rising student populations. Tshwane University of Technology, for example, experienced more than three protests in 2014 alone, in regard to the administration of student loans. The South African Students' Congress, on the other hand, has been advocating for free education and calling for nationwide protests since 2011. Bekezele Phakathi (2014) has argued that the funding of higher education does not address racialized academic exclusion. During this period, the university has responded with increasingly militarized security, and policies have been evoked to criminalize students and their allies, characterized as violent and disruptive, though seldom are the reasons behind such disruptions mentioned. Here the punishment is individualized through video footage, arrests, permit links, and disciplinary hearing processes. The friendships maintained in solidarity, letters, and placards have become thin.

Our concerns are about how social science is produced and reproduced in white academia where black academics are complicit. Focusing on changing institutional culture assumes that the epistemology of social science will change. Our assertion is that it is up to the *native informants* to question how social science is conducted and how it maintains white supremacy. The RMF student movement spoke about changing the curriculum and the culture of the academy. All these debates are valid, but the crucial questions remain. How do the proposed changes position black people in social science? What does the majority presence of black people in the academy mean in relation to radicalizing the academy? After the RMF and #FeesMustFall movements occurred, we witnessed Black scholars being promoted to professor or vice dean in some faculties, while others became members of senate. This is not to take away from the hard-earned efforts yielding promotions for Black academics. The irony however lies in how the system is maintained; the questions posed by Leroke (1994) are yet to be answered.

In this chapter, we draw on our personal experiences to illuminate our arguments as we describe the ways in which Black scholars are trapped in relations with white academics, often disguised as friendship, which are fundamental to the reproduction of white supremacy and anti-Blackness within South African universities. In this context friendship, and intimacy, can be instrumentally used to position Black scholars as objects, and to maintain our role as *native informants*. This binding relationship can incapacitate and has disabled many Black scholars from challenging social science research methods and attendant knowledge-power structures. At the same time, we must confront ourselves as *native informants*, even if we are still asking the same questions two decades later, with the conscious and critical hope to learn from other voices how to transcend the *native informant*.

REFERENCES

Baldwin, James A. 1963. 'A Talk to Teachers.' *The Saturday Review*, December 21: 42–44.

Centre for Research on Evaluation, Science and Technology (CREST), 2014. 'Mapping Social Sciences Research in South Africa.' University of Stellenbosch.

Corneilse, Carol. 2009. *Living Feminism in the Academy: South African Women Tell Their Stories*. PhD Diss. University of Maryland, College Park.

De la Rey, Cheryl Merle. 1999. *Career Narratives of Women Professors in South Africa*. PhD Diss. University of Cape Town.

Duncan, Norman, Mohammed Seedat, Ashley van Niekerk, Cheryl de la Rey, P. Gobodo-Madikizela, L.C. Simbayi, and A. Bhana. 1997. 'Black Scholarship, Doing Something Active and Positive about Academic Racism.' *South African Journal of Psychology* 27: 201–213.

Fanon, Frantz. 1967. *Black Skin, White Masks*. Trans. Charles Lam Markmann. London: Pluto Press.

Khan, Shahnaz. 2005. 'Reconfiguring the Native Informant: Positionality in the Global Age.' *Signs: Journal of Women in Culture and Society* 30 (4): 2017–2033.

Leroke, Windsor S. 1994. '"Koze Kube Nini?" The Violence of Representation and the Politics of Social Research in South Africa.' Paper presented to the Wits History Workshop: Democracy, Popular Precedents, Practice and Culture. Johannesburg. July 13–15.

Mabokela, Reitumetse Obakeng. 2002. 'Reflections of Black Women Faculty in South African Universities.' *Review of Higher Education* 25(2): 185–205.

Mabokela, Reitumetse Obakeng and Zine Magubane, eds. 2004. *Hear Our Voices: Race, Gender and the Status of Black South African Women in the Academy*. Pretoria: Unisa Press.

Mama, Amina. 2003. 'Restore, Reform but Do Not Transform: The Gender Politics of Higher Education in Africa.' *Journal of Higher Education in Africa* 1(1): 101–125.

Mama, Amina. 2015. 'Decolonising Knowledge 101: In the Master's House.' YouTube Video, 1:38:02. May 7, 2015. https://www.youtube.com/watch?v=pXoisspygxU

Mangcu, Xolela. 2015. '10 Steps to Develop Black Professors.' *News 24*. April 29. http://www.news24.com/Archives/City-Press/10-steps-to-develop-black-professors-20150429

Mazibuko, Fikile. 2006. 'Women in Academic Leadership in South Africa; Conventional Executives or Agents of Empowerment?' *Alternation* 13(1): 106–123.

Mdlalose, Bandile. 2014. 'The Rise and Fall of Abahlali baseMjondolo, a South African Social Movement.' *Politikon: South African Journal of Political Studies* 41(3): 345–353.

Phakathi, Bekezela. 2014. 'Funding Aid For Higher Educations Falls Short.' *News 24*.

February 5. http://www.bdlive.co.za/national/education/2014/02/05/funding-aid-for-higher-education-falls-short

Rabe, Maria E. 2003. 'Revisiting "Insider" and "Outsider" as Social Researchers.' *African Sociological Review* 7: 149–161.

Rassool, Ciraj and Leslie Witz. 1996. 'South Africa, a World in One Country. Moments in International Tourist Encounters with Wildlife, the Primitive and the Modern.' *Cahiers d'Études Africaines* 36 (143): 335–371.

Sachs, Albie. 2015. 'The Rhodes Debate: How Can We Have the Last Laugh.' *University of Cape Town*, March 30. http://www.uct.ac.za/dailynews/?id=9064

Sanger, Nadia. 2008. '"Shutting up the Crazies": Reflections on Feminists, Whiteness, Intellectuals and Black Aliens Inside and Outside the Academy.' Presentation for colloquium in honor of Professor Teresa Barnes: *Transforming Higher Education and Knowledge Production since 1994: Perspectives in 2008*. Cape Town. May 30–31.

Showunmi, Victoria and Maylor, Uvanney. 2013. 'Black women reflecting on being Black in the academy.' *International Journal of Qualitative Studies in Education*. DOI unspecified.

Suffla, Shahnaaz and Mohammed Seedat. 2004. 'How Has Psychology Fared over Ten Years of Democracy? Achievements, Challenges and Questions." *South African Journal of Psychology* 34: 513–519.

Vincent, Louise. 2008. 'The Limitations of "Inter-Racial Contact": Stories from Young South Africa.' *Ethnic and Racial Studies* 31: 1426–1451.

Walsh, Val. 1995. 'Transgression and the Academy: Feminists and Institutionalization.' In *Feminist Academics: Creative Agents for Change* edited by Louise Morley and Val Walsh, 86–101. London: Taylor and Francis.

Wierzbieka, Anna. 2011. 'Defining 'the humanities'.' *Culture & Psychology*. 17: 31–46.

Wilderson, Frank B. III. 2010. *Red, White & Black: Cinema and the Structure of U.S. Antagonisms*. Durham, NC: Duke University Press.

NOTES

1   Our use of the capital letter 'B' in 'Black scholars' and elsewhere in the text, is part of the intellectual statement we are making in this chapter on the issue of race and scholarship.

2   The difference between the humanities and social sciences is that humanities focus on studying human experience, including what can happen to people and what people can do, possible ways of thinking, ways of feeling, and ways of speaking; possible motives and possible values (Wierzbicka 2011: 37). In contrast, social science

wants to approach its subject matter (people) in the way that 'scientists' approach theirs (Wierzbicka 2011: 43). By social science, we refer to the scientific approach to the study of society, a tradition usually defined by the trinity of Karl Marx, Max Weber, and Emile Durkheim.

3   However, this is not limited to South Africa, as many scholars have reflected on experiences of being black and women in academia, such as Uvanney Maylor and Victoria Showunmi's (2013) reflective paper on higher education in the United Kingdom.

4   http://jwtc.org.za/resources/docs/salon-volume-9/RMF_Combined.pdf
    https://www.facebook.com/RhodesMustFall/posts/1559394444336048?fref=nf%20
    http://www.uct.ac.za/news/DebatesInHigherEducation/campusupdates/
    https://www.facebook.com/RhodesMustFall/posts/1567409316867894

ACKNOWLEDGMENTS

Every edited collection succeeds on the basis of the dedication of its contributors, but this volume especially has built on years of conversations, exchanges, and friendship, some in person, some online, some through the mediation of scholarship. Without these friendships, this book would not have been possible. These interlinking and rhizomatic connections continue to sustain us, and are the intellectual basis from which this project flows.

In the final stages, we have benefitted from the careful reading and constructive feedback of Kate Elizabeth Creasy, Franco Barchiesi, Veronica Klipp and T. J. Tallie. We were encouraged and challenged by the valuable insights of Mark Hunter, Meghan Healy-Clancy, and the audience at our panel on Race and Friendship at the African Studies Association meeting in 2015. Thanks to Terri Barnes at the same panel, for helping us to see the long history of conversations that this book arises from. We are also indebted to Nadine Gordimer for discussing friendship and fiction with Lewis Nkosi.

At Wits University Press, our brilliant editor Roshan Cader brought patience, intellectual acuity, and creative insight to the process of making this book a reality. Jill Weintroub's close reading and enthusiastic copyediting have made the volume stronger in many aspects. For editing an early version of the manuscript, our thanks go to Casey Burkeholder and Bing Czeng. Our anonymous peer reviewers also contributed erudite and generous observations.

Thanks to the Ernest Cole Family Trust, specifically Ms. Gunilla Knape, for allowing us to use Cole's beautiful photographs. For her brilliant scholarship, and permission to use her poem 'Fanon's Secret', our deepest thanks to Gabeba Baderoon. The poem is reproduced from her collection *A Hundred Silences* by permission of Kwela Books.

In the cover image Mohau Modisakeng is pictured with ghost-like black coal projecting or emanating from his body. His arms are spread wide, as in an embrace or a surrender. He is alone. The image captures a beautiful representation of such a relation of nonrelation – the desire and the impossibility at once. We see the image as one of release, letting go perhaps of the structuring force of racialized categories. Letting go of 'blackness' that is both part and not part of the body.

In South Africa, the contributions to the life of this volume are enormous. I (Jon Soske) am specifically grateful to the organizers of the Love and Revolution conference series (especially Patricia Hayes, Premesh Lalu, G. Arunima) and the participants, especially Thembinkosi Goniwe, Ashraf Jamal, Helena Pohlandt McCormick, and Gary Minkley, all of whom have planted the seeds that inform my thinking about friendship and race in South Africa. I am indebted to Ellene Centime Zeleke and Premesh Lalu for discussions about the relationship between civil society and the 'Native Question'.

Over the past decade I (Shannon Walsh) have been challenged, sustained, and encouraged by an incredible range of friends, scholars, comrades, and activists in South Africa too numerous to name here. I trust that you know who you are. It has been humbling to be invited to share in the rich intellectual and political life of this country. My primary debt in thinking about friendship in South Africa goes to Mandla Oliphant and Wonder Marthinus. The complexities of friendship, intimacy, and race have been made real to me through the love and perspective I have gained from my adopted children, Hlengiwe, Thulani, Mamazana, Ayanda, Lwazi, Luisa, and Thando. Without the intellectual and political engagement of Denis Valiquette, and our shared friends and comrades, I could not have considered the politics of friendship and its relation to everyday life as intensely. Deep gratitude goes to Eugene Arries who sustains me, indulges my ramblings, and makes me an altogether better person. Finally, thanks to Laurel Sprengelmeyer whose empathy, patience, inspiration, and enduring friendship has been the greatest gift of my adult life.

This work has been supported by an Early Career Scheme grant from the Research Grants Council of the Hong Kong Special Administrative Region, China, Project No. 21608915.

CONTRIBUTOR BIOGRAPHIES

Franco Barchiesi is an associate professor in the Department of African American and African Studies at the Ohio State University, a fellow at the W. E. B. Du Bois Institute at Harvard University, and a visiting research associate at the University of the Witwatersrand.

Stacy Hardy is an editor at the pan-African journal *Chimurenga*, and teaches at Rhodes University in the Master's in Creative Writing program. Her writing has appeared in a wide range of publications, and several of her short stories have been published in books, literary anthologies, and catalogues.

Tsitsi Jaji is an associate professor of English and African & African American Studies at Duke University. She is the author of *Africa in Stereo: Modernism, Music and Pan-African Solidarity*, an account of how African American music and literature contributed so profoundly to African notions of solidarity in the twentieth century.

M. Neelika Jayawardane is associate professor of English at the State University of New York-Oswego, and an honorary research associate at the Centre for Indian Studies in Africa, University of the Witwatersrand.

Bridget Kenny is an associate professor of Sociology at the University of the Witwatersrand, Johannesburg. She works on labor, gender, and consumption, with specific focus on service work, precarious employment, and political subjectivity.

MADEYOULOOK is a Johannesburg-based collaborative made up by Molemo Moiloa and Nare Mokgotho who work on tongue-in-cheek interventions that encourage a re-observation of and de-familiarization with the ordinary. Their artworks engage daily urban routine, lived, and practiced by people every day.

Daniel Magaziner is associate professor of History at Yale University. He teaches and researches the intellectual history of twentieth-century Africa and the African diaspora. His new book on art education under apartheid, *The Art of Life in South Africa*, will be published in 2016.

Sisonke Msimang is a South African who writes about money, power and sex. She has been published in the *New York Times*, the *Guardian* (UK), *Newsweek* and a range of media outlets in South Africa. She is a regular contributor to Africa is a Country.

Nomancotsho Pakade has worked extensively in the lesbian, gay, bisexual, transgender and intersex sector in South Africa and is passionate about the narratives of Black African women's lived experiences. She holds a Master's in Research Psychology from the University of the Witwatersrand.

Mosa Phadi is completing her doctoral studies at the University of Johannesburg. She is a researcher at the Public Affairs Research Institute affiliated with the University of the Witwatersrand. Her research interests include race and class.

Lesego Rampolokeng was born in Orlando West, Soweto. He is a poet, novelist, and playwright. His documentary film *Word Down the Line* debuted in 2014. He participates in conferences and literary festivals around the world and teaches at Rhodes University in the Master's in Creative Writing program.

Jon Soske is assistant professor in the Department of History and Classical Studies, McGill University and a research associate at the Centre for Indian Studies in Africa, University of the Witwatersrand.

T. J. Tallie is an assistant professor in the Department of History at Washington & Lee University in Lexington, Virginia. His research interests include settler colonialism, race, gender, religion, and Zulu culture.

Shannon Walsh is a filmmaker and assistant professor in the Department of Theater and Film, University of British Columbia, Canada and a research associate at the University of Johannesburg's South African Research Chair in Social Change.

Frank B. Wilderson III is an award-winning writer, activist, and critical theorist who spent five-and-a-half years in South Africa, when he was one of two Americans who held a position as an elected officer in the African National Congress during the country's transition from apartheid. He worked clandestinely for Umkhonto we Sizwe.

Please consult the ORCiD registry for further information on our authors: www.orcid.org

INDEX

English language writers 9
Entanglement 12
Ernest Cole Family Trust 308
Erwin, Alec 155
Etherington, Norman 122, 123, 124
Ethics 7
European-Native Joint Councils movement
  3, 18, 19
European rule 129
Everatt, David 126, 163, 165
expectations of friendship 4
exploitation 15-17, 20, 24, 152, 158, 217
  capitalist 17, 143
  colonial 109
  domestic workers 232, 238
  economic 134
  socioeconomic 129
*Exploring the Meanings Attached to the Sexual
  Identity of Black Women-Loving-Women in
  Soweto* 296

F
failure of
  civil society 5
  friendship 9
  literary empathy 10
  reciprocity 184
  solidarity 5
  tolerance and humanism 68
Fanon, Franz 58, 70-71, 76, 81-82, 86-89, 93,
  128, 150, 156, 250-251, 291, 294
Fanon's Secret 1, 308
Fees Must Fall campaign 302, 304
feminism
  Black 78
  non-Black 78
  postcolonial 4
Feni, Dumile 51, 59
Ferguson, James 79, 195
Feza, Mongezi 59, 63
fictions of friendship 9-12
First, Ruth 47
framework of colonial friendship 4
framework of friendship 279
Frantz Fanon's War 82

Frederikse, Julie 126
free tertiary education for Africans 86
Freedom Charter 127, 132, 146, 147, 148
friendship(s) 3-30, 32-33, 34, 36, 49-51, 54,
  56, 70-99, 111-118, 128, 130, 156, 158,
  166-191, 194-195, 204, 226, 231, 236, 247,
  263, 265-269, 280, 284, 293-294, 296, 298-
  299, 303-304, 309
  abstract formulation 52
  across race 9, 21-22, 32, 34-35, 266
  across the color bar 68
  affect and friendship 13, 168
  African 114, 115
  and race in post-apartheid South
    Africa 21
  as a coercive gift 22
  as a concept 130
  as gift 106, 107
  between black and white 10, 19, 32,
    152, 194, 288
  between Black scholars and white
    academics 295, 304, 308
  between colonist and colonized 110
  between colonizer and colonized 18
  between madams and maids 216-242
  between students and teachers 195,
    197
  black-white 152
  boundaries 19
  British 107
  by white academics 301
  colonial *see* colonial friendship
  contests of friendship 115
  cross-racial 149
  enmity and friendship 279
  evolution of white friendship 130
  failure of 9
  forms of 5, 115
  framework 148
  homosocial 115
  impossibilities of 21
  in Colonial Natal 100-124
  in South Africa 3-30, 309
  in white academia 288-307
  intellectual 265

Hobe, Hamlet 199-200, 202, 205, 207
Hoernlé, RFA 163
Hogan, Barbara 35
homophobia 274, 286
    intra-racial 96
    racialized 283
homophobic
    policies 269
    structures 283
Horns for Hondo 50
Horrax, OJ 197, 198
Houle, Robert J 124
House of Bondage 221, 222, 223 ill, 224, 225
    ill, 226
human liberation 71
humanitarians 134
Hunter, Mark 7, 308

I

I Shit Diamonds 268
IAS *see* Industrial Aid Society
immigration laws 112
Immorality Act 256
'immorality laws' 7
Imvo Zabantsundu 135
'In Absentia: Mourning and Friendship' 51
incapacity 297
Incognegro: A Memoir of Exile & Apartheid 71
Indaleni *see also* Ndaleni
    Indaleni Training College 196, 207
Indian
    immigration 112, 113
    indenture 5, 17
    migrant laborers 103
Indian Question 102
Indiana, Robert 247
Industrial Aid Society (IAS) 166-167, 185,
    190
Industrial and Commercial Workers' Union
    (ICU) 142, 146, 153
insecurity of workers 169, 172
insider-outsider binaries 292
interconnections 7, 11
international
    labor movement 19

observers 85
whiteness 43
International Labor Bureau 146
International Socialist League (ISL) 142-143
internationalism
    non-racial class 143
    proletarian 142
interracial
    affiliation 145
    affinity 109
    connection 113
    cooperation 145, 146
    dependence 146
    dialogue 132
    drinking 13
    economic interdependence 136
    forums 143
    friendship 9, 32, 36-37, 104-105,
        108-112, 118, 146, 204, 263-264,
        266-267, 284
    interactions 265
    love 264, 283
    marriage 284
    'queer' desire 218, 231, 234
    relations 151
    relationship(s) 9, 10, 13
    respect 32
intimacies/intimacy 5-12, 14, 18, 23, 39, 97,
    98, 171, 177, 185, 194, 195, 216, 218, 222,
    232, 235-237, 244, 246, 248, 250, 252, 258,
    260, 304
    affect and intimacy 5
    and complicities 4
    by black people 249
    clandestine 98
    complexities 309
    geography of intimacy 7
    in liberation politics 14
    love and intimacy 4
    modes of 7, 8, 23
    monstrous 171, 177, 185
    narratives 251
    of precarious labor 170, 171
    policing of intimacy 7
    political economy of 5

imagery of 4
movement 132, 149
politics 14
role of minorities 10
school 76
struggle(s) 68, 165, 267, 279
'LIBERATION BLUES 1974' 64
libidinal
    and emotional forces 5
    economies/economy 71, 264
limitations/limits of friendship 14, 52
Liphosa, Pandeani 244
literature(s) 7, 62, 117, 239
    around precarious work 169
    Black 93, 269
    capacity to reach across the racial
       divide 9
    colonial 64
    historical 22
    on alcohol production and consump-
       tion 113
    South African 10, 49, 59
Loram, CT 146
Lorde, Audre 268
Love 247
love 7, 12, 158, 243-262
    across races 256
    across the color bar 68
    and forgiveness of the oppressed 9
    and intimacy 4
    archives of black love 252-257
    black 12, 23-24, 243-244, 245-261
    Black 93, 95
    for humanity 60
    forms of 5, 246
    impersonal 14
    in contemporary art 246-249
    interracial 264, 283
    intra-Black 93
    public displays of 249
    revolutionary 194
    romantic 243, 246, 247
    same-sex 283
    speaking about 243-262
    white man's 111

    working-class 246
    yourself 88
Love & Revolution conference series 30, 309
lovers
    same-sex 231
loving
    corner loving 243-262
Lowe, Liza 5, 8
LRA *see* Labor Relations Act
Lumumba, Patrice 56
Luthuli, Albert 20, 150

M
Mabusela, Ezekiel 205
Machel, Graça 302
Madam and Eve 241
MADEYOULOOK 23, 243-245, 250, 253-
    254 ill, 259 ill, 310
Madingoane, Ingoapele 58
Magadlela, Fikile 59
Magaziner, Daniel 23, 192, 213-215, 310
Mager, Anne 114
Magona, Sindiwe 31, 39
Mahlangu, Joe 52
Mahlangu, Songeziwe 49
Mahlobo, Samson 205, 206, 214
Mahmood, Anser 41
Mahoney, Michael 114, 123
Maid in Uniform 221
Mailer, Norman 71, 72, 73, 75, 83, 89
Makurube, Peter 58
makwerekwere 266, 267
Malan, Rian 40, 45
Malcolm X 96
The Malcolm X and Dr Betty Shabazz Me-
    morial and Educational Center 96
Malolo, Enoch 204, 214
Mama, Amina 303
Mamdani, Mahmood 122, 164
Mandela, Nelson, President 14, 38, 74, 76,
    85
Mandela, Winnie 97
Mandela-ism 97
Mangcu, Xolela 42, 302, 303
Maori 110

South African Labor Party 143
South African Native Affairs Commission 137
South African Native Congress 135
see also African National Congress
South African Native National Congress (SANNC) 133, 145
see also African National Congress
South African Research Chair in Social Change, University of Johannesburg 190
South African Students' Congress 303
South African War 103
South Africanism 146, 156
South Africans
    African 290, 292
    black 11, 12, 37, 75, 158, 194
    white(s) *see* white South Africans
    writing by white South Africans 3
sovereignty 4
    centered on the rule of law 136
    constitutional 126
    political 132
    state 136
Spillers, Hortense 70, 73, 78, 94, 128
Spinoza, Benedictus (Baruch) 145
Sprengelmeyer, Laurel 309
Spring is Rebellious 303
Staff Rider 13
state domination 182
Stern, Irma 221
Stivale, Charles J 69
Stockholm University of Dramatic Arts 277
struggle
    against apartheid 68
    anti-apartheid 4, 14
    liberation *see* liberation struggle
subjectivities/subjectivity 5-6, 10-11, 129-131, 141, 156, 170, 172, 183, 196, 198
    African 16
    black 18, 130, 136, 185
    native 3, 237
    political 152, 156-157, 185
Swindells, Martin 115
Swisa, Sarit 39

T

Tallie, TJ 22, 100, 308, 311
Tansi, Sony Lab'ou 59
Tate, Greg 66
Tatham Art Gallery 209, 212, 215
temperance laws 116
Thema, Richard V Selope 144-147, 164
Themba, Can 248
ties of friendship 6
TNC *see* Transvaal Native Congress
Touré, Souleymane 21
'traditional customs' 137
transition
    1994 4
    in education 213
transitional democracy 292
Transvaal
    mineral districts 140
    mines 103
Transvaal Labor Commission, 1904 139
Transvaal Native Affairs Society 144, 164
Transvaal Native Congress (TNC) 141-142
tribal
    government 137
    superstition 136
Trump, Donald 85
Tshwane University of Technology 303
Turner, Richard 10-11

U

UDI *see* Unilateral Declaration of Independence
Umkhonto we Sizwe (MK) 55, 68, 71-74, 86, 256-257
Unemployment Insurance Fund 166, 190
Unilateral Declaration of Independence (UDI) 285
Union of South Africa 20, 101, 103, 133, 135-149
Unity Movement 128, 148, 153
universal friendship 19
university campuses 24
University of Cape Town (UCT) 76, 302
University of Pretoria 38, 302
University of the Western Cape 30

University of the Witwatersrand (Wits) 21, 40, 71, 302-303

XYZ

www.ingramcontent.com/pod-product-compliance
Lightning Source LLC
Chambersburg PA
CBHW020244030426
42336CB00010B/611